SOCIAL MEDIA MARKETING

⊛SAGE | 50 YEARS

SAGE was founded in 1965 by Sara Miller McCune to support the dissemination of usable knowledge by publishing innovative and high-quality research and teaching content. Today, we publish more than 750 journals, including those of more than 300 learned societies, more than 800 new books per year, and a growing range of library products including archives, data, case studies, reports, conference highlights, and video. SAGE remains majority-owned by our founder, and after Sara's lifetime will become owned by a charitable trust that secures our continued independence.

Los Angeles | London | Washington DC | New Delhi | Singapore

SOCIAL MEDIA MARKETING

2ND EDITION

Tracy L. Tuten & Michael R. Solomon

Los Angeles | London | New Delhi
Singapore | Washington DC

Los Angeles | London | New Delhi
Singapore | Washington DC

SAGE Publications Ltd
1 Oliver's Yard
55 City Road
London EC1Y 1SP

SAGE Publications Inc.
2455 Teller Road
Thousand Oaks, California 91320

SAGE Publications India Pvt Ltd
B 1/I 1 Mohan Cooperative Industrial Area
Mathura Road
New Delhi 110 044

SAGE Publications Asia-Pacific Pte Ltd
3 Church Street
#10-04 Samsung Hub
Singapore 049483

Commissioning editor: Matthew Waters
Assistant editor: Nina Smith
Production editor: Nicola Marshall
Copyeditor: Kris Bergstad
Proofreader: Sharon Cawood
Indexer: Silvia Benvenuto
Marketing manager: Alison Borg
Design: Francis Kenney
Typeset by: C&M Digitals (P) Ltd, Chennai, India
Printed and bound in Great Britain by Ashford
Colour Press Ltd

Library of Congress Control Number: 2014947247

British Library Cataloguing in Publication data

A catalogue record for this book is available from
the British Library

MIX
Paper from
responsible sources
FSC® C011748
www.fsc.org

ISBN 978-1-4739-1300-4
ISBN 978-1-4739-1301-1 (pbk)

At SAGE we take sustainability seriously. Most of our products are printed in the UK using FSC papers and boards.
When we print overseas we ensure sustainable papers are used as measured by the Egmont grading system.
We undertake an annual audit to monitor our sustainability.

CONTENTS

SUMMARY OF CONTENTS

PREFACE

As you sit in class, you're probably thinking about a lot of things. After all, you are a Master Multitasker. You've spent many of your waking hours (and maybe even some sleeping hours) tuning in to multiple media platforms at the same time. You're probably very comfortable surfing the Web, texting your friends, and perhaps talking on the phone while you sip a latte at the local coffee shop. We suspect you may even check Facebook Messenger during a lecture from time to time!

We have a name for people like you: Digital Natives. That's why this course on social media marketing is so important—it deals with the stuff you do all day long and shows you how to apply it to professional as well as personal activities. Unless you've been living in a cave, you know that platforms like Facebook are about more than just swapping stories with your buds. Marketers use them to talk to you as well—whether you want them to or not. Today marketers have a huge set of new tools to reach digital natives like you. In fact, for most companies now the question is not *whether* to include social media as part of the communications mix, but *how much* to use. Some organizations even question whether they need the "old school" platforms at all when they can easily reach millions of consumers around the world with the click of a mouse.

We don't go quite that far—social media complement other techniques but don't necessarily replace them. Still, there's a lot to learn about what's out there and the best way to integrate these new tools with the tried-and-true.

We hope this book will help you to figure all that out. We were proud (and a little scared) to publish the first textbook on social media marketing—and here we are with the second edition! With the first edition, our goal was to demonstrate how social media could and should take their place in the 21st-century marketer's toolbox. Now, a few years later, that has indeed happened! And what we know about social media marketing, both from an industry perspective and the academic's perspective, has developed.

When we first developed this book, most universities did not have a course on social media marketing. Today, many do and a select few have recognized that social media warrants its own concentration! This text will enable you to provide the content you—and your future employers—crave. Very simply, you need to know even more about social media than you do already. You need to know how to harness the power of these cool tools to succeed in business, nonprofit organizations, and pretty much any kind of situation that involves buyers and sellers, makers and users.

There are so many applications out there—where to start? We've organized the book so that we cover four zones of social media. These four zones—communities, commerce, publishing, and entertainment—certainly aren't mutually exclusive. There are applications that provide a way for marketers to attain two, three, and maybe even all four objectives. This framework will help you to make sense of the booming new world of social media.

Our approach is simple: We start in Section I with a discussion of just what social media means, and how it's changing our lives. We call this change the Horizontal Revolution. By this we mean that social media is about more than new technology. It's helping to fuel a new business model that puts consumers in the driver's seat. All of the cool toys like Androids and iPads are just the means to an end. That end is your ability to play a role as an active partner in the marketing process. Very simply, in the new world of Web 2.0 and social media, companies market *with* us rather than *to* us. We consider implications not only for consumers, but also for organizations that need to include social media as part of their strategic planning process.

The text then dives into the four zones of social media. We start with community (e.g., Instagram), then move on to publishing (e.g., Tumblr), entertainment (e.g., Candy Crush Saga), and finally commerce (e.g., Groupon). We've worked hard to bring a lot of current examples and "real-world" applications to the mix. That's a tough job when the landscape changes even as you write the book. You can see this shift in the second edition. The book includes the latest popular social communities, new examples, and the most relevant research that helps us to understand how to market using social media. Like social media, this text is very much a work in progress. Enjoy the ride!

ACKNOWLEDGMENTS

Several people have been extremely helpful in writing this textbook.

First, we want to thank Matthew Waters, our commissioning editor at SAGE. He recognized the value of this book in educating marketing students around the world about how to use social media marketing in a strategic way. We are very grateful for his vision and commitment. His staff, in particular Nina Smith, have been phenomenal in their availability, responsiveness, and attention. It's been a joy to work with this team.

No book comes to life without help from others and we would like to acknowledge the following individuals for their support, contributions, and assistance:

Ashby Brame
Nik Cochran
Jacquelyn Rae Evans
Sarah Morgan Hunter
Naomi Irvin
Daniel Ladik

Sarah Moran
Brian Pugh
Shanna Rogers
Steven Shugartt
Amanda Steeley
Al Sturgeon

LIST OF FIGURES AND TABLES

Figures

Tables

ABOUT THE AUTHORS

Tracy L. Tuten, Ph.D., is Professor of Marketing at East Carolina University where she teaches social media marketing and advertising. Her first book, *Advertising 2.0: Social Media Marketing in a Web 2.0 World,* was followed by others on using social media and digital marketing for the enterprise, and the book, *Advertisers at Work,* which features interviews with luminaries in the field. Dr. Tuten's publications have appeared in such journals as *Journal of Marketing Communications, Psychology & Marketing,* and *Journal of Business Research.* Prior to her appointment at ECU, she taught at Longwood University and at Virginia Commonwealth University, where her research efforts were recognized with VCU's Excellence in Scholarship award. A two-time Fulbright Scholar, she speaks all over the world on marketing topics. She's been recognized with teaching awards at her respective institutions and with national awards, such as the O'Hara Leadership Award in Direct & Interactive Marketing Education. In 2013, she was inducted into the Incredible Women of ECU series, which highlights female graduates of East Carolina University who have reached exceptional levels of achievement in their respective careers. She is one of only 110 women to achieve this distinction. Her influence in social media marketing is recognized with a consistent ranking in the top 20 listing of marketing professors and top 50 listing of authors of marketing books on Twitter (respectively) by *Social Media Marketing* magazine. Follow her at @brandacity on Twitter or follow her blog at www.tracytuten.com.

Michael R. Solomon, Ph.D., is Professor of Marketing and Director of the Center for Consumer Research in the Haub School of Business at Saint Joseph's University in Philadelphia, Pennsylvania. Professor Solomon's primary research interests include consumer behavior and lifestyle issues, branding strategy, the psychology of fashion, and marketing applications of virtual worlds and other new media. His textbooks include *Consumer Behavior: Buying, Having, and Being; Marketing: Real People, Real Choices*; and *Better Business.* His most recent trade book, *The Truth about What Customers Want,* was published by FT *(Financial Times)* Press. Professor Solomon is frequently quoted in magazines and newspapers, including *Newsweek, The New York Times*, and *The Wall Street Journal.* He has served as a consultant to numerous corporations including Calvin Klein, Intel, Procter & Gamble, Microsoft, State Farm Insurance, and United Airlines on issues relating to consumer behavior, marketing strategy, advertising and retailing.

KEY TO ICONS

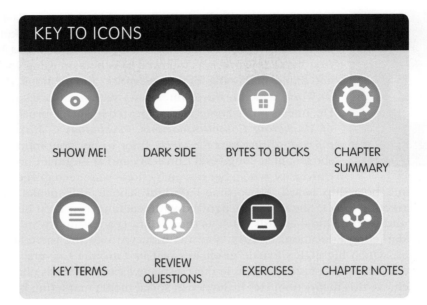

COMPANION WEBSITE

Visit: study.sagepub.com/smm

For instructors per chapter:

- PowerPoint slides

- Instructor manual

- Testbank of multiple choice questions

For students:

- Author-selected YouTube videos per chapter

- Pinterest pins for social media marketing, useful templates, marketing employability and more

- Links to chapter notes

- Six additional case studies

… and remember the hashtag! #smm

For the women in my life who have made this possible:

Hazel Tuten, Susan Brunsdon Tuten, Joyce Tuten Milligan, Jackie Tuten Wynne, Linda Ward Tuten, Betty Perkins, Pamela Kiecker Royall, Dee Congleton, Pat Knotts, Robin Potts, Chloe Tuten, Leia Tuten, Carlene Kincaid, Ayn Rand

PART I

Foundations of Social Media Marketing

1 The Horizontal Revolution

LEARNING OBJECTIVES

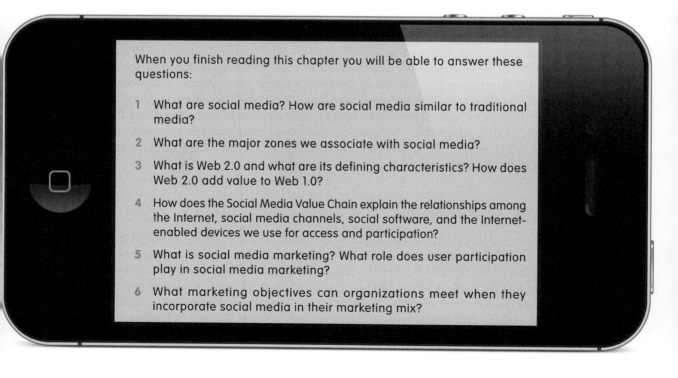

When you finish reading this chapter you will be able to answer these questions:

1 What are social media? How are social media similar to traditional media?

2 What are the major zones we associate with social media?

3 What is Web 2.0 and what are its defining characteristics? How does Web 2.0 add value to Web 1.0?

4 How does the Social Media Value Chain explain the relationships among the Internet, social media channels, social software, and the Internet-enabled devices we use for access and participation?

5 What is social media marketing? What role does user participation play in social media marketing?

6 What marketing objectives can organizations meet when they incorporate social media in their marketing mix?

Greetings, Digital Native

When you woke up this morning, what was the first thing you did? Sure, you may have taken a moment to gulp down some juice or coffee, but odds are you also checked your mobile for texts that came in overnight. Maybe you set your Snapchat Story. Perhaps you scrolled through a few tweets or reviewed your Flipboard to see what's going on in the world. You certainly aren't alone: One recent survey of people ages 18 to 30 from 18 countries reported 90% of them use their smartphone first thing in the morning, often *before* they get out of bed.[1]

Face it—you're a digital native. If you're a typical student, you probably can't recall a time when the Internet was just a static, one-way platform that transmitted text and a few sketchy images. The term *digital native* originated in a 2001 article by Marc Prensky titled "Digital Natives, Digital Immigrants."[2] He tried to explain a new type of student who was starting to enter educational institutions. These students—students like you—were born in an era in which digital technology has always existed. You and your fellow digital natives grew up "wired" in a highly networked, always-on world. It's an exciting time—but it continues to change so constantly that we need to study it carefully.

Today the Internet is the backbone of our society. We call the current version that allows users to interact with senders Web 2.0—we've moved from a fairly simple one-way communications device (that's Web 1.0) to an interactive social system that's available to most of us 24/7. Widespread access to devices like personal computers, digital video and audio recorders, webcams, smartphones, and wearables like "smart watches" ensures that consumers who live in virtually any part of the world can create and share content. Whether you're 18 or 80, odds are you already participate in this wired world.

Information doesn't just flow from big companies or governments down to the rest of us; today each of us communicates with huge numbers of people by a click on a keypad, so information flows *across* people as well. (Hint: How many Facebook friends do you have?) That's what we mean by a horizontal revolution. This fundamental change in the way we live, work, and play is characterized in part by the prevalence of social media. Social media are the online means of communication, conveyance, collaboration, and cultivation among interconnected and interdependent networks of people, communities, and organizations enhanced by technological capabilities and mobility.[3] Does that sound like a complex definition? It is ... because social media exist within a complex and rapidly advancing environment. We'll dive deep into the social media environment, but first let's explore the makings of a social media life—*your* life.

Living a Social (Media) Life

The Internet and its related technologies make what we know today as social media possible and prevalent. Every day the influence of social media expands as more people join online communities. Facebook, a social utility that offers synchronous interactions (which occur in real time, such as when you text back and forth with a friend) and asynchronous interactions (which don't require all participants to respond immediately, such as when you email a friend and get an answer the next day), content sharing of images, video, and music, games, applications, groups, and more, has as of the time of this writing more than 1.2 billion active users.[4] What's more—more than 1 billion of those users are mobile users. If Facebook were a country, it would be the third most populated in the world. Do you wonder why we called Facebook a social utility? A community that got its start as a social network, Facebook offers functionality far beyond basic relationship building. It competes with social channels ranging from video and photo sharing to blogs to e-commerce sites.

People aren't just joining social communities. They are contributing, too! YouTube users upload more than 100 hours of video every single minute of every day.[5] That's roughly equivalent to 500,000 full-length movies uploaded weekly. In less than 30 days on YouTube, more video is broadcast than in the last 60 years on the CBS, NBC, and ABC broadcasting networks combined.[6] Google the phrase "social media stats" and you'll see mind-boggling facts and figures about the number of people who use social media, what they're doing (and when) with social media, and their reach and influence. We've done that for you in Table 1.1. And, take a look at Figure 1.1, an infographic created by Leverage to highlight fun facts about some of the most popular social sites.[7]

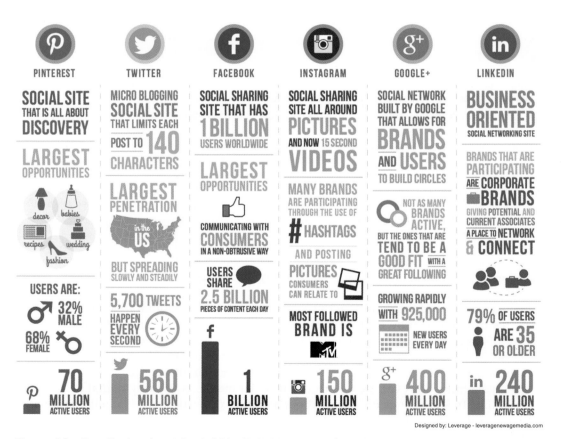

Figure 1.1   Fun Facts about Social Media's Most Popular Sites

Table 1.1   Mind-Boggling Social Media Stats

- It took radio 38 years to reach 50 million listeners. TV took 13 years to reach 50 million users. The Internet took 4 years to reach 50 million people. In less than 9 months, Facebook added 100 million users.

- Social media activity has overtaken porn as the number one online activity.

- 94% of companies use LinkedIn as their primary recruiting tool.

- If you were paid $1 for every time an article was posted on Wikipedia, you would earn $156.23 per hour.[a]

- About 81% of Facebook users reside outside the United States.[b]

- 1 out of 6 couples who married last year met on a social media site.[c]

- Approximately 4 billion pieces of content are shared on Facebook daily.[d]

- 80% of Twitter usage is from mobile devices and 500 million tweets are sent daily.[e]

a. Wikipedia, "Wikipedia: Modelling Wikipedia Extended Growth," May 19, 2014, http://en.wikipedia.org/wiki/Wikipedia:Modelling_Wikipedia_extended_growth, accessed June 26, 2014.

b. Facebook, Company Info | Facebook Newsroom, April 1, 2014, http://newsroom.fb.com/company-info/, accessed July 6, 2014.

c. Chadwick Martin Bailey, "The Evolution of Dating: Match.com and Chadwick Martin Bailey Behavioral Studies Uncover a Fundamental Shift," April 2010, http://blog.cmbinfo.com/press-center-content/?month=4&year=2010, accessed May 24, 2011.

d. E. Protalinski, "Zuckerberg: 4 Billion 'Things' Are Shared on Facebook Every Day," July 6, 2011, http://www.zdnet.com/blog/facebook/zuckerberg-4-billion-things-are-shared-on-facebook-every-day/2020, accessed July 6, 2014.

e. K. Kasi, "Twitter's Mobile Usage Exploding," January 12, 2011, www.dotcominfoway.com/blog/twitters-mobile-usage-exploding, accessed May 24, 2011.

Social Behavior and the Philosophy of Participation

When we introduced the definition of social media earlier, we admitted it's a complicated idea. It's difficult to fully capture the realm of social media because of the expansive nature of sites, services, and behaviors that are a part of this rapidly expanding digital universe. There are simply too many social websites, too many things we can do online, and increasing access using a variety of devices to grasp it all at once.

More generally, however, we can think of social media as the way digital natives live a social life. To sum things up, it's all about a culture of participation; a belief in democracy: the ability to freely interact with other people, companies, and organizations; open access to venues that allow users to share content from simple comments to reviews, ratings, photos, stories, and more; and the power to build on the content of others from your own unique point of view. Here's just a brief look at some of the things you might do with social media:

- Post a status update about plans for the weekend.
- Create a blog to share your favorite recipes.
- Coordinate a book club meeting and negotiate a group discount on the book's purchase price.
- Mobilize a group of people to protest against an unpopular policy on your campus.
- Instant message or voice chat with friends to carry on a synchronous conversation online.
- Share an infographic with your friends.
- Locate the best vegan restaurant in a city you're visiting for the first time based upon reviews by other vegans.
- Make your own animated video and share it.
- Keep a travel diary of a trip abroad complete with photos, videos, journal entries, and destination ratings.
- Raise money for a charity or even find backers for a startup company who are willing to fund part of your costs.
- Find people you used to know and reconnect with them.
- Entertain yourself and your friends with short social games.

This list could go on and on. Our point? Social media enable active participation in the form of communicating, creating, joining, collaborating, working, sharing, socializing, playing, buying and selling, and learning within interactive and interdependent networks. It's an exciting time to be around!

Zones of Social Media

The word media has multiple meanings, but for our purposes we'll simply use it to refer to means of communication.[8] The media we use range from mass media (means of communication that can reach a large number of individuals) such as broadcast, print, and digital channels, to personal media (channels capable of two-way communication on a small scale) such as email, surface mail, telephone, and face-to-face conversations. Social media cross the boundaries of mass and personal media, so they enable individuals to communicate with one or a few people as well as to thousands or even millions of others.

Communication travels using a medium (or channel) such as word-of-mouth, television, radio, newspaper, magazine, signage, Internet, direct mail, or telephone. Within each medium, marketers can choose specific vehicles to place a message. For instance, within the medium of television, marketers may choose *The Walking Dead* as one vehicle to broadcast their message. *Cosmopolitan* and *Fast Company* are vehicles for the magazine medium. Social media also offer a set of online channels with numerous vehicles within each channel.

Part of the complexity of social media is due to the sheer quantity of channels and vehicles, with new ones coming online all the time. These options are easier to compare and contrast if we group similar channels together. In so doing we can conveniently organize the social media space into a compact space that consists of what we call the four Zones of Social Media. Figure 1.2 illustrates the four zones of social media channels, and we've organized the book around these groupings:

- Zone 1 is Social Community.
- Zone 2 is Social Publishing.
- Zone 3 is Social Entertainment.
- Zone 4 is Social Commerce.

You'll note as we discuss various uses of social media for personal and commercial purposes that some areas overlap two or even more zones. That's the squishy nature of social media. All social media are networked around relationships, technologically enabled, and based on the principles of *shared participation*. The four Zones framework isn't set in stone for this reason—but it is a very useful way to cut through the clutter and focus upon the most important functions of each social media platform—including those that haven't been invented yet.

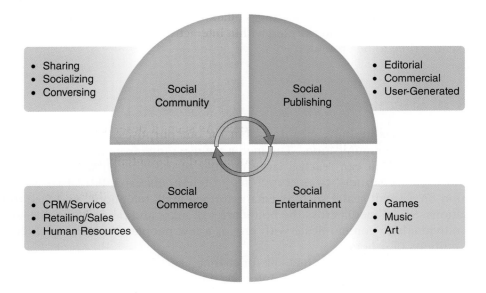

Figure 1.2   Social Media Zones

Zone 1: Social Community

Social communities describe channels of social media that focus upon *relationships* and the common activities people participate in with others who share the same interest or identification. Thus, social communities feature two-way and multi-way communication, conversation, collaboration, and the sharing of experiences and resources. All social media channels are built around networked relationships, but for social communities the interaction and collaboration for relationship building and maintenance are the *primary* reason people engage in these activities.

Many of the channels in which you already participate likely reside in this first zone. The channels in the social community zone include social networking sites, message boards and forums, and wikis. All emphasize individual contributions in the context of a community, communication and conversation, and collaboration.

For example, *social networking sites (SNS)* are online hosts that enable site members to construct and maintain profiles, identify other members with whom they are connected, and participate using various services the site offers. There are a variety of services common to SNS; the focus is on the individual communication and collaboration within the context of connections in the community. Profiles enhance the ability of members to develop a social identity when they add a profile picture or avatar, basic information about themselves, and other customizable options. Members maintain a social presence in the community that may indicate their availability, mood, friend list, and status. Connections, whom we might call *friends*, *followers*, or *fans*, communicate and share content in a variety of ways including *direct messages* (akin to email within the social networking site), *wall posts* (posts to a profile, visible to others), and *chat* or *instant messaging (IM)* options. Thus, SNS offer both synchronous and asynchronous forms of communication, and the resulting content may be either permanent or temporary. We'll delve deeper into these characteristics and uses of SNS and social communities in Chapters 4 and 5.

There are hundreds of SNS vehicles operating at present. You've surely heard of Vine, Instagram, and Pinterest. But are you familiar with Whisper, Secret, Houzz, or Thumb? LinkedIn is the leader in the area of professional networking. The most famous social network is Facebook. We differentiate Facebook from typical SNS though, because of the expansive nature of its offerings. Facebook defines itself not as a social network (although it did begin as one, and retains networking functionality), but as a social utility. Facebook's applications span all four zones of social media. As such, it deserves separate attention that we will provide in Chapter 5.

Forums are perhaps the oldest venue of social media. Essentially they are interactive, online versions of community bulletin boards. They focus entirely on discussions among members. Members establish profiles as they do in SNS and participate by posing content including questions, opinions, news, and photos. Others then respond and extend the conversation as they post responses; this results in a threaded discussion. There are thousands upon thousands of forums active online, most oriented around a common interest. For example, RC Universe (www.rcuniverse.com) is a vibrant community of remote-control hobbyists.

Wikis are collaborative online workspaces that enable community members to contribute to the creation of a useful and shared resource. Wikis can be about anything and everything. A wiki could be created by a family community to share and update family history, or by an appliance manufacturer that is trying to develop the perfect user manual. The software that supports the wiki enables multiple members to collaborate, edit, make comments, and share a variety of content.

Zone 2: Social Publishing

Social publishing sites aid in the dissemination of content to an audience. The channels of social publishing that we will feature in Chapter 6 include blogs, microsharing sites, media sharing sites, and social bookmarking and news sites. Blogs are websites that host regularly updated online content; they may include text, graphics, audio, and video. Blogs may be maintained by individuals, journalists, traditional media providers, or organizations, so they feature a wide range of topics. Thus, there are blogs that operate much like an online news source or magazine, a tabloid, or simply as an online personal diary. Blogs are social because they offer social share tools, and they are participatory because they include the option for readers to leave comments that can result in threaded discussions related to specific posts. Several services are available for formatting and hosting, including Blogger, WordPress, Squarespace, and Weebly.

Microsharing sites, also called microblogging sites, work much like blogs except that there is a limit to the length of the content you can post. A microshare could include a sentence, sentence fragment, embedded video, or link to content residing on another site. Twitter, the most well-known microsharing vehicle, limits posts to 140 characters. Others include Plurk and identi.ca.

Media sharing sites, like blogs, host content but also typically feature video, audio (music and podcasts), photos, and presentations and documents rather than text or a mix of media. Media sharing sites host content searchable by the masses, but within each vehicle are options for following content posted by specific people. Thus, media sharing sites are also networked. Here are some prominent vehicles within different types of media:

- Video sharing: YouTube, Vimeo, Vine, and Vsnap
- Photo sharing: Flickr, Snapfish, and Instagram
- Music and audio sharing: Audiofarm and Soundcloud
- Presentations and documents: Scribd, SlideShare, SplashCast, BrightTalk, and SlideBoom
- Social bookmarking services (i.e., sharing links to other sites): Diigo and Digg

Zone 3: Social Entertainment

The zone of social entertainment encompasses channels and vehicles that offer opportunities for play and enjoyment. The topic of Chapter 7, these include social games and gaming sites, socially enabled console games, alternate reality games (ARGs), and entertainment communities like Spotify.

At this stage in the development of social media, social games are by a substantial margin the most advanced channel in the social entertainment zone. These are hosted online and include opportunities for interaction with members of a player's network as well as the ability to statuscast (post updates to one's status) activities and gaming accomplishments to online profiles. Examples of social game vehicles include Candy Crush and Mafia Wars.

Yet another aspect of social entertainment is entertainment communities. MySpace, once the leading social network, now defines itself as a social entertainment service. Why? Its value lies in the network of musicians and bands and their music the site offers. Though social entertainment is still developing as a channel, we anticipate that social entertainment communities will continue to arise around other traditional areas of entertainment—music, film, art, and sport. We can already see this evolution as cultural institutions like The J. Paul Getty Museum in Los Angeles incorporate social media experiences as a part of their outreach plans.

Zone 4: Social Commerce

Our fourth zone is social commerce. The topic of Chapter 8, social commerce refers to the use of social media to assist in the online buying and selling of products and services. Social commerce influences stages of the consumer decision-making process. Channels include reviews and ratings (on review sites or branded e-commerce sites), deal sites and

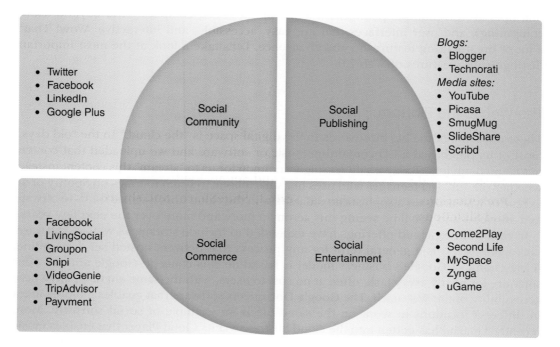

Figure 1.3   Social Media Zones and Exemplar Vehicles

deal aggregators (aggregate deals into personalized deal feeds), social shopping markets (online malls featuring user-recommended products, reviews, and the ability to communicate with friends while shopping), and social storefronts (online retail stores that sometimes operate within a social site like Facebook with social capabilities).

In addition, organizations can socially enable aspects of their traditional e-commerce websites by using tools such as Facebook Connect (a Facebook tool that allows users to log in to other partnering sites using their Facebook identities) and share applications (tools that let users share what they are reading or doing on their status feeds). Examples of review and rating vehicles include Epinions and Yelp. Groupon is an example of a deal vehicle. Yipit, DailyFlock, and 8coupons are deal aggregators. Etsy is an example of a social shopping market. Figure 1.3 illustrates the four zones of social media marketing along with several vehicles prevalent in each zone at this time.

Web 2.0: The Defining Characteristics of Social Media

Chances are you've heard the term Web 2.0 before, but just what is it? This phrase most often is attributed to Tim O'Reilly, a thought leader on the future of technology. In a 2005 article titled "What Is Web 2.0?" O'Reilly wrote, "Web 2.0 refers to developments in online technology that enable interactive capabilities in an environment characterized by user control, freedom, and dialogue."[9] Web 2.0 offers a cost-effective solution that provides access to rich data; the collective wisdom of its users; access to micromarkets; software that operates on multiple platforms (mobile phone, PDA, computer) and beyond (cloud computing); and user interfaces that are easy, accessible, and interactive. Wow! That's a lot of breathtaking features to absorb at once. Let's take a look at the most important distinguishing features of Web 2.0.

The Web Is the Platform

These days one of the big buzzwords in the digital space is "the cloud." In the "old days," most of us purchased a CD containing music or software and we uploaded that content onto our computers. Today it's increasingly common for us to "stream" this content instead; whether the "us" is a teenager who uses her smartphone to listen to tunes on Spotify or an executive who accesses a sophisticated database in the cloud (this is called SaaS—software as a service—and you'll be seeing this acronym more and more over the next few years).

In recent times, cloud offerings have expanded to include storage as well as software. Cloud computing is a general term for any process that delivers hosted services online. A big chunk of Google's business model is based on this concept. Google aims to offer software for nearly every task, often at no cost to users, with the same anytime, anywhere accessibility of the Web itself. The Google Documents software that enables multiple users in different locations to work on the same file is an example of social software. More recently Amazon has gotten into the cloud business via its Cloud Player that enables music lovers to store their tunes on the company's servers and then lets them access the tunes on multiple devices. Dropbox is also a popular cloud storage service.

Web 2.0 reaches well beyond the personal computer today. The Internet is no longer hardware-specific, tied to a physical device in a static location. Rather, we access the Web via tablet PCs and laptops, mobile phones, smart televisions, and even watches and other wearables. This also means that users interact with Web 2.0 services and applications in a host of different situations, locations, and times.

User Participation, User-Generated Content, and Crowdsourcing

Back in the day, many parents pointed with pride to a big bookshelf that displayed several rows of big, musty books; these bound encyclopedias contained a good bit of the world's knowledge. As the Internet started to take off, venerable publishers like *Encyclopedia Britannica* suddenly found their business model on the verge of extinction as consumers began to access information (which could be easily updated) via their computers rather than thumbing through heavy books. To adapt to changing times, many of these reference books (some rather reluctantly) converted their offerings to online versions where some of the content is free but more detailed information is available on a subscription basis.

Although the online material was more accessible than in previous formats—especially because the reader can search very quickly for specific entries—this version of an encyclopedia is still a Web 1.0 creature. It primarily transfers content from an authoritative source (the experts who write the topic entries) to a large audience of users. Contrast that with the Web 2.0 evolution that enabled the development of Wikipedia as the go-to encyclopedia source. Wikipedia is a "crowdsourced," easily updatable resource with tremendous added value to users.

Crowdsourcing describes a process that harnesses the collective knowledge of a large group of people to solve problems and complete tasks. Internet users search for information with *Britannica Online*; Internet users create, publish, rate, edit, and share information with Wikipedia. A small army of zealous volunteers serves as "editors" who verify others' entries—and they do so for "psychic income" in the form of pride, enjoyment, and status only, because they don't receive any direct financial compensation. A single person would not have the resources or knowledge to publish an exhaustive, stellar online encyclopedia, but a mass of individual experts can. Indeed, the willingness of numerous users to provide "free" advice, reviews, and other content provides much of the backbone of social media. This illustrates the importance of participation we described earlier. The odds are you've done it yourself: If you've ever posted a restaurant review on Yelp or "liked" a product on Facebook, welcome to the (Web 2.0) crowd!

As communication is empowered by the capabilities of Web 2.0, we enter the most recent evolution in the history of communication—the horizontal revolution we described at the beginning of the chapter. Communication is no longer one-to-many, mass, and vertically oriented. Instead, communication is now multi-way and multi-directional. Publishers, the media, and traditional marketers now share the power with anyone who can pick up a wireless signal. *This shift is a critical aspect of social media culture.* Web 2.0 levels the playing field between producers and consumers. It invites each of us to be co-creators in product design, delivery, pricing, and promotion. This means that users have a say in what producers and marketers offer in the marketplace.

User-Defined Content

Sites rely on users rather than pre-established systems to sort content. Taxonomies are classifications that experts create; for example, you may have learned (and perhaps forgotten) the classic system that biologists use to categorize organisms (the Linnaean taxonomy) that places any living thing in terms of Kingdom, Phylum, Class, Order, Family, Genus, and Specie. In contrast folksonomies are sets of labels, or tags, individuals choose in a way that makes sense to them, as opposed to using predefined keywords.

Tagging refers to the process social media users undergo to categorize content according to their own folksonomy. This process creates a tag cloud that not only enables others to search and retrieve information using tags that also make the most sense to them personally but also provides information about the popularity of the tags used. For example, many people tag photos of nature with the tag *happiness*. This suggests that those people associate this emotion with images of nature. Figure 1.4 shows a tag cloud of words we used here!

Amazon organizes its shopping site according to a taxonomy of product categories. These include sections such as (1) books; (2) movies, music, and games; and (3) computer and office products. Within the books section, you can further browse by genres such as nonfiction, literature and fiction, children's books, biographies, and more. These categories are part of an established taxonomy. However, Amazon also empowers its users to organize and classify its offerings using their own tags. These tags are entirely user-generated so users can search their own tags and the tags of others. The popular novel *The Hunger Games* by Suzanne Collins is categorized by Amazon's taxonomy as Books: Teens: Science Fiction and Fantasy. In contrast, users categorize it via folksonomy tags as *fandoms, prophecyofseven, worldonfire, amazing, trilogy, fivestars,* and *can't wait to read.* Tags like these, called hashtags and symbolized by the # symbol, are frequently used to add meaning to posts on social media sites like Instagram, Twitter, and Facebook.

according associate categorize choose classifica-tions cloud content create emotion enables example experts family folksonomy forgotten genus happiness im-ages individuals information keywords learned linnaean liv-ing media nature order organisms others people perhaps personally places popularity pre-established predefined process provides refers retrieve search sense sort specie system tag taxonomy undergo used users

Figure 1.4   A Tag Cloud

Source: Created at http://www.tagcloud.com, accessed July 13, 2014.

Network Effects

In Web 2.0, each additional user adds value for all users. Economists refer to this as a network effect. Amazon's ability to recommend books to you based upon what other people with similar interests bought in the past gets better as it tracks more and more people who enter search queries and make purchases. When you're visiting a new city and want to find a great restaurant on Yelp you feel more comfortable with a place that 1,000 diners recommend than one that only 10 users rate. You get more value from Facebook as more of your friends also use the network. Network effects enable organizations to leverage the value of crowdsourcing. Organizations use crowdsourcing to benefit from the collective wisdom of crowds, but the network effect ensures that there is sufficient participation for the crowdsourced solution to be a good one.

Scalability

Suppose a new café opens in your town; it holds only 10 tables but offers a homemade cheesecake that is to die for. As diners sample the dessert, they text and tweet about it and suddenly hordes of other people turn up to check it out. The owner didn't anticipate this response and had baked a limited number of cheesecakes for the evening. She has to turn people away; she's a victim of her own success. Her problem: The café is not scalable.

Scalability means to be able to grow and expand capacity as needed without negatively (or at least minimally) affecting the contribution margin of the business. Many concepts work well until the number of users grows beyond the system's capacity. At that point, system failures occur. Businesses that use Groupon, a social deal service, to offer socially promoted deals may struggle with scalability. Be careful what you wish for: Yes, it *is* possible to have too many customers if all of them take advantage of a special deal you offered to entice people to your store.[10] If the business could not meet the demand created by the social deal, the social media promotion was not scalable. This is an example of how network effects can be both positive and negative for organizations that want to build a Web 2.0 offering. Network effects not only enhance value but also tend to consume massive resources.

Scalability is an issue for organizations that offer services with limited resources. BitTorrent, a peer-to-peer file-sharing company, is an example of a company that sidestepped the issue of limited resources by designing its system in a way that ensured it was scalable. Rather than adding servers to accommodate growing user demand, BitTorrent's system relied upon the users as servers. BitTorrent enables its users to download large files including movies quickly. If the company stored the data and provided the download processing power, it would be limited by the number of users and bits it could download at any point in time given its server capacity. However, BitTorrent works by gathering bits of the files simultaneously from all of its users who have that file in their hard drives. This innovation enabled BitTorrent to solve the scalability dilemma and use the network effect to its advantage.

Perpetual Beta

Web 2.0 is always changing, always responding to the needs of the community. It is in part characterized by a state of being in perpetual beta. In the world of innovations, the term *beta* is used to denote a product in testing. The label enables developers to introduce new features in products even if testing and refinement are not yet complete. In "the old days" we would write the code for a program and put it out in the market. If it had glitches (and most did) we might modify the code when we launched the next release. Users had to bide their time as they waited. For example, many businesses elected not to upgrade to Microsoft's Windows 7 office software. Instead they waited several years for Windows 8; the newer version addressed flaws people found in the earlier program. In Web 2.0, many online services improve and evolve constantly as providers operate in a near constant state of continuous improvement. Google Labs offers numerous services with beta labels for Google users including Google Knol, Google FollowFinder, and more.

Reputation Economy

In Web 2.0, users trust other users as a source of knowledge. As we noted earlier, many active contributors to social media platforms do not get paid a salary—but they do benefit because they earn the respect and recognition of other users. This positive feedback creates a reputation economy where the value that people exchange is measured in esteem as well as in dollars, euros, or pounds. Consider the value of rankings and ratings other users offer as you make shopping decisions. Amazon reviews, eBay's reputation rankings, and other similar forms of collective ratings serve as credibility scores for what we can trust online.

One analyst referred to this ratings system, and other situations where decision making is decentralized to the online masses, as radical trust. This term refers to the trust bestowed on others when organizations shift control to their consumers and users. The trust is radical because those participating are not vetted; anyone and everyone online can participate in making decisions, creating and editing content, disseminating knowledge, and rating content quality. The trust enables organizations to expand beyond their own in-house resources and expertise but also puts them at risk: Will the actions taken by the masses be positive ones? Why would such trust be extended? In part, it's because of the reputation economy. Everyone can participate, but everyone is also charged with policing the content. Further, those who participate gain a form of "street cred" as power users; their reputations are at stake.

Web 2.0 is basically a term that encompasses all the ways that the Internet has developed since the early (Web 1.0) days. These advances make possible the world we know today as social media. Because social media are not possible without this infrastructure, it is the first supporting component we identify in the Social Media Value Chain that we'll talk about in the next section. Importantly, several characteristics of Web 2.0 extend throughout social media. Social media are *networked*, built on connected and interdependent *communities*, and *co-created*.

The Infrastructure of Social Media

The environment of social media is like a volcano that suddenly erupts without warning. Within a few short years we've seen an ever-expanding domain of activities, channels, technologies, and devices that are changing how we think about our lives (e.g., in the old days a "friend" was someone you actually knew in person!). As a student of social media marketing, recognizing the parameters of the field and how the pieces of the puzzle fit together will benefit you as you develop skill at devising social media strategies and tactics. The Social Media Value Chain, shown in Figure 1.5, organizes this complex environment into its core components.

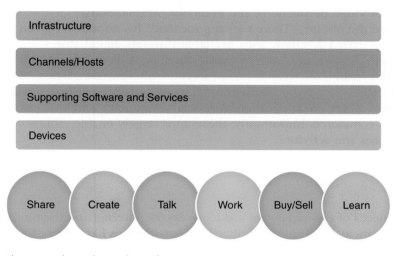

Figure 1.5   The Social Media Value Chain

The value chain illustrates the core activities of social media users and the components that make those activities possible. As a social media user, you are empowered to participate in any way you'd like, from just "lurking" on a site to scripting, filming, and uploading your own video stories. Those activities are made possible by the underlying *infrastructure* of the Internet. Just as in the physical world where we need infrastructure in the form of roads, railroads, TV transmitters, and trained people to operate and maintain these structures, in digital environments the pieces that make up Web 2.0 are crucial. These include the software that provides the programming we need to carry out these activities, the devices (iPads, smartphones, computers) we use to access them, and of course the people whose contributions provide the content we all access. Let's take a closer look at each of these elements.

Social Software

So far we've learned that the social media environment supports many Web 2.0 core activities. But much of what we are able to create or do online is due to a host of social software applications. These are computer programs that enable users to interact, create, and share data online. For virtually everything you'd like to do online, there is a social software program (or several) that can help you accomplish the activity. Interested in planning an event? Use an event planner and invitation service like eVite.com. Want to keep a notebook of wedding ideas that you can share with your bridesmaids? Use Evernote.com, or create a board of hot new wedding gown styles on Pinterest (watch out for those hideous bridesmaids' dresses). Need to keep a newsfeed of all the latest happenings at your school? Use Paper.li or Google Alerts. Social software can facilitate interaction, content creation, sharing, syndicating, saving, analyzing, filtering, sorting, and searching data online. Such tools are certainly useful to individuals, communities, entrepreneurs, and businesses. Examples include Audacity (for producing podcasts and other sound files), Xtranormal (for video production), and Prezi (for presentations).

You've heard the phrase, "There's an app for that!" It's no wonder given that there are currently more than 1.2 billion apps available through digital stores like Google Play. Those apps, also known as widgets (usually downloadable or embeddable), are types of social software. In addition to apps, social software also encompasses application service sites that we call social services. Importantly, social software exists to facilitate *all* social media channels. There are applications for social community activities, publishing, entertainment, and commerce. Importantly, these apps largely enable mobile connectivity to our social spaces and activities.

Devices

Devices are pieces of equipment we use to access the Internet and the range of activities in which we participate online. We utilize hardware devices like tablet PCs, smartphones, Internet-connected game consoles, traditional laptops and desktops, and even televisions, refrigerators, and thermostats (like Nest) for access, but we also rely upon other devices in the creation of social content. In addition to those already mentioned, we can add webcams, flip cams, and digital cameras.

In the world of social media, there is one key attribute of a device that is extremely valuable—portability. At one time, our participation online was limited to the times when we had access to a computer. The computer might have been a desktop in a school computer lab, or if we were lucky, one we had at home. These days many people have access on multiple devices and in many locations. In fact, the location might be anywhere we go as the adoption of smartphones with Internet access increases. Just think—of the more than 1.2 billion Facebook members, one billion access Facebook on their mobile phones.

People

Social media work only when people participate, create, and share content. Journalists, editors, and publishers still matter in social media, but so do everyday individuals. People support social media through their participation. This is why we hear so much about citizen journalists (amateurs who post about newsworthy events) and citizen advertisers (people who share their views about a product or service even though they're not affiliated with the company). Bloggers represent a unique hybrid form of "netizens" in that they may create and share content professionally or personally. Publishing a blog is surely a bigger commitment to sharing content than is posting a status update to your Facebook wall, but both actions generate content and add value to the social media environment.

Show Me the Money!

As wired individuals, we've come to rely on many of the social sites and services available online. And for marketers, social media have created one of the most exciting and efficient opportunities to reach target audiences. But have you ever thought about how those social sites earn revenues? Most sites still feature free access and a buffet of valuable tools and services. Yet those organizations invested in potentially extensive development costs and time, hosting costs, and ongoing maintenance. Though it's standard business practice to invest capital to pave the way for future profitability, how do these organizations earn revenue if many of the platforms are free to use?

THE DARK SIDE OF SOCIAL MEDIA

Are social media wolves in sheep's clothing? Are users so addicted to their laptops, smartphones, and iPads they can't live without them? In Korea, obsessive video gaming is already a big problem; several gamers have actually died because they wouldn't stop playing long enough to eat or drink. The Korean government has established a network of "boot camps" to treat young Internet addicts. In the United States a facility in Washington state called ReSTART offers a similar service to patients like one who spent every waking minute playing "World of Warcraft" and flunked out of the University of Iowa as a result.[11] This type of addiction was even featured in an episode of *Big Bang Theory*, in which Sheldon mentored Penny in the art of social gaming.

A recent project illustrates just how tough a media-free life might be for digital natives. At the University of Maryland, 200 students were challenged to give up their "toys" for 24 hours. That's right, just one day and night with no text messaging or laptops. No Gchatting, no tweeting, no Snapchat, no Instagram. The blogs they wrote about their harrowing experiences betray the signs of addiction: "In withdrawal. Frantically craving. Very anxious. Extremely antsy. Miserable. Jittery. Crazy." One student confessed, "I clearly am addicted and the dependency is sickening." The central role social media play in relationships resulted in feelings of isolation and boredom, even though the participants were still living on a bustling campus. One person wrote, "I felt quite alone and secluded from my life. Although I go to a school with thousands of students, the fact that I was not able to communicate with anyone via technology was almost unbearable."[12]

Can we have too much of a good thing? Are social media like an addictive drug?

Business Models and Monetization

Just like other businesses, social media providers (whether they are social communities, utilities, software providers, or game and app developers) need a monetization strategy.

Monetization refers to how a business earns revenue. It must make money if it is to survive. If a system requires substantial new investment as users adopt it, the break-even point for return on investment is delayed even as it appears to be a success. This plan is part of a company's overall business model—the strategy and format it follows to earn money and provide value to its stakeholders. For example, Google derives most of the revenue from its widely used search engine (where you "google" a term to locate relevant online links) from the fees it charges advertisers to put their messages on the results pages. In contrast, eBay makes most of its money by taking a cut of the proceeds each time a seller fills an order from a buyer on its merchandise pages. Two different business models; both ways to return value to the sponsoring organization.

For decades now, media providers (e.g., the big networks, ABC, NBC, CBS, and Fox) and media conglomerates (e.g., Disney, Viacom, and Time Warner) relied heavily on a business model we call the interruption-disruption model. The goal is to create programming that is interesting enough to attract people to watch it or listen to it. Then, when they have your attention, they interrupt the programming to bring you a commercial message. They sell ad space to marketers who want to gain the attention of a targeted audience, and the audience allows this to happen in return for access to programming they want. The monetization strategy relies upon attracting as many people as possible to the content; the more who pay attention (or who at least tune in even though they may not be paying attention), the more the programmer can charge for the right to insert messages in that vehicle.

In the age of Web 2.0, many online sites still use this same strategy (did you notice the text ads delivered alongside your Facebook newsfeed today?). As we move forward, you'll see how many social media vehicles earn revenues via advertising, following this same approach. But they also recognize the need to find other ways to earn revenues. Importantly, the revenue stream (or source of income) that will ultimately replace the model of "ad space as revenue" probably won't be paid access by subscribers or members. Though hundreds of thousands of households pay monthly for cable access, the resistance to paying for programming is strongly ingrained among many consumers. The exception is when the content is superior to what you can get by other means—and you're willing to pay a premium to receive it without being exposed to ad messages. Anyone who pays a monthly fee to subscribe to XM/Sirius Radio's hundreds of music, talk, news, and sports channels understands this model.

Psychic Income

Should you have to pay for online content? Believe it or not, way back in the old days (i.e., before 1999) it never occurred to consumers that they should *not* pay for content. That's when a college student named Shawn Fanning introduced the Napster site that enabled music lovers to share tracks for free. That party lasted only two years before legalities caught up with the service, but by then the cat was out of the bag. Now, many people (not to point fingers, but especially college students) believe that "information wants to be free," and they gravitate toward technology that enables them to download songs, newspapers, and yes, even textbooks without cost.

As attractive as that sounds, in the long run an entirely free world probably isn't feasible. Remember the old expression, "there's no such thing as a free lunch"? At the end of the day, *someone* has to pay for content and services. Music artists and novelists (and yes, even textbook authors) can't create and receive nothing in return (for long, anyway). However, the currency that we exchange doesn't necessarily have to be money. For example, if you post a restaurant review on Yelp you won't get a check in the mail for your comments. But you may get "paid" by the satisfaction of sharing your foodie opinions with the uneducated masses. You may even receive a rating on some sites that designates you as a star reviewer. These are forms of psychic income (perceived value that is not expressed in monetary form) that help to grease the wheels of social media. Also referred to as social currency, people and brands need to earn a reputation for providing high value—whether that value comes from information, relevance, and/or entertainment.[13]

The Fifth P of Marketing

Social media offer marketers opportunities to reach consumers where they work and live. Just as in the other aspects of our lives we've already discussed, the element of participation is key in this context also: *Social media enable consumers to have more of a say in the products and services that marketers create to meet their needs.*

Let's take a step back: Marketing is the activity, set of institutions, and processes for creating, communicating, delivering, and exchanging offerings that have value for customers, clients, partners, and society at large.[14] The classic view is that organizations accomplish these goals through a marketing mix that includes the so-called Four Ps: Product, Price, Promotion, and Place (or distribution).

As social media marketing techniques continue to sprout around us, today we need to add a fifth P: *Participation*. It's fair to say that just as social media are changing the way consumers live on a daily basis, so too these new platforms transform how marketers go about their business. Whether our focus is to improve customer service, maintain customer relationships, inform consumers of our benefits, promote a brand or related special offer, develop a new product, or influence brand attitudes, new social media options play a role. Social media marketing is the utilization of social media technologies, channels, and software to create, communicate, deliver, and exchange offerings that have value for an organization's stakeholders. We can see this definition play out in emerging trends in social media. While social media marketing initially influenced brands' promotional plans, more recent business applications include social funding (e.g., Kickstarter for funding new business ventures) and social indexing (e.g., preference data from social users from sources like Google+).[15]

Marketing Communication: From Top-Down to Bottom-Up

Just as the horizontal revolution changed the way society communicates, the advent and adoption of social media changes the way brands and consumers interact. Traditional marketing focuses on push messaging (one-way communication delivered to the target audience) using a large dose of broadcast and print media to reach a mass audience. There are minimal opportunities for interaction and feedback between customers and the organization, and boundary spanners (employees who interact directly with customers) mediate these dialogues. The brand message is controlled in a top-down manner by brand leadership within the organization.

Even as digital technology developed in the 1990s and beyond, marketers still essentially applied the traditional Four Ps model to reach customers. Over time they embraced the Internet as an environment for promotion and distribution. E-commerce began to blossom as an alternative to other forms of promotion such as television or radio. Consumers increasingly began to learn about products online—and to purchase them online as well. E-commerce sites are websites that allow customers to examine (onscreen) different brands and to conduct transactions via credit card.

This explosion in e-commerce activity was a boon to manufacturers, retailers, and nonprofit organizations because it offered greater speed, cost efficiencies, and access to micromarkets. A micromarket is a group of consumers once considered too small and inaccessible for marketers to pursue. Suddenly it became feasible for even a small company that offered a limited inventory to reach potential customers around the globe. The Internet enables efficient access to these markets, and in turn allows customers to search for very specialized products (e.g., music tracks by bands that recorded bass line music in Sheffield, England, between 2002 and 2005, or steampunk science fiction novels written by K. W. Jeter). This allows marketers to offer niche products that appeal to small, specialized groups of people.

As it became clear that the Internet was not going to go away, marketers flocked to cyberspace. However, most of them still applied the familiar model of the Four Ps to the digital domain. This form of marketing, tradigital marketing, is characterized by improvements in interactivity and measurement, but it retains the primarily vertical flow of power in the channels of communication and distribution. Digital online messages made it possible for consumers to respond directly to an online display ad by clicking through to the e-commerce website. Search advertising grew during this time too, making it possible for online advertising to target both mass and niche audiences. Direct marketers widely adopted email marketing as a complement to direct mail and telemarketing.

Despite these developments, modes of communication were still primarily vertical, one-way "mass communication," largely impersonal, and delivered from one to many. Whether you read the front page of the *New York Times* online at www.nytimes.com, on the New York Times app on your phone, or peruse the physical newspaper at your kitchen table, the content from the publisher is delivered vertically through the channel of communication.

Both traditional and tradigital marketing work on the basis of the interruption-disruption model we discussed earlier. This means that the source of a communication delivers messages to audiences whether they want to receive them or not, and regardless of whether these messages are directly relevant to their unique needs. By design, an advertising message interrupts some prior activity: a commercial for Axe body deodorant suddenly appears during the latest episode of MTV's *Jersey Shore,* or perhaps a pop-up bubble asks you to click on a link to learn more about low rates on car insurance while you browse a website.

Why would Internet users tolerate these disruptions as they surf the Web? For the same reason television viewers and radio listeners have for decades. The ad as interruption that provides a stream of revenue for the media provider, also enables this sponsor to provide the content of interest at little or no cost to the audience. Television programming exists to draw audiences, which enables the network to sell space to advertisers who wish to reach that audience. The audience in turn accepts the presence of the advertising in order to consume the desired programming. This "you scratch my back and I'll scratch yours" relationship also describes traditional Internet advertising: before you can watch a full episode of *Pretty Little Liars* on your laptop, you might sit through a 15-second ad for Verizon Wireless. Just like television and radio broadcasting, the Web 1.0 Internet relies upon the interruption-disruption model to earn revenue.

In contrast, social media empower consumers. It isn't enough to interrupt the consumer experience and steal a few moments of attention. With social media marketing, the ability for consumers to interact and engage with brands is greatly enhanced. Social media channels give consumers unparalleled access. Consumers discuss, contribute, collaborate, and share—with brands and with each other. The culture of marketing has shifted to an informal one focused on the belief that customers are in control. Marketing guru Peter Drucker once famously said, "The purpose of a business is to create a customer."

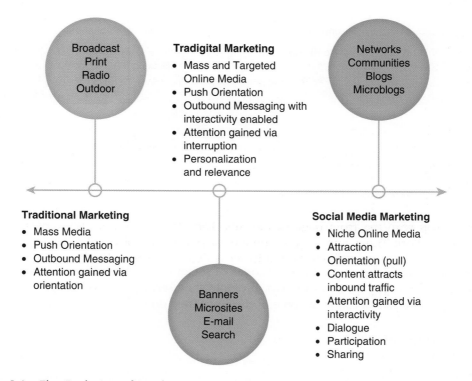

Figure 1.6   The Evolution of Marketing Communications

With the reach and community influence of social media, we can expand this definition: the purpose of a business is to create customers who create other customers.[16] *That participation in the process is the new fifth P of marketing.*

In the few years of social media's existence, social media marketing has expanded rapidly as much for its efficiency given its low absolute costs as for its potential business applications as a tool for garnering customer attention, managing customer relationships, developing new product ideas, promoting brands, driving store (online and off) traffic, and converting consumers to customers. Social media are not a substitute for traditional marketing communications, but they are also more than a complement to traditional methods, as you'll see throughout this book. This shift from traditional to tradigital to social media is illustrated in Figure 1.6.

Social Media Achieves Marketing Objectives

As social media marketing has accelerated over the last few years, the objectives organizations can accomplish have also expanded. Figure 1.6 shows these objectives across a range of marketing activities that include promotion and branding, customer service, relationship management, retailing and commerce, and marketing research. Just as the digital lives

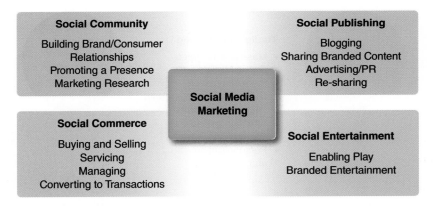

Figure 1.7   Brand Applications Across Social Media Zones

of consumers intersect across the four zones of social media, brands reach consumers in those same spaces to build awareness, promote themselves, and encourage users to try them. Let's take a closer look at some of the ways they do this.

Promotion and Branding

Marketers have many possible techniques to promote goods, services, ideas, places, or people. Though there are potentially dozens of specific promotion objectives marketers may seek to accomplish, there are two overarching objectives relevant to the use of social media marketing as part of a brand's promotional mix:

1   Extend and leverage the brand's media coverage, and

2   Influence the consumer throughout the decision-making process.

When it comes to acquiring space in media to distribute brand messages, marketers have access to three core types of media: (1) paid, (2) owned, and (3) earned. Marketers are assessed monetary fees for paid media, including purchasing space to deliver brand messages and securing endorsements. Paid media are traditionally the purview of advertising, defined as the paid placement of promotional messages in channels capable of reaching a mass audience. Public relations, the promotional mix component tasked with generating positive publicity and goodwill, may also utilize paid media in the form of sponsorships. Television commercials, radio ads, magazine print ads, newspaper ads, billboards, Internet display ads, and search engine marketing (SEM) all represent examples of paid media that may be incorporated in a brand's promotional plan. As we'll see in later chapters, other emerging formats include paying for messages in online games like Happy Pets or offering branded virtual goods to inhabitants of virtual worlds. And traditional sales promotions such as coupons and contests get a new life on social media platforms.

Owned media are channels the brand controls. Corporate websites and e-commerce sites, corporate blogs, advergames, and ARGs all represent forms of owned media. Just as Hollister's brick-and-mortar retail stores are owned and controlled by the organization, so is its website.

Earned media are those messages that are distributed at no direct cost to the company and by methods beyond the control of the company. Word-of-mouth (WOM) communication (called influence impressions in social media) and publicity are important forms of earned media. Companies release content through press releases and paid channels, participate in community events and causes, create stunts designed to generate media attention and buzz, and offer exceptional service quality, all with the hope that a brand message will spread. Table 1.2 explains the forms of paid, earned, and owned media possible in each of the zones of social media marketing.

Do you notice a category missing? That's right. There are forms of marketing that are truly controlled by a social vehicle but that are not paid, earned, or owned. David Armano of Edelman PR calls this media location, "social embassies." For instance, a brand's Facebook profile content is controlled by the brand. Does that sound like owned media? Think again. Facebook dictates the type of content that can be posted. This distinction when the media source is "free" has become more relevant of late as Facebook has announced it will favor paid advertisers in the placement of News Feed announcements. We'll talk more about this in Chapter 5. But for now, this lack of control is why social media experts advise against building your brands on rented land. It's also why it's important to recognize forms of media that do not fall neatly in our buckets of paid, earned, and owned media.

A major objective related to using social media marketing for promotional purposes is to assist in moving the consumer through the purchase process. Marketers target various stages of this cycle to increase brand awareness, enhance brand liking and image, build brand equity, incite desire, and move consumers to action. They can influence consumer attitudes and movement through the process with promotional

Table 1.2   Types of Media

ZONE	PAID MEDIA	EARNED MEDIA	OWNED MEDIA
1: Social Communities	• Ads • Native ads	• Conversations in communities • Shared content • Influence impressions • Likes, followers, fans	• Brand-owned social networks
2: Social Publishing	• Endorsements • Branded channels in media sharing sites	• Embeds • Comments • Shares • Links • Search rankings	• Corporate blogs • Brand-controlled media sharing sites
3: Social Entertainment	• Ads in games or on social music sites	• In-game interactions	• Advergames and branded ARGs
4: Social Commerce	• Sales promotions	• Reviews and ratings • Recommendations and referrals • Group buys • Social shopping interactions	• Social storefronts

messages targeted throughout the social media channels. Ultimately, social media can do more than influence engagement. Social media can influence sales. Researchers from the University of Maryland studied the influence of Twitter activity on sales for several little-known bands. They found a positive association between band social media activity and album sales.[17] Let's take a brief look at how this works at each stage of the purchase process.

1   *Increase Awareness:* Brands can increase awareness with social media marketing by maintaining an active presence in the social spaces where target consumers "live" and by integrating social media into the marketing mix. Such integrations can result in a boost to campaign effectiveness, as was the case when Samsung partnered with the Academy Awards for the 2014 Oscars broadcast. Using a Samsung Galaxy, Academy Awards host Ellen DeGeneres spontaneously snapped and tweeted a selfie. The tweet became the most retweeted post of all time, garnering millions of retweets. Samsung further benefited due to the millions of earned media impressions.

2 *Influence Desire:* Social media promotions can be used much like advertising, catalog marketing, and feature events to persuade consumers to recognize a sense of desire. The fashion brand Lilly Pulitzer posts each new collection on Facebook, Flickr, and YouTube. Visitors can tour pictures of its designs, fresh from each photo shoot. It's like being in the pages of *Vogue*.

3 *Encourage Trial:* Social media can even be used to support sampling and loyalty programs. Sampling means to offer a free trial of a product; these are usually mailed to consumers' homes or distributed in stores or on the street. Social media can be used to recruit interested prospects to qualify for samples. Emergen-C, a health supplement, used this tactic to promote free samples. Whenever a user on Twitter tweeted something like "need energy" or "need to focus," Emergen-C sent a tweet requesting the person's mailing address. A couple of days later, the tired tweeter received a gift of three samples.

4 *Facilitate Purchase:* Social media serve as a distribution channel and venue for many sales promotion incentives, including deals and group offers. Many customers "like" or follow brands in social networks in order to qualify for special deals. Here's a recent tweet from Taco Bell: "We're on @Snapchat. Username: tacobell. Add us. We're sending all our friends a secret announcement tomorrow.! #Shhh." Friends were rewarded with coupons.

5 *Cement Brand Loyalty:* Social media venues offer engaging activities for consumers that can ensure they spend more time with the brand, hopefully resulting in higher levels of brand loyalty. Look no farther than social games that offer rewards for the most loyal visitors. That's just what Foursquare does. Starbucks "mayors" earn one dollar off a cup of coffee when they visit. Tasti D-Lite, a regional ice cream chain, went even farther when it developed its social media loyalty program.[18] Customers use TreatCards—which also double as gift cards—to earn points for purchases, and those who opt into the social media bonuses automatically earn additional points. Twitter and Foursquare accounts are updated each time the card is swiped and points are earned or redeemed. As a customer earns points, he or she can redeem them for free cones.

Customer Relationship Management and Service Recovery

Despite all the hype we hear constantly hear about social media being the "new advertising," there are in fact other applications where these techniques will play an increasingly important role. For one, customer relationship management, or CRM, also finds a home here. CRM practices focus on what we do with a customer after the first sale; it's far more difficult (and expensive) to attract new customers than to keep old ones. That's why many organizations work hard to maintain contact with their customers and to provide additional products and services to them over time. Often they rely on sophisticated databases that keep an ongoing record of what a person buys and other pertinent information so that he or she will receive customized follow-up messages and offers that are likely to meet unique needs. Salesforce.com is among the leading business solutions for social CRM.

FROM BYTES TO BUCKS

Perhaps the best way to illustrate how marketing objectives can be pursued with social media marketing is to kick things off with delicious burritos and tacos. Chipotle is a chain of quick-service, "fast-casual" restaurants in the United States, United Kingdom, Canada, Germany, and France specializing in burritos and tacos. Started in 1993, it positioned its brand on the notion that fast food can be fast and fresh and that sustainable farming matters. With annual advertising expenditures under $10 million per year[19], it successfully competes against other chains with much larger promotional budgets. Panera, for instance, reportedly spent $70 million.[20] How does Chipotle do it? Social media marketing.

Let's take a look at how Chipotle earned publicity with its social media campaign, increased brand exposures on social media networks and media sharing sites, engaged fans for extended periods of time with its social game, and used social media to reinforce its grand position in the market. Chipotle utilizes social communities, social publishing, social entertainment, and social commerce channels in its campaigns and generates earned media from consumers and news media.

Chipotle first gained recognition as a contender in the social media marketing space with its 2012 campaign "Back to the Start."[21] The campaign, which featured Willie Nelson's version of Coldplay's "The Scientist," won the 2012 Cannes Grand Prix for film and for branded content. You can see related videos on our ZonesofSMM YouTube channel. The animated film was broadcast in limited release in paid media outlets including movie theaters, but primarily was shared online via YouTube. The song could be downloaded at iTunes.

In 2013, Chipotle revisited this approach with a new campaign it called "The Scarecrow," and the chain also added to its investment in social media marketing strategy. Chipotle's approach is heavily based on the concept of content marketing, which is the core input for a social publishing (Zone 2) approach to social media marketing. But Chipotle went beyond Zone 2 to develop a social entertainment extension of its message and to participate in social community to espouse its beliefs in sustainable farming.

"The Scarecrow" campaign was launched via a roughly three and a half minute video hosted prominently on the Chipotle webpage and announced through YouTube, as well as on Chipotle's Twitter and Facebook accounts. The ad was also picked up by a variety of news sources due to the high production quality of the ad so it also garnered earned media. Chipotle partnered with Oscar-winning Moonbot to create both the short film and the social game tie-in.[22]

Consistent with Chipotle's 2011 "Back to the Start" film, this effort illuminates the complicated relationships between the food industry and what we put into our bodies. The ad opens with a scarecrow, but scenes from the ad include chickens being injected with a growth hormone that causes them to plump and cows being kept in cages where they are unable to move. The turning point in the ad is when the scarecrow finds a fresh red pepper and returns to farming (as opposed to chemically enhanced food) organic, farm-fresh, seasonal food. Aside from the red pepper, which is a symbol closely associated with the Chipotle brand, the only overt branding in the film is within the closing seconds. The full film can be viewed on YouTube. Those of you who have studied semiotic analysis in advertising courses will appreciate the symbols in this video as Chipotle shares its views on the food production industry and the value of sustainable farming.

The Scarecrow film also came to life in the development of a social game (available at Chipotle's microsite www.scarecrowgame.com), which enabled Chipotle to tie in a social entertainment aspect to the campaign. The Scarecrow social game encourages brand fans to spend more time with the brand message as they participate and to share the brand message with their own social networks. Engagement in social communities including Twitter and Facebook helped

Photo 1.1

to spread the content and brand message. The campaign won three prizes, including a Grand Prix at the 2014 Cannes Festival.

Since the release of "The Scarecrow" campaign, Chipotle has continued to advance its position on the value of organic and locally farmed meats and vegetables by developing content for its own Hulu series called "Farmed and Dangerous." The series includes four long-form, comedy films (22 minutes each); each is consistent with Chipotle's positioning strategy but does not include the brand name. While it's technically a form of branded content, *Social Media Week* dubbed the series "unbranded entertainment." Chipotle's social media approach is consistent with social media best practices to provide content that is valuable, relevant, participatory, and shareable.

But Chipotle went even farther with the campaign as the chain demonstrated how to leverage a theme across many

(Continued)

(Continued)

media platforms. One such extension is a scavenger hunt for its fans with clues provided in social media sites like Twitter. Others embrace offline media as well. For example, the chain uses its food packaging as a medium to offer essays from thought leaders like Malcolm Gladwell.[23] These texts appear on Chipotle bags in stores with accompanying videos on YouTube. Even with the content published offline, the power of social media stands strong, as evidenced by shared images of the packaging essays that pop up on Twitter and other social media sites (check out the Twitter feed @Chipotletweets).

Because of this digital focus, it's not surprising that CRM lends itself to social media applications. Social CRM embraces software and processes that include the collective intelligence of a firm's customers to more finely tune the offer and build intimacy between an organization and its customers.[24] When brands embrace social CRM, they use social media as they were meant to be used. Why do we make this claim? Just as we learned that earned media can result from creative and interactive social messages, companies that do a good job of maintaining strong brand-to-customer relationships will benefit from earned media, as those customers in turn share information and recommendations with their networks.

But this is a sword that cuts both ways. It's ideal when all of our interactions with customers are positive. Unfortunately, things sometimes go wrong. When they do, today's social consumers won't hesitate to share their nasty experiences with others on social platforms. They'll vent their frustrations in the most public of ways. A great example is the sad story of one man's plane trip that resulted in a busted guitar that went viral on YouTube ("United Breaks Guitars" video on YouTube).[25] After he tried unsuccessfully to get United Airlines to repair or replace his guitar, this disgruntled passenger created his own version of the story and set it to music—the video he uploaded about his experience was viewed nearly 10 million times. Obviously this was not a happy event for the airline. This illustration of the potential negative impact on a firm's image underscores how important it is for organizations to take customers' complaints seriously (especially those who are inclined to post about their experiences). It is also vital to have a plan in place to initiate service recovery when things do go wrong (and they will). This term refers to the actions an organization takes to correct mishaps and win back dissatisfied customers.[26] One helpful set of guidelines that some companies use is known as the LARA framework:[27]

- Listen to customer conversations.
- Analyze those conversations.

- Relate this information to existing information within your enterprise.
- Act on those customer conversations.

Service recovery typically has to happen quickly if it's going to have any impact. A firm that can identify a problem in the system (e.g., a product recall, a snowstorm that will ground flights) can nip it in the bud by letting customers know that it's aware of the issue and is taking steps to address it. That's a big reason why social media can play such a big role in CRM: the platforms they can use allow them to communicate quickly and efficiently to large groups of customers or to customize messages to individuals who require follow-up. For example, companies such as Carphone Warehouse, Zappos, Best Buy, and Comcast have turned to Twitter to conduct their social CRM: they can monitor trending topics and preempt problems if they find that a lot of people are tweeting about them (in a bad way). If necessary, they can send their own tweets to explain what happened and provide solutions.

Marketing Research

Social media open exciting new windows for marketing research. Whether to collect insights for the discovery stage of the creative process or to gather ideas for new product development, social media provide new tools to listen to customers as they discuss their lives, interests, needs, and wants. In fact, this social media marketing activity is called social listening. While social listening may be used for social CRM, service recovery, competitive analysis, or even ideas for new product development, it can also be useful for "on the fly" opportunities. An example is this now infamous tweet from Arby's. At the Grammys, Pharrell Williams wore a large hat during his performance of his hit song, "Happy." In real-time, @Arbys tweeted, "Hey, @Pharrell, can we have our hat back? #grammys." Pharrell took the bait and sent a humorous response. This spontaneous and organic exchange was possible due to social listening and resulted in thousands of retweets, favorites, and replies.[28] We'll learn more about conducting research with social media in Chapter 9. Which channels of social media are relevant for social media market research? Potentially all of them, but profile data, activities, and content shared in social communities and content shared via social publishing vehicles are especially valuable for researchers.

Retailing and E-Commerce

The last major application for social media marketing is that of retailing and e-commerce. We've already shared ways that brands can incent trial and purchase using social media promotions. If you are like most consumers, you've used your share of online ratings and reviews before you made a purchase decision. But did you know that you can go shopping in social storefronts or browse on e-commerce sites that enable real-time chat with your friends? That's right. Groups of friends can shop together even when everyone is online—and not necessarily in the same physical location. When brands use social media marketing as a retailing space, create a venue for and/or encourage consumer reviews and ratings of products, and enable applications that help friends shop together online, we're solidly in the social commerce zone. This will be our focus for Chapter 8.

Careers in Social Media

Now you've seen how individuals and organizations including businesses, nonprofits, and governments use social channels. As organizations learn the value of social media for marketing, new jobs come online every day to accommodate the need for skilled social media marketers. Interested? Consider the list of social media jobs in Table 1.3.

Table 1.3   Jobs in Social Media

JOB TITLE	JOB DUTIES
Social Media Editor	Build and maintain our content distribution network by way of social media channels.
	Participate in real-time conversations that surround our content and brand, answer comments, be a mediator.
	Create content for various social media and marketing channels that align with corporate communications goals and calendars.
	Schedule and organize multiple projects that generate content on a daily basis.
	Tag and title content, with an understanding of how the words chosen impact natural search traffic and rankings via recurrent optimized content.
Social Media Marketing Manager	Create and execute social media marketing campaigns.
	Analyze trends in social media tools to increase the use of social media directing consumers to our sites.
	Strategize with marketing team to include and utilize social media as an alternative marketing tool.
Marketing and Communications Associate	Manage key strategic messages, ensuring precise coordination with mission, vision, and positioning.
	Ensure accuracy, timeliness, and consistency of tone.
	Integrate messages into all communication formats with particular emphasis on social media and the website.

JOB TITLE	JOB DUTIES
Project Social Media Manager	Manage the strategy, planning, and execution of the social media initiatives of the brand.
	Work interdepartmentally to select, develop, and promote social content and experiences.
	Consistently report on performance metrics of social media initiatives.
	Monitor and respond to the fan community, as appropriate.
	Optimize the fan experience across social platforms.
	Assist in the continued development of social media strategy.
	Help educate other departments throughout the company on social media.
Social Media Communications Manager	Build and maintain all social media platforms, including Facebook, Twitter, and new/emerging platforms such as location-based social media.
	Establish and grow relationships with key influencers in the digital space, such as bloggers, highly followed personalities, influential YouTube reviewers, and others.
	Lead all digital outreach efforts behind key efforts such as new apps, new original series, priority entertainment verticals, and more.
	Manage all communications with PR team and agency.
	Build and manage Brand Ambassador program.
	On an ongoing basis, measure and report performance of all marketing activities and assess against goals, identify trends and insights, and optimize plan based on these insights.
Social Media Coordinator	Support the day-to-day management and execution of the social media initiatives of the brand.
	Assist in the promotion and development of social content and experiences.
	Handle data entry and tracking of the performance metrics of social media initiatives.

(Continued)

Table 1.3   (Continued)

JOB TITLE	JOB DUTIES
	Monitor and respond to the fan community, as appropriate.
	Support the optimization of the fan experience across social platforms.
Online Communications and Social Media Director	Drive high-profile social media strategies to raise visibility and buzz for the company's major business initiatives, products, and services.
	Develop and implement strategies for the company's official social media channels and platforms.
	Manage PR and social media agencies and vendors to maximize results.
	Shape the company's approach to social media in the short and long term while educating and counseling colleagues, business units, and leaders on social media opportunities, best practices, and key learnings.
	Serve as an external spokesperson and official company representative both for press and within social media channels engaging with bloggers, customers, partners, and prospects on an ongoing basis.
	Develop and nurture relationships with relevant consumer and industry media and influencers.
	Analyze online buzz and discussions as well as emerging social media tools and platforms to develop innovative ideas, programs, and appropriate messaging/response.
	Work with brand marketing teams, legal, business units, and corporate affairs colleagues.
Social Media Communications Specialist	Develop social media strategies and plans to integrate into marketing mix; perform continual updates and adjust plans accordingly to meet business needs.
	Maintain internal communications calendar to consistently deliver new dynamic content to consumers throughout the year.
	Work with cross-functional teams to deliver a consistent brand voice and message across all social media platforms (e.g., Twitter, Facebook, YouTube, blog posts).

JOB TITLE	JOB DUTIES
	Strategize and collaborate with creative team to incorporate captivating social networking features into design templates and content, with distribution through various channels (blog posts, viral video campaigns).
	Research and advise creative team and communications team on trends and best practices involving new media and communications tools.
	Build and maintain content distribution lists by way of social media channels.
	Contribute to public relations activities and efforts by monitoring news on social networks; assist with producing reports of results.
	Compile key metric reports (e.g., tonality, number of fans and followers) on a monthly/quarterly basis that measures effectiveness on social media platforms, including competitors.
	Establish an implementation strategy for leveraging third-party content to enrich the overall user experience and keep the community fresh for frequent visitors.
	Generate titling of content and tags; optimize tags on feeds to include shared sites, search engines, and keyword optimization; understand how words chosen impact natural search traffic and rankings via recurrent optimized content.
	Train customer service representatives on how to respond to customer service issues via Twitter; monitor quality of responses and provide guidance on best practices.
Social Media Intern	Construct and implement social media strategy for the brands' Facebook, Twitter, and YouTube accounts, which will include editorial management and development, blogging, posting, and monitoring website user-generated activity, user experience optimization, and potential development and management of third-party relationships.
Social Media Strategist	Drive strategy, planning, and execution of social media strategies to increase brand visibility, reputation, engagement, and social footprint.
	Develop innovative, comprehensive, and actionable approach for establishing and expanding presence on social networks and perform day-to-day tasks including listening, brand monitoring, social activities, and competitive research.
	Conduct research, monitor, and provide recommendations to enhance social presence and customer engagement.

Source: Used by permission of SimplyHired.com.

CHAPTER SUMMARY

What are social media? How are social media similar to traditional media?

Social media are the online means of communication, conveyance, collaboration, and cultivation among interconnected and interdependent networks of people, communities, and organizations enhanced by technological capabilities and mobility. Like traditional media, social media include several channels, and within each channel there are specific vehicles. For example, television is a broadcast media and *The Today Show* is a vehicle within the medium of television. Social communities are a channel of social media and LinkedIn is a vehicle.

What are the major zones associated with social media?

The major channels of social media include social communities, social publishing, social entertainment, and social commerce. Each channel incorporates networking, communication functionality, and sharing among connected people, but they each have a different focus. Communities are focused on relationships. Publishing features the sharing and promotion of content. Entertainment channels are geared to fun and shared uses of social media. Commerce addresses the shopping functionality of social media applications.

What is Web 2.0, and what are its defining characteristics? How does Web 2.0 add value to Web 1.0?

Web 1.0 provided Internet users with easy access to information, entertainment, and communications tools, but in many ways it was akin to shifting existing programming from traditional media like television broadcasts and magazines to new media online. There were benefits to consumers, but Web 2.0 fundamentally changed the consumers' role as well as the role of providers in delivery information, entertainment, and communications tools. Web 2.0 adds value because it ramps up what we called the "Fifth P" of marketing: participation. When consumers engage in an ongoing dialogue with other people and with companies, their stake in the process increases—this results in more satisfying outcomes for producers and customers. Tim O'Reilly, a leader in technology innovations, defined Web 2.0 as developments in online technology that make interactivity possible as it offers users control, freedom, and the ability to participate in a dialogue. Several characteristics support the meaning of what Web 2.0 is: (1) Web as platform, (2) user participation and crowdsourcing, (3) user-defined content, (4) network effects, (5) scalability, (6) perpetual beta, and (7) the reputation economy.

How does the Social Media Value Chain explain the relationships among the Internet, social media channels, social software, and the Internet-enabled devices we use for access and participation?

The Social Media Value Chain explains that social media are made up of core activities and supporting components. The core activities include the things people do with social media such as converse, share, post, tag, upload content, comment, and so on. The support components include the Web 2.0 infrastructure, social media channels, social software, and the devices we use to interact with social media.

What is social media marketing?

Social media marketing is the use of social media to facilitate exchanges between consumers and organizations. It's valuable to marketers because it provides inexpensive access to consumers and a variety of ways to interact and engage consumers at different points in the purchase cycle.

What marketing objectives can organizations meet when they incorporate social media in their marketing mix?

There are several marketing objectives achievable utilizing social media marketing techniques. Branding and promotion, research, and customer service and relationship management objectives are all viable using social media.

KEY TERMS

advertising
apps
blogs
boundary spanner
business model
cloud computing
connections
content marketing
crowdsourcing
deal aggregators
deal sites
devices
digital native
display ad

earned media
e-commerce
entertainment communities
Facebook Connect
folksonomies
forums
hashtags
horizontal revolution
influence impression
interruption-disruption model
LARA framework
marketing
marketing mix
media

media sharing sites
medium
message boards
microblogging sites
micromarkets
microshare
microsharing sites
monetization
monetization strategy
network effect
niche products
owned media
paid media
perpetual beta

(Continued)

(Continued)

personal media
psychic income
public relations
push messaging
radical trust
reputation economy
revenue stream
reviews and ratings
SaaS (software as a service)
sampling
scalability
search advertising
search engine marketing (SEM)
selfie
service recovery
share applications

social commerce
social communities
social CRM (customer
  relationship management)
social currency
social entertainment
social games
social identity
social listening
social media
social media marketing
Social Media Value Chain
social networking sites
social presence
social publishing
social services

social shopping markets
social software
social storefronts
social utility
statuscast
tag cloud
tags
taxonomies
tradigital marketing
vehicles (media)
Web 2.0
widgets
wikis
word-of-mouth (WOM)
  communication
Zones of Social Media

REVIEW QUESTIONS

1 How do you define social media? Social media marketing?

2 What are the supporting components of the Social Media Value Chain?

3 Identify the characteristics of Web 2.0.

4 What is crowdsourcing?

5 Explain the difference between a taxonomy and a folksonomy. What role does tagging play in creating folksonomies?

6 What does perpetual beta mean for software users?

7 What are the implications of the radical trust adopted by organizations using social media?

8 What are the four zones of social media? How do social media compare to traditional media?

9 Explain the concept of psychic income, also known as social currency.

10 How can brands use social media to develop earned media value?

11 What is social CRM? How is it different from traditional CRM?

EXERCISES

1 What is a monetization strategy? Visit Twitter.com and explain how Twitter monetizes its business. Do the same for Foursquare.

2 Replicate the University of Maryland study discussed in the "The Dark Side of Social Media" feature. Abstain from all social media for 24 hours. That's right—no texting, no tweeting, no snapping. Keep a record of your unwired day and then produce a blog post about your experience.

3 Should online services like Facebook and Google Docs be free? Poll your classmates and friends (including your social network) to find out what they think should be free. Use the polling features available on Facebook to conduct your poll. What do the results say about the possible monetization strategies available to social media providers?

4 Create an account at About.Me or Flavors.Me. Your account will serve as the basis for your social footprint. Begin to link your existing social media accounts to your footprint page. Identify other social communities in which you should develop profiles. Even for channels you choose not to use, you may wish to reserve your profile name.

5 Stuart Elliot noted in his advertising column in the *New York Times* that brands are increasingly including social media lingo in ads designed for traditional media.[29] The practice is known as *borrowed interest*. For example, an ad using this tactic might leverage the word "like" and a thumbs-up symbol or include the word "hashtag" in conversation. Are these "ripoffs" of social media culture effective? Explain.

6 Social funding sites like Kickstarter promise to use crowdsourcing to fund worthy projects. Visit Kickstarter and assess the participation in a project. What do you think spurs participation in the funding process?

CHAPTER NOTES

1   *Cisco Connected World Technology Report*, 2012, http://www.cisco.com/c/en/us/solutions/enterprise/connected-world-technology-report/index.html, accessed July 13, 2014.

2   Marc Prensky, "Digital Natives, Digital Immigrants," *On the Horizon* 9, no. 5 (October 2001): 1–6.

(Continued)

(Continued)

3   There are several definitions of social media proposed by experts in the field. In preparing this definition, we've aggregated the most commonly referenced characteristics of social media and also sought to align the definition with those of traditional media.

4   Facebook statistics, http://www.Facebook.com/press/info.php?statistics, accessed November 15, 2010.

5   YouTube Statistics, YouTube, https://www.youtube.com/yt/press/statistics.html, accessed July 8, 2014.

6   Chloe Albanesius, "YouTube Users Uploading 35 Hours of Video Every Minute," PCMag.com, November 11, 2010, http://www.pcmag.com/article2/0,2817,2372511,00.asp, accessed November 15, 2010.

7   Social Media Comparison Infographic, *Leverage,* April 2014, https://leverage-newagemedia.com/blog/social-media-infographic/, accessed June 8, 2014.

8   *The Free Dictionary,* http://www.thefreedictionary.com/medium, accessed June 8, 2014.

9   Tim O'Reilly, "What Is Web 2.0?" O'Reilly Media, September 30, 2005, http://oreilly.com/web2/archive/what-is-web-20.html, accessed December 31, 2010.

10 Tracy Tuten and Christy Ashley, "Promotional Strategies for Small Businesses: Group Buying Deals," *Small Business Institute Journal,* 7, no. 2 (2011), http://www.sbij.ecu.edu/index.php/SBIJ/article/view/111, accessed August 29, 2014.

11 "Center Tries to Treat Web Addicts," *New York Times*, September 5, 2009, http://www.nytimes.com/2009/09/06/us/06internet.html, accessed May 13, 2010.

12 Quoted in Jenna Johnson, "Fighting a Social Media Addiction," *Washington Post*, April 26, 2010, http://voices.washingtonpost.com/campus-overload/2010/04/fighting_a_social_media_addict.html, accessed May 13, 2010.

13 Mark Ralphs, "Built In or Bolt On: Why Social Currency Is Essential to Social Media Marketing," *Journal of Direct, Data, and Digital Marketing Practice*, 12, no. 3 (2011): 211–215.

14 American Marketing Association, "Definition of Marketing," http://www.marketingpower.com/aboutama/pages/definitionofmarketing.aspx, accessed December 31, 2010.

15 Park Sung-Min, "New Business Applications for Social Networking," January 2012, *SERI Quarterly*, 121–126.

16 Shiv Singh, "Social Influence Marketing Trends for 2010," January 21, 2010, http://www.slideshare.net/shivsingh/social-influence-marketing-trends-2967561?from=ss_embed, accessed December 31, 2010.

17 Yogesh Joshi, Liye Ma, William Rand, and Louiqa Rashid, "How Social Media Drives Brand Engagement and Sales," MSI Insights, *Marketing Science Institute*, December 20, 2013, http://www.msi.org/articles/how-social-media-drives-brand-engagement-and-sales/?utm_source=20141&utm_medium=Email&utm_campaign= Insights/, accessed February 2, 2014.

18 Jennifer Van Grove, "Twitter and Foursquare Become the New Loyalty Program at Tasti D-Lite," *Mashable*, January 13, 2010, http://mashable.com/2010/01/13/tasti-d-lite-tastirewards/, accessed September 7, 2010.

19 Maureen Morrison, "Chipotle Taps GSD&M for Media, Creative," *Advertising Age*, May 29, 2014, http://adage.com/article/agency-news/chipotle-taps-gsd-m-media-creative/293465, accessed June 26, 2014.

20 Brandon Gutman, "Panera Bread Doubles Digital Spend From Last Year," Forbes, February 20, 2013, http://www.forbes.com/sites/marketshare/2013/02/20/panera-bread-doubles-digital-spend-from-last-year/, accessed June 5, 2014.

21 Augie Ray, "Chipotle Scarecrow: Pure Imagination or Pure Manipulation?" *Social Media Today*, September 23, 2013, http://www.socialmediatoday.com/augieray1/1760776/chipotle-advertising-scarecrow-pure-imagination-or-pure-manipulation, accessed September 30, 2013.

22 Nudd, T., "Ad of the Day: Chipotle Makes Magic Yet Again with Fiona Apple and a Dark Animated Film," *Adweek*, September 12, 2013, http://www.adweek.com/news/advertising-branding/ad-day-chipotle-makes-magic-again-fiona-apple-and-dark-animated-film-152380, accessed September 27, 2013.

23 Maureen Morrison, "Chipotle Taps Malcolm Gladwell, Jonathan Safran Foer for Essays on Packaging," *Advertising Age*, May 15, 2014, http://adage.com/article/news/chipotle-taps-gladwell-safran-foer-packaging/293228/, accessed June 1, 2014.

24 Michael Fauscette, "What Is 'Social' CRM Anyway?" January 26, 2009, http://www.mfauscette.com/software_technology_partn/2009/01/what-is-social-crm-anyway.html, accessed September 8, 2010.

25 Josh Bernoff, *Empowered* (Cambridge, MA: Harvard Business Press, 2010).

26 Maria Ogneva, "Why Your Company Needs to Embrace Social CRM," *Mashable*, May 21, 2010, http://mashable.com/2010/05/21/social-crm/, accessed September 7, 2010.

(Continued)

(Continued)

27   Maria Ogneva, "Why Your Company Needs to Embrace Social CRM," *Mashable*, May 21, 2010, http://mashable.com/2010/05/21/social-crm/, accessed September 7, 2010.

28   Eric Melin, "Arby's Biggest Social Win Ever Comes From Listening," *Social Media Today*, January 31, 2014, http://www.socialmediatoday.com/eric-melin/2130416/arby-s-biggest-social-win-ever-comes-listening, accessed February 3, 2014.

29   Stuart Elliott, "Ads That Speak the Language of Social Media," *New York Times*, March 24, 2013, http://www.nytimes.com/2013/03/25/business/media/ads-that-speak-the-language-of-social-media.html?_r=0, accessed January 24, 2014.

 Social Media Marketing Strategy

LEARNING OBJECTIVES

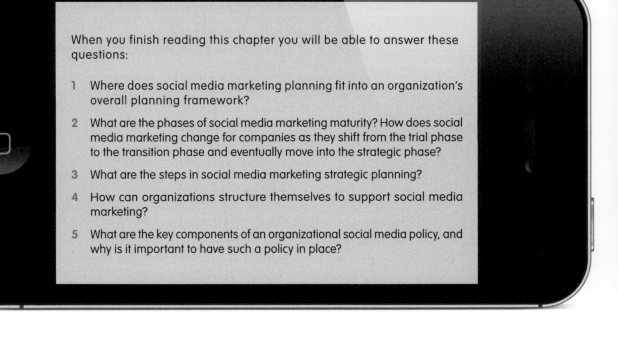

When you finish reading this chapter you will be able to answer these questions:

1   Where does social media marketing planning fit into an organization's overall planning framework?

2   What are the phases of social media marketing maturity? How does social media marketing change for companies as they shift from the trial phase to the transition phase and eventually move into the strategic phase?

3   What are the steps in social media marketing strategic planning?

4   How can organizations structure themselves to support social media marketing?

5   What are the key components of an organizational social media policy, and why is it important to have such a policy in place?

Strategic Planning and Social Media Marketing

Honda is buying into social media, big time. The company has strategically utilized several different social media channels and vehicles in recent years and coordinated these with more traditional tactics like paid broadcast media to maximize impact. The company has an active presence in social communities like Facebook and Twitter, but also runs targeted campaigns on niche community networks like Vine and Pinterest. Honda partnered with Salesforce to manage its social media activity and ensure it could be responsive with fans around the world who use social media to reach out to the brand. We'll hear more about Honda's approach to social media marketing in this chapter.

For marketers like those at Honda, strategic planning is the process of identifying objectives to accomplish, deciding how to accomplish those objectives with specific strategies and tactics, implementing the actions that make the plan come to life, and measuring how well the plan met the objectives. The process of strategic planning is three-tiered, beginning at the corporate level, then moving to the business level, and lastly moving to the functional areas of the organization, including marketing. Planners first identify their overall objectives (e.g., "raise consumer awareness of our brand by 10% in the next year") and then develop the specific tactics they will use to reach those goals (e.g., "increase our spending on print advertising in targeted publications by 15% this year"). A marketing plan is a written, formalized plan that details the product, pricing, distribution, and promotional strategies that will enable the brand in question to accomplish specific marketing objectives. Table 2.1 provides a sample of an overall marketing plan structure.

Table 2.1   The Structure of a Typical Marketing Plan

THE MARKETING PLAN OUTLINE	QUESTIONS THE PLAN ADDRESSES
A PERFORM A SITUATION ANALYSIS 1 Internal Environment	• How does marketing support my company's mission, objectives, and growth strategies? • What is the corporate culture and how does it influence marketing activities? • What has my company done in the past with its: Target markets? Products? Pricing? Promotion? Supply chain? • What resources including management expertise does my company have that make us unique? How has the company added value through its offerings in the past?
2 External Environment	• What is the nature of the overall domestic and global market for our product? How big is the market? Who buys our product? • Who are our competitors? What are their marketing strategies? • What are the key trends in the economic environment? The technological environment? The regulatory environment? The social and cultural environment?
3 SWOT Analysis	• Based on this analysis of the internal and external environments, what are the key Strengths, Weaknesses, Opportunities, and Threats (SWOT)?

THE MARKETING PLAN
OUTLINE

QUESTIONS **THE PLAN ADDRESSES**

B SET MARKETING OBJECTIVES	• What does marketing need to accomplish to support the objectives of my firm?
C DEVELOP MARKETING STRATEGIES 1 Select Target Markets and Positioning	• How do consumers and organizations go about buying, using, and disposing of our products? • Which segments should we select to target? If a consumer market: What are the relevant demographic, psychographic, and behavioral segmentation approaches and the media habits of the targeted segments? if a business market: What are the relevant organizational demographics? • How will we position our product for our market(s)?
2 Product Strategies	• What is our core product? Actual product? Augmented product? • What product line/product mix strategies should we use? • How should we package, brand, and label our product? • How can attention to service quality enhance our success?
3 Pricing Strategies	• How will we price our product to the consumer and through the channel? How much must we sell to break even at this price? What pricing tactics should we use?
4 Promotional Strategies	• How do we develop a consistent message about our product? How do we best generate buzz? • What approaches to advertising, public relations, sales promotion, and newer forms of communication (such as social networking) should we use? • What role should a sales force play in the marketing communications plan? How should direct marketing be used?
5 Supply Chain Strategies	• How do we get our product to consumers in the best and most efficient manner? • What types of retailers, if any, should we work with to sell our product? • How do we integrate supply chain elements to maximize the value we offer to our customers and other stakeholders?
D IMPLEMENT AND CONTROL THE MARKETING PLAN 1 Action Plans (for all marketing mix elements)	• How do we make our marketing plan happen?
2 Responsibility	• Who is responsible for accomplishing each aspect of implementing the marketing plan?
3 Time line	• What is the timing for the elements of our marketing plan?
4 Budget	• What budget do we need to accomplish our marketing objectives?
5 Measurement and Control	• How do we measure the actual performance of our marketing plan and compare it to our planned performance and progress toward reaching our marketing objectives?

On second thought, what's wrong with jumping right into the game? Why should we take the time to plan? Although it's tempting to just follow our instincts, it turns out there is tremendous value in planning. Dumb luck and sweat take you only so far. Planning ensures that an organization understands its markets and its competitors. It helps to ensure that organizations are aware of the changing marketplace environment. When organizational partners participate in the planning process, they are better able to communicate and coordinate activities. Planning requires that objectives are set and agreed upon, which improves the likelihood of those objectives being met. It enhances the ability of managers to allocate limited resources using established priorities. Perhaps most of all, planning enables success to be defined. Success or the lack thereof becomes a measurable outcome that can guide future planning efforts.

It's increasingly common for organizations to include a heavy dose of social media in their marketing plans. Nearly all marketers use social media in some way—one survey revealed 97% of marketers use social media.[1] The use may or may not be integrated, but most are. Whether large or small, B2B (business-to-business) or B2C (business-to-consumer), businesses recognize that social media should be integrated into their marketing plans. One study found that 90% of businesses with revenues in excess of $1 billion felt social media should be an integrated aspect of their marketing.[2] Most are doing so for branding and demand-generation purposes, but social media marketing is also valuable for managing customer service interactions and conducting market research. This upward trend will continue in the coming years.

It makes sense to include social media marketing in a brand's marketing plan. Social media marketing has many applications for marketers. Social media can be a delivery tool to build buzz and word-of-mouth communication. It can efficiently deliver coupons and other special promotional offers. Social platforms can be the primary venue for the execution of contests and sweepstakes. They can collect data to build databases and to generate sales leads. Social media can also serve as efficient channels to manage customer service relationships and to conduct research for new product development. Not to mention, social media are relatively inexpensive ways to increase the reach and frequency of messages that are otherwise delivered via more traditional, big media methods.

Because the creative applications related to social media are somewhat unique, we will suggest an approach for developing an in-depth social media marketing strategy much as advertising plans (also known as integrated marketing communications (IMC) plans or marcom plans) provide in-depth detail on the execution of the (traditional) promotional portion of a brand's marketing plan. In the early days of social media marketing, many plans were developed for stand-alone campaigns that were not fully integrated into the brand's promotional mix. Today, social media marketing campaigns may serve as stand-alones or be a fully integrated media choice in the brand's marcom plan. For simplicity, we approach the sample plan from the perspective of a stand-alone campaign. Table 2.2 provides the structure of a social media marketing plan. We'll begin this process as we explore the strategic development of social media marketing plans. Then we'll cover the steps in strategic planning for social media marketing. Finally, we'll discuss structural approaches organizations can take to be prepared to execute their plans.

Table 2.2   A Social Media Marketing Plan

THE SOCIAL MEDIA MARKETING PLAN OUTLINE

I   Conduct a situation analysis and identify key opportunities

    1   Internal Environment

        a   What activities exist in the overall marketing plan that can be leveraged for social media marketing?

        b   What is the corporate culture? Is it supportive of the transparent and decentralized norms of social media?

        c   What resources exist that can be directed to social media activities?

        d   Is the organization already prepared internally for social media activities (in terms of policies and procedures)?

    2   External Environment

        a   Who are our customers? Are they users of social media?

        b   Who are our competitors? What social media activities are they using and how are social media incorporated in their marketing and promotional plans?

        c   What are the key trends in the environment (social, cultural, legal and regulatory, political, economic, and technological) that may affect our decisions regarding social media marketing?

    3   SWOT Analysis

        a   Based on the analysis, what are the key strengths, weaknesses, opportunities, and threats (SWOT)?

II   State objectives

    1   What does the organization expect to accomplish through social media marketing (promotional objectives, service objectives, retail objectives, research objectives)?

III   Gather insight into target audience

    1   Which segments should we select to target with social media activities?

    2   What are the relevant demographic, psychographic, and behavioral characteristics of the segments useful in planning a social media marketing strategy?

    3   What are the media habits, and especially the social media habits of the segments?

IV   Select social media zones and vehicles

Which mix of the four zones of social media will be best to accomplish our objectives within the resources available?

    1   Social community zone strategies

        a   What approach to social networking and relationship building should we use? How will we represent the brand in social networks (as a corporate entity, as a collection of corporate leadership, as a brand character)? What content will we share in this space?

(Continued)

Table 2.2   (Continued)

THE SOCIAL MEDIA MARKETING PLAN OUTLINE

2		Social publishing zone strategies
	a	What content do we have to share with audiences? Can we develop a sufficient amount of fresh, valuable content to attract audiences to consume content online?
	b	What form should our blog take?
	c	Which media sharing sites should we use to publish content? How should we build links between our social media sites, owned media sites, and affiliates to optimize our sites for search engines?
3		Social entertainment zone strategies
	a	What role should social entertainment play in our social media plan? Are there opportunities to develop a customized social game or to promote the brand as a product placement in other social games? Is there an opportunity to utilize social entertainment sites such as MySpace as an entertainment venue?
4.		Social commerce zone strategies
	a	How can we develop opportunities for customer reviews and ratings that add value to our prospective customers?
	b	Should we develop retail spaces within social media sites? If we socially enhance our own e-retailing spaces, what applications should be used?
	c	How can we utilize social commerce applications like group deals to increase conversions?
V		Create an experience strategy encompassing selected zones
	1	How can we develop social media activities that support and/or extend our existing promotional strategies?
	2	What message do we want to share using social media?
	3	How can we encourage engagement with the brand in social spaces?
	4	How can we encourage those who engage with the brand socially to act as opinion leaders and share the experience with others?
	5	In what ways can we align the zones used as well as other promotional tools to support each other? Can we incorporate social reminders in advertising messages, in store displays, and other venues?
VI		Establish an activation plan
	1	How do we make the plan happen?
	2	Who is responsible for each aspect of implementing the plan?
	3	What is the timing of the elements in the plan?
	4	What budget do we need to accomplish the objectives?
	5	How do we ensure that the plan is consistent with the organization's overall marketing plan and promotional plan?
VII		Manage and measure
	1	How do we measure the actual performance of the plan?

The Phases of Social Media Marketing Maturity

If you keep up with industry news, you might be tempted to think that *every* brand has a social media strategy. Each day seems to bring new stories about a marketing campaign with social media elements. On ads, storefronts, and business cards, we see "Follow me" calls to action as organizations large and small flock to Twitter and Facebook.

Although it seems everyone is talking about social media, it's one thing to claim you *use* social media and quite another to say you have a *strategy* that incorporates social media. In the former case, a group can turn to social media activities to stage stunts (one-off ploys designed to get attention and press coverage) or as activation tools to support other marketing efforts. For example, when Skittles let its social media presence take over its website, that was a stunt. But when Starbucks runs social media promotions, it integrates these promotions with the overall campaign in place.

As organizations develop in their social media marketing maturity, they plan systemati-cally to ensure social media marketing activities are consistent with their marketing and marketing communications plans and are capable of meeting specific marketing objectives. By this we mean that as a result of time and experience we tend to see that applications that start as one-time "experiments" often morph into more long-term and carefully thought-out elements that the organization integrates with all the other communication pieces it uses to reach customers.

Nevertheless, many marketers currently use social media marketing tactics without that level of maturity. A major study of marketers in both Europe and North America found huge differences in the level to which respondents use social media and integrate them with their other initiatives. Many still just experiment with baby steps (like creating a Facebook page) rather than include social media as a fundamental component of their marketing strategy.[3] Companies are eager to jump into the social media game, but many are still in the process of figuring out just how these approaches can go beyond the nov-elty stage and actually help them to meet their objectives. Companies can be thought of in terms of their level of maturity in social media marketing, of which there are three phases: trial, transition, and strategic.[4] Let's take a closer look at each phase.

Trial Phase

The trial phase is the first phase of the adoption cycle. Organizations in the trial phase test out social media platforms, but they don't really consider how social media can play a role in the overall marketing plan. In these early days, most groups focus on learning to use a new form of communication and exploring the potential for social media as a venue.

It isn't necessarily a bad thing to test the waters of social media. Companies need, especially early on, to experiment—to play in the sandbox, so to speak. Doing so helps them to brainstorm ideas to use social media and understand what it takes to succeed in this brave new world. However, the problem with the trial phase is that many companies do not treat it as an exploratory stage of what is really a multi-stage process. Instead they just jump right in and focus only on cool new ways to communicate. Think this couldn't happen? One estimate suggests that 44% of marketers have been using social media less than two years.[5]

SHOW ME!

Photo 2.1

British Airways could be thought of as one example of a company that has not fully embraced social media as a key component of marketing strategy. How do we know? Consider this example. A customer of British Airways, frustrated about his lost luggage (using his Twitter handle @ hvsvn), posted a "promoted tweet" (that's paid media in social vehicle) advising people to avoid flying with British Airways due to its horrendous service. The company didn't respond for eight hours! When it did, it tweeted that customer service hours were standard business hours—9 to 5—and asked that the customer direct message (DM) his baggage claim information to them. What would you think? You got it. Twitter is 24/7. Brands don't have the option of being on only 8 hours per day.[6]

American has been lauded for its use of social media marketing. Headlines make claims like "How American Airlines Gets Social Right," "The Secret to American Airlines' Customer Service Success," and "AA's First Class Twitter Strategy." Sounds good, right? Maybe not. In the transition stage, brands are on the right track but may not have fully formed a strategic approach. We place American Airlines in the transition phase. Why? American Airlines includes automation in its social media response tactics. This means that some of the responses to tweets or Facebook posts (or other social media comments) are programmed. In the industry, these automated responses are sometimes called bots or social media zombies. In and of itself, that's not bad. Automation can help brands be responsive. But if overused or used ineffectively, people will know. And they will resent it. This is what happened to American Airlines. Just after the media announcement that American Airlines would merge with US Airways, a Twitter user tweeted a congratulations (of sorts). The tweet suggested that the new merged organization would be, well, less than a traveler's dream. What did American do? It tweeted (zombie-style) a reply: "Thanks for your support! We look forward to a bright future as the #newAmerican!"[7]

Transition Phase

As organizations mature in their use of social media marketing, they enter a transition phase. During this phase, social media activities still occur somewhat randomly or haphazardly but a more systematic way of thinking starts to develop within the organization. An example? Perhaps American Airlines can serve as one.

Strategic Phase

When an organization enters the final strategic phase, it utilizes a formal process to plan social media marketing activities with clear objectives and metrics. Social media are now integrated as a key component of the organization's overall marketing plan. As we move forward, we'll share insights from Honda's social media campaigns to show why.

Social Media Campaigns: The Strategic Planning Process

Those organizations that have moved beyond the trial and transition phases of social media marketing maturity develop strategic plans for social media that incorporate components of the social media mix as channels to accomplish marketing objectives. As we saw in Table 2.2, the process consists of the following steps:

- Conduct a situation analysis and identify key opportunities.
- State objectives.
- Gather insight into and target one or more segments of social consumers.
- Select the social media channels and vehicles.
- Create an experience strategy.
- Establish an activation plan using other promotional tools (if needed).
- Execute and measure the campaign.

Situation Analysis

The first step in developing the plan is much the same as it is in the creation of traditional strategic plans—research and assess the environment. Good social media planning starts with research on the industry and competitors, the product category, and the consumer market. Once this research is compiled, strategists try to make sense of the findings as they analyze the data in a situation analysis.

The situation analysis details the current problem or opportunity the organization faces. It will typically include a social media audit. In addition to the standard things marketers need to know, the social media audit ensures the team understands the brand's experience in social media. In addition, a review of the brand's SWOT analysis will highlight relevant aspects of the firm's internal and external environment that could affect the organization's choices, capabilities, and resources. This acronym refers to *strengths, weaknesses, opportunities,* and *threats* that the firm should consider as it crafts a strategy. The internal environment refers to the strengths and weaknesses of the organization—the controllable elements inside a firm that influence how well the firm operates. The external environment consists of those elements outside the organization—the organization's opportunities and threats—that may affect its choices and capabilities. Unlike elements of the internal environment that management can control to a large degree, the firm can't directly control these external factors, so management must respond to them through its planning process.

A key aspect of the external environment is the brand's competition. Analyzing competitive social media efforts and how the target market perceives those efforts is a must-do in social media marketing planning. It can be done in much the same way as the social media audit—except the focus is on the competing firms. You can use an internal system or a cloud service such as RivalMap (www.rivalmap.com) to organize competitive information and to monitor news and social activity. When you use RivalMap, you can maintain a search of competitive activity and news mentions online for a small fee.

A competitive social media analysis should answer the following questions:

- In which social media channels and specific vehicles are competitors active?
- How do they present themselves in those channels and vehicles? Include an analysis of profiles, company information provided, tone, and activity.
- Who are their fans and followers? How do fans and followers respond to the brand's social activity?

Importantly, marketers have many approaches to solving problems and taking advantage of opportunities. Here we are concerned with the organization's use of social media, but still, the planner should ask the question, "Given the situation and the problem identified, is social media marketing the appropriate approach?" Especially for organizations that are still in the trial phase, it's tempting to focus on social media "gimmicks" even if other less trendy tactics might in fact be more effective. So, a word of caution: social media often provide effective solutions to marketing problems, but beware of blindly using these tools.

To see how the early stages of the strategic planning process work in the real world, let's return to our example, Honda. Honda relies upon the positioning of each of its sub-brands but seeks to do so in a way that resonates with specific social media vehicles like Twitter, Vine, and Pinterest. We'll focus on Honda's CR-V and the general brand. This campaign will be in line with Honda's selling points of the CR-V, positioned with the tag line, "Get out and move." Honda is one of the most well-known brands in the world, named 20th on the Forbes most valuable brands list. That's not all; the brand has won awards for most trusted car brand, best value brand, and best overall brand! But, Honda faces stiff competition online and off.

THE DARK SIDE OF SOCIAL MEDIA

When brands choose to engage in social media, they need to be sure they understand the commitment. This is especially true for brands in the trial stage of social media marketing maturity. HMV, an abbreviation for His Master's Voice (which makes sense when you see Nipper's image listening to the gramophone)—a staple in the music industry, found this out. As a brand in the trial stage of social media marketing, HMV allegedly had an unpaid intern set up its Twitter account. When the intern was gone, management lost track. But the account was still live and someone held the keys (ahem, the password!). As HMV called a meeting to lay off staff members, one of them live-tweeted the meeting using the hashtag #hmvXFactorFiring. Among the most amusing (of these truly sad tweets) is one about a HMV exec asking how to shut down Twitter![8]

Photo 2.2

HMV closing down © iStock.com/dynasoar

Table 2.3   Honda's Social Media SWOT Analysis

Strengths:	Weaknesses:
• Loyal customers • High brand equity • Affordability • Quality products • High levels of coverage across all forms of media	• Difficulty standing out in a highly competitive marketplace • Reputation issues due to recalls • Reputation issues related to being an old-school brand
Opportunities:	**Threats:**
• Social media as a cost-efficient channel	• Disasters affecting ability to meet demand • Strong brand competition from competitors like Toyota

Identify Social Media Marketing Objectives and Set Budgets

In this stage of the process, the planner elaborates on what is expected of the social media campaign and what financial and human resources are available to meet those objectives. An objective is a specific statement about a planned social media activity in terms of what that activity intends to accomplish. The content of the objective will vary based on the situation and the problem at hand. For instance, the campaign may be designed to amplify other marketing communication efforts the organization uses. Let's say, for example, the brand co-sponsors a concert series. This series is an event marketing strategy built into the overall marketing communications plan. But the organization realizes that promoting the event using social media can build pre- and post-event buzz. In this case, the objective (to create heightened awareness of the event among target customers) relates to other activities in the organization.

The basic assumption is that the campaign can accomplish desired marketing objectives. What are some examples of the basic marketing objectives social media marketers pursue? Here are some important ones:

- Increase brand awareness.
- Improve brand or product reputation.
- Increase website traffic.
- Amplify or augment public relations work.
- Improve search engine rankings.
- Improve perceived customer service quality.
- Generate sales leads.
- Reduce customer acquisition and support costs.
- Increase sales/sales revenue.

In this stage of planning, it's important to state the objectives in a way that will help the planner to make other decisions in the planning process and eventually to measure the extent to which the objective was accomplished at specific points into the campaign. A well-stated, actionable objective should include the following characteristics:

- Be specific (what, who, when, where).
- Be measurable.
- Specify the desired change (from a baseline).
- Include a time line.
- Be consistent and realistic (given other corporate activities and resources).

Here's an example of an actionable objective: *To increase site stickiness in the retail areas of our site by 100% (from 5 minutes browsing to 10 minutes per site visit) with the addition of social commerce sharing applications by the end of the third quarter.* The statement of the objective should include specific elaboration on the individual goals the brand wishes to achieve over the course of the campaign, taking care to state these goals such that they are specific, measurable, realistic,

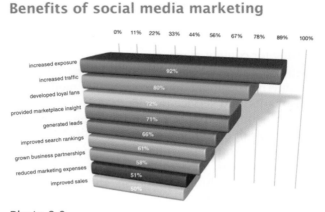

Benefits of social media marketing

Photo 2.3

and time-lined. We don't know Honda's precise objectives but we can gauge that Honda wanted to build a presence on popular social networks, enable its position to resonate in a way that is tailored to those networks, build brand equity, and increase top-of-mind awareness. Particularly for the #Pintermission campaign, Honda clearly sought to drive awareness of the new CR-V launch for users on Pinterest.

There should be a focus on resources. You've probably heard people say that the main benefit of social media marketing is that it's free? When brand managers work with agencies to plan traditional advertising campaigns, the cost of media placement can seem overwhelming. With that as a point of comparison, one can see why many might think of social media marketing as the free alternative to advertising. We will discuss paid media options in social media vehicles, but most of what brands plan is in the earned media realm.

So then, what's the problem? *Social media are not free.* In planning a social media campaign, a budget must be allocated that ensures sufficient resources to accomplish the goals—just like in a traditional ad program. Granted, the media costs are often much lower compared to, say, a national television campaign. But there are other costs associated with social media. Charlene Li, a leading social media strategist, once said, "Social media trades media costs for labor costs."

What does Li's comment mean? To a large extent, the social communities in which brands engage consumers are indeed free to play spaces in terms of *media costs*. But there are other costs we must take into account. Content must be generated, shared, and managed, and the time that that takes requires funding. Strategies in some social media channels of our social media framework require development costs (in-house or with a vendor or agency) such as customizing profiles and developing social games, branded applications and widgets, and microsites. At the end of the day, there's no such thing as a free lunch!

Most organizations to date allocate only a small portion of their marketing budgets to social media. Current estimates are under 10%! Though that budget is expected to nearly double in the next 5 years! Where will this money be spent? Primarily organizations are staffing for content management, ensuring that time is available for content development, blogging, and monitoring of social channels. In addition, organizations are not only creating internal positions to manage social media marketing, they are also hiring agencies, consultants, and service providers. As we described in Chapter 1, the job of social media manager, akin to that of a brand manager, is becoming more commonplace. This person has the role of overseeing, managing, and championing the social media strategy internally. Agencies and other providers can supplement the work of the social media manager (or team) with ideas, ways to integrate social media marketing with the rest of the brand's marcom plan, technical expertise, and measurement.

As with everything else in business, the budget is critical—without funding, the organization can't initiate or maintain the campaign. How much should it allocate? When it comes to social media campaigns, budgets run the gamut from a few hundred to hundreds of thousands of dollars (particularly for complex campaigns like those associated with global alternate reality games, which we'll look at in Chapter 7).

Many companies approach social media marketing budgets as a percentage of their ad spends, which in turn are assigned by planners within the organization according to one of several formulae. The percentage of ad spend method assigns a set portion of the overall advertising budget for the organization to social media activities. Some use a variation, where they allocate a percentage of online marketing funding to social media.

Two other methods are used by companies. The competitive parity method uses competitors' spending as a benchmark. Like advertiser share of voice, competitive parity is based on the belief that spending the same or more on social media marketing will result in a comparable change in share of attention for the brand. When it comes to social media, though, share of voice takes on a new dimension; social media include conversations about the brand from other sources. In contrast, with advertising, increasing share of voice is accomplished by simply purchasing more media time for advertisements.

With social media marketing, the costs of different approaches and platforms vary widely, and even a large spend may not result in widespread buzz or content sharing and viral spread. The resulting share of voice depends in part on the extent to which fans and friends share the message with their own networks. Lastly, the objective-and-task method considers the objectives set out for the campaign and determines the cost estimates for accomplishing each objective. This method builds the budget from a logical base with what is to be accomplished as the starting point.

Profile the Target Audience of Social Consumers

Social media marketing plans, like any marketing plan, must target the desired audience in a meaningful and relevant manner. To do this requires the development of a social media profile of the target audience. The target market for the brand will have been defined in the brand's marketing plan in terms of demographic, geodemographic, psychographic, and product-usage characteristics. The target audience's social profile will take this understanding of the market one step farther. It will include the market's social activities and styles, such as their level of social media participation, the channels they utilize and the communities in which they are active, and their behavior in social communities. You'll learn more about the behaviors and attitudes of social consumers in Chapter 3.

The strategic planner must assess what it means to speak to the audience in the social media space. Who is the core target? How can we describe the key segments of that core target? To whom will the conversations in social media be directed? Of which social communities are the consumers a member? How do they use social media? How do they interact with other brands? The insights from the consumer profile that was done for a brand's overall marketing and marcom plans will be useful to understand the overall profile of the target market.

However, the planner also must understand how and when his or her customers interact in online social communities, as well as which devices they use to do so. In developing a consumer profile, the planner may plot out a typical day for the social media user as well as gather information on the Internet activities of the audience.

Let's see how Honda went through this profiling process. Its strategy for the #Pintermission campaign included specifically targeting Pinterest users. The average user of Pinterest is a female in the age range of 18 to 40.

Select Social Media Channels and Vehicles

Once the organization understands who it wants to reach, it's time to select the best social media mix to accomplish this. The zones of social media make up the channel and vehicle choices available for a social media mix. Similar to a more traditional marketing mix, the social media mix describes the combination of vehicles the strategy will include to attain the organization's objectives.

The social media mix options lie among the four zones we've already discussed: relationship development in social communities, social publishing, social entertainment, and social commerce. Within each zone are many specific vehicles that may be best suited to reach a certain audience. For instance, to meet the desired objectives and the social media patterns of a target audience that includes college students, the planner may determine that the campaign should include social networking, social publishing, and social games. The media vehicles might include Facebook, YouTube, and Flickr. Social publishing may utilize a corporate blog and document sharing sites such as Scribd. The brand may choose to utilize an existing social game. You've seen examples of the choices brands made as they developed effective social media campaigns. It's also a good idea at this stage of planning to map out how the campaign will build earned media and utilize paid and owned media synergistically. In the #Pintermission example, Honda chose to utilize social publishing in the social vehicle, Pinterest. But notably, this is not Honda's only social media approach. It also planned campaigns for Vine and Twitter, as well as maintaining a social media presence on an ongoing basis. See Figure 2.1 for a summary of Honda's zone activity.

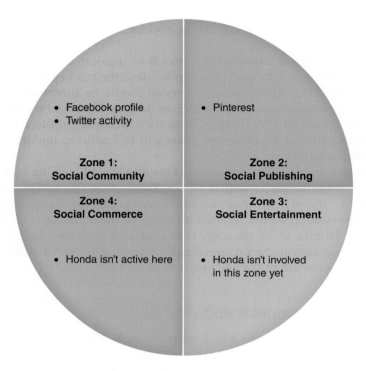

Figure 2.1   Honda's Zones of Social Media Marketing

Create an Experience Strategy

If we were planning an advertising campaign, the next step would be to identify a creative message strategy. Message strategy refers to the creative approach we will use throughout the campaign. This should flow from the brand's positioning statement—a single written statement that encapsulates the position the brand wishes to hold in the minds of its target audience. Positioning statements succinctly capture the heart of what the brand is and what the sponsor wants it to become. Reviewing the position is a necessary step in preparing a social media marketing strategy, because the social media activities the campaign plans and executes need to consistently support the desired message.

Can you identify the brands that go with these positioning statements?[9]

1　The computer for the rest of us
2　Networking networks
3　The world's information in one click
4　Personal video broadcasting network

Answers: (1) Apple, (2) Cisco, (3) Google, (4) YouTube

The message strategy should also be appropriate to meet the campaign's objectives. It is developed from a creative brief—a document that helps creatives channel their energy toward a sound solution for the brand in question. In planning for social media marketing campaigns the design process works similarly; the planners create a brief to guide the development of the campaign. But—because unlike traditional media, social media focus on interactive experiences, social sharing, and engagement—the brief has a somewhat different structure and goes by a different name. Some planners call this document an experience brief.

The concept of an experience brief evolved from the work of website developers who consider the direct impact on users when they design site architecture, imagery, copy, and other site features. Griffin Farley, a strategy planner, uses a different term. He describes the planning document for social media as a propagation brief.[10] He explains that propagation planning means to plan not for the people you reach, but for the people that *they* will reach. In other words, traditional advertising promotes a message to a passive audience, and that audience is the target. Social media invite an interactive experience with an audience of influencers who will then share the brand's message and invite others to the experience. To develop a social experience worthy of participation and worthy of sharing, social media planners ask and answer several questions.[11] The answers become the basis for the brief:

- **What are the campaign goals and/or communication tasks?** Objectives have been set for the campaign and the use of social media identified as a possibility. Here the planner reviews these decisions and provides a succinct overview of the goals.

- **How is the brand positioned? What is unique and special about its position in the marketplace?** As in a traditional creative brief, any campaign work should leverage the brand's positioning strategy and build on the brand's strengths.

- **Who is the target audience?** You've profiled the target already. Now consider what you want the audience to do. Do you want them to talk to the brand? Create and share content? Spread the message to their network? On what devices (e.g., iPad, smartphone, desktop) will they interact with your brand? What could you offer of value in exchange for their cooperation?

- **Is there another group of people who can persuade the target audience to follow them?** This group is your *influencers*—the people who will propagate your message. Why would these people want to share your message with others? What's in it for them?

- **What are the existing creative assets? How can the brand's creative foster a social experience?** Most brands already have some creative assets that drive their paid and owned media. For example, a well-known and popular brand spokescharacter such as the GEICO gecko is a creative asset that the insurance company has developed in its traditional advertising, so he might be employed in a social media campaign to give the company a head start in terms of consumer recognition as it tries to break through the clutter of competing messages. The planner should list the creative assets that already exist and identify the assets he or she still needs to extend the brand's story. How can the creative assets already available be used and/or leveraged in a social media context?

- **How can we integrate with other branded media being used by the organization, and how long do we have to execute?** This is a question that references how the campaign can integrate best with the brand's paid and owned media.

- **What experiences are possible given target market needs and motives, the available channels, and the creative assets? How can we design these experiences to maximize device portability and access?** Creative assets used in social media campaigns should inspire activity and interactivity. These questions ask what types of activities could be engaging for the target audience using multiple devices and worth sharing with their network.

- **What content will be needed?** Social media are content-driven. What content will be relevant to the campaign and what will be the source? Comments? Questions and polls? Video? Images? Stories? Apps?

- **How will experience engagement be extended and shared throughout the social channels?** For instance, will engagement activity auto-post to status updates (e.g., "Tracy likes Cole Haan")?

After the planner goes through the process of discovery and briefing to provide these "must-knows" to the creative team, the creative team will then enter the stage of ideation or concepting. *Discovery* is the term used to describe the research stage of the plan. Planners may rely on secondary and primary research as they seek to discover insights that will be useful to the creative team. These insights will be presented to the team during the briefing. The creative team will spend time brainstorming ideas and developing possible concepts for the campaign. Eventually the chosen ideas will be further refined and designed, and prototypes or mock-ups will be developed. These preliminary executions can then be used for internal review, usability testing, and other pre-testing.

When a brand begins to interact in social spaces, a key decision is how to represent the brand's social persona. This means planners need to define how the brand will behave in the social Web, what voice will be used, and even how deeply the brand will interact in the social space with customers. The decisions made should support the brand's position in the market. To introduce that persona, brands have several creative options. They may involve humanizing the brand (again, think of the GEICO gecko); showing a vulnerability to the customer and working as a steward to customer service (think Dell); or providing a value to the customer whether that value be function, information, or entertainment (think Nike). In Honda's case, the brand's position is brand as corporate entity.

Additionally, the makeup of the brand's social persona may vary. Other brands, such as Zappos, utilize different employee voices in social communities so the online retailer's persona is the sum of its employees. Still others have represented the brand with a person, but with a single individual charged with the brand's social reputation. The brand's mascot may take the social stage as Travelocity has done with its Roaming Gnome. Some brands present themselves as funny, comedic, thought leaders, and friends. There is no right or wrong social persona—it should ultimately be a social representation of the brand's position and of course be consistent with how the brand presents itself in other contexts.

© Jennifer Chong

Photo 2.4

So what did Honda plan? For its #Pintermission campaign, it leveraged relationships with five of the most influential "pinners" on Pinterest. You'll learn more about the nature of influence in Chapter 4, and the specific approach of leveraging influencers in Chapter 6. These pinners are seemingly always on. They pin a lot of content and their curations are so widely respected that each pinner has nearly a million followers. That's some serious street cred. The #Pintermission campaign asked these five pinners to take a break—to take an *intermission* from social media. That was the experience. Why would they? Honda paid and offered a prize for the photos originating from the #Pintermission. The photos had to be tagged #Pintermission and they led back to the Honda website, which enabled measurement. That was Honda's Pinterest campaign, but it also used other social vehicles in its overall plan (as discussed in the Show Me! box on the following page).

Integrate With Other Promotional Components and Establish Campaign Timeline

Traditional media campaigns typically live a designated lifespan with timing tied to the accomplishment of specific objectives. For social media, though, campaigns are not necessarily events with fixed start and stop dates. Conversations in communities continue over time, and a brand's social media marketing presence should do this as well. This is particularly true for brands that rely on social media for customer service and customer relationship management. Some of the most famous social brands, like Dell and Zappos, are "always on" with their social media campaigns. They aim to project a constant presence

SHOW ME!

For instance, Honda launched a campaign that further promoted the company's popular Summer Clearance Sales Event. The campaign creatively combined both Twitter and Vine and used them to increase and engage the company's audience. The whole campaign idea is based around Honda responding in near real-time to unhappy car owners on Twitter with a personalized 6-second Vine video reflecting the message of the original Tweet. Participants had to use the #WantNewCar hashtag for Honda to know that it should respond to it. The more original the message, the higher the probability that the team responded. While all social media initiatives lived online, traditional media coverage was also

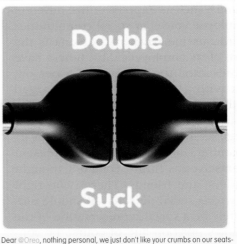

Dear @Oreo, nothing personal, we just don't like your crumbs on our seats- odyssey w available Built-in HondaVAC pic.twitter.com/fG5vN7sZvK

HONDA   @HONDA. TUE, OCT 01 2013 14:20:16   ← REPLY   ↻ RETWEET   ☆ FAVORITE

Photo 2.5

present. That's not all Honda did. It also thoroughly invested in zone 1—social community—by engaging in conversations with other engaged brands on Twitter. Honda sent antagonistic remarks to 15 powerful brands in a humorous way designed to spark engagement and conversation. Take a look at the message Honda tweeted to Oreo.

in the communities in which they participate. Honda uses a mix of short-term campaigns and ongoing presence. Other organizations have also done this.

Execute and Measure Outcomes

In the final stage of the strategic planning process, we implement the plan and measure the results. In Chapter 10, we'll go into detail about the *metrics* we can use to assess the effectiveness of social media campaigns. The data gathered on all aspects of the social media plan are used to provide insight for future campaigns.

As we've seen, many organizations are still "social media wannabes." They're at an early stage in the process and feeling their way in a new environment. So perhaps we can forgive them for the common mistakes they tend to make. Here are some of the biggest offenders:

FROM BYTES TO BUCKS

Ridden on the metro lately? In Melbourne, the Metro is the city's premier rail service. It operates 203 six carriage trains across 803 kilometers of track and transports around 415,000 customers each day. With 15 lines, 218 stations, and services seven days a week, Metro can take you wherever you're headed, whenever you want to go. It is "fully committed to providing a comfortable, safe, and reliable train network as part of an interconnected public transport service, striving to rival the world's best."

What was the background? Metro wanted to reduce train accidents, most of which involved young people. Kids constantly ignore safety messages. To combat their resistance, Metro needed a campaign that catered to this young audience. Something humorous and colorful [with a catchy song] should do the trick! How can teenagers possibly resist dark humor that makes light of a real safety issue? Will it work? Critics said, "Behavior change is a hard thing to market; it's not an easily measurable target—there is no conversion rate, and only time will tell if it's effective. However, in labeling train accidents 'dumb' instead of 'tragic,' this campaign can tap into an important principle for behavior change marketing, and that is that peer pressure and shame can make people change their habits. No one wants to be thought of as dumb."[12]

The campaign pursued three key objectives:

1   To promote railway safety among the general public, specifically the teenage/young adult market

2   To decrease the number of railway related deaths by [at least] 5% next year

3   To connect customers with Metro by showing them that it is a safe and reliable form of transportation

Who was the target audience? All types of individuals use the public transportation system to get around. With that said, it is the younger demographic (e.g., 14 to 20) that is reluctant to pay attention to safety warnings. Maybe it's because they always have their head stuck in a phone, Facebook, Twitter, or some other form of social media. In any event, Metro has to find some way to get through to them.

How could they move forward? The executive creative director for Metro, John Mescall, echoes these sentiments: "Pretty early on, we decided we'd try to create entertainment rather than advertising. For the simple reason that we figured if traditional public service announcements (PSAs) repel people, then we should really try to create one that attracts them."[13]

Metro decided to use three zones—social community (Facebook and G+), social publishing (YouTube video and Tumblr), and social entertainment (branded social game).

The heart of the campaign is in social publishing. Metro developed a video that it released on YouTube, titled *Dumb Ways to Die*. Metro recognized that it would likely attract earned media as marketing

(Continued)

(Continued)

blogs discussed the campaign (assuming it was worthy of discussion and it was!). In fact, not only was the video shared by news media, it was shared by—well, everyone. It became among the most shared viral videos ever. EVER!

Since the target population is teenagers/young adults, it is only natural that the loveable characters become part of a downloadable app for Android on Google Play incorporating part of the social entertainment zone.

Why was this a good experience strategy?

The goal of this campaign was to bring awareness to Metro and its support for railway safety. By making a mockery of the subject on Facebook, Twitter, Google +, YouTube, will kids retain the 'important message' a bit longer? Incorporating cartoon characters, catchy verses, and a "dumb" idea into a 3-minute segment was all part of the strategy. Metro spent around $300,000 on the campaign.[14] What happened? Within 3 months of the campaign's release, Melbourne Metro saw "a 21% reduction in railway accidents and death." In addition, the campaign has generated over 70 million views on YouTube, 12,000 likes on Facebook, 269 followers on Twitter, and 123 members on Google +. It has also won quite a few awards, including seven Webbys, three Sirens, and the Integrated Grand Prix at the Cannes International Film Festival.[15] Let's call that a win.

- Staffing: The initial imperative when it comes to social media marketing is to simply get there—to have a presence in the community of interest. But focusing on presence can result in brand assets that are underutilized and underperforming in terms of the objectives set for the campaign. Organizations in the trial and transition phases tend to focus on establishing Facebook profiles and Twitter accounts, or perhaps on planning a UGC (user-generated content) contest. These companies take an "if you build it, they will come" *Field of Dreams* approach, without addressing ways to build and maintain traffic and interest. Ultimately though, social media marketing is built on the community, content, and technology inherent to social media. To make it successful, the brand must be active in the space—and that means committing staff time to posting, responding, and developing content.
- Content: A related issue is the failure to introduce new, fresh, and relevant content. Developing interactivity, emphasizing relevance, monitoring the asset for needed maintenance, responding to visitor feedback, and providing new content will keep the asset fresh and inspire a curiosity to return among the core audience. Importantly, these components of successful social media marketing require an ongoing commitment of human resources.
- Time Horizon: Social media work differently than do traditional advertising, and may require patience before results are delivered. Although a television campaign can utilize a heavy buy early in its media plan to incite near immediate awareness

and build momentum, social media are just the opposite. It can take months for a social media campaign to build awareness (and there are plenty of social media failures that never gained traction). Assuming the plan itself is sound, organizations must be patient while the community embraces the content and the relationship. Although the results may take longer to see, the overall effectiveness and efficiency of the social media model can be well worth the patience and resources required.

- Focus of Objectives: It's not uncommon for organizations to focus on action steps rather than desired outcomes from social media. In other words, they take a short-term tactical approach rather than a long-term strategic approach. An inappropriate objective might read: "Increase engagement by responding to comments on Twitter and Facebook within 24 hours of posting, posting three status updates per business day, and adding links to social media accounts on the corporate blog." Do you see the error? The emphasis is on the action steps the social media manager will complete (tactical) but there's no focus on what the social media activities should *do* for the brand. There is no value in doing social media marketing for the sake of social media—the value lies in accomplishing marketing objectives. Social media are more than the "flavor of the month"—they have the potential to provide lasting and measurable benefits when campaigns are done right.

- Benefits to Users: Social media live or die on the quality of the content a platform offers to users. That content must add value to the social community. A social media marketing plan answers the question: How will we distribute our content using social media channels? But it also must answer other questions: How can we engage our target audiences in social media communities? What content is valued by our audiences? Do they want content that informs? Entertains? How can we develop an ongoing stream of relevant, fresh content?

- Measurement: Organizations fail to properly measure results. Marketing consultant Tom Peters famously observed, "What gets measured gets done." As social media marketing has developed, some evangelists have encouraged new disciples to keep the faith, emphasizing the growth and popularity of the media as reason enough to develop a presence in the space. In the long term, that's just not good enough. For organizations to succeed in social media marketing, measurement is critical. Measuring outcomes ensures that the organization is learning from what worked and what didn't. Importantly, as organizations begin to shift more marketing dollars from traditional advertising to social media marketing, managers will seek out comparisons on metrics such as ROI (Return On Investment) between social media and other media options.

Develop a Planning Structure in the Organization

So there we have it—a framework to plan a social media marketing campaign. But just how does the planning and execution of a campaign get done—and who does it? These jobs didn't even exist a few years ago; many organizations are scrambling to create a structure that will enable their people to take advantage of these new methods.

Social media personnel can cross several areas of a company's organizational chart. Who has responsibility for the planning, execution, and evaluation of social media marketing strategies? Who should be involved in social media marketing activities? Should there be limitations to social media use within the company? Especially for large companies, different divisions and units may pursue a variety of tactics, ultimately resulting in a disparate collection of pages across social media sites—many ultimately abandoned. Some accounts are abandoned as the campaign component comes to a close. Others quit perhaps due to lack of time, staff, or funding—or simply because their desire to explore the space waned over time.

The Social Media Policy

Companies need to develop, adopt, and publicize a social media policy among employees. A social media policy is an organizational document that explains the rules and procedures for social media activity for the organization and its employees. Just like you, many employees are already engaged in social media. They may be active on social networking sites and microsharing tools like Facebook and Twitter. While employees may use social media to communicate with friends and access entertainment opportunities (maybe even when they're supposed to be working!), there's a good chance they will mention their employers and maybe even vent about office politics or shoddy products. Managing that risk is a must for companies. And many companies will recognize that these employees can act as powerful brand ambassadors when they participate in social media. As we mentioned, Zappos takes advantage of the fact that many of its employees participate in social media vehicles—and these enthusiastic team members promote the company in the process.

Of course, there's no guarantee that an employee (at least on his or her own time) will necessarily say only glowing things about the company. Brands use formal documents to ensure that the company is protected in a legal sense and also to encourage employees to participate in ways that are consistent with the brand's overall strategy. Here are excerpts from three companies' policies:[16]

- *Microsoft:* If you plan to tweet about any professional matters (such as about the business of Microsoft or other companies, products, or services in the same business space as Microsoft), in addition to referencing your alias@microsoft.com email address, whenever possible use the service's profile or contact information to assert that you are a Microsoft employee and/or affiliated with a specific group/team at Microsoft.
- *Sun Microsystems:* Whether in the actual or virtual world, your interactions and discourse should be respectful. For example, when you are in a virtual world as a Sun representative, your avatar should dress and speak professionally. We all appreciate actual respect.
- *Intel:* Consider content that's open-ended and invites response. Encourage comments. You can broaden the conversation by citing others who are blogging

about the same topic and allowing your content to be shared or syndicated … If you make a mistake, admit it. Be upfront, and be quick with your correction. If you're posting a blog, you may choose to modify an earlier post—just make it clear that you have done so.

The Word of Mouth Marketing Association (WOMMA) developed a quick guide to designing a digital social media policy, shown in Table 2.4. Its purpose is to guide how the organization, its employees, and agents should share opinions, beliefs, and information with social communities.[17] Not only is it good business, it can also help prevent legal problems. The WOMMA guide encourages organizations to make several decisions and include those in an organization-wide social media policy. Organizations must decide upon:

- *Standards of conduct:* Standards of conduct in a social media policy refer to the basic expectations for employee behavior in social communities. At a minimum, WOMMA recommends that the standards require that all online statements about the business be honest and transparent. Deceptive, misleading, or unsubstantiated claims about the organization or its competitors must not be issued. Further, good manners must be used in social communities (no ethnic slurs, personal insults, rumors, lies, or other offensive statements).
- *Disclosure requirements:* Transparency is key in online communities. Employees must disclose that they are affiliated with the organization. If they are receiving material compensation or gifts in exchange for posting, this must be disclosed. Disclosing affiliations ensures that readers can still find the posts credible and trustworthy. WOMMA recommends that bloggers include a simple statement: "I received [insert product name] from [insert company name] and here is my opinion …" In addition, when using posts on social networks, WOMMA recommends that the poster use **hashtags** to disclose the nature of relationships reflected in the posts: #emp (employee/employer), #samp (free sample received), #paid (paid endorsement).
- *Standards for posting intellectual property, financial information, and copyrighted information:* Many of the potential legal problems within social media relate to the inappropriate sharing of information. WOMMA recommends that organizations keep all intellectual property and private financial information confidential. Prior to posting copyrighted information, appropriate permissions should be collected.

An Organizational Structure to Support Social Media

Who "owns" social media within an organization? Some brands assign the responsibility to a discipline "silo" such as the marketing department, whereas others rely upon a center of excellence model that pulls people with different kinds of expertise from across the organization to participate. This eliminates the internal political issues relating to who in the company has primary responsibility for social media so it's easier to integrate social media applications with other marketing initiatives.

Table 2.4   WOMMA guidelines

KEY ASPECTS OF THE WOMMA DISCLOSURE FORM

Personal and Editorial Blogs

- I received _____ from _____ sent me _____
- Product Review Blogs
- I received _____ from _____ to review
- I was paid by _____ to review

Additionally for product review blogs, WOMMA strongly recommends creating and prominently posting a "Disclosure and Relationships Statement" section on the blog fully disclosing how a review blogger works with companies in accepting and reviewing products, and listing any conflicts of interest that may affect the credibility of his or her reviews.

Providing Comments in Online Discussions

- I received _____ from _____
- I was paid by_____
- I am an employee [or representative] of_____

Microblogs

Include a hash tag notation, either:
- #spon (sponsored)
- #paid (paid)
- #samp (sample)

Additionally, WOMMA strongly recommends posting a link on your profile page directing people to a full "Disclosure and Relationships Statement." This statement, much like the one WOMMA recommends for review blogs, should state how you work with companies in accepting and reviewing products, and list any conflicts of interest that may affect the credibility of your sponsored or paid reviews.

Status Updates on Social Networks

- I received_____ from_____
- I was paid by_____

If status updates are limited by character restrictions, the best practice disclosure requirement is to include a hash tag notation of either #spon, #paid or #samp. Additionally, WOMMA strongly recommends posting a full description or a link on your social network profile page directing people to a "Disclosure and Relationships Statement." Note that if an employee blogs about his or her company's products, citing the identity of the employer in the profile may not be a sufficient disclosure. Bloggers' disclosures should appear close to the endorsement or testimonial statement they are posting.

Video and Photo Sharing Websites

Include as part of the video/photo content and part of the written description:

KEY ASPECTS OF THE WOMMA DISCLOSURE FORM

- I received_____ from_____
- I was paid by_____

Additionally, WOMMA strongly recommends posting a full description or a link on your video and/or photo sharing profile page directing people to a "Disclosure and Relationships Statement."

Podcasts

Include, as part of the audio content and part of the written description:

- I received_____ from_____
- I was paid by_____

Additionally, WOMMA strongly recommends posting a full description or a link directing people to a "Disclosure and Relationships Statement."

Source: http://womma.org/main/Quick-Guide-to-Designing-a-Social-Media-Policy.pdf, accessed September 2011.

Aside from the organizational structure to support social media marketing efforts, businesses must make decisions on the level of resources to dedicate. Social media are ongoing conversations across potentially several communication vehicles. Some businesses dedicate multiple employees to manage the conversation calendar whereas others assign a single person. The organizational task is to assign the least number of resources needed internally and then supplement those resources with help from the organization's social media agency resources.

There are five basic models for social media structure:[18]

- Centralized
- Organic
- Hub and Spoke
- Dandelion
- Holistic

1   In the centralized structure the social media department functions at a senior level that reports to the CMO (Chief Marketing Officer) or CEO and is responsible for all the social media activations. The potential problem here is that all social media activity may not be adequately represented. Is customer care going to be good if social media marketing is housed under marketing rather than customer service?

2   In the organic structure no one person owns social media. Instead, all employees represent the brand and work social media into their roles. This is implemented through training and used across the organization. The danger here is that the content can end up off message. Any employee can sign up to respond to customer queries on Twitter. That means the company cannot control what employees say. Therefore, the company must have a well-developed social media policy in place to guide employee behavior in social communities.

3   In the hub and spoke (also called the coordinated) model, a team of people who are cross-functionally trained are ready to address various social media needs. This is currently the most popular structure for social media management.

4   The dandelion model is essentially a multi-layered hub and spoke model. It is appropriate for companies with strategic business units (SBUs) that still represent a core brand.

5   The holistic model is currently the least used. It truly refers to a structure within which all employees are empowered to use social media, use social media, and do so according to the company's strategy.

Visit: http://www.web-strategist.com/blog/2010/04/15/framework-and-matrix-the-five-ways-companies-organize-for-social-business/.

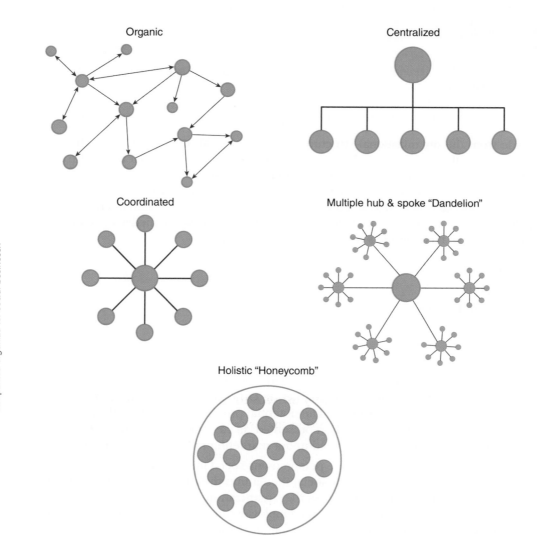

Figure 2.2   A series of images on Organization Structures for Social Media Marketing Management. Images courtesy of the Altimeter Group

Social Media Management Systems

Regardless of the structure a company uses or the policy it develops, it must also devise a day-to-day system for managing the content, content delivery, and response to user-generated content that are all a part of a social media marketing campaign. Companies may utilize in-house systems or may partner with a company like Salesforce for enterprise-level management.

Photo 2.6   Hootsuite University, Social Media Management Certification

Visit: https://learn.hootsuite.com

Whether on a small or large scale, one of the most used systems is Hootsuite. Notably, Hootsuite offers a special program for university users that includes an option to become Hootsuite Certified.

CHAPTER SUMMARY

Where does social media marketing planning fit into an organization's overall planning framework?

Social media marketing should be a part of an organization's marketing plan. Like integrated marketing communications plans, organizations may also develop stand-alone plans offering greater social media marketing.

What are the phases of social media marketing maturity? How does social media marketing change for companies as they shift from the trial phase to the transition phase and eventually move into the strategic phase?

The phases of social media marketing maturity are trial, transition, and strategic. In the trial phase, organizations are pursuing social media tactics in an ad hoc manner, with a focus on gaining experience in social media. The tactics are not well linked to the organization's overall marketing plan and may be haphazardly executed. Organizations in the transition phase think more systematically about how to plan social media activities that support marketing objectives. When an organization enters the final, strategic phase, it utilizes a formal process to plan social media marketing activities with clear objectives and metrics.

(Continued)

(Continued)

Social media are now integrated as a key component of the organization's overall marketing plan.

What are the steps in social media marketing strategic planning?

The social media marketing strategic planning process consists of the following steps:

- Conduct a situation analysis and identify key opportunities.
- State objectives.
- Gather insight into and target one or more segments of social consumers.
- Select the social media channels and vehicles.
- Create an experience strategy.
- Establish an activation plan using other promotional tools (if needed).
- Manage and measure the campaign.

How can organizations structure themselves to support social media marketing?

Companies can structure themselves as centralized, decentralized, hub and spoke, dandelion, or holistic. Each option represents a trade-off of control and responsiveness.

What are the key components of an organizational social media policy, and why is it important to have such a policy in place?

Policies may include several guidelines such as standards of conduct, disclosure requirements, and standards for posting intellectual property, financial information, and copyrighted information. Companies need policies to ensure that social media activity is consistent with the overall brand.

KEY TERMS

activation tools
briefing
center of excellence model
centralized structure
competitive parity method
concepting
creative brief
creative message strategy
discovery
experience brief
external environment
hashtags

ideation
internal environment
marketing plan
message strategy
objective
objective-and-task method
percentage of ad spend
positioning statement
propagation brief
share of voice
situation analysis
social media audit

social media marketing
    maturity
social media policy
social media zombie
social persona
strategic phase
strategic planning
stunts
SWOT analysis
traffic
transition phase
trial phase

REVIEW QUESTIONS

1   Why do some organizations enter the trial phase without planning and research? Is there value in getting social media experience before social media marketing becomes part of the marcom plan?

2   Explain the phases in the social media marketing maturity life cycle.

3   What are the forms of organizational structure used by companies embracing social media marketing? What are the pros and cons of each?

4   Explain the steps in the social media marketing strategic planning process.

5   What approaches to budgeting can be used by organizations planning for social media marketing?

EXERCISES

1   Visit www.thecoca-colacompany.com/socialmedia/ where you'll find Coca-Cola's social media policy, or find the policy for another company. Identify the key components WOMMA recommends be included in a corporate social media policy. How could the policy be improved?

2   Identify a social media campaign for a favorite brand. In what experiences does the campaign invite you to take part? In what zones does the strategy lie? Does the campaign include share technologies to ensure your activities are shared with your network?

CHAPTER NOTES

1   Michael Stelzner, "2014 Social Media Marketing Industry Report," *Social Media Examiner,* 2014, http://www.socialmediaexaminer.com/report2014/, accessed May 30, 2014.

2   "The State of Social: How Brands Staff and Budget," *Wildfire,* 2014, http://www.wildfireapp.com/wp/how-enterprise-brands-staff-and-budget-for-social-infographic, accessed July 21, 2014.

(Continued)

(Continued)

3   "The State of Marketing 2010," *Unica,* http://www.unica.com/survey2010, accessed August 10, 2010.

4   Marketing Sherpa explained these three phases in its Social Media Marketing Benchmarking Report (2010), which surveyed 2,300 marketers. This report has not been updated. Since that time, Altimeter conducted a similar study and identified five phases of development. However, we believe that the path to social media marketing maturity is best understood following Marketing Sherpa's model.

5   Michael Stelzner, "2014 Social Media Marketing Industry Report," *Social Media Examiner,* 2014, http://www.socialmediaexaminer.com/report2014/, accessed May 30, 2014.

6   David Moth, "The Top 16 Social Media Fails of 2013," *Econsultancy,* https://econsultancy.com/blog/63901-the-top-16-social-media-fails-of-2013#i.13hfu23ibbfs9x, accessed July 20, 2014.

7   Moth, "The Top 16 Social Media Fails of 2013."

8   Moth, "The Top 16 Social Media Fails of 2013."

9   "Marketing Artifacts: Brand Positioning Statements?" Leslie Jump (February 7, 2007), http://www.marketerblog.net/2007/02/marketing_artif.html, accessed August 11, 2010.

10 Griffin Farley, "Propagation Planning," May 3, 2010, http://griffinfarley.typepad.com/propagation/, accessed December 1, 2010.

11 Adapted from Griffin Farley, "Revised Propagation Planning Brief," May 3, 2010, http://griffinfarley.typepad.com/propagation/ 2010/05/revised-propagation-planning-brief.html, accessed December 1, 2010.

12 V. Egan. (2012, November 28). "Dumb Ways to Die, Smart Ways to Do Viral," *Econsultancy,* http://econsultancy.com/blog/11204-dumb-ways-to-die-smart-ways-to-do-viral, accessed February 4, 2014.

13 A. C. Diaz. (2013, November 11). "How 'Dumb Ways to Die' won the Internet, Became the No. 1 Campaign of the Year" *Advertising Age,* http://adage.com/article/special-report-the-awards-report/dumb-ways-die-dissected/245195/, accessed February 5, 2014.

14 B. Head, "Smart Ways to Market: Why Online Video Like Dumb Ways to Die Is the Rising Star of Content Marketing" (November 7, 2013), *BRW,* http://www.brw.com.au/p/marketing/smart_content_rising_market_marketing_NHlw9FleN2qxTTOvMaw7zJ, accessed February 6, 2014.

15   D. Collins, "Dumb Ways to Die and a Strange Sense of Success," *Safety and Risk Management* (2013), http://www.safetyrisk.net/dumb-ways-to-die-and-a-strange-sense-of-success/, accessed February 6, 2014.

16   Kimberly Smith, "A Step-by-Step Guide to a Successful Social Media Program," *Marketing Profs,* 2010: p. 9.

17   "The WOMMA 'Quick Guide' to Designing a Digital Social Media Policy," *WOMMA,* http://womma.org/main/Quick-Guide-to-Designing-a-Social-Media-Policy.pdf, accessed December 31, 2010.

18   Jeremiah Owyang, "Most Companies Organize in Hub and Spoke Format for Social Business," *Web Strategist,* November 9, 2010, http://www.web-strategist.com/blog/2010/11/09/research-most-companies-organize-in-hub-and-spoke-formation/, accessed December 12, 2010.

Visit the companion website for free additional materials related to this chapter: study.sagepub.com/smm

3 Social Consumers

LEARNING OBJECTIVES

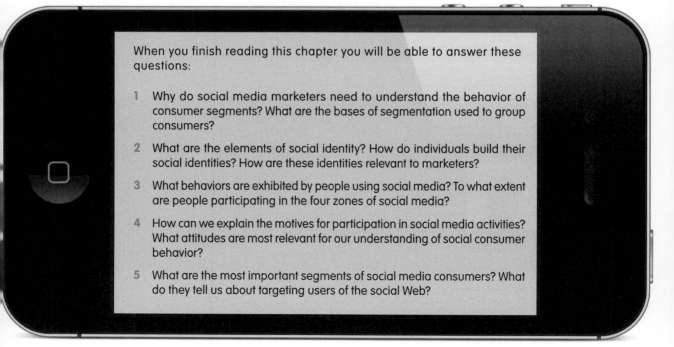

When you finish reading this chapter you will be able to answer these questions:

1   Why do social media marketers need to understand the behavior of consumer segments? What are the bases of segmentation used to group consumers?

2   What are the elements of social identity? How do individuals build their social identities? How are these identities relevant to marketers?

3   What behaviors are exhibited by people using social media? To what extent are people participating in the four zones of social media?

4   How can we explain the motives for participation in social media activities? What attitudes are most relevant for our understanding of social consumer behavior?

5   What are the most important segments of social media consumers? What do they tell us about targeting users of the social Web?

Segmentation and Targeting for Social Media Marketing

In the last chapter, we reviewed the steps marketers use to plan a social media marketing strategy. The steps apply both to campaigns that will be executed entirely in social media as well as those that integrate social media with other media. After analyzing the situation and setting objectives, the planner must gather consumer insight to develop a profile of the targeted consumer segments. This is the focus of Chapter 3. We'll review the basics of segmentation, discuss individual and group behaviors in social media and why those behaviors occur, and detail segments found in social media communities.

Profiling the Targeted Segments

Marketers are rapidly adopting social media marketing strategies and techniques, but social media marketing will work only to the extent that these new media platforms can reach the customers organizations want to talk to in the digital space. Marketers target specific segments whose needs they believe the brand is capable of satisfying in exchange for meeting organizational objectives. Market segmentation is the process of dividing a market into distinct groups that have common needs and characteristics. Marketers use several variables as the basis to segment markets including geographic, demographic, psychographic, benefits sought, and behavior. These characteristics represent the bases of segmentation marketers use when they divide a population into manageable groups.

Marketers utilize these variables to segment and to identify target audiences regardless of what kind of strategy will be used. But when it comes to social media marketing, we need

Photo 3.1

to also take into account how consumers can be segmented according to their digital lives. Although it may seem like everyone is online, and most everyone is on Facebook, the extent to which a person's life is digital varies based on his or her lifestyle, personality, demographics, and even his or her geographic and economic conditions. Understanding these segments and how their attitudes and behaviors differ is a critical component in devising an effective social media marketing strategy. Marketers use this information and insight to develop profiles that help marketers make better campaign choices. Let's briefly review the bases of segmentation and try to understand how these variables translate into the online world.

Geographic Segmentation

Geographic segmentation refers to segmenting markets by region, country, market size, market density, or climate. For example, North Face can expect to sell more parkas to people who live in winter climates, whereas Roxy will move more bikinis in sunny vacation spots. Geographic segmentation is increasingly relevant to social media marketers, not only due to location-based targeting based on a business's distribution channel, but also because social media increasingly incorporate GPS technology, a satellite system that provides real-time location and time information.

This innovation aids local businesses that can use the technology to target specific people based on physical presence. Services such as Foursquare (Gowalla is a similar competitor) position themselves as geo-targeted social media. In other words, Foursquare is part social network, part GPS tracking system. Users log in via their smartphones and other Wi-Fi-enabled mobile devices and "check in" to their location. From there they can see if they have friends nearby (both services will import friends from Facebook and other accounts), and also see links to local businesses. This is where segmentation strategy comes into play.

SHOW ME!

Foursquare Local Offer

As Foursquare members check in, local businesses in that area can reach out to them with special offers and interactive promotions such as free drinks or discounts. Importantly for the local merchants who use the service, Foursquare offers a business "dashboard" that includes metrics on the number of check-ins, the times of day people check in, the most recent visitors, and the most frequent visitors.[1] Other apps utilize geographic targeting too. For instance, Facebook's Nearby Friends app announces when people in your friends list are close. Ads are delivered to your mobile device based on your location. In fact, this is perhaps the most relevant aspect of geographic segmentation for social media marketers—it provides actionable strategies that engage on the social, mobile level. Worried about privacy? We address privacy later in this chapter.

Demographic Segmentation

When marketers employ demographic segmentation they utilize common characteristics such as age, gender, income, ethnic background, educational attainment, family life cycle, and occupation to understand how to group similar consumers together. General Mills creates specialized campaigns for different demographic segments, such as when it launched QueRicaVida.com as an online platform for Latina moms.

How can demographic segmentation benefit social media marketers? Let's take a look at a campaign from Secret deodorant. How would you describe Secret's target market demographically? That's easy—females, aged 12 and up, in North America. Traditionally, a brand such as Secret would target women with print ads in magazines appropriate by age group. In this case, though, Secret has taken a very different route; its strategy highlights the importance of considering demographic characteristics. Here's an overview of the campaign. The Mean Stinks campaign is an anti-bullying campaign sponsored by Secret deodorant. The campaign provides support literature to inform girls and their parents about the dangers of bullying and how to combat those dangers. But more, the campaign has become a community, a channel for creative expression, and a rallying cry of importance to teen girls and their moms. It started simply with a Facebook page

SHOW ME!

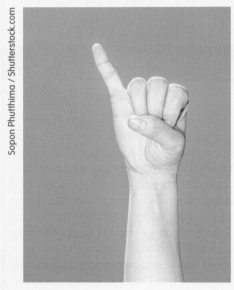

Sopon Phutthima / Shutterstock.com

Secret Mean Stinks

Is this campaign an effective way to reach the target market? The approach suggests the Secret brand really understands the challenges of being female. This is a key component of demographic targeting. It's about more than the basic facts. The marketer takes the demographic knowledge and uses it to understand the needs of the market.

Photo 3.2

and a call to action—girls who believed that "mean stinks" would pinky swear against bullying. How? By painting their pinkies blue! The Facebook page acquired hundreds of thousands of likes in short order. Since then, the campaign has evolved. Using the theme #gangupforgood, Secret empowered girls to use their blue pinkies to let others know they would not bully. Secret then leveraged this content, and its own, in the social community zone (zone 1) and the social publishing zone (zone 2). Profiles are active in Twitter, Facebook, Instagram, and Pinterest. A microsite publishes user-generated content from the social communities, and a YouTube channel and Vimeo (zone 2) channel provide both Secret-produced videos to help parents and teachers combat bullying and user-generated videos.

Psychographic Segmentation

Psychographic segmentation approaches slice up the market based on personality, motives, lifestyles, and attitudes and opinions. These variables may be used alone or combined with other segmentation bases such as demographics. Psychographics tend to provide the richest picture of a consumer segment in that the descriptions of psychographic segments help marketers to know the real person making the consumption decisions.

Let's consider a practical application of psychographics in the social media space. The greeting card industry has experienced declining sales for some time now. Instead of cards, people may send emails, e-cards, or even just a Facebook post! A large-scale study by Unity Marketing identified four psychographic segments among greeting card buyers. Unfortunately for the greeting card industry, a segment called "Alternative Seeker," the largest and fastest growing group the study identified, is also the most eager to find an alternative to the traditional card.[2] Alternative Seekers view social media as an answer to staying in touch with friends and family on both a daily basis and on special occasions such as birthdays and holidays.

Unity's report warns that greeting card companies are at risk as people turn to social media as a replacement to traditional cards. But this change presents an opportunity for others. New entrants in the industry like Wrapp and Givt offer a social form of gift card with mobile redemption features. Even Starbucks enabled a Twitter app that lets you give a cup of coffee to someone with a simple tweet!

Benefit Segmentation

Benefit segmentation groups individuals in the marketing universe according to the benefits they seek from the products available in the market. For example, in the auto industry people who buy hybrids and electric cars look for different benefits from a car than those who buy muscle cars or SUVs.

What benefits do consumers want from their interactions with brands in social media environments? There are competing schools of thought on this issue. Some industry experts argue that consumers want to have meaningful relationships with the brands they use frequently, and particularly with those brands they consider lovemarks. This term refers to brands that inspire passionate loyalty in their customers. Kevin Roberts, CEO of Saatchi & Saatchi, originated the concept; his agency looks for ways to deepen bonds with consumers and thus cultivate these lovemarks. Saatchi & Saatchi even maintains a website that encourages people to nominate the brands that inspire them in different categories. For example, brands in the beverage category include Guinness, Inca Kola, and Boost Juice.[3] You can nominate your own favorites at www. lovemarks.com.

If Roberts and others are right, brands can use social media engagement with customers to build the relationship—conversing, sharing, caring, and interacting in each other's lives over time (just like people do). We'll take a deep look at how brands can engage consumers using social communities (zone 1) in Chapter 5.

Behavioral Segmentation

Behavioral segmentation divides consumers into groups based on how they act with regard to a brand or a product category. When it comes to social media, we leave residues of our interactions with brands and about brands. This behavior can be utilized for targeting of people more likely to want our offering. Actually, our residue, sometimes called social exhaust, can aid marketers in building segments utilizing all of these bases. The information we leave makes up our social identity, a concept we focus on next.

Social Identity: Touchpoints in a Wired Life

Facebook? YouTube? Flickr? Twitter? Which of these sites do you make a part of your digital life? What are you sharing? Thoughts, opinions, activities, photos, videos? When and from where? On the go with a mobile device? From a fixed location using a stationary computer? These days, the answer is most or all of the above. Our online activities and the information we post document our digital identity—the way we represent ourselves via text, images, sounds, and video to others who access the Web. The evidence of these activities also makes up what marketers call social identity. Altimeter defines social identity as "the information about an individual available in social media, including profile data and ongoing activity."[4] In other words, social identity is the way marketers view you given your social media activities. This view of you comes from data available from your social footprint. As time passes, your social identity likely becomes clear. Why? Because you are likely to participate in more communities and in more ways.

This shift is called digital primacy.[5] It reflects a change in the culture of wired individuals like you—digital natives—who turn *first* to digital channels for communication, information, and entertainment. Is this good or bad? Probably a bit of both, as evidenced by submissions to a call for user-generated content issued by PBS and *Smith* magazine. The challenge asked participations to provide six-word insights on their digital lives.

The following posts are a small sample of what people wrote. What might your six-word memoir say?

Countless connections, never a soul meeting

140 characters cannot encapsulate my status

Tweets, keyboards, and mice: my frenemies

My thumbs weren't made to type

Needed to find myself. Used Google

Afraid my phone's smarter than me

Social Touchpoints: The DNA of Social Identity

Perhaps in a typical day you wake up using an alarm clock app on your smartphone. After you snooze the alarm, you might check your News Feed on Facebook Mobile. You leave home and head for school. In transit, you stay connected with your smartphone or even an Internet-enabled car if you drive a new Ford. You might search for reviews on the best place for coffee along your route, or the cheapest source of gas. When you get to class, your professor might ask you to work collaboratively in a wiki on a class assignment or bookmark research for a group project using an app like Evernote. Later that day, you might watch *The Talk* while you get ready for your evening shift at work. When Julie Chen asks for your reaction to today's entertainment news during the #everybodytalks segment, you turn to Twitter to post your opinion—or if you are an innovator, you might use your Google TV to respond right from your television console. Shopping later (or during a lecture?) use an app such as Foursquare and you might score valuable coupons for savings while you shop. See what we mean? Everywhere you go, as long as you have an Internet-enabled device, social media can be a part of your daily life. The opportunities exist as social media touchpoints. You can see the possibilities for these touchpoints in Figure 3.1. These touchpoints leave impressions—we call them social footprints, and they make up the data that marketers use to paint your social identity.

Throughout the day, social media users touch a variety of devices, channels, and sites for many different reasons. Whether we're checking the weather forecast, getting the latest news, relaxing with friends while watching favorite videos, or trying to get a deal on a pizza, social media are increasingly a part of our daily lives.

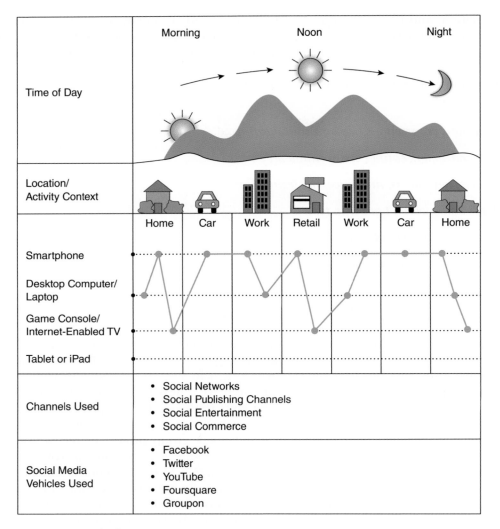

Figure 3.1   A Social Life

Source: Based on Ken Martin and Ivan Todorov, "How Will Digital Platforms Be Harnessed in 2010, and How Will They Change the Way People Interact With Brands?" *Journal of Interactive Advertising,* 10, no. 2 (Spring 2010), http://jiad.org/article132, accessed November 17, 2010.

Social Footprints

A footprint is the impression or mark an object makes when it occupies a physical space. Depending upon the surface material, the impression may remain some time after the indentation was created—when a budding graffiti artist happens upon a patch of drying cement, the rest is history! Similarly, a social footprint is the mark a person makes when he or she occupies digital space. As we visit websites and web communities, we leave a digital trail behind. This social footprint may be subtle or obvious depending upon the quantity and frequency of visits and the activities in which we participate. For example, when you visit your friend's Facebook profile and learn that she's a fan of Juicy Couture, you learn something about what matters to her. This information is one aspect of her social footprint.

Figure 3.2 illustrates a social footprint for one person, Gary. It's clear in this example that the footprint's owner, an artist in Richmond, Virginia, has a sizeable presence on Facebook. There he interacts with friends and colleagues, posts personal messages, and sometimes promotes gallery showings and art for sale. Gary also publishes his film work on the media sharing site YouTube. As he adds photography to his multimedia productions, he frequently uses his iPhone to capture images and upload them to Flickr and Facebook. He further promotes the content he's published by microblogging on Twitter. Gary also posts images and written observations to his blog, Naked Doodles, hosted on Blogger.

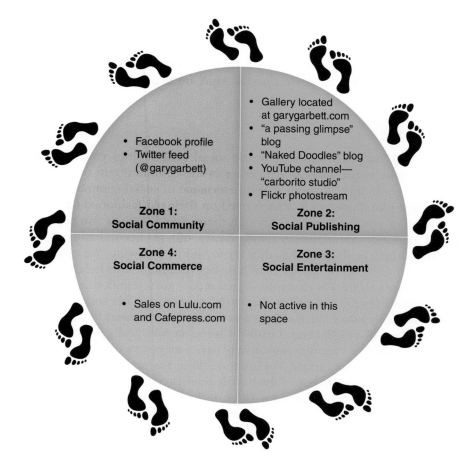

Figure 3.2   Gary's Footprints

He utilizes the social shopping functions of apps such as Snipi on his iPad, which help him to keep track of items he might want to purchase and enable him to run price comparisons across the Web before he does. Over time it's likely that Gary will continue to expand his digital footprint as he becomes involved in other social communities, posts his physical whereabouts on Foursquare, designates his favorite bands on Myspace, and subscribes to news and entertainment feeds using aggregators such as Flipboard. Across all four zones of social media, Gary leads a *very* social digital life as he deposits footprints.

You may or may not leave as many footprints as Gary, but you certainly leave your share. Like Hansel and Gretel who dropped breadcrumbs to mark their way in the forest, you leave traces as you interact online and especially as you share social content. Have you ever "liked" a site, an article, or a product? Footprints. Did you ever shop online? More footprints. Comment on YouTube videos? Download podcasts from iTunes or upload pictures on Instagram? That's right … more footprints. Records of your activities may make up a lifestream (assuming you share enough detail with regularity), which is essentially a diary you keep through your social media activities. And guess what: you're certainly not alone in this particular forest. Lots of people other than your BFFs are interested in these electronic tracks. Savvy marketers follow them to see where you've been and to predict where you are headed and what you might want when you get there. This knowledge helps them ensure that when you do arrive they will be ready to serve you customized, targeted ads and offers that meet your needs. More on that later.

Your Social Brand

You deposit social footprints throughout the social communities you visit. Many social communities require registration as a member of the community in order to access services and join in community activities. Your username in social communities is a handle or nickname, just like those truck drivers used on their old-fashioned CB radios. It may be a pseudonym or your real name. Although many digital natives use pseudonyms that can hide real identities and maintain some privacy, others choose handles that describe something about them in shorthand as they try to build a following. We can think of these IDs as our digital brand name. Rather than hide one's identity, they heighten the meaning associated with one's name. For example, digital media guru Jennifer Leggio, a prominent blogger for ZDNet, uses the handle "mediaphyter" to represent her social digital footprint.

Once you've made that decision, you'll need to ensure that you aren't handle-squatting. This term refers to the use of a digital brand name by someone who really doesn't have a claim to the brand name. Sometimes another person may have a legitimate claim to the name—many of us have names that are not unique. For instance, there are hundreds of men named David Jones in the world. In that case, use of the handle doesn't constitute squatting. On the other hand, a quick search of Twitter for actor Hugh Jackman turns up several people listings, including @RealHughJackman, @JackmanHugh, @HughJackman, and @H_Jackman, among others. Only one is the "real" Hugh Jackman—the others are probably handle-squatters.

Next, you should find out whether your desired username is available in the many social communities. Services like Namechk.com make this easy. A sign of the times—parents are using services like this to choose baby names (to find a unique name) and then register-ing their newborns in social networks to reserve the handle!

Your Social Brand in the Age of Selfies

The first selfie was shared in early 2011, and in just a few years, the hashtag #selfie has been used on Instagram more than 88 million times![6] That's just one social vehicle and one hashtag. People use the hashtag #me just as much! Your selfies are indicators of your social brand and, like your handle, they differ from many other sources of information that make up your social identity. Aspects of your identity over which you have a great deal of control are thought to be active, while activities associated with typical participa-tion in social channels are thought to be more passive.[7] The less control you have over the information, the more passive it is in terms of influencing your identity. A selfie is one of the most active aspects because you are in control. You may take several shots, but you publish only the ones you like—if you publish at all.

We'll explain later in this chapter how marketers can use the information that makes up your social identity to target you more effectively, but what does your social identity say to others? To your friends, family, employers, teachers? That's the question Andy Beal addresses in *Repped*, a book designed to show people how to protect their own reputa-tions in a social economy.[8] Why is it important? Because, as we discussed in Chapter 1, Web 2.0 is a reputation economy. Brian Solis perhaps said it best: "Think about it this way. When you look in the mirror, you see a reflection of who you are right now. What if you could transform that reflection each day into someone you hoped to see staring back at you?"[9] You can with the choices you make. Solis suggests that people conduct their own social activity audit. Does that sound familiar? It should. It's the same exercise marketers can use to assess the situation and their competitors' social presence that we introduced in Chapter 2! A personal audit should categorize social media activity according to the values expressed in the social engagement.[10]

- Vision: a vision post answers the questions, "Did I learn something? Was I inspired?"
- Validation: a validation activity answers the question, "Am I accepted by a group?"
- Vindication: a vindication post informs others, "I am right."
- Vulnerability: a vulnerability post opens one's self to others, "I am approachable."
- Vanity: a vanity post reveals a tendency to narcissism, "Look at me. I am all that."

Footprints should reveal a social identity that is balanced. We all have aspects of these values inside. But when our footprints are focused more in certain areas, we may inadvertently paint a distorted picture of ourselves. To summarize, your *digital footprint* leaves evidence of where you are and where you've been. Your *lifestream* is the journal of your digital life. Taken together, they make up your social brand, what marketers call your social identity. When you look at this evidence, we think you'll agree: *You are what you share!*

THE DARK SIDE OF SOCIAL MEDIA

We've warned that reputation is ever-lasting in the realm of social media. But is that really so? The Court of Justice of the European Union thinks differently. Under the Data Protection Directive, its so-called Right to be Forgotten ruling, the Court declared that people have a right to control, at least to some extent, the access others have to digital information about them.[11] In other words, if you don't like some of the information that makes up your social identity, just ask that it not be found! The ruling puts search engines in the responsible role here in that past information online is mostly found through search. If the ruling stands, people can ask Google to stop indexing information so it no longer appears in search results. And, yes, your public activities in social communities are indexed! Try Googling yourself to see what others could see. While you may appreciate this "do-over" approach to burying past mistakes, it opens the door to digital censorship. Censorship, at its core, is counter to the philosophy of openness and transparency that serves as a cornerstone of digital culture. Plus, it puts the onus on search engines like Google to bear the administrative burden of eliminating indexing on information that may be perceived as invading one's privacy, regardless of whether the information posted was slanderous.

SHOW ME!

Annette Shaff / Shutterstock.com

Photo 3.3

Companies Use Selfies Too!

Dallas Pets Alive decided to leverage the selfie trend to help find homes for homeless mutts. How? With its #Muttbombing campaign! The campaign features real dogs available for adoption. The dogs are featured in "photobombs" using selfies of area celebrities and local people grabbed from Instagram. Fans can submit suggestions for who will be muttbombed next! See the campaign at www.muttbombing.com.

A Wired World: Social Media Usage

Worldwide, there are about 2.5 billion global Internet users today—that's roughly 35% of the world's population. Most Internet users, about 26% of the world's population, are active on at least one social network. That's nearly 2 billion people. Of course, penetration does vary by global region, with the lowest penetration rates reported in Africa and South Asia. Even these areas are expected to experience growth, at least in part due to Internet access via mobile phone. Mobile penetration is 93% worldwide.

Motives and Attitudes Influencing Social Media Activities

Why We Log In

Web users increasingly participate in social networks such as Facebook, play online social games (turn-based, multiplayer games designed to be played within social networks) such as Candy Crush within the network community, comment on the posts of friends, update status messages, and share content. Likewise, brands are joining in on these sites as they add content and try to converse with consumers. What's your motivation for the time you log on social networks? Chances are there are many reasons that drive you to visit these sites. Some of these motives probably seem like no-brainers, but others may surprise you. These are the most common impulses researchers have identified:

- Affinity impulse: Social networks enable participants to express an affinity, to acknowledge a liking and/or relationship with individuals and reference groups. When you use Facebook to stay in touch with high school friends and to make new friends, you are responding to the affinity impulse.[12] This is also referred to as a social function. When people contribute to social communities for this reason, they do so to form friendships and feel a sense of belonging.[13]

- Personal utility impulse: While we tend to think of social media participation truly as community participation, some do consider, "What's in it for me?" This is the personal utility impulse and it may be one of the most important motives for brands to acknowledge. Studies of participation in social communities report that utility, whether in the form of information seeking, incentive seeking, entertainment seeking, or convenience seeking, is a major motive for social media activity.[14] The findings are congruent with others utilizing a uses and gratification approach to understanding social media behavior.[15]

- Contact comfort and immediacy impulse: People have a natural drive to feel a sense of psychological closeness to others. Contact comfort is the sense of relief we feel from knowing others in our network are accessible. Immediacy also lends a sense of relief in that the contact is without delay. Do you feel lost without your mobile phone? Do you feel anxious if you haven't checked Facebook recently? When you reply to a message, do you keep checking for a response? These are indicators of your need for contact comfort and contact immediacy.

SHOW ME!

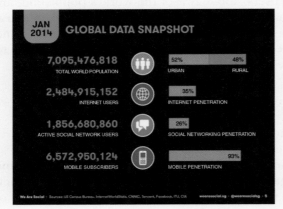

Photo 3.4

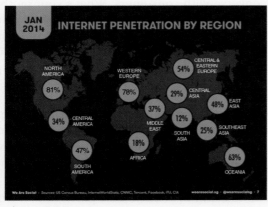

Photo 3.5

Social Use Worldwide

These changes in access to the Internet equate to increased access to target audiences for social media marketers. In other words, our reach is now extensive online. Reach refers to the percentage of the target audience that can be accessed using a form of media. In the early days of the Internet, reach was small and the medium was not considered as attractive. While social media usage is still strongest among younger people, the elderly make up the fastest growing age segment for social media usage.

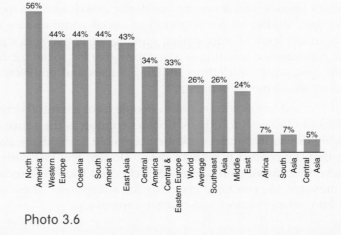

Photo 3.6

- Altruistic impulse: Some participate in social media as a way to do something good. They use social media to "pay it forward." The altruistic impulse is also aided by the immediacy of social media, and this value has been played out in the immediate altruistic responses (IAR) of social media users to aid calls during crises such as the earthquake relief for Haiti or Japan.[16] Individuals want to do good and do it quickly—social media make it easier to contribute in the form of a cash donation or a service to the community. The altruistic impulse serves a value-expressive function in that it enables individuals to express their own moral beliefs through their social media behavior.[17]

- Curiosity impulse: People may feel a curiosity about others and want to feed this interest—this is also known as the prurient impulse. Online, we can satisfy our curiosity by "following" people on Twitter and visiting their profiles. Surely it is the prurient impulse that led millions of Twitter users to follow Ashton Kutcher's daily tweets while millions of others relentlessly track the ups-and-downs of actress Lindsay Lohan—will she prevail, or crash and burn? Curiosity relates to the next impulse—the validation impulse. In fact, they might be thought of as two sides of the same coin. That's because exhibitionism can feed curiosity.

- Validation impulse: Social media focus intently on the individual. You can share as much or as little of your opinions and activities as you like, and comment on those of others. This focus on the self highlights the validation impulse, in other words, feeding one's own ego. That's why the validation impulse is sometimes referred to as the ego-defensive function. This function is thought to be particularly relevant as people seek to eliminate perceived external threats and eliminate self-doubts.[18] Who knows? Perhaps the prevalence of bullying behavior in social media is actually a manifestation of the validation impulse. Certain behaviors are affiliated with people driven by the validation impulse. These include the prevalence of selfies among the mix of posts, a tendency to check to see if posts received likes, a tendency to overshare, and a tendency to impression manage (e.g., promoting the perfect life).[19] These were among the behaviors noted by researchers in a study that investigated types of narcissism in social media. Particularly on Facebook and Twitter, people may use posts to show superiority (particularly by expressing opinions) or to participate in exhibitionism. That's why Brian Solis, a thought leader in the realm of social media, advises to guard against the dreaded disease, "accidental narcissism."

Despite the tendency for vilifying the validation impulse in social media participation, the validation impulse may relate to one's desire to share creative output just as easily as it may relate to one's desire to feed narcissistic tendencies.

Andy Warhol famously said, "In the future, everyone will be world famous for 15 minutes." The legendary artist and visionary understood even way back in 1968 that the media had the power to spotlight almost anybody and everybody. For better or worse, it looks like Warhol was right. With social media, anyone anywhere in the world can earn worldwide fame for a brief time. This seeking for fame and the ease of audience access has given rise to the development of microcelebrities. We'll talk more about this phenomenon in Chapter 7 (on social entertainment).

Despite these motives for participation, there are also motives for not participating! Users may experience guilt for spending what they perceive to be excessive time on social media activities.[20] They may feel guilty "creeping" on other people. Both of these feelings can lead to an increased sense of social media addiction, which we discussed in Chapter 1.

Privacy Salience: How Much Do They Know and How Much Do You Care?

It's helpful for marketers to understand motives for social media participation and sharing as we make strategic marketing decisions, but the residue left behind is also of value. That residue, what we call social footprints, makes up the social identity information that marketers can use to augment other customer information, make assessments, or conduct research.

Are you concerned about privacy as it relates to your social media activities? The extent to which worries about sharing too much information impact our online behavior is known as privacy salience. Interestingly, privacy salience doesn't necessarily explain whether social media users take steps to protect their privacy. Because of the disparate relationship, researchers call the phenomenon the privacy paradox.[21] The privacy paradox describes people's willingness to disclose personal information in social media channels despite expressing high levels of concern for privacy protection. Privacy concerns also take on multiple forms including social privacy and institutional privacy. Social privacy refers to concerns about disclosing personal information to others. A desire for social privacy is the antidote to the curiosity impulse and "creeping" behavior. Institutional privacy is privacy from the use of data by the institution providing the service and third parties. Research suggests that people are taking steps to protect their social privacy. Common strategies include excluding contact information, untagging and removing photographs, and limiting contacts to known others. While it's still common to disclose (and perhaps overshare) intimate information, people may feel comfortable sharing because they've taken steps to protect social privacy. Despite the concern over social privacy, social media users seem less concerned about *institutional privacy*. Is this because of an acceptance of business use and access to big data or a lack of understanding?

Some suggest that privacy is viewed differently by different generations. In particular, today's teens, Generation Z, exhibit lower levels of privacy salience. According to Pew, teens share a lot of information in social channels:[22]

- 92% have posted their real name to the profiles they use.
- 91% have posted a selfie.
- 82% have posted their birth date.
- 71% have posted the name of the school they currently attend.
- 71% have posted the name of the town in which they live.
- 64% who use Twitter have a public profile.
- 53% have posted their email address.
- 20% have posted their mobile phone number.
- 16% have allowed sites to auto-post their location.

Why so much sharing? It may be the view of the social context. If social media communities are viewed as private, the expectation is that social norms will prevent inappropriate use of the content and people should feel comfortable disclosing sensitive information. If these spaces are viewed as public rather than private communities, users may disclose more carefully, recognizing that the content may have a broad reach beyond the intended audience. People, particularly young people, may view social media profiles as forms of "produced self" and tend to see social communities as public venues.

Whether due to a lack of privacy salience or a distinction in whether the media used to communicate is public or private, social media users may be guilty of oversharing. To date, research on oversharing suggests that this behavior may be motivated by the validation impulse, the affinity impulse, or the contact comfort impulse. For instance, a study

FROM BYTES TO BUCKS

How Marketers Use Social Identity

You are one person, but the reality is that you have many selves. There's the real self, though you may choose to reveal different parts of that as you move through different social situations. For example, you may come off as a serious, quiet person when you sit in class but as a fun-loving party animal on Saturday night. Then there's your ideal self that you construct online—many of us are very selective about the information and photos we post as we try to convince others about who we really are. In social media others construct an image and perception of who you are based on the footprints you leave. When marketers assess this information, the portrait they paint of you is called a social identity. Just as direct marketers have long known that a more complete customer profile can lead to better targeting of offers, marketers now recognize that utilizing social data can further enrich these profiles. Marketers can use this information to identify new leads, convert prospects to customers, resolve service issues, and more. Altimeter, the leader in helping businesses utilize social identity data, sees social identity as an evolution in social CRM.[23] The data enable brands to learn about customers in a more relevant way than simple transaction data or even the cookie data captured when consumers browse the Web. For example, if a brand can associate an Instagram user who posts a picture with a complaint caption with a customer who has purchased often in the past, it is positioned to build higher customer lifetime value. Altimeter believes using social identity data helps brands to build richer customer profiles, efficiently use marketing budgets, and engage across channels. In fact, cross-channel engagement is one of the hottest topics in marketing today. Brands can use social identity data at all points in the purchase funnel, whether they seek to identify prospects, nurture leads, tailor recommendations, follow up with customers to enhance retention, or reward loyalty.

of oversharing among Facebook users found that the content was self-oriented with an apparent goal of attention-seeking.[24] As one author put it, these oversharers treat Facebook like a drive-thru window where they can get their fast, cheap pick-me-up.[25] People who have trouble expressing their "true selves" may also overshare. The true self is made up of qualities a person possesses but has difficulty expressing to others. Social media may provide the venue for expression.

Privacy salience may also vary by cultural region. A study by marketing research firm Ipsos found just that! You might be surprised by the outcome, though. When asked for a descriptor of how much they share online, nearly one in four people around the world said they share everything.[26] The United States, Canada, United Kingdom, France, and Germany all under indexed while countries such as Saudi Arabia over indexed. There may be a relationship between Internet penetration and oversharing. Nearly all of the countries reporting oversharing are in areas with lower Internet penetration, while the countries that undershare are primarily European, where Internet penetration is high.[27]

Social Media Segments

Because social media are such new areas, marketers are still figuring out just how to use them, and to what extent they should rely on these platforms when they identify their target markets and try to communicate with them. One brand may add a social media piece to a broader strategy when it creates a Facebook page, whereas another may replace virtually all of its traditional advertising with "new media" messages. Decisions regarding just how much to rely on social media and how to design programs that will be effective require us to understand as much as we can about just who participates in social media and how they may differ from one another. We need to address these questions:

- In what online communities do these consumers participate?
- What activities do they participate in online and in social communities, specifically?
- What role does social technology play in their lives? Is it for keeping in touch with friends and family, a productivity tool, a stress reliever?

Knowing the answers to these questions will help you to ensure that the social media marketing strategies and tactics you plan have a shot to resonate with the target market. There are countless examples of social media marketing campaigns that have failed. In fact, Gartner, a research firm specializing in technology, claims that half—that's right, 50%—of social media campaigns fail.[28] Why the huge number of bombs? Probably a major reason is simply that the social strategy is not matched to the target audience. A contest that requires players to upload original video content will not succeed with a target market that primarily consumes content but does not create its own. A promotion for a free song download offered on Twitter will not work if the band's fans tend to hang out on MySpace instead. A stunt from Skittles to feed live streams from social media communities to its website will not appeal to parents if the live feed includes profanity inappropriate for their children.

How then should we identify and define social segments? The segmentation schemes of consumers participating in social communities online are still in their infancy. We'll take a look at three typologies of digital consumers, each of which offers insights into the lives of social consumers.

Social Technographics

Forrester Research introduced the concept of social technographics based on research it conducted on the social and digital lives of consumers. This work became the foundation for a book, *Groundswell*, by Charlene Li and Josh Bernoff.[29] From that first study, Forrester identified six types of people (of those online) based on how those people use and interact with social media. Because the types reflect increasing levels of involvement in social media, Forrester used the image of a ladder to illustrate the segments (see Figure 3.3). The system classifies people into the types based upon their social activities within the past month. The types are not exclusive—some people fit into more than one category based on their activities. Still, the ladder is indicative of the level of involvement in social media people have reached given their activities. Forrester continues to collect data as social media further penetrate our culture, and to study the social technographics of specific groups, including businesses.

Creators are categorized as such because—guess what?—they create content. They add value to the social Web and their social communities as they contribute content to be shared with others. User-generated content (UGC) is one of the defining cornerstones of the social Web, as we discussed in Chapter 1. What constitutes creating content? UGC may refer to a broad range of content ranging from video, photos, blogs, vlogs, comments, podcasts, forum discussions, online product reviews, wiki contributions, and consumer-generated advertising. The technographics profile categorizes people as creators if they recently published a blog entry, wrote and posted an article online, maintained a personal webpage, and uploaded video or audio they created to a site such as YouTube. In other words, creators are those who at least in part provide the ammunition with which the rest of the social community interacts.

Forrester added conversationalists to the social technographics ladder as the company recognized that people were *talking* through social media and doing so frequently (at least weekly). What does this mean? Simply, conversationalists maintain discussions with their friends via Twitter and Facebook updates and comments. Generally, conversationalists are the youngest of the segments, and more likely to be female.

Critics are reactors to content, rather than creators of content. They interact socially primarily by posting comments, ratings, or reviews and editing wikis. Although critics are not creating original content at the same level as creators, their contributions are highly valued in their social communities. Reviews and ratings are among the most utilized sources of information in the social Web. Critics are more than consumers of content; they embellish the content others contribute and thus create consumer-fortified media, also known as *augmented content*.

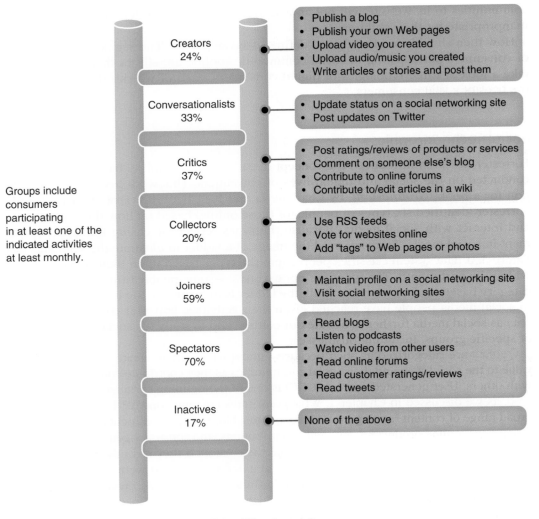

Base: US online adults

Figure 3.3   Social Technographics Ladder

Source: 2011 Social Technographics® for Business Technology Buyers, http://forrester.typepad.com/groundswell/2010/01/conversationalists-get-onto-the-ladder.html, accessed May 28, 2011.

As we move down the technographics ladder, the segments become less responsible for content and more involved in the *consumption* of content. Of course, creators and critics are also consumers of content, but they are defined more by their contributions than by their consumption.

Collectors tend to be efficient and organized users of social content. They use RSS feeds (syndicators of content that send content directly to subscribers) to receive regular updates on the information they want; bookmark and share online content; add tags to content such as bookmarked articles, photos, and videos; and "vote" for content. Historically, collectors were not thought of as contributors in the sense that creators and critics are. Their social activities ensured that they were regular consumers of content and helped the communities to which they belong by sorting and rating the content others post. But this has changed as curation has become a valued social media skill. Just as curators in art galleries carefully select pieces based on a collection's mission, curators in social media use their knowledge of a subject matter to skillfully orient a collection of social content. Collectors may not give the social audience a cool new video on YouTube, or publish poetry on WeBook, but they do add value when they help to organize content in a way that benefits the social network as a whole.

Joiners maintain a profile on one or more social networking sites and visit those sites on a regular basis. Joining is fun. Joining is easy. It takes advantage of the enhancements available in Web 2.0 technologies and social software that make it simple for even technophobes to participate in social networks.

Spectators consume content. They read, watch, and listen. Spectators treat online content like that available in other media—television, magazines, and radio. Inactives are online, but they aren't social participants. Some people spend time on the Internet and still avoid social communities. Being inactive is largely a by-product of generation. Of those users in developed countries worldwide who are in the under-35 age group, only 10% fall into the inactives category.

When an organization develops a social media marketing campaign, it can use Forrester's Social Technology Profile Tool to identify which tactics will fit with its target audience's social media usage category. The idea is to match your media strategy with how your target market uses social media to maximize the likelihood you will connect with your intended customers.

For example, it wouldn't be too smart to set up a UGC contest that requires entrants to film and upload their own video if your target market is composed primarily of spectators. Or at the other extreme, there is the danger of unintentionally excluding some segments from the experience. For instance, Unilever launched an initiative that solicited ads from consumers for several of its brands. The winners won cash and prizes, as well as a trip to a London film festival. However, the campaign focused on creators. The microsite provided information only for video creation rules and uploading guidelines. Judges chose the winners. There were no planned participation routes for the other technographic segments. Only a small percentage of the online population are creators, whereas the market for brands such as Ben & Jerry's and Dove is quite broad. Thus, even though Unilever developed an interesting social media promotion with an experienced partner, the company unwittingly ensured that about 76% of its online target audience wasn't able to engage.

Unilever's campaign reminds us that in many cases the target audience will include more than a single technographic type. For this reason it's key to offer multiple ways to participate. For example, the *Crash the Super Bowl* contest offers opportunities for several forms of participation. Creators contribute videos to the contest site and share the videos on other media sharing sites such as YouTube. Critics rate and vote on the videos submitted. Conversationalists talk about the videos. Collectors share the video links using channels such as Twitter and Facebook and tag the videos so that others can find them. Joiners and spectators view the videos but may not help to promote them. Still, they add to the overall impact of the contest.

Social technographic behavior does vary around the world. Table 3.1 explains the percentage of the online population in each region that participates in the specified category. It's clear to see that Koreans are avid in their social media participation.

Table 3.1 Social Technographics by Region (percentage)

CATEGORY	AUSTRALIA (%)	KOREA (%)	EUROPEAN UNION (%)	UNITED STATES (%)
Creator	23	49	14	24
Critic	31	46	19	37
Collector	14	19	6	21
Joiner	50	48	29	51
Spectator	64	76	49	73
Inactive	22	9	40	18

Forrester's social technographics segments are useful for understanding how people may interact with social media and how brands should engage them. But a simpler approach may be possible. Researchers at Ryerson University in Toronto studied the commonalities among behaviors like those included in the social technographics segments and found that the number of meaningful segments could be reduced to three.[30] Social media participation centered around (1) creating, (2) socializing, and (3) information seeking. Social media users will spend more time socializing and information seeking. This is because social media activities exist along a continuum of active-to-passive with online reading and viewing demanding less involvement and cognitive effort compared to the active creation of content.[31]

Pew Internet Technology Types

The Pew Internet & American Life Project published a paper called "The Mobile Difference."[32] As increasing numbers go online and participate in social communities from mobile devices, this Pew report sought to better understand consumer views of mobile Internet access. In the study, participants were asked about their attitudes toward a variety of online activities as well as their motives. What resulted was a typology of 10 digital lifestyles for the American consumer. In this scheme, digital lifestyle groups are based on two characteristics: (1) whether they hold a positive or negative view of digital mobility and (2) their relationships with assets (gadgets and services), actions (activities), and attitudes (how technology fits in their lives).

Pew defines digital mobility in terms of whether the individual welcomes mobility as a way to delve further into digital communications or keeps Internet communication technologies at a distance. Five groups have an increasing reliance on mobile technologies as a way to connect with others online; the other five groups are "stationary" in their use of Internet communications. The research suggests that when it comes to social media strategies, marketers should target those with positive views of mobility. The use of social media is associated with their use of the Internet and mobile devices, whereas the stationary groups are less likely to be heavily engaged in social media. Table 3.2 summarizes the 10 groups Pew identified.

Table 3.2   Pew Internet Technology Types

MOTIVATED BY MOBILITY

- **Digital collaborators:** Digital collaborators have the most gadgets of any group and use them to work, play, create, and share by visiting social networks with their mobile devices. Key demographics: mostly male, late 30s, well educated, relatively high incomes.
- **Ambivalent networkers:** Ambivalent networkers use mobile devices to visit social networks and for texting, but they also feel like people need breaks from so much connectivity. Key demographics: male (60%), young (late 20s), ethnically diverse.
- **Media movers:** Media movers create content such as photos and share them on social networks using their mobile devices. For them, digital is all about being social and connecting with others. Forty-six percent have a social network profile. They are managers of content and have a high attachment to the Internet. Key demographics: male (56%), mid-30s, family oriented, middle income.
- **Roving nodes:** This group wants to be connected but primarily for work. They use texting and email and rely upon their mobile devices for productivity. Social networking is not a key concern. This group relies on voice communication, texting, and email for communication. Key demographics: female (56%), late 30s, well educated, high incomes.
- **Mobile newbies:** This group is relatively new to mobile connectivity to the Internet. Overall, they are more focused on old media than new. Key demographics: female, 50s, lower educational and income levels.

STATIONARY MEDIA PREFERRED

- **Desktop veterans:** Content to use desktop computers with high-speed Internet access. Key demographics: male, mid-40s, well educated, relatively high incomes.
- **Drifting surfers:** Infrequent online users who wouldn't mind giving up the Internet and their mobile phone. Key demographics: female, early 40s, middle income.
- **Information encumbered:** This group suffers from information overload. They prefer old media such as television to the Internet. Key demographics: men (66%), early 50s, average education, lower-middle income.
- **Tech indifferent:** This group is made up of light users of the Internet who would be willing to give up their digital connectivity. Key demographics: female, late 50s, lower income.
- **Off the network:** This group is made up of people who do not use the Internet and do not have mobile phones. They may have had some experience in the past, but did not choose to continue participation. Key demographics: low-income seniors.

Source: Adapted from John Horrigan, "The Mobile Difference," Pew Internet & American Life Project, March 2009, http://pewinternet.org/Reports/2009/5-The-Mobile-Difference-Typology.aspx, accessed March 27, 2010. Used by permission of Pew Internet & American Life Project.

Microblog User Types

Microblogs like Twitter are thought to differ from other social networks. Members may seek to align by interests rather than relationships. The patterns go even deeper though, as Pew Research Center found in its study of Twitter topic networks.[33] It discovered six specific archetypes of social media participation in its analysis of Twitter conversations:

- Polarized Crowds
- Tight Crowds
- Brand Clusters
- Community Clusters
- Broadcast Networks
- Support Networks.

The two most critical for marketers are brand clusters and support networks, but before we get into that, let's take a look at the meaning of each archetype. Polarized crowds are people who are passionately discussing an issue. There are two sides and people do not cross the party lines! Tight crowds are characterized by highly interconnected people such as hobbyists, fans, or professional groups. Brand clusters are talking about brands but the people talking are not talking with each other. Community clusters typically feature news relevant to specific groups. Broadcast networks exist when many people repeat prominent news. The news sources are the hub, but the news is spread through retweets. The support network is one in which customer complaints are handled by one or more members. It produces a hub-and-spoke structure but the members are largely disconnected.

Brand clusters are relevant for social media marketers because these conversations are occurring around brand topics. There is an opportunity to engage. The support network archetype is relevant to brands seeking to use social media as a customer service channel.

CHAPTER SUMMARY

Which bases of segmentation are relevant to target wired consumers in a social media context?

The traditional bases of segmentation marketers rely upon are still useful in social media applications. Geographic segmentation is segmenting by market location or location characteristics. In particular, social media tools with geo-targeting such as Foursquare are useful to businesses that employ geographic segmentation. Demographic segmentation includes common personal characteristics such as age, gender, income, and educational attainment. Benefit segmentation is based on the benefits consumers seek from products. Some brands are developing mobile apps to pro-vide added value to consumers; we call these branded applications brand butlers. Behavioral segmentation uses consumer behavior as the basis for segmentation. Psychographic segmentation utilizes personality, activities, interests, and opinions to categorize individuals. Many of the existing social media segmentation schemes available to date are psychographic in nature.

What are the aspects of social identity? How do individuals build their social identities? How are these identities relevant to marketers?

Social identity is the information marketers collect using our social footprints (the residue from our social media activities). We build our social identities anytime we share online. Marketers can use this information to augment other consumer data.

What behaviors are exhibited by people using social media? To what extent are people participating in the four zones of social media?

Increasingly our lives are spent online checking email, shopping, banking, watching videos, playing games, and socializing in social networks. In zone 1, consumers interact and communicate with others in their networks. In zone 2, we publish our own content as well as consume the content produced by others (both commercial and user-generated). If you've watched videos on YouTube, you've spent part of your online activity in zone 2. Playing games online is a major activity of zone 3 and shopping online is a prelude to zone 4.

How can we explain the motives for participation in social media activities? What attitudes are most relevant for our understanding of social consumer behavior?

There are several motivations for consumer participation in social media activities. The affinity impulse is our need to acknowledge a liking or relationship with indi-viduals or reference groups. The prurient impulse is the curiosity we feel—curiosity that can be fed by observing social media activity. Contact comfort is our need to feel close to others. The immediacy impulse is our need to have contact without delay. The altruistic impulse is the need to do something good for others. The validation impulse is the need to feed our own egos.

What are the most important segments of social media customers? What do they tell us about targeting users of the social Web?

Several typologies of digital consumers exist, including the social technographics profiles from Forrester Research, Pew's Internet technology types, and the archetypes of Twitter participation. Each provides insight into online social behavior.

KEY TERMS

affinity impulse
altruistic impulse
bases of segmentation
behavioral segmentation
benefit segmentation
collectors
consumer-fortified media
contact comfort
contact immediacy
conversationalists
cookies
creators
critics
demographic segmentation
desktop veterans
digital brand name
digital collaborators
digital identity

digital mobility
digital primacy
drifting surfers
geographic segmentation
GPS technology
handle
handle-squatting
immediacy impulse
immediate altruistic responses
  (IAR)
inactives
information encumbered
joiners
lifestreams
market segmentation
media movers
mobile newbies
off the network

oversharing
personal utility impulse
privacy paradox
privacy salience
prurient impulse
psychographic
  segmentation
reach
roving nodes
RSS feeds
social footprint
social media addiction
social media touchpoints
social privacy
social technographics
spectators
tech indifferent
validation impulse

REVIEW QUESTIONS

1 Define digital primacy. Do your media choices reflect the claim of digital primacy? Explain.

2 What is the difference between a social footprint and a lifestream?

3 What is a social identity?

4 Define the major variables marketers use to segment consumers, and provide an example of how each variable can be applied in a social media application.

5 What are the primary motives that drive social media participation?

6 Describe the seven types of people characterized by the social technographics ladder. Which of the types is the most important to marketers using social media marketing? Why do you say so?

7 Why is the concept of mobility relevant to social media marketers?

8 What differences exist between the Pew Internet technology types who are motivated by mobility and those who prefer stationary media?

9 What is privacy salience? Why is it of concern to social media marketers? What is the difference between social privacy and institutional privacy?

EXERCISES

1. Begin a social footprint audit. Make a list of your online memberships. Start by "googling" yourself to find out where you've left your mark online. Then evaluate your presence using the personal audit suggested by Brian Solis. Are you painting the social identity you wish to portray?

2. Evaluate the Social Technographics ladder as it relates to your own behavior. In which of the categories do your activities fall? What would this mean for marketers targeting you?

3. Find an ongoing social media marketing campaign. Assess the components of the campaign in terms of whether and to what extent it offers a participation route for the social technographics segments. How could the campaign be improved to better engage people of varying levels of social media involvement?

4. Visit Twitter and read the stream of user posts (this is known as the tweet stream) for a few minutes. Can you see activities related to the archetypes in the chapter? How are you able to identify them?

5. Write six words on your digital life. Do your ideas relate to the concepts in the chapter?

6. How do you feel about privacy? Do you take steps to protect your social privacy? What about your institutional privacy? Ask a few friends and establish a plan to protect your privacy that fits with your own view.

CHAPTER NOTES

1. Erick Schonfeld, "Foursquare Becomes More Business Friendly," *Tech Crunch*, April 22, 2010, http://techcrunch.com/2010/04/22/foursquare-business-friendly/, accessed August 7, 2011.

2. "Changing Demographics and Psychographics of the Greeting Card Market Reveal New Opportunities—and Challenges—for Card Marketers and Retailers," *Market Wire*, February 4, 2010, http://www.marketwire.com/press-release/Changing-Demographics-Psychographics-Greeting-Card-Market-Reveal-New-Opportunities-Challenges-1112522.htm, http://www.marketwire.com/press-release/changing-demographics-psychographics-greeting-card-market-reveal-new-opportunities-challenges-1189051.htm, accessed August 7, 2011.

3. Lovemarks, http://www.lovemarks.com/index.php?pageID=20015&lmcategoryid=17&additions=2&require=100, accessed May 21, 2010.

(Continued)

(Continued)

4 Altimeter's Social Identity Use Cases, Andrew Jones, "Leveraging Social Identity," A Market Overview Report, *Altimeter Group,* June 12, 2014.

5 Feed: The Razorfish Digital Brand Experience Report, 2009, http://feed.razorfish.com/downloads/Razorfish_FEED09.pdf, p. 17, accessed August 7, 2011.

6 Ambuj Gupta, "I. Me. My Selfie," Simplify360, http://simplify360.com/i-me-myselfie-ebook, accessed July 30, 2014.

7 A History of the Selfie, *BBC News Magazine,* June 6, 2013, http://www.bbc.com/news/magazine-22511650, accessed July 30, 2014.

8 Andy Beal, *Repped: 30 Days to a Better Online Reputation*, 2014, CreateSpace.

9 Brian Solis, "Hello, It's Nice to Meet You Again: Your Digital Reputation Precedes You," February 18, 2014, http://www.briansolis.com/2014/02/digital-reputation-precedes/, accessed March 5, 2014.

10 Brian Solis, "This So-Called Digital Life: Re-Evaluating the Value of Social Media," October 27, 2013, http://www.briansolis.com/2013/10/re-evaluating-the-value-of-social-media/, accessed July 30, 2014.

11 Rory Cellon-Jones, "EU Court Backs 'Right to Be Forgotten' in Google Case," May 13, 2014, http://www.bbc.com/news/world-europe-27388289, accessed July 30, 2014.

12 A. Quan-Haase and A. L. Young, "Uses and Gratifications of Social Media: A Comparison of Facebook and Instant Messaging," *Bulletin of Science, Technology and Society,* 30 (5), 2010, 350–361.

13 T. Daugherty, M. Eastin, and L. Bright, "Exploring Consumer Motivations for Creating User-Generated Content," *Journal of Interactive Advertising*, 8 (2), 2008, 1–24.

14 Yongjun Sung, Yoojung Kim, Ohyoon Kwon, and Jangho Moon, "An Explorative Study of Korean Consumer Participation in Virtual Brand Communities in Social Network Sites," *Journal of Global Marketing,* 23 (2010), 430–445.

15 Quan-Haase and Young, "Uses and Gratifications of Social Media."

16 Scott Brown, "Scott Brown on How Twitter + Dopamine = Better Humans," *Wired*, April 19, 2010, http://www.wired.com/magazine/2010/04/pl_brown_karma/, accessed August 7, 2011.

17 T. Daugherty, M. Eastin, and L. Bright, "Exploring Consumer Motivations for Creating User-Generated Content," *Journal of Interactive Advertising*, 8 (2), 2008, 1–24.

18 Daugherty, Eastin, and Bright, "Exploring Consumer Motivations for Creating User-Generated Content."

19 Elliot Panek, Yioryos Nardis, and Sara Konrath, "Mirror or Megaphone?: How Relationships Between Narcissism and Social Networking Site Use Differ on Facebook and Twitter," *Computers in Human Behavior*, 29 (September 2013), 2004–2012.

20 Clodagh O'Brien, "The Emergence of the Social Media Empowered Consumer," *Irish Marketing Review,* 21 (1), 2011, 32–40.

21 Alyson Leigh Young and Anabel Quan-Haase, "Privacy Protection Strategies on Facebook," *Information, Communication, and Society*, 16 (4), 2013, 479–500.

22 Mary Madden, Amanda Lenhart, Sandra Cortesi, Urs Gasser, Maeve Duggan, Aaron Smith, and Meredith Beaton, "Teens, Social Media, and Privacy," May 21, 2013, *Pew Research Center,* http://www.pewinternet.org/2013/05/21/teens-social-media-and-privacy/

23 Andrew Jones, "Leveraging Social Identity," A Market Overview Report, *Altimeter Group,* June 12, 2014.

24 Gwendolyn Seidman, "Expressing the 'True Self' on Facebook," *Computers in Human Behavior,* 31 (February 2014), 367–372.

25 Julie Beck, "Study: People Who Overshare on Facebook Just Want to Belong," *The Atlantic,* June 16, 2014, http://www.theatlantic.com/health/archive/2014/06/study-people-who-overshare-on-facebook-just-want-to-belong/372834/, accessed July 30, 2014.

26 Caitlin Dewey, "Where Do People Overshare Most Online? Hint: It's Not the US," *The Washington Post,* accessed July 15, 2014.

27 Caitlin Dewey, "Where Do People Overshare Most Online? Hint: It's Not the US," *The Washington Post,* accessed July 15, 2014.

28 Caroline McCarthy, "Analyst: Half of 'Social Media Campaigns' Will Flop," CNET News, October 6, 2008, http://news.cnet.com/8301-13577_3-10058509-36.html, accessed December 20, 2010.

29 Charlene Li and Josh Bernoff, *Groundswell: Winning in a World Transformed by Social Technologies* (Cambridge, MA: Harvard Business Press, 2008).

30 Mary Foster, Bettina West, and Anthony Francescucci, "Exploring Social Media User Segmentation and Online Brand Profiles," *Journal of Brand Management*, 19 (1), 2011, 4–17.

31 G. Hutton and M. Fosdick, "The Globalization of Social Media: Consumer Relationships with Brands Evolve in the Digital Space," *Journal of Advertising Research*, 51 (4), 2011, 564–570.

32 John Horrigan, "The Mobile Difference," *Pew Internet & American Life Project,* March 2009, http://pewinternet.org/Reports/2009/5-The-Mobile-Difference-Typology.aspx, accessed March 27, 2010.

33 Marc Smith, Lee Rainie, Itai Himelboim, and Ben Shneiderman, "Mapping Twitter Topic Networks: From Polarized Crowds to Community Clusters," *Pew Research Center,* February 20, 2014, http://www.pewinternet.org/2014/02/20/mapping-twitter-topic-networks-from-polarized-crowds-to-community-clusters, accessed May 2, 2014.

Network Structure and Group Influence in Social Media

LEARNING OBJECTIVES

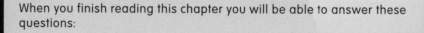

When you finish reading this chapter you will be able to answer these questions:

1 Why are relationships critical to social media and the basis for leveraging the network effect in social media marketing?

2 How are social networks structured?

3 What are the characteristics of online communities?

4 How do ideas travel in a community? What role do opinion leaders play in influencing social networks?

5 What role does social capital play in the value of social media communities? What types of ties do we have to others in our communities?

Community Structure

Though infrastructure, channels, devices, and social software make social media possible, it's people like you that make it a living, breathing part of everyday life. Social media are first and foremost about *community:* the collective participation of members who together build and maintain a site. We've previously asked you to audit your own participation in social media. You built an early iteration of your social footprint. Chances are that you already participate in Facebook or other social networking sites. Maybe you post comments to a blog on music or fashion, or perhaps you take on the role of an orc or a warrior in a multiplayer game such as World of Warcraft or Everquest. If so, you're one of the billions of people worldwide who are part of online communities.

Defining exactly what an online community is and what it isn't has been a difficult task for researchers. Though different approaches exist, we'll refer to online communities as a group of people who come together for a specific purpose, who are guided by community policies, and who are supported by Internet access that enables virtual communication. Here is a brief sampling of online communities; there may be some out there just waiting for you!

- Qzone
- Google+
- Tencent Weibo
- WhatsApp
- YouKu

In some ways, online communities are not much different from those we find in our physical environment. The *Merriam-Webster Dictionary* (online version, of course) defines community as "a unified body of individuals, unified by interests, location, occupation, common history, or political and economic concerns." In fact, one social scientist refers to an online community as a cyberplace where "people connect online with kindred spirits, engage in supportive and sociable relationships with them, and imbue their activity online with meaning, belonging, and identity."[1]

Networks: The Underlying Structure of Communities

When we first presented the social media value chain to you, we emphasized that all of social media is networked. Though we'll talk more in the next chapter (and throughout the text) about social networking sites, in fact *all social communities are social networks.* Networks underlie the premise of social media. So, before we move on, let's cover the basics of social network theory, the theory that explains how networks (whether online or off) work.

Social Networks

A social network is a set of socially relevant nodes connected by one or more relations.[2] Nodes are members of the network. Members (whom we also refer to as network units) are connected by their relationships (or ties) with each other. Relationships are based on various affiliations such as kinship, friendship and affective ties, shared experiences, professional relationships, and shared hobbies and interests.

When we think of community, we tend to think of people, but members of a network can be organizations, articles, countries, departments, or any other definable unit. A good example is your university alumni association. The association is a community of networked individuals and organizations. Social networks are sometimes called social graphs, though this term may also refer to a diagram of the interconnections of units in a network. LinkedIn offers members a mapping tool that creates a visual representation of members' social graphs at www.inmaps.linkedinlabs. com. Photo 4.1 illustrates a LinkedIn member network. Circles in the image represent nodes

Figure 4.1   LinkedIn Network Map

(members of LinkedIn) who are connected via ties. LinkedIn also supplies information on degrees of separation between members. People with direct connections are separated by one degree. A friend of a friend has a two degree separation, and so on. The degrees of separation show what a small world we live in.

SHOW ME!

Photo 4.1

The game The Six Degrees of Kevin Bacon illustrates the small world concept. It's based on the premise that everyone (not just movie stars like Kevin Bacon) is connected to everyone else by no more than six ties, called the six degrees of separation. The principle draws from the mathematical model known as a small-world network that illustrates that most nodes in a social graph are not directly linked to one another but instead indirectly connected via neighboring nodes.

Nodes in a network experience interactions; these are behavior-based ties such as talking with each other, attending an event together, or working together. If you have a conversation on Twitter, you are a node engaging in an interaction with another node.

Node-to-Node Relationships

We use many terms to refer to connections in a social networking site or SNS, including *friend*, *fan*, *follower*, *colleague*, and *contact*. The biggest predictor of whether someone will become active in a social network space, regardless of the site's primary function, is the presence of a critical mass of friends. If your friends are present and active in the space, you probably will be too because you will have someone with whom to interact and to reward you for your participation. Your level of activity is based on a mix of the *people* with whom you are connected, the content (called *artifacts)* you produce on the site, the *feedback* you receive from others, and the *distribution* of the artifacts and feedback throughout the network.[3]

Of these four elements of SNS participation, three are dependent upon the nodes in your network. If your contacts are not active in your experience, your own activity in the network will be stunted because you won't have people with whom to interact, you won't receive sufficient feedback, and your content will not be redistributed. Some nodes will have more connections than others and some will take part in more interactions. These nodes will tend to have greater influence in the network. We'll talk more about influence and the types of nodes later in this chapter. Interactions are participative in nature—they are shared activities among members in the network.

Flows occur between nodes. Flows are exchanges of resources, information, or influence among members of the network. On Facebook you share news, updates about your life, opinions on favorite books and movies, photos, videos, and notes. As you share content, you create flows among those in your network. In social media these flows of communication go in many directions at any point in time and often on multiple platforms—a condition we term media multiplexity. Flows are not simply two way or three way, they may involve an entire community, a list or group within a network, or several individuals independently.

Photo 4.2

Flows of communication also occur outside the community platform. While the online community exists within a web space, the flows of communication may extend to other domains such as emails, text messages, virtual worlds, and even face-to-face meetups where members of an online network arrange to meet in a physical location. Increasingly we find that social connections online result in face-to-face connections offline. In fact, that's what the company Meetups does. It's scheduled more than 10 million events worldwide since its start. While a social media, online site, the purpose is to connect people offline. Wondering about monetization? Meetups' revenue comes from fees from organizers and attendees.

For marketers, flows are especially important because they are the actionable components of any social network system in terms of the sharing of information, delivery of promotional materials, and sources of social influence. Word-of-mouth communication flows from node to node. Whether the flow changes behavior or attitudes depends on the social influence of the initiating node. The extent of social influence (where one person's attitudes or behavior change as a result of others' attempts) varies depending upon the power or attractiveness of other nodes. We'll take a deep look at influence and how someone develops it later in the chapter.

The Characteristics of Online Communities

All communities, whether they exist online or in the physical world, share important characteristics: participants experience a feeling of membership, a sense of proximity to one another (even though in online groups other members' physical selves may be thousands of miles away), and in most cases some interest in the community's activities. Members may identify with one another due to a common mission (e.g., a Twitter campaign to donate money for Japan's earthquake relief) or simply because they come from the same neighborhood or belong to the same sorority (e.g., Classmates.com connects people who attended the same high school).

Social object theory suggests that social networks will be more powerful communities if there is a way to activate relationships among people and objects. In this perspective an *object* is something of common interest and its primary function is to mediate the interactions between people. All relationships have social objects embedded in the relationship. In the online world, a site such as Facebook provides venues for several object formats to ensure that relationships can thrive within the site's framework. One factor that drives Facebook's stunning success is that it offers so many objects for users to share; these include events, family and friends, quizzes, and so on.

Other social networking sites (SNSs) provide a more specialized or focused set of objects. For example, consider how each of the following SNSs incorporates objects as part of its mission. On Instagram users participate because they want to share photos. These images are the objects that give meaning to the platform and motivate people to visit. Video is burgeoning. It's no wonder that social media vehicles that previously focused on photos have expanded to include video. Instagram and Snapchat are two examples.

SHOW ME!

Photo 4.3

Social object theory explains that shared objects give meaning to a social vehicle and motivate member engagement.

On Diigo, the objects are URLs. On Foursquare, the objects are places. On Dogster, the objects are our canine companions. On Whisper, secrets are the object.

Object sociality, the extent to which users can share an object in social media, clearly relates to an audience's unique interests. It ties the site relationships to a specific object such as photos of people's dogs or bookmarked websites that provide details about the history of alternative music. The audience becomes specialized, at least to a degree. Importantly, though, SNSs oriented around object sociality are likely to be passion-centric. That is, the people who join those communities probably not only share an interest in the object in question; chances are they are passionate about the object. We all know people who devote countless hours to a hobby or who (to an outsider) seem insanely obsessed about the fine details of *Star Wars* characters, vintage wines, or warring guilds in World of Warcraft.

In industry terms, vertical networks are sites designed around object sociality. The term refers to the narrow, deep focus of SNSs that differentiate themselves because they center on some common hobby, interest, or characteristic that draws members to the site. These vertical networks do not attract the same traffic typical of general sites, but one might argue that the members are more involved because of the common interest that initially brought them to the site. They function much like so-called niche markets in the physical world. The term *niche* refers to marketplaces that offer a relatively small number of items to buyers who tend to be loyal to these outlets (e.g., big-and-tall men's stores or tandem bicycles built for two).

Communities help members meet their needs for affiliation, resource acquisition, entertainment, and information. Above all else, communities are social! Whether online or offline, they thrive when the members participate, discuss, share, and interact with others as well as recruit new members to the community. Members do vary in their degree of participation, but the more active the membership, the healthier the community.

Social media provide the fuel that fans the fires of online communities. In the Web 1.0 era, people visited a lot of websites to get content that interested them. But these really weren't communities—the flow of information was all one way. In today's Web 2.0 environment all that has changed as interactive platforms enable online communities to exhibit the following basic characteristics:[4]

Conversations

Communities thrive on communication among members. Though social media provide online space for what are essentially digital conversations, these conversations are not based on talking or writing but on a hybrid of the two. The immediate nature of the written word is perceived more like a spoken conversation even without the soundtrack. For this reason, if you communicate with a friend via AIM or Facebook chat, you may feel that you actually "talked" to her.

Presence

Though online communities exist virtually rather than at a physical location, the better ones supply tangible characteristics that create the sensation of actually being in a place. This is particularly true for virtual world communities that include three-dimensional depictions of physical spaces, but it also applies to visually simplistic online communities such as message board groups. Presence refers to the effect that people experience when they interact with a computer-mediated or computer-generated environment.[5] Social media sites enhance a sense of presence when they enable interactions among visitors or make the environment look and feel real.[6]

Virtual communities do not develop and thrive without a foundation of commonality among the members. Just as your offline communities revolve around family, religious beliefs, social activities, hobbies, goals, place of residence, and so on, your online communities also need commonalities to create bonds among the members. These groups come together to allow people to share their passions, whether for indie bands, white wines, or open-source apps.

Community content (whether simple dialogue, shared recipes, event photos, or something else entirely) is generated, shared, consumed, fortified, and promoted by community members. The contributions of members add value for the general membership group. Community members seek out ways to be connected. The site encourages new members to connect. It's critical to encourage participation among new members; these contributions continue to build the value of the platform for all members. If a social media site starts to lose visitors, it resembles a deserted mining town in the Old West—empty saloons, banks, and stores with (digital) tumbleweed blowing across the streets.

Democracy

The political model of most online communities is democratic (that's with a small d, not the Democratic Party); leaders emerge due to the reputation they earn among the general membership. In this context democracy is a descriptive term that refers to rule by the people. The community appoints or elects leaders based on their demonstrated ability to add value to the group.

SHOW ME!

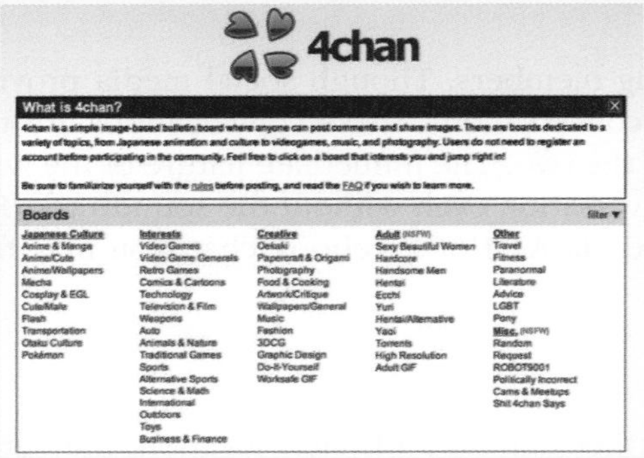

Photo 4.4

In the online community 4chan, an online bulletin board devoted to the sharing of images related to and discussion of Japanese *anime* (graphic art stories), members widely acknowledge that the person who posts under the name of "moot" is a leader. His leadership comes from his role in the creation of the community as well as from his ongoing participation and the quality of his contributions. Even though leaders emerge in online communities, the power structure of the community is decentralized. Majority rule applies. New leaders can emerge as they choose to escalate their levels of involvement.

Because of the horizontal structure of social media (remember, this is all part of the horizontal revolution), we typically find that control over what appears on the platform shifts from a small elite to the larger mass. Media democratization means that the members of social communities, not traditional media publishers such as magazines or newspaper companies, control the creation, delivery, and popularity of content.

Standards of Behavior

Virtual communities need norms, or rules that govern behavior, in order to operate. Some of these rules are spelled out explicitly (e.g., if you buy an item on eBay you agree that you have entered into a legal contract to pay for it) but many of them are unspoken. Without these rules, we would have chaos. Imagine the confusion if a simple norm in the offline world such as stopping for a red traffic light did not exist!

In the online world people also need to observe norms and they may arouse others' anger when they don't. A simple example is the practice of flaming, when a POST CONTAINS ALL CAPITAL LETTERS TO EXPRESS ANGER. Some norms such as flaming are pretty minor; they just help ensure a more pleasant online experience. Others relate to more serious matters; they help ensure protection for those who participate in terms of fair use of information (such as posting content that belongs to others), privacy, and etiquette. Two issues in particular are important in this context:

- Open access sites enable anyone to participate without registration or identification. This can be valuable for participation on sensitive topics as well as for ease of use. However, open access also lowers the barriers for misbehavior because it ensures anonymity to users. Just as people tend to "act out" at a costume party when no one knows who they really are, visitors to these sites may post things they might avoid if others knew their real identity.

- The social contract is the agreement that exists between the host or governing body and the members. You engage in a social contract when you indicate agreement to a "terms of use" clause for a site. Social contracts set forth expectations for user behavior as well as for the host or governing body. Some sites such as Facebook, however, come under fire when they make changes to the social contract without user input. The specific concern is typically for the protection of membership privacy.

Level of Participation

For an online community to thrive, a significant proportion of its members must participate. Otherwise the site will fail to offer fresh material and ultimately traffic will slow. Participation can be a challenge, though, because most users are lurkers, people who review site content but don't actually contribute. Researchers estimate that only 1% of a typical community's users regularly participate and another 9% do so only intermittently. The remaining 90% just observe what's on the site, so they don't add a lot of value—other than adding to the number of "eyeballs" the site can claim when it tries to convince advertisers to buy space.

Sound familiar? This disparity roughly parallels the larger pattern we often observe in marketing contexts called the 80/20 rule—that roughly 20% of a brand's users buy 80% of the product. Marketers label these faithful "heavy users." In many groups or consumer segments, a relative handful of people account for most of the activity; this hard-core group is often the most valuable for organizations to touch because they are the real movers and shakers. Thus a person's participation is influenced by 20% or less of their network. Just as opinion leaders influence other types of decisions, they also can influence how active others are in a given social community.[7]

How can a site convert lurkers into active users? The easier it is to participate, the more likely it is that the community can generate activity among a larger proportion of visitors. In part, this means ensuring that there are several ways to participate. Ideally, at least one or more of these pathways are quite easy so that "newbies" don't get discouraged. Facebook is an example of an online community that has figured out how to offer a variety of options: Members can post status updates (very easy), make comments, upload photos, share notes and links, play social games, answer quizzes, decorate their profiles, upload videos, and create events (a bit harder), among other forms of participation. There is a way for everyone to participate actively in the community.

How Ideas Travel in an Online Community

Earlier we saw that social communities are built on networks, and these networks include nodes that are connected by ties and through which content and experiences flow.

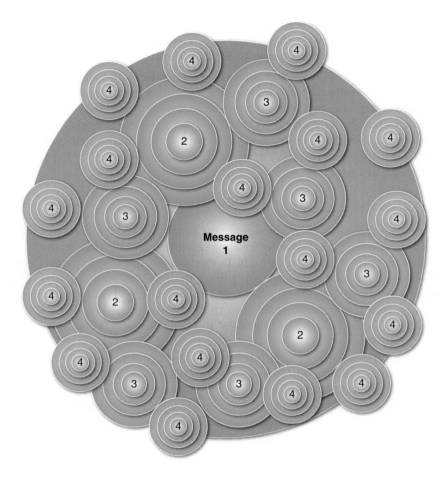

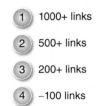

① 1000+ links	Bloggers who exert a larger "sphere of influence" have a broad ripple effect.	
② 500+ links		
③ 200+ links	Bloggers at the lower ranking levels also influence, but their ripples are smaller. Bloggers with smaller "influence ripples" tend to be higher in volume.	
④ −100 links		

Figure 4.2   An Influence Network

Understanding what flows occurred and how extensively disseminated was first based on a framework called the two-step flow model of influence. It proposed that a small group of *influencers* are responsible for dissemination of information because they can modify the opinions of a large number of other people.

More recent research has tweaked that basic idea; now it suggests that influence can be driven by both influencers and by interactions among those who are easily influenced. These people communicate the information vigorously to one another and also participate in a two-way dialogue with the opinion leader as part of an influence network. These conversations create cascades of information, which occur when a piece of information triggers a sequence of interactions (much like an avalanche), as Figure 4.2 shows.

A message originates at Level 1 and is sent by the influencer to his or her contacts (Level 2). The message may travel on from some Level 2 contacts to their contacts (Level 3), and so on.

Word-of-Mouth (WOM)

Word-of-mouth (WOM) communication is product information individuals transmit to other individuals. Because we get the word from people we know, WOM tends to be more reliable and trustworthy than messages from more formal marketing channels. And unlike advertising, WOM often comes with social pressure to conform to these recommendations.[8]

Photo 4.5

Ironically, despite all of the money marketers pump into lavish ads, WOM is far more powerful: it influences two thirds of all consumer goods sales.[9] In one recent survey, 69% of interviewees said they relied on a personal referral at least once over the course of a year to help them choose a restaurant, 36% reported they used referrals to decide on computer hardware and software, and 22% got help from friends and associates to decide where to travel.[10]

If you think carefully about the content of your own conversations in the course of a normal day, you will probably agree that much of what you discuss with friends, family members, or coworkers is product related: when you compliment someone on her dress and ask her where she bought it, recommend a new restaurant to a friend, or complain to your neighbor about the shoddy treatment you got at the bank, you engage in WOM.

Marketers have been aware of the power of WOM for many years, but recently they've been more aggressive about trying to promote and control it instead of sitting back and hoping people will like their products enough to talk them up. Companies such as BzzAgent (https://www.bzzagent.com/) have thousands of online "agents" who try new products and spread the word about those they like.[11] And many sophisticated marketers today also precisely track WOM.

The ongoing *TalkTrack* study reports which brands are mentioned the most by consumers in different categories. Based on online surveys of 14,000 women, it reports that middle-aged (Baby Boomer) women talk about Kraft more than any other packaged goods food brand, and they discuss Olay the most among beauty products.[12]

The influence of others' opinions is at times even more powerful than our own perceptions. In one study of furniture choices, consumers' estimates of how much their friends would like the furniture was a better predictor of purchase than what *they* thought of it.[13] In addition, consumers may find their own reasons to push a brand that take the manufacturer by surprise. That's what happened with Mountain Dew; we trace its popularity among younger consumers to the "buzz" about the soda's high caffeine content. As an advertising executive explained, "The caffeine thing was not in any of Mountain Dew's television ads. This drink is hot by word-of-mouth."[14]

WOM is especially powerful when the consumer is relatively unfamiliar with the product category. We would expect such a situation in the case of new products (e.g., medications to prevent hair loss) or those that are technologically complex (e.g., laptops). One way to reduce uncertainty about the wisdom of a purchase is to talk about it. Talking gives the consumer an opportunity to generate supporting arguments for the purchase and to garner support for this decision from others. For example, the strongest predictor of a person's intention to buy a residential solar water-heating system is the number of solar-heat users the person knows.[15]

You talk about products for several reasons:[16]

- You might be highly involved with a type of product or activity and simply enjoy talking about it. Computer hackers, avid football fans, and "fashion plates" seem to share the ability to steer a conversation toward their particular interests.

- You might be knowledgeable about a product and use conversations as a way to let others know it. Thus, word-of-mouth communication sometimes enhances the egos of those individuals who want to impress others with their expertise (we all know someone like that!).

- You might initiate a discussion out of genuine concern for someone else. We like to ensure that people we care about buy what is good for them or that they do not waste their money.

Word-of-mouth is a two-edged sword that cuts both ways for marketers. Informal discussions among consumers can make or break a product or store. Furthermore, consumers weigh negative word-of-mouth more heavily than they do positive comments.

According to a study by the White House Office of Consumer Affairs, 90% of unhappy customers will not do business with a company again. Each of these customers is likely to share his or her grievance with at least nine other people, and 13% tell more than 30 people about their negative experience.[17]

Word-of-mouth has long been an influence on consumer decision making. Recognizing the ease and speed with which people share brand experiences, recommendations, and product-related opinions with others online, both negative and positive, led marketers to invent the phrase word-of-mouse. With the added accessibility to our networks brought about by SNSs, peer-to-peer influence has taken on even more power in terms of the sources that may influence a consumer decision. Some of the brands using social media most avidly are those that recognized early on social media's value in terms of creating a customer service communication channel and service recovery venue.

These brand-specific conversations also have value in terms of their media equivalent, known as the ad equivalency value. In other words, when brands use paid media, they have an estimate of the value of the advertising in the form of the fees they paid to place the ads. But in social media, most of our promotional value comes from earned and owned media. Therefore, we may try to establish a value and relate that value to the cost of buying equivalent paid media. This is the meaning of ad equivalence value—what would the value of the mention be if it had come through a paid advertising placement rather than a volunteered comment?

Forrester Research labels these brand-specific mentions "influence impressions"; we discussed these in Chapter 1. We generate influence impressions whenever we discuss brands openly online. In advertising lingo, an impression refers to a view or an exposure to an advertising message. In social media, brands may benefit from influence impressions as well as ad impressions. An influence impression is an exposure to a brand via another person—in other words, it's the impressions that are generated through social sharing. Forrester estimates that each year among U.S. consumers 256 billion influence impressions are generated as people talk about their lives with each other, telling stories and experiences that invariably include brands.[18] Further, the brand activity in the social media space, whether in the form of tweeting, blogging, social networking, or virtual commerce, encourages people to incorporate this information into their own communication exchanges.

Opinion leaders in social communities are most likely to deliver these influence impressions: only 6.2% of social media users are responsible for about 80% of them. Forrester calls these influencers mass connectors, paying homage to Malcolm Gladwell's popular book *The Tipping Point*. Gladwell posits that three factors work to "tip" a trend, in other words to ignite interest in an idea, behavior, or product: the law of the few, stickiness, and the power of context.[19]

1 The law of the few proposes that three types of people help to spread viral messages:
- Mavens are people who are knowledgeable about many things.
- Connectors are people who know many people and communicate with them.
- Salesmen are people who influence others with their natural persuasive power.

2 If an idea is sticky, this means it has memorable impact and it stays with us for a long time. Indeed, web designers use the term "stickiness" to describe the extent to which a website captures people's interest so that they stay on the site for a long time.

3 Lastly, Gladwell acknowledges that ideas spread more easily when conditions are right—that's the power of context.[20]

The Viral Spread of Social Content

When content, whether a simple opinion, video, or trend, spreads through social networks rapidly, we say that it *went viral*. Viral content may or may not be branded, but it will be content that a large number of people in one or more social communities deemed relevant, valuable—or just plain too bizarre not to share with friends. Those community members then influenced the spread of the content by sharing it with their own social graphs and by participating in WOM about the content.

SHOW ME!

Debby Wong / Shutterstock.com

Recent examples of viral content include the songs, "What Does the Fox Say?" and "Gangnam Style," the use of the hashtag #yesallwomen, and the spread of the "First Kiss" video.

https://www.youtube.com/watch?v=jofNR_WkoCE

https://www.youtube.com/watch?v=9bZkp7q19f0

http://time.com/114043/yesallwomen-hashtag-santa-barbara-shooting/

Photo 4.6

When viral content evolves within a social community, it becomes a meme. A meme is a snippet of cultural information that spreads person to person until eventually it enters the general consciousness. These snippets may include songs, phrases, ideas, slang words, fashion trends, or shared behaviors. An example of a meme is the plethora of *Harlem Shake* videos available on YouTube. After the initial video spread, groups around the world made their own versions (e.g., www.youtube.com/results?search_query=harlem+shake).

It's easy to understand how a meme spreads if you use the medical analogy of a virus: memes spread among consumers in a geometric progression, just as a virus starts off small and steadily infects increasing numbers of people until it becomes an epidemic. The leap from person to person occurs as people share and imitate the meme. The memes that survive over time tend to be distinctive and memorable. The most enduring ones evoke earlier memes that may relate to legends and well-known stories and tales. For example, the *Star Wars* movies evoke prior memes that relate to the legend of King Arthur, religion, heroic youth, and 1930s adventure serials.

Show Me!

Photo 4.7

Some memes "infect" numerous kinds of people and truly take on a life of their own—at least until the next meme takes over. *Rickrolling* is a great example: this term describes a prank that involves sending someone a link to click on—but when they do they're instead taken to a link to Rick Astley's campy video of his 1987 hit song "Never Gonna Give You Up" on YouTube. The first rickroll happened in 2007 when visitors to the YouTube trailer for the video game Grand Theft Auto IV were instead served Astley's video. YouTube got in on the fun itself for April Fool's Day 2008 when the site rickrolled every user who viewed a clip on its homepage.[21] Rick Astley performed an in-person rickroll at the Macy's Thanksgiving Day Parade in 2008 and live rickrollings have since popped up at university basketball games and protest events.[22]

http://www.cultofmac.com/183192/apple-says-goodbye-to-youtube-by-rickrolling-developers/

Group Influence and Social Capital

Although consumers get information from personal sources, they do not usually ask just *anyone* for advice about purchases.[23] If you decide to buy a new sound system, you will most likely seek advice from a friend who knows a lot about this topic. This friend may own a sophisticated system, or may subscribe to specialized magazines such as *Stereo Review* and spend her free time browsing through electronics stores. However, you may have another friend who has a reputation for being stylish and who spends his free time reading *Gentleman's Quarterly* and shopping at trendy boutiques. You might not bring up your sound system problem with him, but you may take him with you to shop for a new fall wardrobe.

Opinion leaders (also known as influencers or power users in some communities) are people that others view as knowledgeable sources of information. They have a strong communication network that gives them the ability to affect purchase decisions for a number of other consumers, directly and indirectly. Five characteristics help to describe them: (1) activists, (2) connected, (3) impact, (4) active minds, and (5) trendsetters.[24] In other words, opinion leaders develop a network of people through their involvement in activities. They are active participants at work and in their communities. Their social networks are large and well developed. Others trust them and find them to be credible sources of information about one or more specific topics. They tend to have a natural sense of intellectual curiosity that may lead them to new sources of information.

Opinion leaders exist in all social communities. It is a natural pattern for some members to be more active and to acquire positions of authority within a group, whether offline or online. The source of the influence itself, however, originates from the power bases an influencer may possess.

How can someone acquire power? French and Raven identified in their classic article, "The Bases of Social Power", several sources of power individuals can accrue in organizations.[25] These sources of power include:

- Reward power: one's ability to provide others with what they desire
- Coercive power: the ability to punish others
- Legitimate power: organizational authority based on rights associated with a person's appointed position
- Referent power: authority through the motivation to identify with or please a person
- Expert power: recognition of one's knowledge, skills, and ability
- Information power: one's control over the flow of and access to information

Of course, marketers always want to identify opinion leaders and get them on their team. These people often are the linchpin in a communications strategy; once an opinion leader decides he or she loves your product it's just a matter of time before others in that person's networks hear about it as well.[26] Thus for purchase decisions, opinion leaders are extremely valuable information sources due to their social power:

- They are technically competent so they possess expert power.[27]
- They prescreen, evaluate, and synthesize product information in an unbiased way, so they possess knowledge power.[28]
- They are socially active and highly interconnected in their communities.[29]
- They are likely to hold positions of leadership. As a result, opinion leaders often have legitimate power by virtue of their social standing.
- They tend to be similar to the consumer in terms of their values and beliefs, so they possess referent power. Note that although opinion leaders are set apart

by their interest or expertise in a product category, they are more convincing to the extent that they are *homophilous* rather than *heterophilous*. Homophily refers to the degree to which a pair of individuals is similar in terms of education, social status, and beliefs.[30] Homophily can predict collaborative online relationships and connectivity, whether in professional collaborations like a new product development project or in reciprocal kindnesses among friends in an online network of musicians.[31]

- Effective opinion leaders tend to be slightly higher in terms of status and educational attainment than those they influence but not so high as to be in a different social class.

- Opinion leaders are often among the first to buy new products, so they absorb much of the risk. This experience reduces uncertainty for the rest of us who are not as courageous. Furthermore, whereas company-sponsored communications tend to focus exclusively on the positive aspects of a product, the hands-on experience of opinion leaders makes them more likely to impart *both* positive and negative information about product performance. Thus, they are more credible because they have no "axe to grind."

FROM BYTES TO BUCKS

Opinion leaders often play a crucial role in B2B marketing. Take the case of a study for the pharmaceutical industry to identify physician opinion leaders who could influence other physicians to adopt (in the form of prescribing) a new drug.[32] Using sociometric techniques, the researchers showed that physicians who were most frequently identified by other physicians as experts were also the most influential. Traditional measures of opinion leadership among medical doctors tended to utilize measures of expertise in the form of journal publications or self-reported measures. The study showed that peer opinion leaders—those who were active in the community—were most influential and those docs voted as influencers by the network were not the same doctors who self-reported as opinion leaders. Doctors who were central in the network structure were more influential. Using the analysis and mapped network image, the pharmaceutical company could identify who to target with sales calls. Further, the company could also be more efficient. Because the map revealed that several opinion leaders had the same followers, the company could choose to target only one influential doctor in each cluster of connected nodes.

A recent reexamination of the traditional perspective on opinion leadership reveals that the process isn't as clear-cut as some researchers thought.[33]

Social Capital

When people form community relationships, these affiliations allow them to accumulate resources that they can "trade" for other things. In the offline business world, we clearly see how this process works in the golf subculture. Although many people do love to hit that ball around, the reality is that a lot of business is transacted on the course and executives profit from their membership in this community (some business schools even offer academic courses on "golf etiquette"!).

We call these resources social capital or *social currency* because their value lies in providing access to others.[34] The resources may be actual or virtual, and they may be held by a group or an individual. For instance, they might include useful information, relationships, the ability to organize groups, employment connections, and more.[35] Do you know anyone who landed a job interview due to the intervention of a friend of a friend? This is an example of social capital at work—especially since jobseekers who know larger numbers of people who already work at high-level jobs are more likely to be able to trade on these connections. Social capital tends to be a limited and protected resource. To return to the golf example, at many country clubs it's not enough just to be rolling in money: you also need to be recommended by current members so that the organization controls (fairly or not) just who gets to hobnob on the links and in the locker room.

Typically, a community is healthier and more desirable when it is able to offer a lot of social capital as an inducement for people to join. Communities build capital through reputation and structure. Reputational capital is based on the shared beliefs, relationships, and actions of those in the community such that norms, behaviors, and values held and shared by individuals ultimately support a community reputation. You can think of this like a big, beefy nightclub bouncer who decides whom he will admit past the velvet rope.

In fact, like exclusive country clubs, online gated communities that selectively allow access to only some people may offer a high degree of social capital to the lucky few who pass the test.

SHOW ME!

Consider "exclusive" dating sites such as hotenough.org that weed out unattractive people. The site's homepage claims, "Through our screening process, we have filtered the masses leaving only your area's most attractive, fit, trendy singles and have now included an exclusive section for our 40+ singles, the 'BABY BOOMER SECTION.' Hot Enough offers three tiers of hotties, so if you're fit and trendy, then rest assured there is a place for you."[36]

(www.hotenough.org)

Let's use Klout as an example to understand how online social capital works. Klout is a social reputation indicator that measures relative influence across several social communities including Twitter, Facebook, LinkedIn, and Foursquare. Klout assigns a Klout Score between 0 and 100 to each user, with higher scores denoting greater levels of influence in social media.

Network size, member activity, activity quality indicators such as network feedback like number of "favorites," and information flows from a member through his or her network all serve as variables to calculate a Klout score (https://klout.com/brandacity). Network size is a variable because it promotes the viability of the *network effect* we discussed in Chapter 1 and the chance that content will cascade through the community. Member activity reveals the importance of participation. Quality indicators and information flow serve as evidence of value and relevance. All of this is based on community participation. If and when people participate less in a given social community, the social capital of influencers in that community will diminish as well. As social capital declines, the community experiences decline in its own strength as measured by participation, adherence to norms, perceived reputation, and trust among members.[37] Hopefully you can see that influencers in a community have a lot at stake in keeping the community active and even growing it.

Interestingly, this is the very phenomenon researchers at Princeton University used to predict the ultimate demise of Facebook.[38] Just as we discussed the way viral content spreads like a disease, we can also view community participation and membership much like the spread of infection. Using data on the adoption and abandonment of memberships and activity in MySpace, the study built a model using Google Trend data on social network search queries. The model suggested that social networks follow a life cycle (much like a product life cycle) through which social communities will grow, mature, and ultimately decline. The prediction that Facebook would lose 80% of its active members by 2017 went viral, and Facebook researchers responded with their own study of Princeton enrollment. Using data from Google Scholar and a similar approach to modeling, Facebook's team built a model illustrating that Princeton would lose all student enrollments by 2021.[39] Given the low probability of the latter prediction, Facebook was able to humorously debunk the Princeton study. Nonetheless, it is true that Facebook's meteoric growth is stabilizing, especially as many younger people abandon it in favor of more private networks like SnapChat.

SHOW ME!

Although billions of people worldwide love to share on Facebook, not everyone wants details about their private lives to be available to lurkers (especially to curious parents). In recent years sites like SnapChat that delete posts after a certain amount of time have gained in popularity. What do you predict to be the future of Facebook?

Snapchat: 360b / Shutterstock.com

Photo 4.8

Strong and Weak Ties

Emotional support is one form of social capital. For example, people who struggle to lose weight or fight addictions often prevail because they are part of a group that helps them with these battles, such as Weight Watchers or Alcoholics Anonymous. We call this kind of emotional support bonding social capital.

This resource easily accrues online because of our accessibility to people who can help us with a variety of issues even though we may not know them personally. In contrast, our core ties, those people with whom we have very close relationships, may or may not be in a position to provide solutions to some problems we face (or we may not want them to know about these in some cases).[40] Interestingly, through the course of giving and receiving bonding social capital, we may come to develop core ties, or at least significant ties (somewhat close connections, but less so than core ties), with others in the community.

Online communities can also provide other kinds of support. This is particularly true of those that increase the accessibility of so-called weak ties. This term refers to contacts with people where your relationship is based on superficial experiences or very few connections. For instance, you have a strong tie with your best friend. Perhaps you and she went to high school together and so you have a history of shared experiences and friendships from your past. You then attended college classes together and again you were able to share experiences. You also joined the same sorority so you are bound by your relationship in the context of the organization. In this relationship, there are at least three connection streams between you and your friend that extend over several years and multiple shared experiences—we'd say this is a fairly strong tie.

In contrast, you likely have *weak ties* among your Facebook friends, many of whom are just casual acquaintances or even friends of a friend whom you've never met. Weak ties may also be more prevalent when someone is connected to several otherwise dispersed networks of people. In other words, rather than being central in a few tightly connected networks, the person serves as a node in several relatively unconnected networks.[41]

However, we can assure you that weak ties also have value. They may provide bridging social capital, the value we get from others who provide access to places, people, or ideas we might not be able to get to on our own.

In fact, many of the connections we make on SNSs are not active ties at all. Rather, they are latent ties: pre-existing connections that we've discarded. [42] Maintained social capital refers to the value we get from maintaining relationships with latent ties. You've probably heard your parents say they've reconnected with old high school friends on Facebook ("I can't believe how bald he is now!"). This is a perfect example of latent ties—as we move through life, some people stay in our lives, but others lose relevance as we develop and change. SNSs are valuable connectors for latent ties because they represent a low-involvement, low-effort channel to maintain these bonds. In fact, researchers discovered that college students use Facebook as a way to preserve their network of latent ties.[43] Some of your high school friends may have chosen the same university you did. Others went elsewhere. With sites such as Facebook, you are easily able to stay in touch with these friends, despite the shift in lifestyle and geographic location. Those connections may come in handy if you visit an unfamiliar place or need to find a job.

SHOW ME!

Consider a recent plea circulated on Facebook to help fund an operation for Memphis, an abandoned pit bull in Cummins, Georgia. His foster family couldn't afford to fund Memphis' surgery so they turned to Facebook to

The world's platform for change

74,502,796 people taking action. Victories every day.

Start a petition

Photo 4.9

make a plea to their friends, those friends shared the appeal with their friends, and so on. In just a few days, the dog had his surgery. Luckily for Memphis, his owners tapped into bridging social capital—they used nodes to build a bridge to otherwise unconnected nodes.

https://www.change.org/

Note: Earlier we talked about weak and strong ties in communities. Latent ties are not necessarily weak ties. Your BFF in the sixth grade was once a strong tie, but she might now be a latent one. Before the social media era, it's likely you would have just lost track of her unless you both happened to hobble into your 25th class reunion. Now, you can keep your old connections on the radar screen, even if you don't necessarily talk or write to them on a regular basis. SNSs enable members to maintain relationships across tie types.

The Evolution of Online Communities

Online communities are of course a fairly recent phenomenon. How did these new digital structures form? Historically, physical closeness was key to defining a community; indeed the large majority of people were likely to be born, grow up, and die in the same place so they were likely to see members of their relevant groups (extended families, religious clans, etc.) just about every day.

In fairly recent times, people became increasingly mobile and technologies advanced in ways that shifted personal interactions from *outside* the home in a neighborhood to *inside* the home via telephones and computers. As this happened, sociologists worried that we would lose the value communities provide in terms of feelings of belonging in a neighborhood and among family members. These concerns are not unique to the 21st century, of course. Indeed, back in 1897 the well-known sociologist Emile Durkheim warned of a condition he called anomie, a condition of modern industrial life that alienates individuals from society and (potentially) results in suicide.[44]

These worries were largely unfounded, though many would argue that modern society does make it more difficult to connect with others (hence the popularity of social media dating sites!). Still, over time sociologists recognized that technological innovations can actually help us to maintain and support a number of community relationships despite physical distances and other limitations. Marshall McLuhan, the English professor at the University of Toronto who wrote the seminal work *Understanding Media*, once made the famous statement, "One's village can span the globe." Sure enough, we now define communities in terms of their social networks rather than in terms of the physical space they occupy.[45] One sociologist who has studied communities for a long time observed, "I define 'community' as networks of interpersonal ties that provide sociability, support, information, a sense of belonging, and social identity. I do not limit my thinking about community to neighbourhoods [sic] and villages."[46]

On the other hand, several years ago a controversial book titled *Bowling Alone* warned of a society that is increasingly disconnected from community.[47] As we become more mobile and connected screen-to-screen rather than face-to-face, the book argued, community structures and our involvement in them would decline. From thousands of interviews,

THE DARK SIDE OF SOCIAL MEDIA

The man allegedly responsible for several murders and a shooting spree in 2014 that injured several others in Santa Barbara, California, posted a user-generated video on YouTube (since removed) titled "Elliot Rodger's Retribution."[48] We learned in Chapter 1 that anyone can use social publishing sites to publish content and Rodger did just that. The video promised revenge and explained Rodger's feelings of loneliness after women rejected him. Rodger's influence in the social community of YouTube was weak and the content did not spread until the video was discovered following the shootings. The discovery of the video and spread of news of the killings led to an intense conversation across social media sites on misogyny, harassment, and rape culture.

Later the same day, the Twitter #hashtag #yesallwomen spread as people posted tweets criticizing a culture that would lead men to feel entitled to women. Within 2 days, the hashtag appeared in more than 700,000 tweets. Geo-tagged tweets enabled tracking of the global spread of the hashtag revealing that posts using the hashtag were originating from countries in Europe, Africa, Australia, India, and Asia.[49] Twitter members made such statements as:[50]

- "Because every single woman I know has a story about a man feeling entitled to access her body. Every. Single. One. #yesallwomen."

- ""I have a boyfriend' is the easiest way to get a man to leave you alone. Because he respects another man more than you. #yesallwomen."

- "#yesallwomen b/c putting someone in the friend zone should not make me feel guilty."

Ultimately the social community of Twitter and the viral spread of #yesallwomen gave rise to a voice for people all over the world.

the author showed that people today meet less often with others in person and are less involved in community groups than in the past. He noted that people are even more likely to bowl alone, rather than in leagues—a clear sign that the digital connections we have do not encourage us to form strong bonds with others.

So, what's the verdict? Are online communities as strong—or stronger—than the traditional kind? The jury is still out. We do know that people can engage in civic activities online, and modern political campaigns testify to the power of social media to mobilize voters. (President Obama's 2008 campaign set a new standard for this participation among young people.)

One study of civic engagement and social networks found that online communities neither hindered nor encouraged the sharing of community resources.[51] The Pew Internet & American Life Project offered positive support for the role online networks can play; it noted that the Internet provides us with access to the right people with the right information. In fact, the Pew report even showed that the more we see members of our network in person and talk on the phone, the more likely it is that we will *also* communicate with those people online.[52] The more connected you are, the more connected you will become!

CHAPTER SUMMARY

Why are relationships critical to social media and the basis for leveraging the network effect in social media marketing?

At the heart of social media are links among members of social communities. Because social media enable participation and sharing, their success is strongly tied to the network and the relationships among those in the network.

How are social networks structured?

Online communities are built on foundations of networks. These networks are made up of nodes connected by ties. The nodes experience interactions and flows of resources, information, and influence occur between nodes. Some nodes are more influential than others. Some ties are stronger than others. Some information flows more deeply and widely.

What are the characteristics of online communities?

Communities are often built around social objects—objects of mutual interest among community members. Social communities thrive on conversations. They instill a sense of presence for those who participate. Community members share a collective interest, and governance is based on democracy. Community members follow standards of behavior that may be presented as rules and as norms accepted by the membership.

(Continued)

(Continued)

Participation is necessary for the health of the community but most members are not active. Community participation is typically characteristic of the 80/20 rule whereby only a small percentage of members participate for the benefit of all.

How do ideas travel in a community? What role do opinion leaders play?

Information travels in the community via flows between nodes in the network. Word-of-mouth communication about brands, known as influence impressions, travel this way. Opinion leaders have more influence in communities and consequently information shared by opinion leaders may be more influential and spread farther and deeper through the social network. The content may go viral. When a viral piece of information enters the general consciousness of the community and is adapted by the community members, it is called a meme.

What role does social capital play in the value of social media communities? What types of ties do we have to others in our communities?

Opinion leaders possess sources of social power such as expert power, reward power, and authority power. Social capital refers to the valuable resources people (individually or in groups) have within the context of a community. The capital may be actual or virtual and can include reputational capital, bonding social capital, bridging social capital, and maintained social capital. People's networks always include strong and weak ties. Both have value. Even weak ties can create social capital for network members.

KEY TERMS

ad equivalency value	flaming	mavens
anomie	flows	media democratization
bonding social capital	homophily	media multiplexity
bridging social capital	impression	meetups
cascades	influence network	meme
coercive power	influencers	negative word-of-mouth
community	information power	network units
connectors	interactions	niche markets
core ties	latent ties	nodes
cyberplace	legitimate power	norms
democracy	lurker	object sociality
80/20 rule	maintained social capital	online communities
expert power	mass connectors	online gated communities

open access sites	significant ties	strong tie
opinion leader	six degrees of separation	ties
passion-centric	small-world network	two-step flow model of
power users	social capital	influence
presence	social contract	vertical networks
referent power	social graphs	weak ties
reputational capital	social network	word-of-mouse
reward power	social network theory	word-of-mouth
salesmen	social object theory	communication

REVIEW QUESTIONS

1   What is the underlying structure of a network?

2   How does information flow in a network?

3   What are the characteristics common to communities, whether offline or online?

4   Explain the meaning of social capital.

5   What is an opinion leader? What sources of power might accrue to opinion leaders?

6   Why are social communities relevant for word-of-mouth communication?

EXERCISES

1   Visit the following communities: (1) lugnet.com, (2) ivillage.com, and (3) chatipad.com. What do you see in common among these communities? What's different? Does each so-called community really seem to be a unified group with a common culture? Explain.

2   Review the list of friends you have on Facebook. How many of your friends are "weak ties" and how many are "strong ties"? Identify the relationship bonds you share with those in your strong tie group. Does Facebook help you to strengthen both kinds of relationships? Why or why not?

3   Identify a current meme and track its origin.

4   Search Twitter for hashtags related to a brand (e.g., #dunkindonuts). What kinds of influence impressions appear for the hashtag you searched? Can you identify key influencers who are sharing tweets with this specific hashtag?

5   Discussion: How can we explain the Six Degrees of Kevin Bacon game as an example of social network theory?

CHAPTER NOTES

1   Barry Wellman, "Physical Place and Cyberplace: The Rise of Personalized Networking," *International Journal of Urban and Regional Research* 24, no. 2 (2001): 227–252.

2   Alexandra Marin and Barry Wellman, "Social Network Analysis: An Introduction," in *Handbook of Social Network Analysis* (London: Sage, 2010).

3   M. Burke, C. Marlow, and T. Lento, "Feed Me: Motivating Newcomer Contribution in Social Network Sites," ACM CHI 2009 Conference on Human Factors in Computing Systems, 2009, pp. 945–954.

4   John Coate, "Cyberspace Innkeeping: Building Online Community," 1998, http://www.cervisa.com/innkeeping, accessed December 31, 2010.

5   T. B. Sheridan, "Further Musings on the Psychophysics of Presence," *Presence: Teleoperators and Virtual Environments* 5 (1994): 241–246.

6   Matthew Lombard and Theresa Ditton, "At the Heart of It All: The Concept of Presence," *Journal of Computer Mediated Communication* 3, no. 2 (1997), http://jcmc.indiana.edu/vol3/issue2/lombard.html, accessed December 31, 2010.

7   Michael Trusove, Anand Bodapati, and Randolphe Bucklin, "Determining Influential Users in Internet Social Networks," *Journal of Marketing Research* (August 2010), 643–658.

8   Johan Arndt, "Role of Product-Related Conversations in the Diffusion of a New Product," *Journal of Marketing Research* 4 (August 1967): 291–294.

9   John Gaffney, "Enterprise: Marketing: The Cool Kids Are Doing It. Should You?" *Asiaweek*, November 23, 2001, p. 1.

10 Douglas R. Pruden and Terry G. Vavra, "Controlling the Grapevine," *MM* (July–August 2004): 23–30.

11 BzzAgent, http://about.bzzagent.com/word-of-mouth/index/about-bzzagent, accessed December 31, 2010.

12 Les Luchter, "Kraft, Folgers, Olay Top Baby Boomer Gals' WOM," *Marketing Daily*, November 18, 2008, http://www.mediapost.com/publications/?fa=Articles.showArticle&art_aid=95000, accessed November 18, 2008.

13 James H. Myers and Thomas S. Robertson, "Dimensions of Opinion Leadership," *Journal of Marketing Research* 9 (February 1972): 41–46.

14 Ellen Neuborne, "Generation Y," *BusinessWeek*, February 15, 1999, p. 86.

15   Dorothy Leonard-Barton, "Experts as Negative Opinion Leaders in the Diffusion of a Technological Innovation," *Journal of Consumer Research* 11 (March 1985): 914–926.

16   James F. Engel, Robert J. Kegerreis, and Roger D. Blackwell, "Word-of-Mouth Communication by the Innovator," *Journal of Marketing* 33 (July 1969): 15–19; see also Rajdeep Growl, Thomas W. Cline, and Anthony Davies, "Early-Entrant Advantage, Word-of-Mouth Communication, Brand Similarity, and the Consumer Decision Making Process," *Journal of Consumer Psychology* 13, no. 3 (2003): 187–197.

17   Chip Walker, "Word-of-Mouth," *American Demographics* (July 1995): 38–44; Albert M Muñiz, Jr., Thomas O'Guinn, and Gary Alan Fine, "Rumor in Brand Community," in Donald A. Hantula, Ed., *Advances in Theory and Methodology in Social and Organizational Psychology: A Tribute to Ralph Rosnow* (Mahwah, NJ: Erlbaum, 2005).

18   "Introducing Peer Influence Analysis: 500 Billion Peer Impressions Each Year," *Empowered*, April 20, 2010, http://forrester.typepad.com/groundswell/2010/04/introducing-peer-influence-analysis.html, accessed December 31, 2010.

19   Malcolm Gladwell, *The Tipping Point* (Boston, MA: Little, Brown, 2000).

20   Malcolm Gladwell, *The Tipping Point* (Boston, MA: Little, Brown, 2000).

21   "The History of RickRolling: Infographic," *Huffington Post*, June 1, 2010, http://www.huffingtonpost.com/2010/06/01/the-history-of-rickrollin_n_596064.html, accessed December 31, 2010.

22   Evelyn Nussenbaum, "The 80's Video That Pops Up, Online and Off," *New York Times*, March 24, 2008, http://www.nytimes.com/2008/03/24/business/media/24rick.html?_r=1, accessed December 31, 2010.

23   Some of the material in this section was adapted from Michael R. Solomon, *Consumer Behavior: Buying, Having, and Being*, 9th ed. (Upper Saddle River, NJ: Prentice Hall, 2010).

24   Ed Keller and Jon Berry, *The Influentials* (New York: Simon & Schuster, 2003).

25   J. R. P. French and B. Raven, "The Bases of Social Power," in D. Cartwright and A. Zander, *Group Dynamics* (New York: Harper & Row, 1959).

26   Everett M. Rogers, *Diffusion of Innovations*, 3rd ed. (New York: Free Press, 1983); see also Duncan J. Watts and Peter Sheridan Dodds, "Influentials, Networks, and Public Opinion Formation," *Journal of Consumer Research* 34 (December

(Continued)

(Continued)

2007): 441–458; Morris B. Holbrook and Michela Addis, "Taste versus the Market: An Extension of Research on the Consumption of Popular Culture," *Journal of Consumer Research* 34 (October 2007): 415–424.

27 Dorothy Leonard-Barton, "Experts as Negative Opinion Leaders in the Diffusion of a Technological Innovation," *Journal of Consumer Research* 11, no. 4 (1985): 914–926.

28 Herbert Menzel, "Interpersonal and Unplanned Communications: Indispensable or Obsolete?" in Edward B. Roberts, Ed., *Biomedical Innovation* (Cambridge, MA: MIT Press, 1981), 155–163.

29 Meera P. Venkatraman, "Opinion Leaders, Adopters, and Communicative Adopters: A Role Analysis," *Psychology & Marketing* 6 (Spring 1989): 51–68.

30 Rogers, *Diffusion of Innovations*.

31 Asim Ansari, Oded Koenigsberg, and Florian Stahl, "Modeling Multiple Relationships in Social Networks," *Journal of Marketing Research* (August 2011), 713–728.

32 Raghuram Iyengar, Christophe Van den Bulte, John Eichert, Bruce West, and Thomas Valente, "How Social Networks and Opinion Leaders Affect the Adoption of New Products," *New Theories* 3, no. 1 (2011), 16–25.

33 Watts and Dodds, "Influentials, Networks, and Public Opinion Formation."

34 James S. Coleman, "Social Capital in the Creation of Human Capital," *The American Journal of Sociology* 94 (1988): 95–120.

35 Pamela Paxton, "Is Social Capital Declining in the United States? A Multiple Indicator Assessment," *The American Journal of Sociology* 105 (1999): 88.

36 Quoted on http://www.hotenough.org, accessed June 27, 2010.

37 Nicole Ellison, Charles Steinfield, and Cliff Lampe, "The Benefits of Facebook 'Friends:' Social Capital and College Students' Use of Online Social Network Sites," *Journal of Computer-Mediated Communication* 12 (2007): 1143–1168.

38 John Cannarella and Joshua Spechler, "Epidemiological Modeling of Online Social Network Dynamics," January 2014, working paper, Princeton University, http://arxiv.org/pdf/1401.4208.pdf, accessed January 27, 2014.

39 John Constine, "Facebook Hilariously Debunks Princeton Study Saying It Will Lose 80% of Users", *TechCrunch*, January 23, 2014, http://techcrunch.com/2014/01/23/facebook-losing-users-princeton-losing-credibility/, accessed January 27, 2014.

40   Lee Rainie, John Horrigan, Barry Wellman, and Jeffrey Boase, "The Strength of Internet Ties," Pew Internet & American Life Project, January 25, 2005, http://www.pewinternet.org/Reports/2006/The-Strength-of-Internet-Ties.aspx, accessed June 23, 2010.

41   McKinsey & Company, "The Strength of Weak Ties," Report, http://www.mckinsey.com/insights/high_tech_telecoms_internet/the_strength_of_weak_signals?cid=other-eml-nsl-mip-mck-oth-1403, accessed February 12, 2014.

42   Fred Stutzman, "Activating Latent Ties," May 2007, http://chimprawk.blogspot.com/2007/05/activating-latent-ties.html, accessed December 31, 2010.

43   Ellison, Steinfield, and Lampe, "The Benefits of Facebook 'Friends.'"

44   Emile Durkheim, *Suicide* (1897; repr., Glencoe, IL: Free Press, 1951).

45   Marshall McLuhan, *Understanding Media: Extensions of Man* (New York: McGraw-Hill, 1964).

46   Quoted in Barry Wellman, "Physical Place and CyberPlace: The Rise of Personalized Networking," *International Journal of Urban and Regional Research* 25, no. 2 (2002): 228.

47   R. Putnam, *Bowling Alone: The Collapse and Revival of American Community* (New York: Simon & Schuster, 2000).

48   Nolan Feeney, "Last IDs Made in Calif. Killings," *Time,* May 25, 2014, http://time.com/113948/Elliot-rodger-ucsb-santa-barbara/, accessed July 10, 2014.

49   Elias Groll, "What Do #YesAllWomen and #BringBackOurGirls Have in Common?" Foreign Policy, http://blog.foreignpolicy.com/posts/2014/05/27/what_do_yes_all_women_and_bringbackourgirls_have_in_common, accessed July 10, 2014.

50   Nolan Feeney, "The Most Powerful #YesAllWomen Tweets," *Time*, May 25, 2014, time.com/114043/yesallwomen-hashtag-santa-barbara-shooting/, accessed July 10, 2014.

51   Josh Pasek, Eian More, and Daniel Romer, "Realizing the Social Internet? Online Social Networking Meets Offline Civic Engagement," *Journal of Information Technology & Politics* 6, no. 3 & 4 (2009).

52   Rainie, Horrigan, and Boase, "The Strength of Internet Ties."

Visit the companion website for free additional materials related to this chapter: study.sagepub.com/smm

PART II

The Four Zones of
Social Media

5 Social Community

LEARNING OBJECTIVES

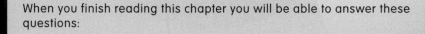

When you finish reading this chapter you will be able to answer these questions:

1. How do social networking communities enable user participation and sharing?

2. Why is engagement a goal of brands using social media marketing? What are the benefits of engagement?

3. In what ways can brands utilize social networking communities for branding and promotion?

The Social Community Zone

In this chapter we dive deeper into the zone of social community, the first zone in our model, shown in Figure 5.1. Recall that *all* zones in the social media mix are built on social networks, technologically enabled, and based on the principles of shared participation.

As we plan, we want to devise a way to encourage customers to participate and to share and to do so within the zones within which we operate. What will invite participation and sharing? That's our experience strategy. Where will they participate and share? Within the zones. Of course, we may use any of the four zones. But in this chapter our focus is on the first zone, the zone of social community. Let's think of zone 1 as the *relationship zone*. Social media networks provide a structure for social interactions. They focus on acquiring and maintaining relationships above all else. Conversation and collaboration are the principal activities in this zone, though we often converse and collaborate around content, whether provided by brands, users, or others. Brands encourage this participation through engagement.

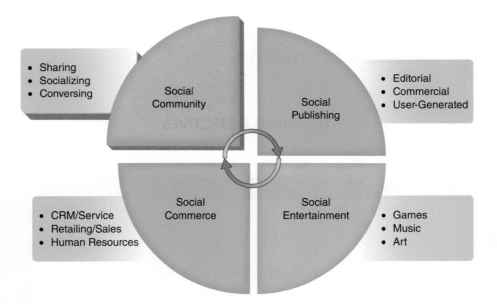

Figure 5.1   The Social Community Zone

Participation in Social Networks

Social networking sites are the community vehicles that house and enable social engagement. Facebook is the juggernaut of social networks, with the most members worldwide.

Even Facebook recognizes that social media participation has been shifting from a one-stop shop approach to one preferring specific types of interactions in what could be thought of as boutique social settings. While Facebook, as a social utility, enables sharing, conversation, and participation around many forms of social objects, including pictures, videos, events, and games, it is investing in more narrowly focused social networks to create a portfolio of social vehicles.[1] Its acquisitions of WhatsApp and Instagram as well

SHOW ME!

World Map of Social Networks

The map illustrates that Facebook is dominant around the world—in fact, it is the most used social vehicle in 127 countries! But, Facebook is growing at a decreasing rate. In the product life cycle, this is the stage known as the maturity stage.

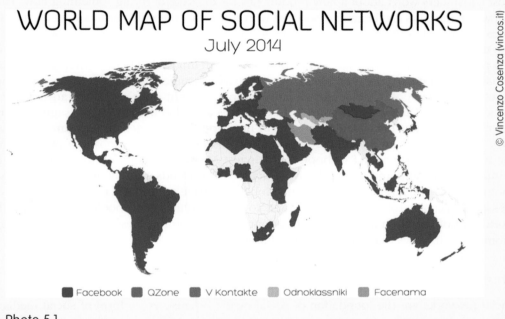

WORLD MAP OF SOCIAL NETWORKS
July 2014

© Vincenzo Cosenza (vincos.it)

■ Facebook ■ QZone ■ V Kontakte ■ Odnoklassniki ■ Facenama

Photo 5.1

as its development of Messenger are examples of this commitment to micro-oriented social channels. Facebook has more than a billion users. WhatsApp has more than 500 million users, while Instagram and Messenger each have more than 200 million.

Diffusion of (Digital) Innovations

There are thousands of social networks in existence, and even more mobile apps. The companies providing these social channels and software must acquire a critical mass of users if they are to survive. Once adoption passes a tipping point (the point at which a series of small changes becomes significant enough to cause a larger change), the network effect takes over, helping to ensure success, at least by usage measures. What influences whether something will be adopted? To help us approach these questions, let's review a classic perspective on how people deal with new products and new ways of doing things.

Roger's diffusion of innovations theory presents characteristics of innovative products that explain the rate at which people are likely to adopt these new options.[2] These characteristics include:

1   The relative advantage of the innovation (i.e., does it provide a greater benefit than the existing alternatives?)
2   The ability to observe and try the innovation
3   The innovation's compatibility (how easily it can be assimilated into the person's life)
4   The innovation's simplicity of use

Most consumers won't adopt a new product just for the sake of trying something new. They will weigh the costs and benefits associated with adoption—does the product solve a problem? Does it work with other products consumers already own? Do they see other people using it? Can they try it without risk? Is it easy to use or is there a learning curve involved in the adoption process? To the extent that marketers can make an innovation better, while also making it easy to integrate, try, use, and see in use, the faster consumers will accept the new product.

Let's use Facebook's Messenger as an example. Does it offer a relative advantage? It does if you use Facebook on your mobile devices and also use direct messaging within the network. That's because Facebook will not support messages on its primary mobile app. Thus, there is an advantage to adopting Messenger. Can we observe others using the innovation and try it? Facebook will suggest Messenger as an option as you use its primary mobile app and let you know which of your friends already use Messenger. Is it compatible? If you already use Facebook Mobile and have an Android or Apple phone, yes, Messenger is compatible. Lastly, is it simple to use? Absolutely. Facebook has increased the likelihood of adoption and the rate of adoption by designing Messenger and Messenger promotions in ways that address these characteristics.

Characteristics of Social Networking Sites

Social networks are the foundation of social media because every form of social media is based on participation from a *community* of members. Still, it is useful to compare and contrast social networks and to understand how their defining dimensions affect our ability to market brands within the social space. This is particularly relevant as we see a trend to users utilizing more social channels for specialized purposes. Social networking sites all maintain the basic network structure we discussed in Chapter 4—nodes that interact with one another, flows between node members, and graphs connected to others by way of node relationships. However, social networking sites vary in terms of three important dimensions:

1   Audience and degree of specialization
2   The social objects that mediate the relationships among members
3   Degree of decentralization or openness

Audience Specialization

Social networking sites can be internal or external, general or specialized. Internal sites are those a specific organization builds for its own use and limits to members of the organization. Rather than hosting several subcultures within a larger social networking site, an internal social network provides a method of communication and collaboration that is more dynamic and interactive. This is a lot like the *intranet* that many companies provide their employees. For instance, Nissan launched a site for its employees called N-Square. The network enables employees to post profiles, maintain a blog, participate in discussion groups, and share files.[3] Microsoft uses a network it calls TownSquare, IBM has the BeeHive, and Yahoo! employees meet in the Backyard. In contrast, an external social network is open to people who are not affiliated with the site's sponsor.

Social networks are, of course, about networking—participating in the kinds of activities that enable members to build and maintain their relationships with other people. However, the nature of those relationships also affects the characterization of the social network. LinkedIn is a professional social network that emphasizes career experience and the need to maintain connections to those we know professionally. The primary benefit is to be able to call upon one's network when looking for a consultant, employee, job, or other career-related search. There are several professional networks held together by industry, purpose, and personal career goals. Care2 is a social network for people who want to help with social causes. Focus is a network for business and technology experts. Den provides a social network where architects and designers congregate.

Just because a social network focuses on personal relationships over professional ones doesn't necessarily mean that it has a broad target. For instance, Jdate.com is a dating social network for Jewish singles. Its mission is social, but it still targets a niche audience. There are several networks designed around specific target audiences defined by demographic characteristics including age (e.g., ClubPenguin, Webkinz), marital status (e.g., MarriedLife, MarriedPassions), income (asmallworld.net, affluence. org), and so on.

Social Objects and Passion-Centric Sites

In industry terms, sites designed around object sociality, the ability of an object to inspire social interaction, are known as vertical networks. The term describes the narrow, deep focus of social networking sites that differentiate themselves because they emphasize some common hobby, interest, or characteristic that draws members to the site. These vertical networks do not attract the same traffic typical of general sites, but one might argue that the members are more involved because of the common interest that initially brought them to the site. They function much like so-called *niche markets* in the physical world; this term refers to marketplaces that offer a relatively small number of items to buyers who tend to be loyal to these outlets.

Decentralization

As social media sites continue to proliferate around the Web, they experience "growing pains" because we are still trying to figure out how to manage all of this new activity. Some people seem to spend most of the day just updating their Facebook profiles, responding to email (if they still use that instead of texting), and checking out the *site du jour* that everyone is talking about (today). Can we have too much of a good thing? One of the big issues social media need to confront is how to let people easily access multiple sites and to understand where they go and why.

Openness and Identity Portability

Social networks can be closed, gated communities entirely controlled by the vendor that offers the platform. At the other extreme they can be accessible to any members or developers who wish to participate. Many social networking sites require new members to register for membership and to use login specifications to access the community. It often makes sense for a social networking site to keep a record of membership even if anyone is allowed to join. This information can be invaluable for purposes of member management, product development, promoting the site, and utilizing the member data for other purposes. How might social networks utilize member data? Because social networks have access to vast amounts of detailed data about members' preferences, friends, and activities, they may eventually license that data to external marketers who could use the data to target potential customers. For now, the social community site with the most data, Facebook, isn't selling member data, but some speculate that it will.[4]

Complaints about the lack of centralized communities have given rise to the terms social networking fatigue and social lock-in. The fatigue comes in part from the need to manage multiple community accounts (and to forgo some due to the required investment) as well as from the steady streams of content flowing from multiple networks. Rather than experiencing a single social stream, those with multiple networks have several streams flowing at any point in time. Social lock-in occurs when a user is unable to transfer social contacts and content from one social network to another.

This problem is similar to one we often encounter in the physical world when we use a mediocre product, but it's too complicated or expensive to drop it in favor of a better one. For example, a student who has a revelation at the beginning of her senior year that she'd rather be a marketing major than an accounting major may decide to just stick it out with balance sheets because it would require several additional years to complete the course requirements for a new major. Economists would say that in this situation the switching costs are too high. It's much the same in the world of social media; once our social graph is firmly engrained in a particular host community, the time and effort to shift may outweigh the benefit we think we will get if we move to a new community service.

How can social media minimize the switching cost problem? One widely discussed solution is to develop a system of identity portability such that a single profile would provide access across social networking sites with a single login and shared information. This is the goal of OpenID, an authentication protocol that works across participating sites. Unfortunately, OpenID works only on OpenID-enabled sites, limiting the portability for users. Sites can also choose to enable authentication with Facebook Connect, an option that has been more widely adopted.

Open Source

The decision as to whether to grant access to outside developers (and how or if to share in the revenue these applications produce) is one of the most important strategic issues in business today. For example, Apple uses a fairly closed model; the company maintains strict control over "apps" that outsiders can sell for its iPhone and iPad and it takes a hefty commission (30 percent) on each sale. Similarly, Sony shares its code for its PlayStation game with only a selected set of licensed developers.

Other companies follow the open source model that turns some of our conventional assumptions about the value of products and services on its head. This model started in the software industry where the Linux system grows by leaps and bounds—even IBM uses it now. Unlike the closely guarded code that companies such as Microsoft use, open source developers post their programs on a public site and a community of volunteers is free to tinker with them, develop other applications using the code, then give their changes away for free. For example, the company that gives out (for free) the Mozilla Firefox Internet browser that competes with Microsoft commands over 20% market share among users.[5]

Google believes that the more outside developers it can attract, the faster its business will grow. The company offers what it calls OpenSocial code. This term refers to a set of common APIs that enable developers to write software for applications that will run on multiple social websites. API stands for *application programming interface*. It's a programming model that enables a piece of software to interact with other software. When private APIs are used, only licensed developers can provide applications. When social networking sites make their APIs freely available, development of tools and features from outside the community can flourish. This has been the case with Facebook; it doesn't use Google's OpenSocial proactively, but it has encouraged freelance developers to contribute to Facebook's community. This has resulted in hundreds upon hundreds of special applications such as Citizen Sports, Where I've Been, Flair, Bumper Sticker, My Family, iLike, Dogbook, and more.

Social Network Activities

Interaction is the currency of social networking sites. How do we interact with others on social media platforms? We addressed this question in Chapter 3. But especially for the zone of social community, the answer has three parts: we mingle, we chat, and we share.

We can think of social networks as communication hubs; virtually all of them offer users access to a contact list and an interface that makes it easy for people to talk to one another. However, most sites offer more features than these basic ones. The new standard for social networking sites is to offer tools, widgets, applications, and features that encourage social sharing; sites provide people with the tools they need to reveal elements of their digital identities. These elements include information about us or things that we create—such as our opinions, photos, videos, songs, and artworks. They may also take the form of secondary content—things that others create we feel are worth redistributing to our social networks, such as retweets, links to a celebrity blog, or even brands we "like" on our Facebook page. Mark Zuckerberg, president and CEO of Facebook, said this about sharing: "People have really gotten comfortable not only sharing more information and different kinds, but more openly and with more people. [This is a] social norm that has evolved over time."[6]

Social media empower us and because of them we all have the capacity to share something if we choose to do so. In Chapter 3, we learned about the social consumer segment we call *creators*. Creators are the social media users who actively produce content in the form of video, podcasts/music, stories and articles, and blog posts. They may publish their own website.[7] Creators are a busy bunch—24 hours of YouTube video is posted every minute. The rest of us may not possess the technical skill or the desire to produce original content. We're happy leaving that work to others—many of whom are professionals.

Still, we certainly are avid consumers of the content—YouTube videos alone get billions of views every day.[8]

Although not everyone is a creator who develops artifacts such as videos and podcasts for distribution in their social network, anyone *can* join a network, update a status, post secondary content from others, and provide feedback on the content others post in their networks. Remember that analysts estimate lurkers—those people who consume content by reading posts and watching videos, but who do not contribute to the flow of content— make up about 90% of any online community.[9]

The act of sharing changes this dynamic, because even lurkers can redistribute secondary content to a larger network of people. In this sense even fairly passive participants can extend their reach well beyond their own social graph. ShareThis, a provider of a widget that enables visitors to easily share content they discover online, found that though almost half of users preferred email for sharing interesting content with others, most of the remainder preferred to use a social media channel to share.[10] Applications such as ShareThis minimize the investment of time and effort necessary to share secondary content on a social network, so it's more likely that content will spread rapidly.

A study of social media users found that 75% of people are likely to share content via social media channels. The top three reasons people share content "socially" are because they find it interesting and/or entertaining, they think it could be helpful to others, and

THE DARK SIDE OF SOCIAL MEDIA

Do the posts you read on your favorite social media sites influence your mood? Turns out, they do. Scientists at Facebook set out to determine whether emotions expressed in status updates could affect the emotions of those reading the posts. Called the "emotional contagion" experiment, news feeds for hundreds of thousands of Facebook users were systematically manipulated to increase or decrease the level of positive or negative messages that appeared. When people saw fewer positive messages and more negative messages, they produced more negative messages. When people saw more positive messages and fewer negative messages, they generated more positive posts, too.

The study concluded that emotions are influenced by the emotions of others on Facebook. Perhaps you are thinking that this isn't surprising. We are often times influenced by the moods of those around us. But past research on emotional contagion suggested that emotions were influenced by in-person interaction that included nonverbal cues. The Facebook experiment debunks that belief.

The study also suggests that Facebook can manipulate the user experience on a massive scale, and yet very intimate level. It also presents a potential opportunity for marketers. News feeds could potentially be manipulated to induce feelings of fear, guilt, and other emotions used as advertising appeals. With Facebook's help, advertisers can create on demand emotion-fueled marketing opportunities.[11]

to get a laugh. Although the content can be virtually anything you can send in digital form, most people reported sharing family pictures and video, news about family and friends, funny videos, news articles and blog posts, and coupons and discounts.[12]

How do social networking sites encourage participation and sharing by members? They make sharing engaging and they make it easy. Brands enhance participation by providing experiences for users that are worth participating in and telling others about. Experiences may involve any of the four zones, but the zone of social community is where conversations take place in and around the experiences.[13]

Engagement

What does it mean to engage? People differ on their explanation of this. In all likelihood this is because engagement means different things. Just as being satisfied might mean being satisfied across a host of specific areas, being engaged may so too. Still, that's what we must do. Engagement is the very essence of social media. Without it, social media might as well be television. Engagement is the heart of it all.

Engagement takes on many forms. From a customer perspective, engagement means customers' behavioral manifestation toward a brand or firm, beyond purchase, resulting from motivational drivers.[14] How do customers behave when they are engaged? They may exhibit positive word-of-mouth behaviors, provide recommendations, help others make decisions, blog … in other words, they become brand ambassadors.

At a minimum, brands want consumers to friend, follow, or like the brand's social presence. Do consumers make friends with brands? If we use the growing trend of online "friending" as an indicator, the answer is yes. According to Razorfish, a leading digital marketing agency, 40% of online consumers have become a friend or fan of a brand on a social networking site. Even more have interacted with brands in other ways; 70% report having read a corporate blog, 67% watch branded videos on YouTube, and 65% play a branded game online.[15]

Consumers may also seek help from trusted brands to help them manage their lives. Mobile apps are commonplace, but brands can matter by providing apps that fit strategically with the brand and consumer needs. These apps are called brand butlers.[16]

The growing popularity of mobile apps provided by brands, such as the GEICO Glovebox app, are examples of how brands can serve as butlers. This app enables customers to view their insurance card with their phone, pay their insurance bill, report accident information, find instructions for what to do in roadside crisis situations, and call for taxis and rental car reservations. By making activities that are sometimes necessary but always a hassle to consumers easy and accessible, GEICO provides a benefit to its time-starved customers. The idea of seeking out brands to serve in the role of brand butler is consistent with a key principle of marketing—that of offering value to customers. Brands that provide supporting services via social media add value to their product offering.

Besides wanting an emotional bond and valuable services, consumers may also want to simply save money. Razorfish's *Feed* report found that 44% of those who follow a brand on Twitter and 37% of those who had friended a brand on Facebook did so exclusively to be privy to special deals and offers. The popularity of location services such as Foursquare supports this reasoning; as we've seen, users are rewarded with deals when they check in with local business venues. Brands with successful track records in the social media space often use these platforms to aggressively offer incentives that motivate people to choose the brand because they can save money. Take JetBlue, for instance. To celebrate its 10th anniversary, it promoted $10 fares on Facebook, targeting Facebook users who were fans or friends of JetBlue and those who had a vacation-related status message on their Walls.[17]

Brand engagement, of course, may encompass many levels from mild to evangelistic, and brands should seek to grow fans at the lower levels, investing in them so they become true fans.

Ideally, brands will develop brand fans. This may be based on pure love of the product offered or some other aspect of the brand. Brands can develop fans by helping them move from lower levels of engagement to higher ones. The higher the engagement the more positive outcomes for the brand in terms of positive word-of-mouth, enhanced perceptions of brand equity, and possibly sales. All of those positive benefits of engagement occur when brands are able to encourage people to become brand fans.

Brand Fans

With millions of Facebook fans and thousands of Twitter followers, these brands participate in friendvertising—a brand's use of social networking to build earned media value—and purposefully cultivate brand fans. The word *fan* refers to a person who is enthusiastic about something or someone. Fans display their loyalty and affection for celebrities, sports teams, and musicians in the physical world when they buy T-shirts or other licensed products, join fan clubs, and flock to concerts or stadiums. In a social network, a similar display of loyalty may be as simple as clicking Facebook's "Like" button and "joining" a sponsored page in the networking site. An online fan community is a fandom.

The brands with the strongest social followings around the world include:

- Coca-Cola
- Red Bull
- Converse
- Samsung Mobile
- Nike Football
- Playstation
- Starbucks
- Oreo
- Walmart

Curious how your favorite brand stacks up across the major social channels of Facebook, Twitter, YouTube, and Google+? Visit www.socialbakers.com to search its free social statistics area.

For brands to truly leverage social networks as places to build relationships with customers, fan relationships should strive to mimic those found among strong fan communities such as Trekkers and Trekkies (members of the *Star Trek* fandom) and Gladiators (fans of the television show *Scandal*). Fans who define their own individual identities at least in part by their membership in a fandom share five key characteristics:[18]

1   *Emotional engagement:* The object is meaningful in the emotional life of the fan. For example, fans of *Scandal* may feel that they relate to one or more of the characters.

2   *Self-identification:* The fan personally and publicly identifies with like-minded fans. *Scandal* fans identify themselves as Gladiators and feel a sense of belonging with other Gladiators. They may tweet while watching episodes and use the hashtag #gladiators to identify themselves to others.

3   *Cultural competence:* The fan has a critical understanding of the object, its history, and its meaning beyond its basic functionality. Gladiators may follow the show on Twitter and Facebook, read the show blog, read articles about the actors, and participate in chats with the actors. They know key facts and common expressions like "It's handled" or "Shut this down" used in the script.

4   *Auxiliary consumption:* The fan collects and consumes related items and experiences beyond the basic object. Gladiators can buy clothes, mugs, and other items that sport the *Scandal* logo.

5   *Production:* The fan becomes involved in the production of content related to the object. Gladiators post their favorite clips (unofficially), and write predictions for future episodes. Some Gladiators run their own *Scandal*-focused blogs.

It's really too soon to tell whether the fans being amassed by brands active in social networks are true fans who define themselves by their participation in a brand community, or just brand users who are willing to acknowledge some affiliation with a brand. That's because it's become so easy to like, follow, or become a fan. Liking a brand is an easy, low-involvement step and it's one that frequently comes after exposure to an ad requesting a "like" as a call to action.

The fan base is an indicator of the brand's success in establishing a known presence within a community. But to build brand equity and lasting loyalty, brands need more than brand awareness and recognition or even brand affiliation. As brands embrace social media marketing, they acknowledge that a strong relationship exists between brand and customer when the customer has a high level of brand engagement.

We can think of engagement as a continuum. At one end, people may affiliate with a brand online simply because they want to acknowledge the brand. For example, you might affiliate with Oreos because you have a nostalgic connection to the brand based on childhood experiences. It doesn't mean that you plan to buy Oreos now or that you are otherwise engaged with the brand. At the other end, affiliates may want to interact with a brand in meaningful ways, perhaps even working with the brand to develop new products and services. Lego fans, for instance, are infamous for their high levels of brand engagement. Brands with strong fan bases even build museums for fan visits! Cadbury,

Ben & Jerry's, Tabasco, Volkswagen, and Crayola have all provided a physical destination for passionate brand fans. And somewhere in between are fans who want special offers and find they benefit from branded content.

Why might people engage with brands? One possible reason is the aspirational value of brands in people's lives. Brands help people build their ideal selves and engagement with the brand online is a path to that self. In other words, the brand is a reflection of the fan's idealized self. That's just what PhaseOne Communications found in a study of 75 brands across six vertical markets. They concluded that users engage with brands based on how they wish to be perceived by their own social graph.[19] Research suggests that increasing brand knowledge and emotion increases the perceived value of the brand in the mind of the consumer. As a consumer's knowledge increases, so too does his or her emotional attachment to the brand.[20] Brands can also leverage fans to get new fans. Fan activity on social profiles can engage new fans.[21]

Level of engagement makes a big difference in terms of the buying decision process. One study found that purchase intent for a brand with interactive profiles was higher than for brands without such profiles.[22] Another study by Syncapse specifically measured the value of being a brand's Facebook fan. It found that people spend about $72 more on a product for which they have a social network affiliation than for one they do not. Fans are also 28% more likely than nonfans to continue using a brand, and 41% more likely to recommend a fanned versus nonfanned product to a friend.[23] Fans in the study also said they felt connected to their brands.

Importantly, brands that use social media to develop a relationship with customers need to find ways to provide a return on emotion for the fans. Return on emotion conceptually assesses the extent to which a brand has delivered a value in exchange for the emotional attachment fans have awarded it.[24] Traditionally, the relationship between brand and consumer is asymmetric, with more effort invested by the fan. One industry study suggests that for brands to succeed as social friends to consumers, building heightened engagement and loyalty, consumers must feel that their efforts are reciprocated and the relationship is symmetric.[25] To do so, brands should socialize with fans and participate in conversations using a credible and authentic brand voice.

Ultimately, this social media marketing approach seeks to drive awareness and liking of brands while also building earned media. As we suggested earlier, brands should use social spaces to give consumers reason to share positive stories and product information. To encourage this, brands can offer branded assets such as downloads, shareable widgets and wallpapers, and invitations for consumers to co-create branded content. Brands should also be sure to provide value to the fans by using the branded page as an information hub to announce new products, company news, contests and promotions, and career opportunities.

Marketing Applications in the Social Community Zone

As we discussed earlier, the social community zone focuses on relationships. By becoming an active participant in these channels, brands can leverage social networks to meet several marketing objectives including promotion and branding, customer service and customer relationship management, and marketing research.

In social networks, brands can purchase paid space for advertising and utilize share technologies to further leverage the value of the advertising impressions. In contrast, earned media are those messages that are distributed at no direct cost to the company and by methods beyond the brand's control. Brands participate in social networks to generate brand awareness and knowledge and positive word-of-mouth communication. There's an added bonus, too. Links to brand-related online content shared via social media affect the search engine rankings delivered by search engines such as Google and Yahoo! So not only can consumers be influenced by brand interactions and references to brands made by those in their network, they also can be led to branded content via search listings. That's a topic we'll cover further in Chapter 6 when we discuss search engine optimization.

Social Presence: Brands as Relationship Nodes

Brands must create a brand profile within the selected social networking communities in which they wish to command a presence. In this way, the brand acts as a node in the network's social graph. Doing so increases the opportunities for interactions with customers and prospects and also encourages people to talk about the brand with each other.

When a brand launches a profile on social networking sites, the brand exists much as people do on the sites. Friends can interact with the brands; share information, photos, and videos; and participate in two-way communication. As we discussed in Chapter 2, brands may participate as a corporate entity, as one or more people representing the brand, or as a mascot. Whichever the choice, the brand will develop a profile to represent its persona and then should interact in keeping with that profile—like a good actor, it should "stay in character." Building brand personas strengthens brand personality, differentiates brands from competitors, and sets the stage for a perceived relationship. Assuming the brand's persona is likeable and credible, it can facilitate message internalization (the process by which a consumer adopts a brand belief as his or her own). It is a natural expansion of the trend for brands to create personalities for themselves, both through the use of creative language—including style, imagery, tone, and creative appeals—and music.

The most social brands in the world might already be among your "friends." Many social network users *like*, *friend*, or *fan* brands. The most popular brands include Starbucks and Coca-Cola. And who could resist being friends with Oreo cookies? That's a friendship that lasts a lifetime! These brands maintain a social presence in online communities as they invite people to interact and share content related to the brand.

What does it take to devise a good brand persona? Brand personas should be consistent with the brand's style guide. Social media are still components of an integrated marketing communications program and as such, the decisions made for the brand's style guide still apply. The "voice" of the brand in social channels will need to be consistent, whether the approach is humanized or corporate. The social media aspects of the style guide will enable multiple people to create content and converse with fans in the role of the brand. It will ensure that brand representation is consistent. It will include indicators like brand personality traits.

SHOW ME!

Hanka Steidle / Shutterstock.com

Photo 5.2

Travelocity's Roaming Gnome Stays in Character

Consider the Travelocity Gnome and its brand profiles. The Gnome is quirky, fun, and irreverent. He speaks with an accent and likes to go places! The Gnome wants to inspire people to see the world … and potentially use Travelocity to do it. What's his story? He was kidnapped! One day he was a bored gnome on a lawn in England, the next, he was traveling all over the world with his kidnapper. Even after he was free, the Gnome enjoyed it so much that he just kept traveling.

https://twitter.com/RoamingGnome / @RoamingGnome

The personality and fit with the brand overall is clear in all social media communications. Brian Solis, author of *Engage*, recommends that brand managers build the brand's social media persona on a foundation of eight decisions:[26]

1   What are the brand's core values?
2   What are the brand's pillars, or social objects that illustrate these values?
3   What has the brand promised to its customers?
4   What are the brand's aspirational attributes?
5   What traits are associated with the brand?
6   What opportunities exist?
7   How does the brand align with the company's overall culture?
8   What stories can help bring the brand's personality to life?

There is a lot of clutter and fragmentation in social media. It can be hard for a brand's voice to be heard. There are several applications that can help brands analyze their social profiles and identify strengths, weaknesses, and opportunities. Some examples include Likealyzer, Fanpage Karma, and Cscore. The social vehicles also offer insights to aid page development.

Earned Media

Brands earn value in social media when they engage consumers over time (relationship marketing) and when they encourage consumers to interact with the brand and share

SHOW ME!

Brands develop their profiles within the confines of the social vehicle. That's why a brand profile isn't truly owned media, which is under complete control of the brand. Still, brands can leverage the features of different social vehicles to develop a meaningful social presence. Zara is a good example. It posts often and focuses posts on fashion trends. It maintains a Lookbook app within the profile for fans to use to stay up to date on the latest styles. The interactive app includes photos and videos and is optimized for mobile.

Photo 5.3

The city of Philadelphia used this strategy to build its brand equity and awareness for tourism. The destination marketing organization (DMO) is called Visit Philly and its core mission is to bring more people to Philadelphia and encourage them to spend money during the visit! Visit Philly created profiles on Instagram, Twitter, Facebook, and Pinterest and linked those accounts with its owned media site at www. visitphilly.com. The presence is meant to build the brand equity of Philadelphia as a destination, increase [ad] impressions of the city to tourists, and influence tourists' desire to visit. Visit Philly focuses on the use of photography to spotlight its brand

Photo 5.4

offering. As such, Instagram serves as the primary network for the brand's persona. Still, images are pushed out to Twitter, Facebook, and Pinterest too. A gallery of the best images and images provided by Philly fans organically is maintained on the website.

Visit Philly builds love on Instagram: http://instagram.com/visitphilly#

those interactions with others. Brands stand to benefit from heightened brand loyalty among engaged consumers and a more expansive reach for brand-related messages. The earned reach (the breadth and quality of contact with users) gained when people share positive brand opinions and branded content with others is invaluable because of the influence attributed to individual, personalized brand endorsements. Yes, we're talking about word-of-mouth communication. How can brands encourage interaction? Three strategies are at the forefront: conversations, real-time marketing, and contests and requests for user-generated content.

Brands Talk

When we say "brands talk," we mean they talk! That's right. If brands want to engage consumers in conversation, they have to converse. Can this approach be effective? Ask Beyonce. She eschewed traditional marketing for the launch of her album, turning to her Instagram followers instead. With a simple post, "Surprise!" she incited a storm of demand for her new music, available via iTunes. In record time, the album beat sales of her past albums and all without any use of traditional media.[27]

And no one knows the power of conversation better than Taco Bell. It's used its social presence (yes, to even try to influence earned media, the brand must be present) to present itself as a hip and fun friend. While brand managers may worry that this kind of investment of resources won't result in sales, that doesn't seem to be an issue for Taco Bell, which reportedly sold 100 million Doritos Locos Tacos in the first 2½ months of sales—with, you guessed it, a launch via social media. How is Taco Bell managing this? Its social presence is humanesque and it starts conversations! These conversations could be with you, me, or any other follower, but they are entertaining and engaging! Take, for example, this exchange with @menshumor:

@menshumor: *"This morning I gave birth to a food baby and I think @tacobell is the father."*

@tacobell: *"I want a DNA test."*[28]

When Universal Pictures wanted to promote *Endless Love* it used Whisper, a social network in which people remain anonymous, to share messages related to the movie's theme. Whispers with movie images were posted with questions like "What are three words to describe your first relationship ever?" That particular message brought more than 10,000 whispered replies.[29]

Real-Time Marketing (RTM)

What is real-time marketing? It's kind of like social media conversation on the fly. Brands post messages that resonate with the moment, whether that moment is planned or spontaneous. Here's a planned example. As we discussed earlier, brands can provoke conversation in social networks. With RTM, the brands leverage current events to do so. Remember the Gladiators? Tide laundry detergent leveraged the online chatter around a viewing of *Scandal* to engage those watching. Using the same hashtag #gladiators, Tide posted a provocative image of a blood-stained blouse with the promise that Tide can get any stain out. This is a message with a short life-span. Even shorter than the typical 30-second advert! But it works because of its timeliness and relevance.

SHOW ME!

What about a spontaneous example? Oreo is the king of RTM, perhaps even being the first brand to incite the use of this technique. During the 2013 Super Bowl, game play halted during an unexpected power outage. Oreo's digital agency, 360i, responded fast, tweeting a picture with the caption, "You can still dunk in the dark." Even though Oreo had no paid advertising during the broadcast, it was able to leverage the experience in real-time to share its brand message.

View a short video explaining Oreo's Blackout Tweet here: http://www.360i.com/work/oreo-super-bowl/.

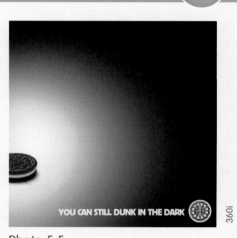

YOU CAN STILL DUNK IN THE DARK

360i

Photo 5.5

Brands can also utilize this approach to establish a sense of conversation, as GM did during the 2014 Super Bowl. It tweeted personalized messages to people who mentioned its commercial on Twitter. This provided a hybrid approach that resonated well with the audience.

For an example of Chrysler's real-time, personalized tweets, see: http://t.co/qR7DfTTtGP.

FotograFFF / Shutterstock.com

Photo 5.6

Contests and Requests for UGC

Brands can seed many forms of content in social communities as they try to boost engagement and sharing. One of the most popular tools is the user-generated contest campaign (also known as a *UGC contest*). UGC campaigns offer a way for brands to invite consumers to engage and interact while they develop shareable content. The lexicon of online marketers includes many commonly used phrases and accompanying acronyms related to user-generated content, also known as consumer-generated media. Consumer-generated media (CGM) or UGC are the catch-all phrases for user content. User content is organic when its creation is motivated by an intrinsic intent on the part of its creator rather than incentivized or guided by the brand itself. Organic brand-oriented UGC, at least when promoting the brand in a favorable light, is valuable and suggests highly engaged customers. For example, a YouTube video espousing one's love for one's iPad is organic UGC—Apple didn't invite or incent the fan to create and post the content.

Is it effective? Studies show that user-generated social media communication positively influences brand equity and attitude toward the brand and contests are a tried and true method for generating that communication.[30] A comparison of movie ticket sales among groups who were exposed to a movie-themed microsite, a social media contest for the movie, or both, found that using both as a combined approach was most effective.[31]

A UGC campaign is sometimes called participatory advertising. Brands invite content, set mandatory guidelines and specifications, and possibly also provide participants with selected *brand assets* such as footage from prior commercials that ran on TV. Brands must pay attention to vehicle rules. Whether the campaign will run on Pinterest, Instagram, or Facebook, each vehicle has published guidelines. UGC contests encourage people in the target audience to develop and submit content related to the campaign. The content is then shared on social sites in the form of a gallery, which others can view and pass on to their respective networks.

UGC contests engage consumers and spread the message by leveraging consumer networks. It takes work to organize and oversee the process and promotion to activate these contests, but on the other hand they provide interesting content at a relatively low cost to the brand—especially compared to what professional advertisers charge to create commercials! Depending upon the contest design, UGC contests can also offer ways to engage different types of consumers—creators, joiners, conversationalists, and collectors. In addition, they provide content for journalists to include in stories about the brand, so ultimately this enhances a brand's public relations profile.

The most frequently used manifestation of CSM is the request for a personal story and/or photo. For example, in the Hanes campaign, "Undercover Color," women shared the color of their underwear on Twitter. The campaign fit with the brand's core product and also related to the target audience, because a woman's color choice is a reflection of her personality and mood. Another variation is the "create your own ad" contest, which has been used by numerous brands including Frito-Lay, Dove, and Chevy. Sponsors encourage submissions with incentives such as prize money or the chance for the winning entry to be broadcast on television.

Paid Media in Social Networks

Just as brands may advertise on websites throughout the Web, they may also choose to advertise within social communities. Paid advertising in Facebook alone is expected to reach nearly $5 billion per year by 2015. These ads may take the form of standard display or video ads, ads in mobile apps, or may be more integrated in the form of native advertising. Native advertising is a type of paid advertising that is based on a form unique to the vehicle within which it is placed. Sponsored posts in Facebook and promoted tweets in Twitter are examples.

Display ads may include text, graphics, video, and sound much like traditional print ads and commercials but they are presented on a website. Whether the ads are text-oriented (e.g., a classified ad in a newspaper), text and graphics (e.g., a print ad in a magazine), or rich media (e.g., a television commercial), they are enhanced with a response device in that viewers can click the ads (called a clickthrough) to reach a target landing page. A landing page is the first page that a person sees when he or she clicks through an ad to reach a brand's target site. It's an important page for marketers, in that the content on the landing page will influence whether visitors stay at the site or move on to another page.

Social ads are online display ads that incorporate user data in the ad or in the targeting of the ad and enable some form of social interaction within the ad unit or landing page. In these applications, user data are harnessed to deliver messages that should be relevant to the recipients based on their online behaviors. These ads often customize the ad content; they may even incorporate references to friends of the target. The ads are personalized using details from user profiles, images, relationships among users, data gathered from applications, and interactions within a user network. Like other online display ads, they incorporate a response device, enabling interested viewers to click through to a landing page (which could be the brand's social profile). But unlike conventional display ads, social ads are interactive—viewers can play with the ad, share it, or comment on it. According to research from Nielsen, social ads are more effective than non-social ones. In a study of 70 Facebook campaigns, social ads generated a 55% lift in ad recall.[32] There are variations of social ads:[33]

1   A social engagement ad contains ad creative (image and text) along with an option to encourage the viewer to engage with the brand (e.g., a clickable "Like" button or a link).
2   A social context ad includes ad creative, an engagement device, and personalized referral content from people in the viewer's network.
3   Organic social ads are shared on a person's activity stream following a brand interaction (such as liking the brand). Organic social ads occur only when people are interacting with the brand and are thought to carry enhanced credibility.

Newsfeed stories of brand interactions, called derivative branded content, are just one way to seed content using the network. When organic social ads are combined with social engagement or context ads, effectiveness improves. A limitation is that organic social ads occur only when community members have interacted with the brand's social ads, on the brand's own profile, or with some branded application or game. If few people choose to interact, few organic social ads will be generated. In this case, paid media seeded the interaction necessary to generate additional impressions. But marketers can also utilize seeding to foster consumer engagement and interactivity though nonpaid media activities. Whether the ads are based on apps, photos, engagement options like links or likes, or video, they can be served in the traditional digital context and/or in the mobile delivery of the network experience. Dashboards are provided for advertisers to illustrate how effective the ad was in terms of characteristics like reach, engagement, and sentiment. We discuss these measures further in Chapter 10.

Paid ads in social networks can be targeted using geographic segmentation, demographic segmentation, psychographics, and behavioral targeting. Companies can merge email addresses from their customer databases and website visitor data to target social media users directly. Facebook offers the creation of "lookalike audiences" that match the characteristics of known customers. A popular technique is to use targeted ads to "retarget content," also called remarketing. The concept is to increase the frequency of exposure of the brand's message.

FROM BYTES TO BUCKS

How can marketers make the most of relationships and generate earned media? They are tasked with creating and delivering persuasive messages that are relevant, engaging, interactive, personalizable, and shareable. To put it simply, the challenge is to create marketing messages that are so cool, funny, or interesting that people *want* to see them and share them. That's why social media marketers sometimes call the creative design of social media campaigns experience design. The term underscores the desire to create more than a passive ad—the goal is to launch an experience that people will *want to share*.

Photo 5.7

Breaking Bad's "Name Lab" campaign is a great example of creativity that motivates the receiver to get involved with the message and help to spread it to others. Rather than delivering a static commercial (online using paid media or on the AMC network using owned media) using the interruption-disruption model, visitors to the AMC.com website were invited to have their name transformed into element symbols like the show's logo.

The app is a seed. It gave *Breaking Bad* fans a reason to interact with the brand and resulted in a segment of produced content that could be shared online using social networks. When the name images are shared, they become earned media. Some of the people who see the images become intrigued with the *Breaking Bad* story—and maybe, just maybe, they tune in for the next episode.

To explore the app, visit: http://www.amctv.com/shows/breaking-bad/name-lab.

You can see from the example the importance of ensuring that paid and earned media support each other. AMC utilized paid media in social networks and earned media to promote the app (the seed). Users could take that seed and create something that is unique to them while also resonating imagery associated with the show. Figure 5.2 illustrates how paid and earned media work together in social media to promote brand messages.

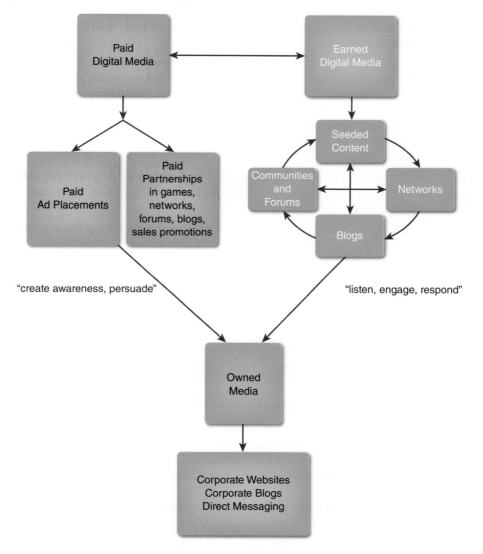

Figure 5.2   The Relationship Among Owned, Paid, and Earned Media

Is the Brand Ready for Social Relationships?

Clearly, there is a lot to be gained for brands operating in social media, and from friending customers in social networks. Managers should ask these questions before deciding whether social relationships will work for a specific brand.

- Is the brand set up for engagement? Mark Kingdon, CEO of Organic, Inc., a digital marketing agency, said that "Brands have to allow for and anticipate dialogue, because consumers very much want to engage with brands and not all brands are set up for engagement. A lot of brands are simply set up to broadcast their message to an audience."[34] Some brands will be safer with one-way communication.

- If the traditional brand participates in social media, where should the brand be? Should the brand have its own dedicated social network space (e.g., Nike's Joga)? Or will the brand have the best chance of creating consumer dialogue and engagement by using an existing network such as Gather or Facebook? Is there a social networking site that is well suited to the brand? For example, Purina is perfectly suited to advertising on Dogster, but its message may not be as effective on Glue.

- How can the brand's profiles be developed in such a way as to reflect the brand's personality? With what voice will the brand speak? How will the brand interact within the site?

- If "fan pages" exist among brand loyalists on social networking sites, how can the brand leverage the fan sites to better meet its objectives?

- How can the brand integrate its social network presence into other campaign components? Integration may start with simple steps such as including a Facebook icon in other brand messages and develop into utilizing the social network for sales promotions such as coupon distribution and contest administration.

CHAPTER SUMMARY

How do social networking communities enable user participation and sharing?

Social networks encourage participation by providing easy-to-use tools, including share buttons, applications, uploading functionalities, embed codes, and activity streams. Most importantly, people participate around experiences. Brands aid in this by providing experience strategies that relate to their marketing objectives.

In what ways can brands utilize social networking communities for branding and promotion?

Brands have three key ways of utilizing social networking communities for branding based around owned, earned, and paid media. Brands should develop a social presence in the chosen social networks. This is not truly owned media but it is a brand's representation of itself in the social communities. Brands can earn media by participating in dialogue, using real-time marketing, and creating opportunities to encourage user-generated content using techniques like contests. Lastly, brands can purchase paid advertising opportunities.

Why is engagement a goal of brands using social media marketing? What are the benefits of engagement?

Engagement is the active involvement between consumer and brand. It implies an emotional attachment and serves to build the relationship. Ideally, brands will engage consumers in ways that develop the level of fan experience. Engaged consumers are more likely to purchase, exhibit loyalty, and share positive word-of-mouth communication about the brand.

KEY TERMS

APIs
brand butlers
brand engagement
brand fans
brand profile
clickthrough
consumer-generated media (CGM)
derivative branded content
diffusion of innovations
display ads
earned reach
embed codes
experience design
external social network

fan base
fandom
friendvertising
gallery
identity portability
internal social network
landing page
message internalization
native advertising
open source model
OpenID
OpenSocial code
organic social ads
participatory advertising
response device

return on emotion
rich media
secondary content
seed
social ads
social context ad
social engagement ad
social interaction
social lock-in
social networking fatigue
social sharing
switching costs
tipping point
user-generated content campaign
vertical networks

REVIEW QUESTIONS

1 What social activities are the focus of participation in social communities?

2 How can brands create identities in social communities?

3 What are the types of social networks in social media?

4 What are the characteristics of social ads? How effective are social ads?

5 How can brands engage consumers in social communities?

6 What is earned media? How do brands encourage earned media with their social networking activities?

7 What are the characteristics of brand fans?

EXERCISES

1   Discussion: Should a social network own our social data? Is it an invasion of privacy for social networks to collect and use the information we leave as we deposit digital footprints in a site and around the Web?

2   Discussion: Is it a good thing to "friend" your professors? Why or why not?

3   Discussion: Are Facebook friends the same as real friends? Are Facebook fans real fans? Explain.

4   Analyze a brand profile on Facebook. Identify all the brand assets on the page. What techniques are being used by the brand to engage consumers? Do the brand fans seem passionate and engaged? Why or why not? How could the brand improve its profile?

5   Interview three people who are passionate about some interest. Document the time and resources they spend to engage with this object. Despite their passion for very different objects, what similarities or common patterns do you observe among them? Do they engage in this interest in social communities? Do you see the five characteristics of fans exhibited in their behavior?

CHAPTER NOTES

1   Austin Carr, "Facebook Everywhere," *Fast Company,* July/August 2014, 56–68.

2   Everett M. Rogers, *Diffusion of Innovations* (New York: Free Press, 1962).

3   "Nissan Launches 'N-Square' Internal Social Networking Site," Internal Comms Hub, November 17, 2007, http://www.internalcommshub.com/open/news/nissan.shtml, accessed December 20, 2010.

4   Mark Sullivan, "How Will Facebook Make Money?" *PC World*, June 15, 2010, http://www.pcworld.com/article/198815/how_will_facebook_make_money.html, accessed December 31, 2010.

5   Tom Espiner, "IE Slips Further as Firefox, Safari, Chrome Gain," CNET, February 2, 2009, http://news.cnet.com/8301-1023_3-10154447-93.html, accessed June 8, 2010.

6   Quoted in Marshall Kirkpatrick, "Facebook's Zuckerberg Says the Age of Privacy Is Over," Read Write Web, January 9, 2010, http://www.readwriteweb.com/archives/facebooks_zuckerberg_says_the_age_of_privacy_is_ov.php, accessed December 21, 2010.

7   Jackie Rousseau-Anderson, "The Latest Global Social Media Trends May Surprise You," Forrester Blogs, September 28, 2010, http://blogs.forrester.com/jackie_rousseau_anderson/10-09-28-latest_global_social_media_trends_may_surprise_you, accessed December 20, 2010.

8   "Timeline," YouTube, May 2010, http://www.youtube.com/t/press_timeline, accessed December 19, 2010.

9   Jakob Nielsen, "Participation Inequality: Encouraging More Users to Contribute," AlertBox, October 9, 2006, http://www.useit.com/alertbox/participation_inequality.html, accessed December 18, 2010.

10   Debra Aho Williamson, "Brand Interactions on Social Networks," eMarketer, June 2010, http://www.emarketer.com/Report.aspx?code=emarketer_2000694, accessed December 20, 2010.

11   Gregory McNeil, "Facebook Manipulated User News Feeds to Create Emotional Responses," *Forbes,* June 28, 2014, http://www.forbes.com/sites/gregorymcneal/2014/06/28/facebook-manipulated-user-news-feeds-to-create-emotional-contagion/, accessed June 29, 2014.

12   Josh Mendelsohn and Jeff McKenna, "Social Sharing Research Report," *Chadwick Martin Bailey,* September 2010, http://www.cmbinfo.com/cmb.../Social_Sharing_Research_Report_CMB1.pdf, accessed October 15, 2010.

13   Christian Crumlish and Erin Malone, *Designing Social Interfaces* (Sebastopol, CA: O'Reilly Media, 2009).

14   J. Van Doorn, Kay Lemon, V. Mittal, S. Nass, D. Pick, P. Pirner, and C. Verhoef, "Customer Engagement Behavior: Theoretical Foundations and Research Directions," *Journal of Service Research* 13, no. 3 (2010): 253–266.

15   Feed: The Razorfish Digital Brand Experience Report 2009, http://feed.razorfish.com/downloads/Razorfish_FEED09.pdf, p. 9, accessed August 7, 2011.

16   "Time-Starved Consumers Seek Brand Butlers," Marketing Charts, March 29, 2010, http://www.marketingcharts.com/direct/time-starved-consumers-seek-brand-butlers-12437/?utm_campaign=rssfeed&utm_source=mc&utm_medium=textlink, accessed April 12, 2010.

17   Christopher Heine, "Facebook Ads Provide Big Win for JetBlue's $10 Campaign," ClickZ, May 12, 2010, http://www.clickz.com/3640312, accessed May 18, 2010.

18   Robert Kozinets, "Brand Fans: When Entertainment + Marketing Intersect on the Net," in Tracy Tuten, ed., *Enterprise 2.0: How Technology, E-Commerce, and Web 2.0 Are Transforming Business Virtually* (Santa Barbara, CA: Praeger Publishers, 2010).

19   Tom Troja, "Social Is About Aspirations: How to Get People to Aspire to Your Brand," May 8, 2012, *iMedia Connection,* http://blogs.imediaconnection.com/blog/2012/05/01/social-is-about-aspirations-how-to-get-people-to-aspire-to-your-brand/, accessed June 15, 2013.

20   N. Sinha, V. Ahuja, and Y. Medury, "Corporate Blogs and Internet Marketing: Using Consumer Knowledge and Emotion as Strategic Variables to Develop Consumer Engagement," *Database Marketing and Customer Strategy Management* 18, no. 3 (2011): 185–199.

(Continued)

(Continued)

21   B. Jahn and W. Kunz, "How to Transform Consumers Into Fans of Your Brand," *Journal of Service Management* 23, no. 3 (2012): 344–361.

22   David Evans and Eden Epstein, "Comparing User Engagement Across Seven Interactive and Social Media Ad Types," Psychster and All Recipes, 2010, http://psychster.com/library/PSYCHSTER_Allrecipes_Widget_Whitepaper_Mar10_FINAL.pdf, accessed December 31, 2010.

23   "The Value of a Facebook Fan: An Empirical Study," Syncapse, June 2010, http://www.brandchannel.com/images/papers/504_061810_wp_syncapse_facebook.pdf, accessed December 20, 2010.

24   Anna Farmery, "What Is Your Return on Emotion?" The Engaging Brand Blog, July 2009, http://theengagingbrand.typepad.com/the_engaging_brand_/2009/07/what-is-your-return-on-emotion.html, accessed December 31, 2010.

25   "Fluent: The Razorfish Social Influence Marketing Report," Razorfish, 2009, http://fluent.razorfish.com/publication/?m=6540&l=1, accessed December 21, 2010.

26   Brian Solis, "The Social Media Style Guide," June 14, 2010, http://www.briansolis.com/2010/06/the-social-media-style-guide-8-steps-to-creating-a-brand-persona-2/, accessed June 30, 2010.

27   "Beyonce Rejects Tradition for Social Media's Power," *New York Times,* March 9, 2014.

28   Ann Handley, "Marketing Trend for 2014: Smaller Messaging Has a Big Impact," *Entrepreneur.com,* http://www.entrepreneur.com/article/229806, accessed August 29, 2014.

29   Ryan Tate, "How Facebook Can Make Money From Your Gossip," *Wired*, April 25, 2014, http://www.wired.com/2014/04/whisper-gets-ads/, accessed May 1, 2014.

30   B. Schivinski and D. Dabrowski, "The Effect of Social Media Communication on Consumer Perceptions of Brands," *Journal of Marketing Communication* 1, no. 20 (2014): 1–26.

31   Emily Mabry and Lance Porter, "Movies and Myspace: The Effectiveness of Official Websites versus Online Promotional Contests," *Journal of Interactive Advertising,* 2014, http://www.slideshare.net/emabry1/movies-and-myspace-the-effectiveness-of-official-websites-versus-online-promotional-contests, accessed August 29, 2014.

32   "Ads With Friends: Analyzing the Benefits of Social Ads," *Nielsen Newswire,* March 2012, http://www.nielsen.com/us/en/insights/news/2012/ads-with-friends-analyzing-the-benefits-of-social-ads.html, accessed August 29, 2014.

33   Jon Gibs and Sean Bruich, "Advertising Effectiveness: Understanding the Value of a Social Media Impression," Nielsen Company and Facebook, April 2010, http://uk.nielsen.com/site/documents/SocialMediaWhitePapercomp.pdf, accessed December 21, 2010.

34   E. Steel, "Using Social Sites as Dialogue to Engage Consumers, Brands," *Wall Street Journal*, November 8, 2006, B2D.

Social Publishing

LEARNING OBJECTIVES

When you finish reading this chapter you will be able to answer these questions:

1   What are the channels of social publishing?

2   Who creates the content published in social channels? What kind of content can be published?

3   What content characteristics enhance perceived content quality and value? How can marketers plan and organize their efforts as they embrace a social publishing strategy?

4   What is the role of social publishing in social media marketing? How do social media marketers utilize search engine optimization and social media optimization to meet marketing objectives?

5   How can social content be promoted? What role do social news and social bookmarking sites play in content promotion?

The Social Publishing Zone

In this chapter, our focus shifts to the second zone of social media. The social publishing zone, as shown in Figure 6.1, includes those channels that allow people and organizations to publish content including blogs, media-sharing sites, microblogs, and information and news networks. Blogs are websites that host regularly updated content. Microblogs are similar to blogs, except that the content is limited to short bursts of text and links. Twitter is one example because it limits posts to 140 characters. Media-sharing sites include video-sharing sites such as YouTube, Vimeo, and Ustream; photo-sharing sites such as Flickr and Instagram; audio-sharing sites such as Podcast Alley; and document- and presentation-sharing sites such as Scribd and SlideShare. Facebook, as a social utility, also offers multimedia sharing functionality with videos, photos, and links to content.

In this chapter, you'll learn some basic principles of content creation and distribution via blogs and media-sharing sites; how marketers can design content for search engine and social media optimization; and how to promote social content using social media press releases, microblogs, and social news and bookmarking sites.

Publishing Content

Content is the unit of value in a social community, akin to the dollar in our economy. It provides a social object for community participation. Its importance is the reason content marketing has evolved as a core aspect of marketing communications. According to

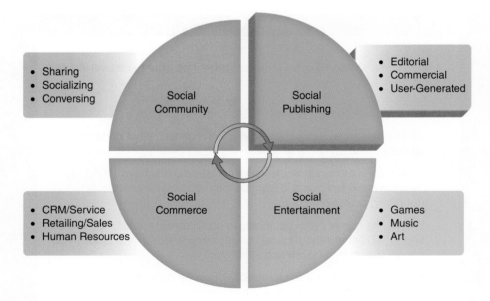

Figure 6.1   The Zones of Social Media

the Content Marketing Institute, content marketing is a "marketing technique of creating and distributing valuable, relevant and consistent content to attract and acquire a clearly defined audience—with the objective of driving profitable customer action." The philosophy of content marketing emphasizes that brands should publish content in their owned media channels, but publishing in social channels can build awareness, influence brand attitudes, and help drive traffic to owned media.

Types of Content

Content may include opinions, catchphrases, information, fashion photos, advice, art, or photos from that wild party last week. It may be curated or original.

Social media content may begin with content published for some other purpose, such as a broadcast commercial, entertainment film, or news story. Or the content may be entirely original contributions that community members produce and publish. Ideally, social media content should do more than repurpose offline content for digital display, although we often do find this kind of "secondhand content" on some sites, for example, when people retweet a news article they find interesting.

Content appears in a variety of different formats such as:

- Blog posts and feature articles
- Microblog posts
- Press releases
- White papers, case studies, and ebooks
- Newsletters
- Videos
- Webinars and presentations
- Podcasts
- Photos

Content can be any of these and more. Increasingly, however, we see more content that is multilayered; it offers several applications based on a meme or a piece of factual information. For instance, suppose *Travel & Leisure* magazine publishes an article on fashionable solutions to travel clothing dilemmas. The online magazine site also publishes the article, but now it includes several social features including a comment option, a Share This widget, a bookmarking option, and a game called Pack and Play. The content began its life as a piece of content in the traditional press. It was repurposed for use in the online magazine. But it didn't become social until the content was fortified with interactivity, participation, and shareability. Note too that the social components of the content added value to everyone connected to the content. The original publisher gained additional readers through the sharing option and enhanced the stickiness of the site (making the site more attractive to online advertisers) because it offered social features. The readers were able to better use the information in the article because they could share it, store it for later reference, and practice the tips offered in the Pack and Play game application.

Channels of Content Distribution

Blogs

Blogs have been around for more than a decade. They began as simple online logs posted in reverse chronological order, and developed into a widely used publishing venue for individual and corporate use. With hundreds of millions of blogs in existence, blogging is clearly a publishing venue here to stay. However, blogging has evolved: once a way to simply share opinions via text postings, today many blogs also include video and images. Blogs are primarily owned media. The blogger controls the website and the blog's content. However, some social media vehicles enable a form of blogging that does not fall into the owned media category. For instance, Tumblr blogs are truly social media, rather than owned media with social functionality. Bloggers may be hobbyists, part-timers, corporate bloggers, or self-employed bloggers. According to Technorati, the top 100 bloggers publish 500 times the number of posts of the average blogger.[1] As a group, bloggers seek to promote their blogs much as other content providers promote content. To do so, many use Twitter to drive traffic to their blog site.

Blogs offer an opportunity for individuals to express their opinions, share their expertise, make money by selling on-site advertising, and attract clients for consulting work. They also offer opportunities for organizations to establish thought leadership on a topic, increase traffic to targeted websites such as an organization's e-commerce site, build links to other corporate sites, and build brand awareness.[2] For example, Heather Armstrong's blog, *Dooce*, established her as a creative writer capable of providing her readers with insight and amusement into the life of a typical woman.[3] David Armano's *Logic + Emotion* blog grew his reputation as a visual thinker and experience designer.[4] Blogging may be an outlet for creative expression but can also be a business! The top bloggers in the world earn hundreds of thousands of dollars each month. In fact, one of the best sources of information on social media marketing strategies, *Mashable*, is a blog. Its founder, Pete Cashmore, is among the top earning bloggers in the world with revenues estimated at $600,000 per month. The blog began in Cashmore's bedroom in

Photo 6.1

Scotland when he was just 19.[5] Another favorite blog is *Dogshaming*. This popular blog publishes images of dogs (like the shown in photo 6.1) who have misbehaved. The images are submitted by its readers and so are based on user-generated content.

Most revenue from blogs is earned from paid ads, but bloggers can earn money in other ways too. We'll talk more about that and the related issues later in the chapter.

Media-Sharing Sites

Like blogs, media-sharing sites enable individuals and organizations to publish content online. However, whereas blogs are typically in the realm of owned media, media-sharing sites are earned media because their environments are not directly controlled by the person or organization posting the content. Instagram, Pinterest, and YouTube are all media-sharing sites. Often the choice of which media-sharing site to use is dictated by the type of content to be distributed. The style of content should be customized for the site's personality, too. Some media-sharing vehicles are serious, others quirky.

SHOW ME!

Ford maintains a corporate hub for its social media content called Ford Social, but video content is shared on its YouTube channel, photos are shared on its Flickr photostream and on Instagram, fact sheets and other corporate content are shared on Scribd, and news are shared on its Twitter feed. Reviews, covered in Chapter 8, are also a form of content that can be published using media-sharing sites. Media-sharing sites like Pinterest and Instagram may be used to drive sales as well as customer engagement.

Visit: http://social.ford.com/.

Content Producers: What Is "Authentic"?

Content can take so many forms that it's sometimes difficult to categorize. This is especially true in the online world, where the lines between what is real and what is not become increasingly blurred. For example, people often share YouTube clips of outrageous or racy commercials with their friends—but in many cases these spots were not produced by the company (sorry to disappoint you). In fact, the proliferation of untruths and exaggerations (or so-called urban legends) is so widespread that specialized websites do nothing but verify or refute them. The website Snopes.com is the best-known of these.

This ambiguity also exists when we try to identify the sources or distributors of content. At one time, it was easy to classify a message as either editorial or commercial. An editorial message is objective and unbiased; the source expresses an opinion or provides information and does not intend to carry out the agenda of an organization. The most obvious example is the editorial page of a newspaper, where a writer presents an argument that may criticize a government, a company, or a politician. This section of the paper is clearly marked as editorial.

In contrast, a commercial message such as an advertisement makes it clear that the intent is to persuade the reader or viewer to change an attitude or behavior; the source has paid a fee to place the message in a medium. So, it's obvious in a traditional newspaper that a half-page plea, say, to pass environmental legislation or carry out sanctions against governments that permit whaling, is sponsored and paid for by an identifiable organization.

For news and educational content, traditional press organizations hire journalists to research, verify, and write credible, objective, trustworthy stories. These media outlets then deliver that content to a paying audience via newspapers, newsletters, magazines, and radio and television programs. The traditional press controlled the message and the channel, but it adhered to accepted industry guidelines and norms. Similarly, traditional entertainment companies or production houses created and distributed their own content. Broadcast networks commissioned the development of programs and movies they showed on the stations they owned. And the transition from editorial to commercial content was clear: "And now a word from our sponsors." Of course, even before the explosion of social media these lines blurred—for example, many critics label cartoon shows that feature product-based characters (such as those on popular Yu-Gi-Oh trading cards) as a "program-length commercial."[6]

Though content from traditional media sources is still valuable, today these sources struggle as consumers increasingly turn to other places to access their news and entertainment. People no longer need to subscribe to the local newspaper in order to get credible news. Instead they can read email, Twitter posts, blogs, and updates to social networking sites, all from their smartphones. This seismic shift has forced the closing of media providers around the world as they fail to find new ways to monetize their businesses. Major newspapers such as *The San Francisco Chronicle* have closed, while other traditional media vehicles merge with online companies—for example, the venerable print magazine *Newsweek* was recently acquired by *The Daily Beast*.

Other traditional content providers adapt to the new media environment as they shift from delivering their messages on a printed page (or, as some new media people like to say, "dead trees") to mobile applications. *Gourmet* responded by evolving into the first mobile magazine. It closed operations due to declining subscriptions and ad revenues. *Gourmet Live* instead delivers articles to foodies on their mobile phones. But, unlike the old dead tree delivery system, this content is also social—subscribers can interact, share, and play games within the application.

In addition to a blurring of the lines between editorial and commercial messages, today we witness an explosion of user-generated content (UGC)—which, as we've seen, is the lifeblood of emerging social media. In many cases, everyday people create and post this content for personal reasons rather than to receive financial reward. A proud father shoots video of his son's high school graduation and shares it with the family. An expecting young mother chronicles the story of her pregnancy and birth. A retired couple keeps a photo log of their yearly trips where they explore the world together.

What's new about this consumer-generated content? In one sense, absolutely nothing! People throughout history have written stories, commissioned portraits, kept diaries, and more recently taken photos and videos of family events. What is new is that due to the social media value chain, people can share this content with those beyond their immediate area. Today they post photos to Flickr or perhaps a less-than-flattering video from last night's raucous party on YouTube. This content is largely shared in the context of social communities (zone 1), but it is also published content, crossing into the realm of zone 2.

In terms of the content itself, UGC is powerful because it often attracts our attention to things we wouldn't otherwise watch (sometimes it's like watching a train wreck—you know it's terrible but you can't tear yourself away). You may stumble upon this content while you search for specific information about a product or brand, discovering it accidentally. And, because of the power of social media, these inputs may well impact what others think or even change a firm's marketing activities. In this form of cultural co-creation, co-created meanings (among both producers and consumers) fold back into the culture. Jones Soda, for example, enlists its consumers' input on packages and flavors so that the products it makes are the outcome of collaboration with its customers. That helps to explain soda flavors such as Blue Bubble Gum and Turkey with Cranberry Sauce, not to mention such favorites as Sweat and Dirt![7]

It's useful to distinguish between UGC that people voluntarily publish and content that appears because some organization has invited contributions from users. Organic content is content that a person feels intrinsically motivated to prepare and share. In contrast, incentivized content is encouraged by the offer of an *incentive*, such as the chance to win a contest, receive free merchandise, or even earn cold hard cash. In these cases the contribution is a response to a call to action. This term refers to a direct request in a marketing message for a specific behavior. You've observed a similar technique in TV infomercials, where a host reminds you to "Call right now. Operators are standing by!" That's a call to action. In social media marketing, calls to action ensure that people participate in the social media campaign.

Consumer-solicited content (CSC) refers to invited but non-compensated citizen advertising, which is another way to describe marketing messages that actual consumers create. Sometimes marketers call this approach participatory advertising; brands invite submissions, set mandatory guidelines and specifications, and possibly provide participants with selected brand assets such as footage of the brand in use or logos and former commercials. CSC can be incentivized by the sponsoring brand. It functions just as non-incentivized citizen-advertising campaigns except that the sponsor encourages submissions with incentives such as prize money. Perhaps the most famous example is the Crash the Super Bowl contest, which gives citizen advertisers the chance to win $1 million and see their ad on air. The winner in 2014 was called "Time Machine," which cost just $300 to make. That seems to have paid off for Doritos in terms of ad effectiveness, with two of the ads measured in the top 10 for memorability and likeability. That's pretty impressive when you remember that the Doritos spots were "homemade" and cost so little to create.

Sponsored conversations refer to *paid* consumer content. Consumers are paid for their content creations, and brands may actively seek out certain people like bloggers, videographers, and artists to participate in the campaign. For example, the company

PayPerPost pays bloggers to endorse products. Bloggers who post sponsored conversations as their sole reason to contribute to a conversation are known as spokesbloggers. These bloggers may also participate in other paid forms of endorsement, like hosting events. This is particularly common in the fashion industry where bloggers like Aimee Song (of the blog, *Song of Style*) command a great deal of respect for the influence they have with their readers.

Counterfeit conversations occur when an organization plants content that masquerades as original material an actual consumer posted. The Lonelygirl15 YouTube phenomenon was a planned, strategic marketing ploy to promote the capabilities of its producers who hoped to use their 15 minutes of fame to land other jobs in the video industry. Bree, aka Lonelygirl15, was allegedly a home-schooled 16-year-old. She started a *vlog* on YouTube that for a time was the most viewed video on the site.[8] Eventually the hoax was uncovered, but only after the videos achieved millions of page views and the phenomenon generated several news articles on the story. Such hoaxes may be user-generated too. Consider the case of Linda Tirado, who wrote a blog post about her experiences with poverty. The post went viral and was reprinted on the *Huffington Post* website, where it received millions of views. Tirado created a GoFundMe page for donations that reportedly net her $60,000. Turns out, Tirado isn't poor. The post was a scam but it worked. She has since been a guest at the White House and she has a book deal for her story.[9]

So, the lines have blurred and merged across authentic and counterfeit sources. For instance, typically we think of bloggers as independent writers who publish their thoughts, activities, opinions, and information. The blog is historically an online diary of sorts—in fact, its name comes from a combination of the words "web log." Yet many traditional press organizations support bloggers as a part of the information content they provide. The *New York Times*, certainly a stalwart of the traditional press, hosts several blogs on its website on topics that range from the cultural *ArtBeat* and the humorous *WordPlay*, to the socially conscious *Green*. These writers are bloggers, but they post on behalf of a commercial publisher.

What's more, even the seemingly independent blogger can shift from noncommercial to sponsored content. If a blogger accepts Google AdWords on his or her site so that Google places ads there, or takes freebies or payment to blog about specific topics, that content shifts from editorial to commercial. For example, Walmart established *Moms*, a group of independent bloggers who receive free samples and then review the products. These women post on other topics as well, but these sponsored reviews live alongside the other content in their blogs. As we'll see later in the book, one important issue for social media is to clearly identify content as either editorial or commercial so that users understand just where it came from and what the poster's intent may be.

Because our cultural expectation for blogs (and other forms of content in the social media space) is that they present independent, nonfunded, noncommercial content, the FTC (Federal Trade Commission) introduced specific guidelines for social media content producers. The intent of the guidelines is to protect the public from advertising disguised as social media by ensuring that sponsorships are transparent. For instance, the FTC investigated Cole Haan's use of a user-generated content contest on Pinterest. The contest asked players to create a Pinterest board called "Wandering Sole" and to ping images from Cole Haan's board along with favorite places to wander. All pins needed the hashtag #wanderingsole. The FTC concluded that the pins were Cole Haan endorsements and that viewers would not be aware that the content was incentivized and the participants had not disclosed the relationship.[10]

Developing and Organizing Content

As they develop content to post on social media platforms, there are several guidelines marketers should consider. First, the content must match the brand's overall personality and strategic objectives. To manage workload, authors will need to be appointed and their duties assigned. Content development and responses to content feedback should follow established organizational policies like those we discussed in Chapter 2. An important component of social publishing is identifying relevant topics, types of content, publication venues, and a schedule for publication (in the form of an editorial calendar). Developing an editorial calendar helps bloggers and other content producers to forecast the time needed to manage the content development process, including researching topics, creating content, and promoting the content using the social publishing strategies discussed here. Figure 6.2 provides an example of such a calendar.

Organizations may have a set of editorial calendars including a master calendar and others for specific activities. The master calendar will provide an overview of all content planned by day and by week over the course of the plan. It will track key dates such as events and activities that could provide topics for sharing with the target audience. It will also consider the planned distribution for content throughout the channels of social publishing.

As in any other media, not all content is created equal. Some is trash; some is important. Some content is fun, some inspiring, and some just titillating (anyone for "Keeping

	A	B	C	D	E
1		Important Dates	Blog Post	Content Type/Event #1	Content Type/Event #2
2	Week of August 16				
3	Monday, August 16, 2015				
4	Tuesday, August 17, 2015				
5	Wednesday, August 18, 2015				
6	Thursday, August 19, 2015				
7	Friday, August 20, 2015				
8					
9	Week of August 23				
10	Monday, August 23, 2015				
11	Tuesday, August 24, 2015				
12	Wednesday, August 25, 2015				
13	Thursday, August 26, 2015				
14	Friday, August 27, 2015				
15					
16	Week of August 30				
17	Monday, August 30, 2015				
18	Tuesday, August 31, 2015				
19	Wednesday, September 01, 2015				
20	Thursday, September 02, 2015				

Figure 6.2   A Master Editorial Calendar

Up With the Kardashians"?). As Figure 6.3 shows, we can characterize content in terms of its originality and substance according to a content value ladder.[11] Let's take a closer look at this form of classification.

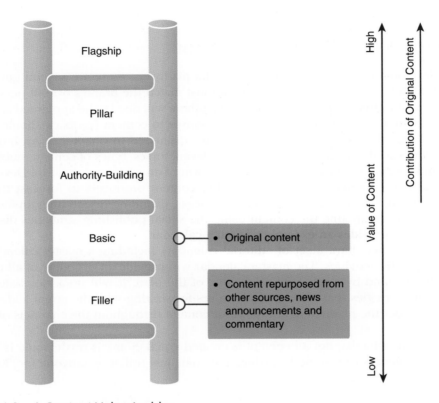

Figure 6.3   A Content Value Ladder

- At the lowest step in the ladder we find the least important type of materials. Filler content is simply information that people copy from other sources. A site called ArticlesBase.com is a free online article directory. It hosts articles that have been contributed by authors hoping to expand the reach of their work online. Others can use the articles posted on ArticlesBase at no charge. They just search for the topic of interest, copy and paste the article to their own site, and cite the contributing author. Filler content can also come from other content providers (blogs and posts on media-sharing sites) and syndicated sources such as PRNewsWire and the Associated Press.

- All other content on the ladder is original content. This level refers to contributions that originate with the poster. At the lowest level, this content is original, but not "weighty" enough to establish the creator as an authority in the topic area or serve as a reference piece for the audience.

- If that original content positions the sponsoring entity as an authority on the subject in question, then we call it authority-building content.

- If a source creates a solid foundation of original content, the foundation blocks are known as pillar content. Typically pillar content is made up of educational content that readers use over time, save, and share with others. As more and more people refer to these posts, they enable a sponsor to grow in readership, followers, and friends. The content's impact grows exponentially over time as other people share it through reposting, citations, and retweets. Table 6.1 elaborates on some of the most important kinds of pillar content that blogs can publish.

- Flagship content is also authority-building content. This term refers to seminal pieces of work that help to define a phenomenon or shape the way people think about something for a long time. Those pieces of content create a draw for years to come. Tim O'Reilly's 2005 article "What Is Web 2.0?" that continues to be a reference piece for those who study social media, is an example of flagship content.[12]

Table 6.1 Types of Pillar Content in Blogs

TYPE	DESCRIPTION	EXAMPLE
"How-To" Article	This form of content is the most popular type posted, according to an analysis of content shared on several news sites including Digg and StumbleUpon.[13]	*How to Make Brownies in a Crockpot*
Definition Article	This type of post defines a concept. Although this is a straightforward approach, it provides a high level of utility for those interested in the concept being defined	*What Is Web 2.0?*
Glossary Article	This form of article includes a series of definitions related to each other and creates a resource guide on the topic.	*A Glossary of Literary Terms*
Theory Article	Theory articles offer some unique insight into a topic but the content is opinion. They are equivalent to opinion-editorial pieces in your local newspaper.	*Media Aren't Social*
List Article	These forms of content use bullets for easy readability and consumption. They may draw on humor or education in detailing the list.	*Top 10 USB Thumbdrive Tricks*

Source: Based on Yaro Starak, "How to Write Great Blog Content—The Pillar Article," *Entrepreneurs-Journey.com*, February 9, 2008, www.entrepreneurs-journey.com/845/pillar-article/, accessed December 25, 2010.

Great Content Provides Value

For marketers, content should be of value to the target audience. The content will then be sought after and shared. In fact, great content is a useful lead generation tool! Most content can be parsed to fit in multiple social sites, all of which drive traffic back to the brand's owned media. Importantly, content can be original or can be curated. Content curation refers to developing a valuable form of content that draws from the collection of existing content. The value is in the collection of a group of items produced by others. For instance, a curated Pinterest board of top shoes for fall draws on other content but the value is in the collection.

Let's look at some examples of how brands have successfully launched social publishing strategies.

Velocity Partners used social publishing to reach its clients. A B2B marketing agency based in the UK, Velocity Partners wanted a way to emphasize its culture to prospective clients. The traits it values in customer relationships became the basis for an ebook, *The B2B Marketing Manifesto*, which it published on its website. The ebook can be downloaded (once prospects enter basic contact information, which feeds Velocity's lead generation funnel), comments are enabled on the site, and the link can be shared using Twitter, Facebook, and other social sites.

Indium Corporation provides materials used to produce electronics. Are you thinking how could a company like that use social publishing? Well it did! It created a blog called *From One Engineer to Another* that provided guidance and training to its target audience.

The fashion company French Connection wanted a way to provide advice to its target audience the way a personal shopper would. It built a YouTube channel called YouTique that provides short videos on fashion advice.

Lauren Luke started out as a part-time cosmetics salesperson in Newcastle, England. She developed a YouTube channel with instructional videos to help her sell more products. The videos have millions of views and catapulted Luke to a thought leader in the cosmetics industry. Just 5 years later, she has her own brand of makeup and a series of books.

Home Depot created a DIY Tips & Trends channel on YouTube. The channel provides instructional videos tailored by season and region that, of course, use products easily available at your nearest Home Depot.

Fashion brand Tory Burch created *The Tory Burch Blog* to engage with fans. The blog has it all—tips, heart, and personality. With it, Tory Burch is well on its way to being a true lifestyle brand, rather than just a fashion brand. *Mashable* called the blog "one of the leading manifestations of ongoing, brand-developed content." And the Content Marketing Institute named it "the blog to see" in the fashion world.[14]

Blue Cross Blue Shield of North Carolina developed a campaign called Let's Talk Costs. The campaign provides individuals with information on health care and health-care cost management in a language the average person can understand. The content is published on BCBSNC's owned media microsite, letstalkcosts.com, but is socialized (with comments and interactions on site) and shared using Twitter, Facebook, and YouTube.

Are you seeing a pattern here? Whether the marketing is B2B or B2C, the content adds value. It's relevant. It's not about selling. It's about providing something that people can participate in and share that experience with others. The core of the content may be published in owned media and made shareable or it may be published in a media-sharing site or it may have elements of both. But the content is engaging and relevant. It is content people want to share because it's just that good.

Social Publishing Strategies

For marketers there is a twofold goal for social publishing: (1) to increase exposure to the brand's messages and (2) to use the content to drive traffic to the brand's owned media. The social publishing process is similar to the media planning process we see for traditional advertising campaigns. In those cases the media plan designates how the campaign's creative content will be disseminated to the target audience using specific media vehicles such as radio or billboards. The media planner sets specific goals for what is to be accomplished through the ad placements in terms of audience reach, exposure to the message, and desired outcomes. Social publishing works much the same way except the creative content seeking exposure is not necessarily an ad (in the traditional static or rich media formats) and the distribution of that content is accomplished with inbound links or link chains to the content from search engine results, other websites, and social media communities. In other words, traditional media plans utilize paid media to achieve marketing objectives. Social publishing relies upon owned media and earned media online to reach these goals.

Just as traditional media plans vary considerably in terms of complexity and sophistication, so too do social publishing strategies. Marketers must determine what content to publish and where and then develop a strategy to maximize exposure to the content through search engine rankings and social sharing. In fact, we can identify two types of optimization that an organization can use (either individually or in combination) with on-site and off-site optimization tactics. Table 6.2 summarizes these levels.

Using search engine optimization (SEO), the process of modifying content, site charac-teristics, and content connections to achieve improved search engine rankings, marketers develop and publish content in ways that improve the likelihood that search engines will rank the sites well in response to search queries. Whereas SEO is all about increasing the prominence of a site on search lists using on-site and off-site tactics, social media optimization (SMO) is a process that makes it more likely for content on a specific social media platform to be more visible and linkable in online communities.[15] If the content is valuable and engaging, other sites will link to it. And people will share it, post it, rank it, tag it, and augment it with their own stories about your brand.

All of this linking activity in turn increases the credibility of the marketer's message— exactly the goal of social publishing. SMO not only provides additional visibility for a marketer's message, it benefits search rankings because it increases the likelihood that others will link to it. Thus, SEO focuses on earning higher organic search engine rank-ings whereas SMO focuses on earning organic links to content. SMO is used by search engine optimizers because those links also improve rankings. The optimization process is so important that it has created an entirely new field of specialists who help organiza-tions to stay afloat in the growing sea of content. Let's take a closer look at each level of social publishing.

Table 6.2   Media Optimization Matrix

TYPE OF OPTIMIZATION	ON-SITE	OFF-SITE
Search engine optimization	Optimizing content value, tags, keywords, titles, URL	Publishing related content elsewhere with links to original
		Creating a linkwheel structure
Social media optimization	Including share tools and RSS feed options	Promoting on social news and social bookmarking sites
		Microblogging
		Promoting social media press releases

Level 1: Social Publishing and Search Engine Optimization

The first level focuses on ways the brand can increase exposure to its online content and drive site traffic by publishing related components of the content across several social sites. These placements include links back to the targeted site. This cross-promotion to the branded content is accomplished with owned media and the placement of related content on media-sharing sites (earned media).

How can a business use different elements of social publishing to multiply its exposure in an inexpensive way? Let's consider the brand SOS (SellOurStuff). SellOurStuff is an eBay reseller of luxury goods. As a promotional tool, SOS might create a branded article, an article that is written to promote SOS's expertise in the field, on "7 Ways to Spot Luxury that (re)Sells." The article is a promotional piece that educates the company's prospects on the types of items SOS could auction successfully while it encourages them to retain SOS as their auctioneer.

The article is a good piece of content—but it won't help SOS unless prospects are exposed to it. SOS publishes the piece on its main website at SOS-SellOurStuff.com, and the company also posts a teaser to the article with a link to the original content on the SOS blog. Next, SOS takes the images from the article and posts them to Flickr (again with a link to the original) and also creates a Prezi slideshow of the content to share at the Prezi site (with again, you guessed it, a link

eBay: © iStock.com/manley099

Photo 6.2

back to the original). Finally, SOS creates a badge that its top clients can post on their own personal webpages to show visitors that they have an "Eye for Luxury." That is, SOS designates these top clients as people who already know the rules for spotting luxury that resells. The SOS badge also links back to the branded content on the SOS website. In this example, SOS created content that promotes its brand message. It then shared the content on its own site and on other sites where it had some control as to what was presented and how it linked back to the branded content. Publishing in multiple places creates additional "opportunities to see" (OTS) for the target audience and brand-controlled links to the targeted site.

At this point, the brand can utilize search engine optimization to improve how its content is listed in response to search queries. These listings are crucial—as you probably know from experience, most people tend to follow up only on the first few results they get from a query. SEO is a complicated technical process, and it's also a bit of a cat-and-mouse game. For example, #1 site Google uses a secret algorithm (a mathematical formula) to decide which sites will appear at the top of a search list. The company changes this formula on a regular basis, so SEO experts engage in a constant contest to figure out the algorithm and then modify their sites to keep up with Google's changes.

Consumers love their search engines. The rankings these search engines generate are crucial because they drive site traffic—and of course traffic is social media's lifeblood. No traffic, no interest. No interest, eventually no site. Sites that attract heavy traffic are valuable for two reasons:

1 A large number of visitors makes it more likely the sponsor will benefit from a higher rate of conversion (i.e., the person browsing actually purchases, so he or she is converted from a browser to a buyer).

2 The more "eyeballs" the site attracts, the more advertising revenue the site can generate (assuming it sells ad space to other advertisers).

SEO is the key tool used for search engine marketing (SEM). SEM refers to a form of online marketing that promotes websites by increasing the visibility of the site's URL in search engine results, both organic and sponsored. Incidentally, there are hundreds of search engines, and some sites that do not feature search as their primary function also offer search engine capabilities. YouTube and Facebook, for instance, are also used for search.[16]

When someone enters a query, the search engine turns to its index for the best matches and then returns a search results list to the user. The results list includes the organic results, which are listings ranked in order of relevance based on the search engine's ranking algorithm, and the sponsored results, which are paid advertising links.

How Do People Use Search Results?

Let's say you've dreamed of owning a high-end designer handbag—the Hermès Birkin. Celebrities and fashionistas carry it, it's always in scarce supply, and a new one can set you back a year's tuition. A brand new Birkin is out—too expensive—but maybe you

FROM BYTES TO BUCKS

Fuse Chicken used social publishing techniques to drive traffic to its Kickstarter campaign for a product called Une Bobine, which is an accessory product for smartphones. At the time of the campaign, the iPhone 5 had not yet been revealed and the blogosphere was abuzz with speculation. Fuse Chicken co-opted this social touch point by creating iPhone 5 computer-generated concept images and even fake specifications. Fuse Chicken pushed the design concepts out into the blogosphere with the requirement that any reposting would include the Fuse Chicken name and a link in the article. The phone concepts were picked up and soon went viral, eventually being covered by news outlets like *Business Insider* and *Mashable*. This generated a lot of traffic to the Fuse Chicken website, which then directed people to the Kickstarter campaign. In the end, the Une Bobine campaign ended up funding to the tune of $212,000, over 20 times the campaign's goal.

can find a used one online. You might visit Yahoo! and enter the search query, "hermes handbags." The search results list leads off with sponsored, or paid, links. In this case, e-retailers such as DesignerPurseOutlets.com and Bluefly.com have paid for sponsored listings. The search results then provide a series of organic listings for Hermès as well as e-tailers such as eBay and The Purse Blog. These sites did not pay to be listed; they are based on the search engine's model for delivering relevant search results. However, in addition to these retailers you may see several merchants that offer counterfeit versions of the bag. Why? Those sites were listed in part because Yahoo!'s algorithm indicated that the content was a good match to your search query. (We'll go into more depth on how this works in a bit.) You might now refine your search, but if it turns out you'd consider a Birkin replica, you might click through to one of the listed sites (and possibly make a purchase, or at a minimum build the site's traffic figures, which will help it earn ad revenue).

As you can imagine, it's very important for a brand or site to appear in a search list so that the shopper will at least consider clicking on the link. Although search engine marketers can buy paid listings from search engines, it's preferable to earn organic results. One reason is that these results have no pay-per-click fees. These are the fees a marketer pays when someone clicks on an online display ad. Organic results also tend to generate more site traffic, presumably because people view them as more credible referrals from the search engine.

Organic entries, especially the first few, garner most of the attention in a typical search. Clickthroughs taper off pretty rapidly, so few people tend to go beyond the first 10 or so. Of course, pages and pages of search results could be returned for any given search—but again, for the most part these won't generate much traffic. For example, the search on Hermès handbags returned a whopping 1,900,000 listings.

We know that people tend to look at the first searches in a list rather than the entire list (few of us would make it to listing number 1,900,000 no matter how badly we wanted that Birkin bag). Still, it's helpful to understand more about which links the user is likely to follow. Researchers use eye-tracking studies to help identify the characteristics of a search page that determine this. They borrow this method from more traditional advertising researchers, who for many years have hooked respondents to sophisticated devices that follow the precise movements of eyeballs as they scan ads on TV or computer screens.

This method shows clearly that most search engine users view only a very limited number of search results. When typical respondents look at a search page, their eyes travel across the top of the search result, return to the left of the screen, and then travel down to the last item shown on the screen without scrolling. On most screens, this means that every user will view the first three search results, but they may or may not scroll down. Search engine marketers call this space on the screen where listings are virtually guaranteed to be viewed the golden triangle.[17] So the real value—the sweet spot—is in earning a list rank that is on the first page, and preferably one of the top three listings ranked. How can a source enhance the probability that its listing will appear near the top? For many organizations, this is (literally) the million dollar question! And that's exactly the point of search engine optimization.

How Search Engines Work

Search listings are produced by search engines using indexed data and an algorithm that determines a listing's relevance to the search query. Search engines use web crawlers (also known as *spiders* and *bots*); these are automated web programs that gather information from sites that ultimately form the search engine's entries. The programs are called crawlers because they crawl websites. They follow all the links, site after site, collecting data until the link network is exhausted. After the bots gather this information, they index (classify) it using labels the sites provide. The indexed data include tags and keywords derived from site content. Then, when someone enters a search query, the search engine applies its algorithm to determine the sites that are most relevant to the search query. This algorithm determines which sites are identified in the search listing and the ranking of the sites presented.

On-Site Optimization

You can see that optimizing content in order to improve search engine rankings is an important marketing task. How do marketers optimize? They use one of two key approaches: (1) on-site optimization or (2) off-site optimization. This is because the bots look for cues on-site, especially tags, and for off-site indicators such as links from other sites as they index data.

On-site, coders try to optimize certain site characteristics (called on-site indicators) that the search bots and the search engine index. In plain English, this means they tinker with elements of the site to make indexing more efficient and ensure that the web crawlers will classify the site the way the developers intend. The primary on-site variables are keywords embedded in the page's tags, title, URL, and content.

Keywords tell the bot what information to gather and specify the relevant topic. The bot will collect this information for the search engine to use in indexing. The keywords explain to the search engine when to deliver your site as a search result. Consequently, choosing the right keywords is critical to ensuring a site shows up in relevant searches. Once you have selected your keywords, you will work them into the areas crawled by the bots—the site's tags, title, URL, and body copy (or content).

For example, say your website sells vintage comic books. To ensure that a buyer who wants to snag a pristine copy of *Adventure Comics #77* featuring Superboy and the Legion of Super-Heroes, published in 1967, will visit your online store, you might code your site with these labels:

- Meta tag: code embedded in a webpage. Meta tags are visible to site visitors but only by viewing the source code for the page. Meta keywords should include three or four of the targeted keywords. The meta description should include two or three sentences that summarize the page content. The description is shown with the search engine listing. The vintage comic book store might include meta tags such as adventure comics, Superboy, superheroes, and vintage.

- Title tag: an HTML tag that defines the page's title. The title is displayed in the browser's title bar, in search engine results, and in RSS feeds. Title tags should include no more than 12 words, with at least two keywords. For example, your website title tags might read: Comics Direct Sales Rare Comics/Vintage Comic Books—Vintage Comics offers comic book collectors vintage adventure comics.

- Heading tag: an HTML tag that is used to section and describe content. Heading tags should include keywords. Tags for heading levels are designated as H1, H2, H3, and so on. Within the webpage, major headings (named for keywords) will be designated with code such that the sections are recognizable to the bots. For example, the first heading on the page will be designated "<h1>This is heading 1</h1>".

- Title: your headline—the main indicator of your page's content. It should be loaded with keywords. Writing optimized titles may seem difficult to some because the style of an optimized title is quite different from that of a story headline a journalist might write. A traditional headline may be indirect; the idea behind a traditional headline is to engage the audience without giving away the story. For instance, a print magazine article about Hermès Birkin bags and the prevalence of high-quality replicas might be titled "High Fashion Replicas Indistinguishable From the Real Thing." An optimized title might read "Shop Wise: 5 Tips for Ensuring That Birkin Is Real, Not Fake, Fashion" to ensure that the search would index on keywords such as Hermès, Birkin, and shop. Another difference is that the title needs to be more literal than the one we might use in an article: bots are pretty smart, but they don't understand metaphors or puns.[18] "Cute" titles such as "How to Keep Birkinstock" or "Counterfeit Hermès Bags Are Birkin Up the Wrong Tree" just won't cut it.

- URL: the website address. To optimize the URL, use a static URL and include the title of the article or the keywords in the URL. Static URLs do not change and they do not include variable scripts. Dynamic URLs are generated from scripts and change over time, making it difficult for people to return to your content later.

Ideally, you'll have a story or topic in mind around when you devise the content. For example, SOS's owner knew that a story explaining how to determine which luxury items will sell and which will bomb would have high value to eBay hobbyists. The story itself should help to determine the keywords, but it shouldn't be the only source. You will also want to include keywords that reflect popular search terms. Before writing the story, the first step is to research the keywords that will help ensure the bots will index the site's data and the algorithm will show relevance to search queries. So, if your "story" is "Sell your luxury used goods with SOS" you may also want to include more general keywords such as "consignment" to be sure potential resellers find it when they search.

How can you generate a strong list of keywords? Keyword research! This process is a critical step to design the content and the site's page for successful search engine optimization. Keyword research involves answering these questions:

- What is the topic of your article? What words and phrases best describe the article?
- What terms are your competitors using as keywords? You can find this out when you analyze their article titles, meta tags, and body copy.
- What words are suggested by keyword generators such as Google AdWords Keyword Tool or The Free Keyword Tool?
- What are the derivatives of your keywords? For example, SOS might pick derivatives of handbags such as bags, purses, clutches, totes, and so on. Free SEO tools such as Google Suggest will offer variations on search terms you may not have thought of.
- How much search volume does the keyword generate compared to other keywords you might use? Is it worth using given the resulting search volume? You can check Google Trends to see how much interest there is in your keywords. This useful tool will show how often the keyword was searched and from which geographic regions.

SEO marketers may want to use long tail keywords. This term refers to multi-phrase search queries.[19] They are much more targeted than a general keyword because they may say exactly what the searcher wants to find. For instance, the long tail keywords for the keyword topic Hermès handbags might include "finding a gently used Hermès Birkin bag," "identifying a fake Birkin," and "best deals on designer handbags." Because the long tail keywords are actual search queries (and you can use the same tools to find these queries as you did to identify your basic keywords), they help to optimize the site.

Off-Site Optimization

Bots don't look only at site information as they index data and feed information back for the search engine's algorithm. They also use other indicators off-site to determine the value of a site's content. These off-site indicators include the number of links to a website from other sites, the credibility of those sites, the type of site promoting the link, and the link text (called anchor text) these sites use. Therefore, search engine optimizers will not stop at tweaking on-site characteristics like the title and meta tags. They will also strive to earn links from high quality sites.

Links are the building blocks of social publishing. The more links to your content, the higher the ranking you will probably receive during a search engine query. There are two approaches to building links. The first approach is to publish related content and links across other sites (branded sites and social media channels). These venues are under the control of the marketer—it is simply a matter of developing the content and identifying where related content and links can be placed to promote traffic to the original site. The second approach is to encourage other, unaffiliated sites to link to the brand's content. This can be accomplished in different ways, such as using affiliate marketing, but we'll address how social media optimization builds unaffiliated links when we discuss level two of social publishing.

Building affiliated links to content is an extension of the first level of social publishing, in which the brand publishes related content with links back to the main site among several branded sites and social media outlets. This is exactly what SOS did in our earlier example. In addition to using links from related content, the marketer will also strategically formulate these links to form a linkwheel. Linkwheels increase the number of links back to a site. They are built on a hub-and-spoke system that uses web properties (i.e., link pages) as spokes to send one link to the home site and another link to the next property. Several properties are set up as spokes; the targeted page is the hub.

Figure 6.4 shows a sample linkwheel for SOS. The linkwheel system ensures that if a user comes to a site and clicks on a link, that site will connect the user to the next hub site and to the next spoke site, and so on. The spoke sites can also be used as a hub in a new linkwheel as new content is developed and published. The result of this tactic is that the main site gains links from other sites with branded content using the linkwheel. When other sites link back to the content, it's called a backlink or a trackback. The site's search ranking benefits then from the increase in the link quantity (this is called link juice). Further, all of the new sites used by the main site to promote it can also be indexed and ranked in searches. If done well, a search engine query could produce a results list with several links to sites owned by the same company.

Linkwheels and other SEO tactics can be used appropriately, but there is room for abuse in this system. Have you watched an episode of *Gunsmoke* on TV Land or an old western on Hulu? Cowboy with a white hat—a hero. Black hat—a villain. This western analogy applies to SEO culture. Social media insiders classify SEO marketers as white, gray, or black hats:[20]

- White hats play by the rules of the system, striving to provide good quality content, with the best use of keywords and tags, and earned links at reputable sites. They create site maps so that every page is linked to every other page and search engine bots can crawl every page.
- Gray hats take some liberties with the system. For example, they will utilize a keyword density (the number of times the keyword is used in the body of a page) that is beyond that of the typical usage of keywords, but below that of true keyword

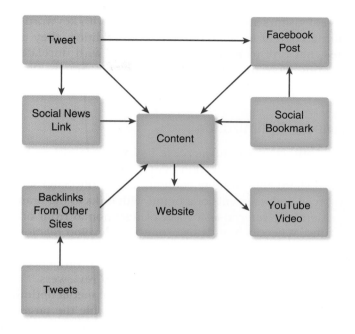

Figure 6.4   SOS Linkwheel Structure

stuffing (the insertion of a superficially large number of keywords throughout a site's content and tags). Gray hats also duplicate content at multiple sites and create link exchanges, where sites agree to link with each other. They may also utilize three-way linking, ensuring that their own sites link to each other in sequence and then back to the original site, and paid links, which are considered somewhat unethical in that linking should be the realm of earned media, not paid.

- Black hats manipulate the system by utilizing several tactics considered unethical in the realm of search engine optimization. For example, with linkwheels, the more spokes in the wheel, the more links to the hub site. Because the search engines rank in part based on number of links, black hats simply set up a massive number of property sites linking to the hub and using the same anchor text. It works. And, it's easy and inexpensive. Software can be used to automatically build thousands of links using social media properties such as Tumblr and WordPress while RSS feeds populate the content. Especially for smaller search engines, a black hat linkwheel can send a site soaring to the top in search rankings. Big search engines such as Google combat the black hats by changing the crawler criteria and the indexing algorithm. If Google sees hundreds of links to a site, it will devalue the link, assuming there's a black hat operating behind the scenes.

Black hats also keyword stuff and place keywords in hidden text by making the font color of keywords the same color as the page background. They may also utilize gateway pages (pages that real visitors are directed past) stuffed with keywords and cloaking (the display of misleading content to search engines). In addition, they utilize link farms—groups of websites that link to each other and pages with unrelated links solely for the purpose of creating more links to the targeted pages. Finally, black hats may spam websites with links.

Level 2: Social Media Optimization

Just as SEO tactics optimize a site to increase its exposure (through links) and search engine rankings, social media optimization (SMO) employs tactics to increase the likelihood that others will share and promote content. Essentially, SMO seeks to leverage the network effect to spread endorsements of a brand with links to the brand's content. These shared links are essentially referrals—a form of testimonial from other players in the social publishing zone. Whereas brands use zone 1 to develop relationships and engage consumers to garner influence impressions, the word-of-mouth communication in zone 2 gains influence posts and referrals to the brand's content. Influence posts are word-of-mouth content from published sources like bloggers and reviewers.

What's the difference between search engine and social media optimization? Both have the same goals—to support inbound marketing and enable the target audience to find and consume the brand content. But SEO is more about finding ways to ensure search engines index the site and to calculate a good result ranking for the content, whereas SMO is about encouraging the sharing of the content.

In other words, SEO focuses on manipulating the processes controlled by the search engines (because even in this social world, Internet users rely heavily on search engines to find information online). In contrast, SMO focuses on building community. SEO efforts target machines. SMO targets people. SMO is especially valuable to marketers because it improves search engine rankings. This happens because bots prefer links, especially high-quality ones. For now at least, search engines tend to rate social media links as higher quality.

As we've seen, sharing behavior is a cultural norm in most online social communities. Content can be promoted on social networks, blogs, microblogs, and social bookmarking and on news sites that use aggregators such as FriendFeed. People can also share links to content in these channels by email. As a result, the potential impact for a piece of content can be huge. That's because as people share links to content with their network, some of those people will consume the content, and some of those will also share the content with their network, and so on.

How do we optimize for social media? As with SEO, there are on-site and off-site tactics.

On-Site Tactics

SMO is all about encouraging people who are exposed to your content to share, promote, and recommend it. To do this, the content needs to be valuable, interesting, or entertaining enough that someone wants to endorse it. We're back to the importance of good content, and you'll learn more about developing good social media content a bit later in this chapter. Aside from the issue of good content, though, we can use the title (as we did with SEO) and other site features to encourage endorsements and sharing. Search engines also consider the quality of a linking site and its type. A site will rank better in search engine results listings if independent sites link to it, and if those sites are of high quality and high relevance.

Let's return to SOS for an example of this process. SOS is a reseller of many types of luxury items. Suppose that one of its blog posts on fashion tips for moms on a budget is picked up by *Dooce*, a funny "mommy blog" that's consistently rated among the top 50 parent blogs online. *Dooce* does a post on the tips article with a link to SOS. It's not long before hundreds of other mommy blogs have linked to the SOS post. Because each of these blogs have their own linkwheel to drive traffic, SOS has a lot of potential to further spread the original post beyond this audience. *Dooce*, for instance, maintains a presence on Facebook and Twitter. A reader might link a *Dooce* tweet to her blog, see the SOS reference, and then link to SOS.

SOS has a winner here in terms of quantity of links. But are these links of high quality? The search engine would rather see links from industry-related sites. Since SOS is a luxury reseller, links from other fashion sites such as *The Bag Blog* would hold more value in the indexing algorithm. That's true unless the linking site is a power site. This label refers to a site with enormous readership, such as CNN.com. If CNN.com runs a story on how moms increasingly focus on saving money but still wish they could feel fashionable, they might reference SOS as a great site for deals. That link is going to be worth a lot of link juice to the search engine.

Title

Our goal is to persuade people to access our content. How do users initially decide whether a site is worth checking out? The most likely candidate is simple: the title. We can enhance interest in content when we compose a catchy title. Social media pros refer to the careful crafting of a title that markets the content as linkbaiting.

To continue the fishing metaphor, let's look more closely at techniques that make linkbaiting effective. You can guess what's coming next: we choose a hook that increases the likelihood that the intended audience will click. Hooks are used to position the content for the target audience. For example, consider this blog post title: "Andy Hagan's Ultimate Guide to Linkbaiting and SMM." Andy could have titled the post, "The Basics of Linkbaiting," but he realized that including a full name, the qualifier "ultimate," and the keywords SMM and Linkbaiting would optimize the title and increase clickthrough rates.

- The resource hook is a common type in social news sites. It refers to content written with the intent to be helpful to the target audience. For example, the Serta mattress company might create an article titled "5 Methods to Ensure a Restful Night's Sleep."
- The contrary hook refutes some accepted belief. Challenging the belief incites people to read the content if only to argue the point. For instance, Weight Watchers might post an article titled "Lose Weight With Chocolate"; the company recognizes that

this will spark an interest from those who believe chocolate cannot possibly be part of a weight loss plan (just too good to be true).

- The humor hook is designed to show that the content will entertain. For example, the *DietBlog* posted a blog called, "Obese Skunk Cuts Out Bacon Sandwiches."[21]
- The giveaway hook promises something for free. In other words, it embeds a sales promotion, an incentive offered to encourage a specific behavior response in a specific time period, into the content. For example, our Weight Watchers' article could have been titled "Save $50 Doing What's Good for You!"
- The research hook offers a claim about something of interest. For example, our Weight Watchers' article might claim, "66% of Americans are overweight, but you don't have to be."

Titles are just as important to video content! That's why the viral video for Smart Water touted the title, "Jennifer Aniston Sex Tape."

Share Tools

People are more likely to connect to our content (using that call to action we discussed earlier) if we make it easy for them to follow through. Share tools are plug-ins that appear as clickable icons on a website and enable the viewer to bookmark or share the page with many social networking, social news, and social bookmarking sites. Plug-ins are third-party applications that "plug in" to a main site to add some form of functionality. In this case, the functionality is the ability to easily share the site's content with external sites. Many social media sites offer their own site-specific plug-in (Facebook has a Like plug-in; Twitter offers a Tweet This button; Digg has a Smart Digg button) or a site may wish to utilize a multi-share tool such as Share This or Sexy Bookmarks.

Social media are about community, so reciprocity matters. Remember the Golden Rule you learned as a child: "Do unto others as you would have them do unto you." You'll want to reward those who link to you by including trackbacks, which promote those who promote your content. When someone links to your site, you'll post a trackback on your site to theirs. The trackback gives attribution to sites linking to you. It can be a method of communication between bloggers but, importantly, it provides an easy way to acknowledge those who send traffic to the brand's site by reciprocating their kindness.

RSS Feeds

Syndicate content with an RSS feed, a tool to automatically feed new published content to subscribers. Enhancing the ease of content distribution with an RSS feed makes it easy for others to consume new content as it is offered by having that content feed directly into their feed reader or email.

Off-Site Optimization

Social media suffer from an embarrassment of riches—there's way too much content available for people to process on their own. Millions of tweets are posted daily. There are hundreds of thousands of blogs. There are also corporate white papers, articles from online publishers, and other valuable content available online. Thus, the average consumer can easily be overwhelmed or simply miss valuable sources of information. That's why it's important for social media marketers to optimize their socially published content. We can optimize off-site for social media in three key ways. First, we can publish a social media press release to promote our content. Second, we can use a microblog to encourage sharing of our announcements. Third, the content can be promoted on social news and bookmarking sites.

The Social Media Press Release

A press release is an announcement public relations professionals issue to the news media to let the public know of company developments. For social media marketers, a release is also a key tool, but a social media press release is structured a bit differently. It should have an optimized title, good keywords and tags, links to the main site landing page, RSS feed options, share buttons, and embeddable multimedia content that can be shared on several networks, in addition to the typical press release content. That's right—a press release is social when it has been prepared in a way that ensures the content is shareable. Figure 6.5 provides a template for a social media press release.

An organization can publish a social media press release on distribution sites such as PRWeb and Pressit, both social media news release services. In addition, organizations with a corporate blog should also post the social media press release on the blog so that it can be indexed easily by search engines.

Microblogs

Whereas blogs share a story, microblogs share headlines. That's probably one reason that Twitter, the leading microblog service, defines itself as a real-time information network. Microblog posts can be useful for reminder communications and ensuring top-of-mind awareness, but they can also provide valuable links, direct traffic, and build credibility and reputation. Brands can post their own links, but social media optimization comes into play when brands figure out ways to encourage others to retweet the message. This may be as simple as offering content valuable enough that others wish to retweet it or asking followers to retweet. Or it may mean offering an incentive to share the links.

Social News and Bookmarking Sites

Have you read current news on Digg or bookmarked online articles for research using Diigo? Digg and Reddit are two leading social news communities. Social news communities

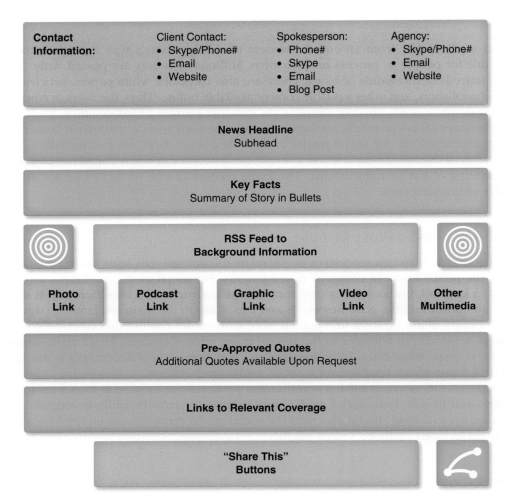

Contact Information:	Client Contact: • Skype/Phone# • Email • Website	Spokesperson: • Phone# • Skype • Email • Blog Post	Agency: • Skype/Phone# • Email • Website

News Headline
Subhead

Key Facts
Summary of Story in Bullets

RSS Feed to Background Information

Photo Link	Podcast Link	Graphic Link	Video Link	Other Multimedia

Pre-Approved Quotes
Additional Quotes Available Upon Request

Links to Relevant Coverage

"Share This" Buttons

Figure 6.5   A Template for a Social Media Press Release

share and promote online news. Diigo is a social bookmarking site. Social bookmarking sites save your bookmarks online so they are always available wherever you have online access. They are social because these bookmarks can be shared and the collective intelligence can promote a bookmark to other interested members. They are very similar, with social news focused more on content distribution and social bookmarks more intent upon the organization of content.

Social news and bookmarking communities play an invaluable role, because they filter vast amounts of information into sets that individuals can manage. In many cases this process is as simple as if a trusted friend told you she personally visited 10 ski resorts, and then she suggested the three she was sure you would like. You still might pick and choose among the three, but there's no way you could have considered the original 10 anyway, so you're happy to take her word for it. Imagine how much happier you'd be if five other friends gave you the same recommendations!

Social news websites are social communities that allow their users to submit news stories, articles, and multimedia files including videos and pictures so the submissions can be shared with other users and the general public. Submissions receive enhanced attention and visibility if they get a lot of votes from users. Social bookmarking communities are similar to social news communities in that users can share material from around the Internet with each other, and the size and influence of a user's network affects the ultimate influence of the resource in question. However, those who use social news sites put a priority on message promotion, whereas those who use social bookmarking sites place a priority on organizing the links they want to save and store. Users store and organize bookmarks (using tags) to online source materials within the social bookmarking site (instead of storing bookmarks with one's Web browser) to make the information easily sortable, retrievable, and accessible.

These communities uphold the principles of media democratization. Individuals determine what material is disseminated throughout the community, as well as the value ratings associated with the material. Users act as editors; they identify what material should be pushed to the featured areas of the site. The process supports the wisdom of crowds perspective we discussed in Chapter 1, in that individual users recommend and vote on submissions. The site then uses algorithms to filter content and determine the popularity of a story. The algorithms include number of votes received as well as other factors such as the richness of the discussion related to the story. The system ensures each individual has a voice, if he or she chooses to use it, but it also enables some voices to be heard louder than others. The most active and respected participants, the influencers or opinion leaders that we discussed in Chapter 4, come to hold positions of high authority in the community.

Although there's always the potential to manipulate the voting system (like ballot box stuffing in the physical world), the algorithms minimize this threat by seeking to identify voting campaigns (in which voters are incentivized to vote for a story). In addition, some social news websites have editorial staff who review stories and award featured positions for relevant, newsworthy stories (though bookmarking sites generally do not). There are more than 100 such sites. Digg, Reddit, Mix, Propell, Diigo, and Furl are some of the major players.

Planning a Social News Campaign

Choosing the communities to seed and target can be difficult. There are several social news sites and social bookmarking sites, just as there are several social networks. Depending on the campaign's objectives and target audience, it may make sense to focus on the leading sites or alternatively to find a niche site that attracts a smaller number of passionate participants. The community should also be evaluated for quality and engagement. Inactive or weak communities will not offer the social support necessary to propel a successful social news marketing campaign. Consider this list of community characteristics when evaluating the desirability of a community target:

1   What is the community's focus (general news, specific topics)?

2   How many active users are involved in the community? What kind of traffic does the site receive?

3   How active are the top users on the site?

4   How many comments on average are generated for each new submission?

5   How many votes are required to earn front page status on the site?

6   Are stories on the site's front page recent? How rapid is story turnover?

7   Are there limitations for branded content in the community's Terms of Service?

8   What have others (such as bloggers) said about the social news site?

Just as journalists receive pitches for content from public relations specialists who pitch stories that promote specific brands, influential social news users may receive pitches for branded content. The influencer's referral is valuable because she provides an unbiased, third-party word-of-mouth endorsement of the content. The process of influencing the influencers follows the traditional public relations model that gets information to be distributed into the hands of those in a position to distribute it to a large number of people. The key to success is to ensure that the content pitched is relevant to the people it targets.

Just as most people do not appreciate hearing from a friend only when she needs a favor, influencers as a group are unlikely to respond well to obvious pitches from social media marketers. Just like a good salesperson in the physical world, the effective social media marketer understands that it's important to build a relationship with the other person *before* he or she offers a sales proposition. Some care must be taken to introduce oneself, acknowledge the contributions the influencer makes to the community, and flatter the influencer's judgment and expertise in making high-quality content submissions. The influencer will be helping the brand by virtue of the content submission and vote, so it can be useful to help the influencer by offering other content that will be perceived as desirable prior to pitching the branded content. And don't simply send along your social media press release. Instead, a more personal pitch that emphasizes knowledge of the influencer's recommendation patterns and the marketer's relationship to the branded content is likely to be effective.

THE DARK SIDE OF SOCIAL MEDIA

John Chow is a blogger and Internet entrepreneur who lives in Vancouver, British Columbia. He has 50,000 Twitter followers; on a typical day he shared with them a photo of his lunch, discussed the local weather, linked to a new post on his business blog—and then earned $200 by advising his followers where to buy customized M&M's candies. How does he make these hookups? He partners with specialized companies that link his Twitter stream to advertisers that want to plug in to his base. The co-founder of one such firm, Peer2, defends this practice: "We don't want to create an army of spammers, and we are not trying to turn Facebook and Twitter into one giant spam network. All we are trying to do is get consumers to become marketers for us."[22]

It's fine to get employees to "seed" content, so long as they identify themselves as such and avoid sockpuppeting. Sockpuppeting is the term used to describe people who take on a fictional identity when promoting content online. Such behavior crosses an ethical line.[23] But is it ethical to "bribe" supposedly objective bloggers to endorse your content with money or freebies? The Federal Trade Commission (FTC) doesn't think so. The practice of compensating bloggers who write product reviews for categories from diapers to movies has become so widespread that the FTC was forced to issue guidelines to regulate it. For example, Microsoft got into hot water a few years ago when it gave away free laptops to potential reviewers. The rationale for the company to hand out valuable hardware is pretty obvious: It's hard to bite the hand that feeds you, so people may be more inclined to post a positive review of a product they got courtesy of the manufacturer.

Now the FTC says that bloggers must disclose any compensation they receive in exchange for a product review—these rules already apply to broadcast TV, newspapers, and magazines. An FTC official observes, "We look at it from the perspective of the consumer and the principle being that a consumer has the right to know when they're being pitched a product. It doesn't matter whether it's an email or Twitter or someone standing on a street corner." A blogger who violates this edict risks a fine of up to $11,000 per incident. He'd need a lot of freebies to make that worthwhile. The guidelines don't worry power users who already disclose this information. For example, as we mentioned earlier, the *Moms* bloggers are a group of moms Walmart put together who receive free merchandise from the retailer's suppliers; they have been flown to special events by Frito-Lay, Johnson & Johnson, and other companies. Christine Young, one of the moms, already disclosed these relationships on her posts, and she agrees with the new rules: "The brands and companies directly working with bloggers need to be held accountable. While some companies may choose not to work with us now, I would much rather work with companies that wanted us to be open in the first place." However, other bloggers question the limits of these guidelines. As one observes, "If I get a free tube of toothpaste in the mail and say nice things about it on Twitter, Facebook, or in a PTA meeting, do I have to disclose it as a freebie or pay the $11,000 fine the FTC imposes? What kind of disclosure can one fit into a 140-character Twitter message, anyway?"[24]

CHAPTER SUMMARY

What are the channels of social publishing?

The channels of social publishing include blogs, media-sharing sites, microsharing sites, social bookmarking sites, and social news sites, as well as owned media sites with social components.

Who creates the content published in social channels? What kind of content can be published?

Anyone can create the content published in social channels. Content can be editorial, commercial, or user-generated. Content appears in a variety of different formats such as blog posts and feature articles, microblog posts, press releases, white papers, case studies, ebooks, newsletters, videos, webinars and presentations, podcasts, and photos.

What content characteristics enhance perceived content quality and value? How can marketers plan and organize their efforts as they embrace a social publishing strategy?

As Figure 6.3 shows, we can characterize content in terms of its originality and substance. The higher the level of originality and substance, the higher readers will perceive the content's quality and value to be. The lowest level of quality and value is associated with filler content, which is content resourced from elsewhere. Original content is of higher value than filler content, but can range from basic original content to the highest quality level, called flagship content. Marketers can utilize an editorial calendar to organize their ideas and content across several publishing sites.

What is the role of social publishing in social media marketing? How do social media marketers utilize search engine optimization and social media optimization to meet marketing objectives?

Social publishing enables marketers to distribute branded content. Also called content marketing, this approach helps to bring consumers to the brand's sites. Because consumers utilize search engines to find information online, using search engine optimization to improve search engine rankings is an important marketing task. Thus, when we publish content, the content should be optimized for search engines. We also want people to link to our site; a form of referral. This is the goal of social media optimization.

How can social content be promoted? What role do social news and social bookmarking sites play in content promotion?

Social content can be promoted with social media press releases, microblog posts, and social news and social bookmarking sites. The press release and microblog posts encourage sharing among interested people and provide links to the original content. Social news sites enable a way to share links to the content and to promote the content through community rankings. Social bookmarks also enable shared links and a form of content quality ranking.

KEY TERMS

AdWords
affiliate marketing
aggregators
algorithm
anchor text
authority-building content
backlink
black hats
call to action
citizen advertising
cloaking
commercial message
consumer-solicited content
   (CSC)
content
content value ladder
contrary hook
conversion
counterfeit conversations
cultural co-creation
definition article
dynamic URLs
editorial calendar
editorial message
eye-tracking studies
filler content
flagship content
gateway pages
giveaway hook

glossary article
golden triangle
gray hats
heading tag
hook
humor hook
incentivized content
indexed data
keyword generators
keyword research
keyword stuffing
keywords
link exchanges
link farms
link juice
linkbaiting
links
linkwheels
list article
long tail keywords
media plan
meta tag
microblog
off-site indicators
on-site indicators
organic
organic content
original content
paid links

pay-per-click
pillar content
plug-ins
power site
research hook
resource hook
search engine marketing (SEM)
search engine optimization
   (SEO)
share tools
social bookmarking
social media optimization
   (SMO)
social media press release
social publishing zone
sockpuppeting
spokesbloggers
sponsored
sponsored conversations
theory article
three-way linking
title
title tag
trackback
urban legends
URLs
voting campaigns
web crawlers
white hats

REVIEW QUESTIONS

1 What is social publishing? What kinds of content can be published socially?

2 Explain the difference between inbound and outbound marketing.

3 How can social publishing, along with SEO and SMO, help to meet marketing objectives?

4 How can a site be optimized for search engines?

5 Why is it important to achieve a top three ranking in a list of search engine results?

6 Explain the concept of the linkwheel.

7 What are the different types of tags that are used by search engine optimizers to influence search engine indexing?

8 What role does social media optimization play for search engine optimization? How are the two concepts related?

9 Explain the five types of linkbait and why linkbaiting is important.

10 Is there a difference between social news sites and social bookmarking sites? Explain.

EXERCISES

1 Visit a website of your choice.

A Go through the website to identify the components that were strategically optimized using SEO and SMO techniques. What could have been done to optimize the site further? Print out a screen image and label the page for in-class discussion.

B Identify the keywords you think would be good tags for the site.

C Run a search query using the keywords. Does the site show up in the first page of rankings? In the top three? Why do you think the site was successful (or not)?

D While you're on the search results page, take a look at the sponsored and organic results listings. How do they differ? Which would be most influential if you had been conducting a real search?

2 Visit Blogger or WordPress and sign up for a free blogging account. Complete your profile and add the standard blog components to your blog layout.

A Now write your first post (your instructor may assign a topic or you can start with one of the review questions).

B Optimize your post using the techniques described in the chapter.

C Create your own social media linkwheel with the pages you have in your digital footprint.

D   Try to get your content to spread through the network effect by seeding the content and drawing upon the influencers already in your network.

3   Register for a social bookmarking site and a social news site. You can choose which ones you wish to use. Once you've completed your profiles on the two sites, be sure to add your new activity to your digital footprint.

4   Visit the social bookmarking site you joined and look up a topic of interest for you. Select 10 headlines that have been saved by other users. Classify the headlines according to the type of linkbait used in their title. Anecdotally, does it seem like there is a relationship between the number of users who have bookmarked the content and the type of linkbait used? Explain.

5   Visit Google's free SEO tools, listed below. Enter several search terms to see how they present information to you on keywords, trends, and phrases.

A   Google Suggest

B   Google Keywords

C   Google Trends

6   Read the FTC "Guides Concerning the Use of Endorsements and Testimonials for Advertising" at www.ftc.gov/os/2009/10/091005revisedendorsementguides.pdf. How will the guides affect your own brand mentions in social spaces?

CHAPTER NOTES

1   "State of the Blogosphere Report," *Technorati*, November 3, 2010, http://technorati.com/blogging/article/state-of-the-blogosphere-2010-introduction/page-3/, accessed December 25, 2010.

2   "Who's Blogging What: Better Business Blogging in 2011," *HubSpot*, http://www.hubspot.com/ebooks/better-business-blogging-in-2011/, accessed December 19, 2010.

3   Heather Armstrong, *Dooce*, http://www.dooce.com, accessed January 1, 2011.

4   David Armano, *Logic + Emotion*, http://darmano.typepad.com/, accessed January 1, 2011.

5   Annika Darling, "The 10 Top Earning Bloggers in the World," *The Richest*, February 2, 2014, http://www.therichest.com/rich-list/world/worlds-10-top-earning-bloggers/, accessed March 5, 2014.

6   David Silverman, "FCC Increasing Fines for Violations of Children's Programming Rules—Fines as High as $70,000 per Station Issued," *Broadcast*

(Continued)

(Continued)

Law Blog, May 29, 2010, http://www.broadcastlawblog.com/2010/05/articles/childrens-programming-and-adve/fcc-increasing-fines-for-violations-of-childrens-programming-rules-fines-as-high-as-70000-per-station-issued/, accessed June 25, 2010.

7   Susan G. Fournier, Michael R. Solomon, and Basil G. Englis, "Brand Resonance," in B. H. Schmitt and D. L. Rogers, eds., *Handbook on Brand and Experience Management* (Cheltenham, UK, and Northampton, MA: Edward Elgar, 2009).

8   Jon Fine, "Lonelygirl15: A Likely Scenario," *BusinessWeek.com*, August 27, 2006, http://www.businessweek.com/innovate/FineOnMedia/archives/2006/08/lonelygirl15_th_1.html, accessed December 31, 2010.

9   Ryan Grim and Arthur Delaney, "Linda Tirado, Author of Viral Essay on Poverty, Invited to White House," *Huffington Post*, April 30, 2014, http://www.huffingtonpost.com/2014/04/30/linda-tirado-white-house_n_5239833.html, accessed May 5, 2014.

10 Shannon Harrell, "#Sweepstakes and #Contest #Entries on Pinterest Are Endorsements, Says FTC; Implications Beyond Pinterest," *Information Law Group,* http://www.infolawgroup.com/2014/04/articles/ftc/sweepstakes-and-contest-entries-on-pinterest-are-endorsements-says-ftc-implications-beyond-pinterest/, accessed May 28, 2014.

11 Chris Garrett, "Diggbait, Linkbait, Flagship Content and Authority," *chrisg.com*, February 11, 2008, http://www.chrisg.com/diggbait-linkbait-flagship-content-and-authority/, accessed December 25, 2010.

12 Tim O'Reilly, "What Is Web 2.0?" *O'Reilly Media*, September 30, 2005, http://oreilly.com/web2/archive/what-is-web-20.html, accessed January 1, 2011.

13 "What Type of Content Is Most Popular on Digg, Reddit, Propeller, Delicious, and StumbleUpon," *Social Media Trader*, December 29, 2007, http://socialmediatrader.com/analysis-what-type-of-content-is-most-popular-on-digg-reddit-propeller-delicious-and-stumbleupon/, accessed June 24, 2010.

14 Joe Pulizzi, "100 Content Marketing Examples," Content Marketing Institute, http://www.contentmarketinginstitute.com, accessed May 15, 2014.

15 Rohit Bargava, "5 Rules of Social Media Optimization (SMO)," *Influential Marketing Blog*, August 5, 2006, http://rohitbhargava.typepad.com/weblog/2006/08/5_rules_of_soci.html, accessed January 1, 2011.

16 comScore, January 15, 2010, http://www.comscore.com/Press_Events/Press_Releases/2010/1/comScore_Releases_December_2009_U.S._Search_Engine_Rankings, accessed December 25, 2010.

17 Chris Sherman, "A New F-Word for Google Search Results," *Search Engine Watch*, March 7, 2005, http://searchenginewatch.com/3488076, accessed June 29, 2010.

18 "SEO for Journalists: Headlines & Body Copy," *SEOMoz.org*, April 13, 2007, http://www.seomoz.org/ugc/seo-for-journalists-headlines-body-copy-part-2-of-5, accessed June 29, 2010.

19 "How to Find and Target Long Tail Keywords for More Search Engine Traffic," *Dosh Dosh*, http://www.doshdosh.com/how-to-target-long-tail-keywords-increase-search-traffic/, accessed July 1, 2010.

20 Linking Strategies, http://www.webhostingtalk.com/wiki/Linking_strategies#Three-way_linking, accessed December 25, 2010.

21 Ali Hale, "Obese Skunk Cuts Out Bacon Sandwiches," *The Diet Blog*, January 2, 2010, http://www.diet-blog.com/10/obese_skunk_cuts_out_bacon_sandwiches.php, accessed December 25, 2010.

22 Quoted in Brad Stone, "PING: A Friend's Tweet Could be an Ad", *New York Times*, November 21, 2009, www.nytimes.com/2009/11/22/business/22ping.html, accessed July 6, 2010.

23 Brad Stone and Matt Richtel, "The Hand that Controls the Sock Puppet Could get Slapped", *New York Times*, July 16, 2007, www.nytimes.com/2007/07/16/technology/16blog.html, accessed January 1, 2011.

24 Quoted in Amy Schatz and Miguel Bustillo, "U.S. Seeks to Restrict Gift Giving to Bloggers", *Wall Street Journal*, October 6, 2009, http://online.wsj.com/article/SB125475547130664753.html, accessed July 6, 2010.

7 Social Entertainment

LEARNING OBJECTIVES

When you finish reading this chapter you will be able to answer these questions:

1 How can social media marketers use social entertainment to meet branding objectives? What are the types of social entertainment? Why is social entertainment an effective approach for engaging target audiences?

2 What is branded entertainment? How is it distinguished from content marketing used in social publishing?

3 What are the characteristics of social games and gamer segments? How can marketers effectively use social games? How are alternate reality games different from other social games?

4 In what ways are marketers using social music, social television, and social celebrity to share brand messaging?

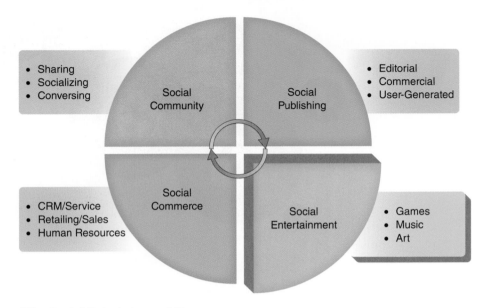

Figure 7.1   Social Entertainment Zone

The Social Entertainment Zone

Have you played Candy Crush? Felt addicted to Pet Rescue Saga? Maybe you get your music fix on Spotify and watch and chat about your favorite television shows on TVTag. The third zone of social media is social entertainment. Broadly, social entertainment encompasses the digital and social forms of media that are otherwise addressed by the entertainment industry. By that, we mean that social entertainment channels are digitally connected, participatory, and shareable. As such, social entertainment includes social games, socially enabled video games, alternate reality games, social music, and social television and film. Marketers can use aspects of social entertainment in several ways. As paid media, marketers can buy advertising space in and around the source of entertainment. This is not truly social media but instead feeds on the power of social entertainment properties. Product placements within social entertainment vehicles can also be arranged. Brands can sponsor entertainment content in social channels. Lastly, brands can create *owned* vehicles of social entertainment by creating branded content (a category of branded entertainment) whether it be games, music, or film. This option is known as branded entertainment. We will focus on *social* branded entertainment but keep in mind that branded entertainment also exists in traditional media.

Branded entertainment is a subset of content marketing. Content marketing is also the basis for social publishing strategies utilizing relevant, high-value information desired by the target audience, as we discussed in Chapter 6. However, for branded entertainment, the content seeks to capture attention and retain that attention for a prolonged period of time (at least compared to the standard 30-second ads) and to do so by entertaining the audience. Social branded entertainment goes a step farther to encourage the audience to interact with the content and to share the content and their interactive experience with the content with their social graphs. Social branded entertainment is thought to generate word-of-mouth communication about the respective brand as social interactions occur among users.[1] In Chapter 1, Chipotle's extensive use of social media was highlighted. One core aspect of that approach was social branded entertainment

Photo 7.1

in the form of a social game and a film series published on Hulu. Branded entertainment, whether social or not, is original content (just as we discussed in Chapter 6).

The value of owned content with social capabilities is clearly noted not only by brands using this approach to market non-entertainment offerings but also by content producers.

For instance, Netflix has repositioned itself as a developer of original content with Netflix Originals programming produced and distributed exclusively by Netflix, like *Orange Is the New Black* and *House of Cards*. The Netflix Social Sharing app enables viewers to share and discuss what they're watching in Facebook. The social component enhances the viewing experience while providing a channel for word-of-mouth (WOM) communication about the show and Netflix. Media-sharing sites traditionally thought of as social publishing venues with social media components built in are creating their own entertainment vehicles. This can be seen with YouTube's entry into original content.

Brands can also produce curated entertainment, just as they can develop curated content that is informative. Rather than buying ads in and around entertainment properties or producing original branded entertainment, the value of curated entertainment for the target audience is the access to a collection of entertainment that is relevant for the consumer. The value for the brand is the ability to use the social entertainment zone without the expenses of paid media space or content production.

This brings us to the need to distinguish between social publishing and social entertainment. Both utilize the principles of content marketing to some extent (but not entirely). Just as advertising has been associated with the goals of informing and/or entertaining, so too is content marketing. The content marketing aspects of social publishing are focused on the goal of informing. The content marketing aspects of social entertainment are focused on the goal of entertaining. As a review, remember that social publishing is most akin to traditional media in that any one (whether brand, news organization, or individual) can publish content in online channels. These channels may be part of a media-sharing site or owned media such as a blog. Across socially published content, the primary goal is to express a point of view (POV) via information. For brands, this POV is an opportunity to build reputation, encourage positive WOM about the brand,

and share relevant information. Social entertainment is most akin to the entertainment industry, which provides amusement, distraction, and escape to audiences. In the marketing context, brands add value by producing social entertainment venues or leveraging popular social entertainment venues to reach an audience.

Social Entertainment as Play

Entertainment can be thought of in the context of play and brands that utilize entertainment as a channel (whether via paid or owned media) are ingratiating themselves into the consumers' realm of play.[2] Individuals voluntarily choose to actively participate in entertainment media just as they may other enjoyable activities – they play! Play and the motivations for individuals to participate include power, identity, fantasy, and frivolity. These four aspects of play are present in social entertainment and make Play Theory relevant for our study of the social entertainment zone: social entertainment that builds on the 'play as power' concept provides participants with a competitive task. Play as identity provides symbolic benefits to the participant in that the form of entertainment is self-expressive, reveals affinities and interests, and provides for a sense of affiliation. Social music and social film are largely thought to be most relevant to those who are motivated by play as identity. Play as fantasy encourages participants to engage in creative, imaginative experiences. Play as frivolity provides for fun, plain and simple. The goal is not challenging but relaxing. These four aspects of play are easily identifiable in all components of social entertainment. To the extent that we can understand why consumers engage in social entertainment, as marketers, we can then find ways to provide value for those target audiences that are consistent with our brand message and marketing objectives.

Social Entertainment and Marketing Objectives

Why are brands turning to social entertainment? Edelman's Brand Engagement in the Era of Social Entertainment Survey found that 34% of people and 52% of those between 18 and 34 years old perceive value in online branded entertainment.[3] It is because of this perception of value that people seek out social entertainment and choose to engage with it. All forms of social entertainment, whether branded or not, provide for a more immersive and longer-lasting experience with the brand. In this chapter, we'll explore how brands can use social games, social music, and social television to meet branding objectives.

Social Games

Social games make up the largest active area of social entertainment. At their core, they are games but, importantly, they are social—that is to say, they are digital, interactive, and shareable online with one's network. The context of a social game revolves around goal-oriented activity with defined rules of engagement and online connectivity among a community of players. Estimates vary but one source claims that 500 million people play social games. Social game revenues worldwide are estimated at $12 billion.[4]

What makes a game social is largely what makes *any* form of social media social—the existence of and participation in a community and sharing within the community. Games are social when players share their game play with others. This means that by definition social games are multiplayer games. The social components of the game will be enhanced if there is communication among the players, tools to share activities and achievements, and methods to encourage others to join in the play. Therefore, we define a social game as a multiplayer, competitive, goal-oriented activity with defined rules of engagement and online connectivity among a community of players. Most social games include a few key elements:

- *Leaderboards:* a listing of the leaders in the game competition
- *Achievement badges:* symbols awarded to show game levels achieved and shared with the community
- *Friend (buddy) lists* with chat: a list of contacts with whom one plays and the ability to communicate within the game

The characteristics that appeal to serious gamers—the sense of competition and immersion within a dedicated community of players—can be heightened with the addition of social elements. And, people who once felt games were nothing more than a waste of time for teenage boys who huddle in basements among discarded pizza boxes now find casual, social games an enjoyable way to chase away boredom, spend time online with friends, and, quite simply, play.

Gamer Segments

At one time, we could easily categorize gamers based on the centrality of gaming in their lives. Gamers were either casual or hardcore, and the games they played reflected this division within the gaming community. Casual gamers played casual games and hardcore gamers played core games. Casual games are distinguished by low barriers to entry. They require only a small amount of time per session, are easy to learn, and are readily available online. For example, someone who wants to play Pet Rescue Saga can just hop online and start matching gemstones for whatever brief time he or she has available. Most casual, social games even offer a mobile app for those who want to play while they wait in line at the grocery store. That's because mobile use of casual, social games is the most popular game variant. Among active gamers, 44% report playing games on a smartphone. In fact, estimates suggest that 32% of the time people spend on a smartphone is dedicated to game play.

In contrast, a core game such as Call of Duty: Ghost requires a much larger time investment. Core games typically require extended lengths of time per game-play session (90 minutes to several hours), are highly immersive, and demand advanced skills for ongoing play. They may be available online, or may have specific hardware and software requirements. Hardcore gamers value realism in the game's contextual clues and challenge in the game's activities; casual gamers value ease of use and immediate gratification. Although the stereotypes of casual versus hardcore gamers still hold some truth, social games are blurring the distinctions between these two types, and indeed they are bringing new gamers (and crossover games) into the mix.

Gaming is not limited to male teens, as most of us assume. Jason Allaire, co-director of the Gains Theory Gaming Lab said, "There is no longer a 'stereotypical game player,' but instead a game player could be your grandparent, your boss, or even your professor."[5] Let's take a look at the demographic characteristics of gamers.[6] Today a staggering 72% of American households play computer and video games. The gender mix of gamers no longer skews male (52 % male, 48% female). As a rule, women tend to prefer games that stress relationships (such as The Sims). The average gamer is 31 years old with 14 years of gaming experience. Thirty-nine percent of gamers are over 35. The number of female gamers 50 and older is a fast-growing segment that is expected to continue growing as seniors recognize the value of gaming as a social entertainment experience. Historically, casual gamers trend older and female whereas hardcore gamers skew younger and male. Early studies on social gamers suggest that a single profile would paint a picture that looks very similar to that of the casual gamer (and most social games share the characteristics of casual games). That said, the sheer number of people playing social games means that social games pull from both types of gamers (as well as recruiting a new breed of gamer who developed an interest in games within the context of social media).

There are differences in the dedication of gamers to their respective games, but overall games exhibit a high degree of stickiness. As a reminder, stickiness describes the ability of a medium to attract an audience and keep that audience. Game designers attribute stickiness to design: games are designed with a compulsion loop such that every action you experience produces a response that makes you want to do it again.[7] When we feel pleasure, a substance called dopamine is released in our brains. Common addictions including sex, nicotine, and gambling all stimulate dopamine production. Gamers as a cohort tend to be dedicated hobbyists who spend countless hours embroiled in intense games (yes, in some cases even while they pretend to work at the office or study in the library). People are passionate about games. In fact, gamers spend more time gaming online than they do on the Internet in all other activities except social networking—which is increasingly linked to game activity.[8] Online gaming even surpasses email in terms of average time spent weekly on the activity.

Casual gamers do spend less time on games each week than do core gamers, but even in these cases eMarketer estimates that 34% of gamers spend more than 4 hours a week playing games, 8% spend about 3 hours, 17% spend about 2 hours, and 9% spend 1 hour. That's a lot of game time—and a lot of opportunities for brands to interact with prospective customers.[9]

Gaming involves more than an investment of time, however. These activities require attention and active involvement. Unlike many other forms of media consumption, players are not likely to be multitasking during a game or consuming multiple forms of media simultaneously. Gamers aren't texting, talking, or using the remote to channel surf when they're engrossed in killing orcs or acquiring farmland. Many gamers play through *game consoles*.

The game console is one of the reasons we increasingly see a socialization of other forms of broadcast media. The Entertainment Software Association reported that 50% of people with a game console also used the console to watch movies and 26% also used the console to watch television programming. All in all, we can safely say that gaming is a viable medium to market promotional messages. Games meet all of the criteria for viable market segmentation:

- The market is substantial, reachable, and measurable.
- The gaming demographic has broadened so that games are now considered viable vehicles to reach women and older consumers as well as young males.
- Gamers spend sufficient, dedicated time with games to achieve valuable ad impressions.

How We Categorize Social Games

Game design is built upon several layers, including platform, mode, milieu, and genre.[10] In fact, any platform can potentially support a social game environment. If the game can operate as multiplayer and includes online connectivity for communication and sharing among the players, it is social. Let's take a closer look at the dimensions we use to characterize games.

Game Platforms

A game platform refers to the hardware systems on which the game is played. Game platforms include game consoles (consoles are interactive, electronic devices used to display video games such as Sony's PlayStation, Microsoft's Xbox, and Nintendo's Wii), computers (including both online games and those that require software installation on the player's computer hard drive), and portable devices that may include smartphones or

devices specifically for game play such as the Sony PSP or Nintendo DS.[11] However, it's important to keep in mind that social games often appear on multiple platforms: gamers have a strong tendency to use two or more platforms, so marketers can reach them as they move back and forth.

Game controllers © iStock.com/MrKornFlakes

Mode and Milieu

Mode refers to the way the game world is experienced. It includes aspects such as whether a player's

Photo 7.2

activities are highly structured, whether the game is single player or multiplayer, whether the game is played in close physical proximity to other players (or by virtual proximity), and whether the game is real-time or turn-based.[12] Milieu describes the visual nature of the game, such as science fiction, fantasy, horror, and retro.

Genres

The genre of a game refers to the method of play. Popular genres include simulation, strategy, action, and role-playing. Each of these genres is represented in the game market whether the games are casual, core, or social games.

- Simulation games attempt to depict real-world situations as accurately as possible. There are several subgenres including racing simulators, flight simulators, and "Sim" games that enable the players to simulate the development of an environment. Among social games, simulations include FarmVille, Pet Resort, and FishVille. Gamers trace most of the innovations in today's simulation games to the pioneering Sim City game.
- Action games consist of two major subgenres: first-person shooters (FPS) where you "see" the game as your avatar sees it and *third-person games*. Contextually there is little difference in these subgenres given the extent to which gamers identify with their avatars. The avatar acts as a virtual prosthetic connecting the player and the environment.[13] Action games are performative in that the player chooses an action that the game then executes. The actions may revolve around battles, sports, gambling, and so on. Examples of social action games are Epic Goal (a live-action soccer game), Paradise Paintball (a first-person shooter social game), and Texas Hold'Em (a social gambling game).
- Role-playing games (RPGs), games in which the players play a character role with the goal of completing some mission, are closely tied to the milieu of fantasy. Perhaps the best-known RPG started its life as a tabletop game—Dungeons and Dragons. Players adopt the identity of a character in the game story and go about completing tasks and collecting points and items as they strive to accomplish the intended goal. MMORPGs—*massive multiplayer online role-playing games*—are a type of RPG that truly encompasses the social aspects of gaming. For years, World of Warcraft was the largest of these with millions of paid subscribers. However, in recent years, the entry of "free to play" games and the popularity of The League of Legends has resulted in a decline in popularity for the once juggernaut game. The League of Legends has grown into the most played PC game in North America and Europe with more than 67 million people playing each month.[14]
- Strategy games are those that involve expert play to organize and value variables in the game system. These games may involve contextualizing information available from secondary sources outside the game itself, including previous experience with game play. Later in this chapter we will discuss alternate reality games as a game form for marketing. Although these games stand apart from other social games due to their complexity, they are also strategy games that involve the solving of puzzles and the systematic evaluation of new information and choices to be made

to continue in the game. Puzzle games, a common variant in the realm of social games, are also a type of strategy game. Social strategy games include Kingdoms of Camelot, Highborn, KDice, Word Cube, and Lexulous. Of course, there is quite a bit of blurring between the genres; you can play other games strategically even though they may best be categorized as sims, action, or role plays.

It's clear that play theory, explained earlier in the chapter, is useful for understanding the design of these games and gamer motivations for playing. More than 50 million gamers are active daily and the most popular social games currently are Candy Crush (93 million users), Farm Heroes Saga (11.28 million users), Pet Rescue Saga (10.18 million users), Hay Day (9.39 million users), and Criminal Case (6.58 million users).

Game-Based Marketing

Brands can utilize social games for marketing in several ways—and they should! Games offer a targeted audience, large reach, a high level of engagement, low intrusion methods of promotion, and a way to interact with brand fans.

The Social Gaming Market Global Industry Analysis Report from Transparence Market Research suggests that worldwide revenues will reach $17.40 billion by 2019, with the largest revenues earned in the Asia Pacific region ($7.59 billion).[15] Ad revenues represent just a portion of these revenues as game producers also earn revenues from the sale of virtual goods in games and game purchase or subscription fees. Revenues are growing most rapidly in the mobile game market, largely due to the popularity of tablets.

Brands have many choices when it comes to marketing with social games. They may choose to promote a brand's message in an existing game property. In these cases the brand can advertise in and around the game using display advertising and product placements, sponsor aspects of the game, and integrate the brand into game play. In addition, a brand can take an even bigger step and develop its own advergame, a game that delivers a branded message. We'll review each approach.

In-Game Advertising

In-game advertising is promotion within a game that another company develops and sells. Ads delivered in social games (online and mobile) have higher clickthrough rates, higher completion rates, and higher engagement rates than do other online ads.[16] Brands advertised in games have higher rates of recall, too.[17] Marketers can choose from among three general methods for in-game advertising:

1 Display ads are integrated into a game's environment as billboards, movie posters, and storefronts (depending of course on the game's context), or simply as ad space within the game screen. The display advertising may be static or dynamic and include text, images, or rich media. Rich media advertising can run pre-roll (before the game begins), interlevel (between stages of the game), or post-roll (at the game's conclusion), though interlevel is the most common placement.

2   Static ads are hard-coded into the game and ensure that all players view the advertising. The Obama campaign ran ads in 18 games including Burnout Paradise prior to the 2008 election.[18]

3   Dynamic ads are variable; they change based on specified criteria. This technique is managed by networks such as MediaSpike and Massive, which offer insertion technology to place ads across multiple games. The networks contract with game publishers to place advertising in their games. By combining games from several publishers, networks create a large portfolio of in-game media opportunities for advertisers. The network works with publishers to strategically embed advertising, sell the placement to advertisers, serve the ads into the games in the network, and manage the billing and accounting for the process.

Dynamic advertising is valuable because of the high degree of control and real-time measurement it offers. In addition, this approach makes it possible to develop an ad network within game families. It makes it possible to aggregate numerous games, platforms, and genres into the ad network. Massive Inc. conducted a series of research tests to gauge the impact of dynamic in-game advertising. It found that in games using dynamic advertising, brand familiarity, brand ratings, purchase consideration, ad recall, and ad ratings all increased significantly compared to a control group. The study, which involved more than 1,000 gamers across North America, included tests of several advertising categories, including automotive, consumer packaged goods, and fast food.[19]

Is in-game advertising effective? You be the judge. A report by MediaBrix gives these highlights:[20]

- Ads in social games achieve an average clickthrough rate (CTR) of 3.8% online or 3.2% mobile, while the average online ad earns just 0.2% or less and a Facebook sponsored ad between 0.3% and 3.2%.

- A rich media ad placed in a social game earns an average clickthrough rate of 11.5% online or 10.0% on mobile, while the rate for the average online rich media ad is just 3.3%.

- Do you finish watching video ads served to you online? You aren't alone. Video completion rates for ads online is under 58%. But video ads delivered in social games are completed 89% of the time.

- And the rate for "value-exchange ads" (those are the ads that offer you game-related goods)? These are opened 100% of the time online and 91.4% for mobile play.

Product Placement

A product placement is simply the placement of a branded item in an entertainment property such as a television program, movie, or game. A placement can be very simple—involving nothing more than having a brand visible in a scene—or it can be heavily integrated into the entertainment property (and then product placement begins to overlap with immersive in-game advertising, which we discuss later).[21]

Screen placements that visually incorporate the brand into the scenery are the most common form of product placement. The placement may be as simple as a brand of soda present in the background or branded attire on in-game characters. For example in *FIFA*, players may wear Adidas shoes.

Script placements take the process one step farther: they include verbal mentions of the brand's name and attributes in the plot. In the Japanese version of Metal Gear Solid: Peace Walker, the character could drink Mountain Dew, eat Doritos, and spray himself with Axe to recover or develop additional strength for game play. Gamers note that product placements that are realistic enhance the game's realism and make the game more enjoyable.

Transactional advertising is more integrated into the game. This form of in-game advertising rewards players if they respond to a request.[22] This technique is part product placement, part direct response advertising, and part sales promotion. The offers can be for virtual goods (which players can use in the game or offer as gifts to friends), currency (used to advance in the game), or codes (used to unlock prizes and limited-access player experiences). Players are rewarded with the virtual goods, currencies, or codes if they take certain actions such as interact with the brand in the game, make a purchase, "like" the brand on Facebook, watch a commercial, or perhaps answer a survey. A more unusual take on transactional in-game advertising was used by Pizza Hut in Everquest II. Players could order pizza straight from the game by using the "/pizza" command. The pizza was charged to the player's monthly subscription bill.[23]

Entertainment Arts (EA), one of the most successful social and mobile game developers, identified four types of advertising it offers for marketers who wish to place their brands in EA games: (1) traffic drivers, (2) quests, (3) store tabs, and (4) media integrations. All are forms of transactional in-game advertising. Traffic drivers seek to drive players to a brand's Facebook page in exchange for a free virtual good. For instance, in EA's *The Sims Social*, players could download Dove Hair Spa virtual goods with a visit to the Facebook page. Quests involve multiple tasks in game during which the player interacts with the brand. Toyota used a quest integration for players to earn a virtual Prius. Store Tabs are sections of the virtual store in-game that are totally dedicated to the brand. Media integrations require players to watch a short video advert to unlock a virtual good. Some of the brands that have used one or more of these tactics in EA games include Dunkin Donuts and Wendy's.

Bounty developed a transactional in-game approach for the social game, Restaurant City. Players completed quests to unlock rolls of Bounty towels that clean more quickly than the game's standard paper towels. A more challenging quest unlocked a Bounty janitor who was 30% more effective at cleaning than the standard janitor. More than 2.5 million players unlocked the paper towels and more than one million scored the janitor. The campaign is also credited with the addition of 500,000 "likes" to the Bounty Facebook page. There is evidence that this interactive form of brand engagement pays off in sales, too. For instance, EA commissioned a Nielsen study to assess sales impact related to Gatorade in-game ads in sports games. The study found that spending on Gatorade increased by 24% in households that had seen the in-game ads.[24]

Brand Integration

In-game immersive advertising opportunities include interactive product placements, branded in-game experiences, and game integration between the game and the brand. In the film industry this is known as a plot placement. Plot placements involve situations in which the brand is actually incorporated into the story itself in a substantive manner. Whether a plot placement or some other form of integration, research suggests that brands achieve enhanced brand attitudes, recall and recognition, and purchase among consumers exposed to the brand message in-game.[25]

The campaign to launch the release of the *Public Enemies* DVD illustrates how a brand can integrate its marketing messages very closely into a game. The movie studio that released the film worked with the social game Mafia Wars to create a truly integrated game experience. Players in Mafia Wars start their own Mafia family, run their empires,

THE DARK SIDE OF SOCIAL MEDIA

Gatorade Portrays Water as the Enemy

What's your favorite workout beverage? Water? Gatorade? While Gatorade is known to provide benefits to hydrating athletes in extreme situations like marathons or professional play, for most of us, water is the better choice. Gatorade took action when it learned that one of its key target audiences—teenage athletes—tended to choose water during practice because they believed it provided the hydration they needed. Gatorade responded by integrating the brand and an anti-water message into an existing mobile game called Bolt! Bolt, developed by Rock Live, Inc., features athlete Usain Bolt, a Gatorade-sponsored athlete. The brand integration explained that Gatorade helped Bolt (already identified as the fastest man in the world) have even better performance but that water was the enemy, hurting performance. In the game, players make choices that affect how fast Bolt's character moves through the course. Gatorade resulted in faster times and higher scores while water slowed Bolt down. The game was downloaded more than 2 million times, played as many as 87 million times, and resulted in 4 million new online fans. Overall, 820 brand impressions were served, reinforcing the message that Gatorade is better than water at enhancing athletic performance. The game integration was a Bronze winner in the 2013 Interactive Advertising Bureau's MIXX awards. Seventy-three percent of players were 13 to 24 years old, consistent with the brand's key demographic.[26] Gatorade's in-game advertising successfully delivered the misleading message that water is the enemy to its teenage target audience. The case study video submission was posted on the IAB MIXX website with other winners until it was removed shortly after following outcries about the ethics of the tactic from nutritional bloggers and journalists.

and fight for the position of most powerful of Mafia families. During a one-week campaign, Mafia Wars featured Public Enemies Week. Players could complete tasks to unlock branded virtual goods such as wooden guns and prison stripes. After they completed tasks, players saw movie clips and trivia about the movie characters. A success? You bet. Nineteen million players took part in Public Enemies Week: they completed 44.5 million branded tasks, watched 1.5 million movie clips, and posted 7.6 million news feed posts on game tasks and virtual goods. The promotion also generated 25,000 Facebook "likes" and 26,000 comments on the Mafia Wars Facebook page.[27]

Advergames

With advergaming, the game itself is a form of branded entertainment. It is designed by the brand to reflect the brand's positioning statement. Advergames are almost exclusively available online rather than in hard media because of the desire to have a cost-effective method of distributing the game to a large audience. Likewise, they tend to be casual rather than core games because of the costs associated with creating and promoting core games. When they include social components like friend lists, sharing of experiences and results, and badges, they are known as social advergames. In Chapter 1, we shared the social media strategy for the global, fast-casual restaurant brand Chipotle. Its Scarecrow campaign included a social advergame. The campaign won a 2014 Grand Prix and two Gold Lions at Cannes, possibly the most prestigious award for creativity. In addition to being well integrated with the social publishing aspects of the campaign, the game also included a social commerce element in that players achieving average to high marks in the game earned coupons for redemption at Chipotle locations.

The shift to social games is a boon to advergaming given the goal of the game—to spread a branded message. Studies on the effectiveness of social advergames found that when advergames were social they resulted in more positive brand attitudes and more positive word-of-mouth communication about the brand than when the advergame was not social.[28] There are developmental costs to be considered, but advergames are sometimes "reskinned" versions of existing games. This means that a game is reprogrammed to contain brand logos or other sponsored images. The key to success in the advergaming market is the quality of the game and the congruence between the brand and the game context. Gamers tend to be thought of as people who eschew traditional advertising, but they welcome a good game, whether or not it appears as an advergame.

Perhaps because advergames are not intended to make money, but rather to serve as a promotion vehicle that builds awareness for the sponsoring brand, many have lagged behind in terms of their technical sophistication compared to social games. However, some success stories illustrate the potential for advergames. Take, for example, Swiss watchmaker Tag Heuer.

It created a social game, working with French social media agency KRDS, called Mystery on Board available via Facebook for mobile, tablet, or desktop play. The game story is set on the Glacier Express, tied to the sub-brand name of the timepiece, the Aquaracer Glacier Express. Similarly, Longchamp used an online game to show its Fall 2013 collection. The campaign, "Bigger than Life," featured a giant model walking through the streets of New

York carrying a Longchamp bag. Captain Morgan developed a mobile social game called Captain's Quest that included geo-location technology incorporating Foursquare and QR code readers that unlocked virtual goods when bar codes on bottles of Captain Morgan were scanned. Social advergames aren't just for B2C marketers. IBM developed its *CityOne* social advergame to target city managers and urban planners. Players are tasked with solving a city's most pressing problems in the areas of banking, retail, energy, and water with technology.[29] The game has an underlying goal of teaching city planners about new technologies and examining the consequences of possible choices they make in addressing common urban issues. Thousands of people in more than 100 countries have played since the game launched.

Jane Chen of Ya Ya Media, a video game developer, had this to say of advergaming's potential: "It is one of the few advertising mediums that effectively reaches target audiences in all day-parts—including hard-to-reach at-work hours … The most effective advergames push deeper down the purchase funnel and can serve to qualify buyers and incentivize consumers to visit retail outlets or even purchase directly online. The natural interactivity of games provides the perfect stimulus and ongoing communication channel between brands and their customers."[30]

The Bottom Line: Why Do Social Games Work for Marketers?

Social games have the potential to be a major weapon in a marketer's arsenal. As gaming continues to explode as a consumer activity, we expect to see many more of these vehicles—and you should too. Players tend to be in a receptive mood when gaming and branding efforts result in more positive brand attitudes. And, it's relatively inexpensive to use this medium, brand exclusivity is available (where a sponsor is the sole advertiser in a gaming environment), and metrics are available to measure just how well the game works to attract players.

Of course, like any advertising medium games do have some negatives that the industry has to deal with. One is game clutter; like the pervasive problem of *advertising clutter* in other formats, this means that there are way too many games out there that compete for players' attention. Facebook alone offers hundreds of social games, and this number multiplies when you consider the massive inventory available on games offered on game networks (such as Pogo.com), microsites, and via consoles and software. Unlike advertising clutter, however, the problem is compounded by the time investment involved in playing a game. You can either look at or not look at a popup ad on a website and move on, but if you choose to play a game you need to devote time to learning the rules and mastering its tricks. Even for avid game geeks, there are only so many hours in a day (OK, a few more if you skip class to play your favorites). Another issue is available inventory for advertising in-game. Granted there are numerous game titles and genres, but the inventory of space available for display advertising, product placement, and brand integration is still in limited supply.

There are some key characteristics of games—in addition to cost and ease of targeting—that make this domain especially attractive to marketers going forward:

1   *Gamers are open to advertising content in games.* It's not that they're "adverholics"— just that they crave realism and many real-world venues (for better or worse) like stadiums are saturated with marketing messages. In fact, a study by Nielsen Entertainment conducted on behalf of Massive Inc. revealed that after exposure to in-game ads on Massive's advertising game network, brand familiarity, a measure of brand recognition, increased 64%.[31] In addition, the study found that positive attitudes toward the brands studied increased by 37% and purchase consideration increased by 41%. The advertising itself also performed well; respondents reported an increase in advertising recall and a positive attitude toward the ads they encountered in the games. These results are consistent with other research on the effectiveness of ad placement, which found that placing ads in creative locations such as games over traditional placements such as magazines resulted in positive feelings toward the brand.[32]

2   *Brands benefit when they associate with a successful game.* When players love a game, some of these positive feelings rub off on the brands they encounter within it; we call this spillover a transference effect. This is the same thing that tends to happen with event sponsorships. Brands often try to link to sports and music events like the Olympics or a Rihanna concert to gain residual benefits from the brand–event association. The only difference is that a game/brand linkage is more intimate; the player encounters the sponsoring product on his or her screen rather than in an arena packed with 10,000 other fans. Like event sponsorship, a prerequisite for success is congruence between the brand's image and the image and atmosphere the game conveys. It's unlikely that a conservative clothing chain such as Talbot's would sponsor a Lady Gaga tour, and similarly the U.S. Army is probably a better candidate to create a role-playing military game like Call of Duty than is, say, the Methodist Church. In other words, there must be a good fit in order to maximize the value of the association. To pick the right game, marketers must choose the game (or game concept) just as they would choose any other media and vehicles for a media plan—they need to consider the demographic profile of game players, the size of the player market, and the quality and content of the game franchise. Ford or Chevrolet in Grand Theft Auto? Probably not a great idea.

Not only do brands benefit from association with the game, but they can also achieve outcomes similar to when they use celebrity endorsers. Famous people whom the target audience admires also create a transference effect. That's why companies pay millions to movie stars; they hope that the knowledge that an admired person likes the brand will in turn encourage the star's fans to like it as well. Internalization occurs when members of the target market accept the beliefs of an endorser as their own. In a game context, the characters in the game's story and setting can act as brand endorsers.

The meaning transfer model states that consumers associate meaning with the endorser and then transfer the meaning to the brand in question.[33] The consumer first chooses to assign the meaning associated with the endorser to the product or brand. Thus, meanings attributed to the endorser become associated with the brand in the consumer's mind. For game advertisers, the meaning transfer model suggests that a character's attributes can be transferred to a brand a character uses in the game as part of an in-game product placement. The key to using character endorsers successfully parallels the choice of celebrity endorsers. The character endorser should have the appropriate set of characteristics the brand desires.

3 *Players identify with the brands their characters use, and this increases their brand involvement.* Players may be particularly invested in their characters because they spend weeks, months, and even years on building their character identity and developing the attributes that will enable the character to compete at the highest possible level of the game. Even the name of the RPG genre itself, "role-playing," implies just how involved players are with their characters. When brands are embedded using immersive techniques such as enabling players in a racing game to choose their brand of race car, the players can actively interact with brands during the game experience. This "bonding" results in a heightened sense of brand identification.

4 *Branding within a game's story is an unobtrusive way to share a brand's core message.* In many ways, games approximate the immersive experience of watching a movie. Games, like movies, are capable of transcending barriers of class and culture. However, games offer more than stories told through film and literature, in that they allow the audience to actually participate in the story. When spectators become actors, they are less likely to sit back and think of reasons why the advertising message on the screen doesn't apply to them (psychologists call this common process counterarguing). Narrative transportation theory explains how even imagined interactivity can build positive brand attitudes. This theory proposes that mental stimulation through narrative storytelling encourages players to become lost in the story. Once immersed in the plot, players are distracted from advertising embedded in the game. They do not counterargue against these messages, and as a result they are more likely to form attitudes toward the brand simply based on the positive feelings the story evokes.[34]

5 *Targeting is possible for most in-game ads using gaming ad networks like Rock You and MediaSpike.* Social games were already a high value for effective reach based on game/player fit, but ad networks can tailor and customize product placements dynamically to deliver different ads based on geographic location and other segmentation variables.

6 *Marketers can measure a game's promotional value.* For both game advertising and advergaming, the game environment creates a higher impression value for the ad compared to that earned from traditional media placements. This is attributed to the frequency of exposure, the potential for interactivity with the brand's message, and the entertainment value of the platform. Millions of advertising impressions can be delivered in just a few weeks of game play at a cost as low as 25 cents per impression. In addition to the low cost, there is little advertising

clutter in games, particularly when compared to other media choices. But what's equally or even more important is that marketers know how well a game works to deliver these impressions. Unlike many other forms of advertising, a sponsor can measure who saw the message and in some cases even link these exposures to sales of its product. We'll talk more about the vital issue of measuring marketing results in Chapter 10.

Industry and academic research supports the use of social games for branding purposes. Though there are many factors involved in whether this approach will be successful, studies suggest that brands affiliating with social games are more memorable, talked about more often and more positively, and are better liked than if a social game were not used. Effectiveness can be influenced by game–brand congruity, target audience, type and realism of brand integration, and individual factors of the players.[35]

Alternate Reality Games: A Transmedia Genre

So far in this chapter we've focused on social games. But in addition to all the Mafia Wars and World of Warcraft players out there, other people are getting into an even newer genre that's even more immersive—one that vividly demonstrates the stunning potential of digital media. We refer to alternate reality games (ARGs). Unfiction.com, a leading website for the ARG community, defines an alternate reality game as "a cross-media genre of interactive fiction using multiple delivery and communications media, including television, radio, newspapers, Internet, email, SMS, telephone, voicemail, and postal service."[36] ARGs are still social games, with a community of geographically dispersed players who compete and collaborate to solve a complex puzzle. These games are like others of the strategy genre—but on steroids. When a sponsoring brand develops an ARG it also resembles an advergame. And, because ARGs involve two or more different media, they are transmedia social games.

The Marketing Value of ARGs

Brands such as Levi Strauss, McDonald's, Nine Inch Nails, and Audi have used ARGs for marketing. In fact, to date, the most successful ARGs in terms of participation are brand-sponsored. Most ARGs are tied to entertainment properties such as movies, books, and video games (yes, games to promote games!). For instance, the movie *The Dark Knight* was promoted with an ARG called Why So Serious? that was played by more than 11 million people in 75 countries. It's natural that story-oriented products would promote themselves using a story-based promotional tool, but other brands can benefit from ARGs too. The key, just as with other forms of social games, is to ensure a high level of congruence between the game and the brand.

The movie launch of A.I. (Artificial Intelligence) in 2001 started it all with the ARG game *The Beast* that a Microsoft team created. This groundbreaking promotional vehicle was set in the year 2142, 50 years after the events in the movie. This game offered three rabbit holes:

1 A clue hidden among the credits for *A.I.*
2 A trailer for the movie that invited players to call a phone number in order to receive a clue by email
3 A promotional poster the producers sent to technology and media outlets that contained another clue

The prevalence of brand-initiated ARGs is at least in part due to the funding necessary to build an intricate, multimedia, multi-channel narrative with characters and clues spread online and off. Take, for instance, The Art of the Heist ARG that Audi used to promote its A3 model. ARG-related expenses ran about $5 million.[37] Compared to television advertising, the cost of an ARG is minimal. Still, the resources required are substantial enough to warrant the need for a brand sponsor. However, this investment can pay off handsomely. For instance, Audi claims that 500,000 consumers, in its target audience of 25- to 35-year-old, upper-income males, participated in its Art of the Heist ARG, with average exposure of 4 to 10 minutes spent on numerous websites and pages used to embed game clues.[38] Hits to Audi's website increased 140% during the game with the most hits originating from game sites. Its dealers earned 10,000 qualified sales leads, and 3,500 test drives could be attributed to the game.[39]

Although an ARG benefits from a sponsor's deep pockets, many of the games do not identify who is behind the effort. Instead, players play until the mystery is solved (or the sponsorship is inadvertently discovered and leaked to the community) and the brand sponsor is revealed. This type of branded ARG is known as a dark play ARG; it's one of the ways that brands can use dark marketing, which refers to a promotion that disguises the sponsoring brand. Some say it's an ethical question whether brands should acknowledge their role in an ARG (or other dark marketing promotional stunts), but thus far, both brands and players seem to recognize that the game is best left as pure play space. In the end, players have a sense of gratitude toward the brand for the game experience that translates into more positive brand attitudes, along with potentially stronger brand knowledge because participants stick with the game for days, weeks, or even months before they solve the mystery. Table 7.1 on page 222 summarizes the pros and cons of the ARG strategy. All of this sounds pretty complicated, so let's first review the characteristics and vocabulary of ARGs.

Characteristics of ARGs

ARGs begin with a scripted scenario. However, over time an ARG will also become a form of consumer-fortified media as the network of gamers participates in the game by discovering clues, sharing information with others, and literally changing the structure and plot of the game with their responses. In an ARG, players not only share tips, clues, and accomplishments with the player community, they also help to direct how the story underlying the game develops. In fact, that's why sometimes ARGs are referred to as immersive fiction. For branded ARGs, marketers have an unmatched opportunity to share a brand story with the audience.

The games unfold over multiple forms of media and utilize many types of game elements, each tailored to specific media platforms. ARGs may utilize websites (story sites and social networking sites), telephone, email, outdoor signage, T-shirts, television, radio play, and more to reveal story clues, compose scenes, and unite gamers.

ARGs are ideally suited to social media because it would be impossible to solve the puzzle alone. Among players, the term "collective detective" acknowledges the need for a team approach to solve the mystery. Because players from around the world participate, online communication is a necessary component to play. Many ARGs use other media channels including live events, television, radio, and so on, but social media ensure a hub of communication for the players. We summarize the basic characteristics of ARGs as follows:

- ARGs are based on a fictional story. Game characters, events, places, and plot are imagined and explored by the game writers, known as puppet masters.

- ARGs are strategy/puzzle games. The story unfolds as a mystery that invites players to solve clues before more of the narrative is revealed.

- Because they are transmedia social games, ARGs offer clues on multiple platforms that range from traditional media like television and newspapers to text messages and messages hidden in code in movie trailers or even concert T-shirts.

- The story is fictional as are the game characters, but the game space is not. The players are real people and the clues are revealed in real time. Consequently, *real life is itself a medium.* This characteristic has led to the ARG "TINAG" credo—"This is not a game!" Telephone numbers, websites, and locations revealed in-game are all real and functioning. Oh—and if you meet an ARG enthusiast, beware. He or she won't take kindly to references to ARGs as games (even though they are).

- Players collaborate to unravel the meanings of the clues offered but they also compete to be the first to solve layers of the mystery. Players are geographically dispersed, sometimes worldwide.

- The story unfolds, but typically not in a linear fashion. The speed of disclosure is influenced by the players' success and speed in solving clues and sharing them with the player population.

- ARGs are organic; the story may not unfold as initially conceived. Because players interact with the game, and player response can dictate the next scene in the story, stories are fluid and unpredictable.

- Players rely on the Internet, and especially social communities including forums, as the hub of communication.

- The desire for players to share information with each other and even for the story to be followed by observers attests to the viral nature of ARGs.

The Vocabulary of ARGs

ARGs have their own vernacular—understanding the lingo is the first step to understanding the culture of alternate reality gaming. The website Unfiction.com is a major clearinghouse for ARG fans. The site summarizes the basic lexicon of alternate reality gamers:[40]

- *Puppet masters:* The authors, architects, and managers of the story and its scenarios and puzzles.
- Curtain: The invisible line separating the players from the puppet masters.
- Rabbit hole: The clue or site that initiates the game.
- *Collective detective:* A term that captures the notion of collaboration among a team of geographically dispersed players who work together to flesh out the story.
- Lurkers *and* rubberneckers: Lurkers follow the game but do not actively participate, whereas rubberneckers participate in forums but do not actively play. Consider this common line from brand-sponsored sweepstakes: "You don't have to play to win." From a branding perspective, lurkers and rubberneckers are just as critical to the success of an ARG as are the active players. Unfiction.com estimates that the ratio of lurkers to active players can range from 5:1 to 20:1, depending upon the game.
- Steganography: The tactic of hiding messages within another medium; the message is undetectable for those who do not know to look for it.
- Trail: A reference index of the game including relevant sites, puzzles, in-game characters, and other information. Trails are useful for new players coming late into a game and to veteran players who eagerly try to piece together the narrative.

Evaluating the Effectiveness of a Brand-Sponsored ARG

How can we measure the effectiveness of ARGs as a branding tool? ARG effectiveness measures are similar to those used for other social media approaches with a focus on site traffic and participation. We'll discuss these in greater depth in Chapter 10. The most common indicators for ARGs include:

- Number of active players
- Number of lurkers and rubberneckers
- Rate of player registration from launch or from specific game event
- Number of player messages generated
- Traffic at sites affiliated with the ARG
- Number of forum postings (at sites like Unfiction.com)
- Average play time
- Media impressions made through publicity generated about the ARG

Social Music

Just as marketers can use social games as vehicles for in-game ads, integrated placements, or fully branded games, similar options are available for social music. This category of social entertainment has developed substantially in recent years with the entry of social,

FROM BYTES TO BUCKS

Disney's The Optimist

The heart of Disney is immersive storytelling so it shouldn't come as a surprise that Walt Disney Imagineering Research and Development planned and executed an ARG, Disney's The Optimist. Imagineering, the laboratory that brings Disney stories to life in the form of park attractions, believes storytelling is in its DNA. It developed The Optimist ARG as a 6-week game culminating in a live version of the game at the 2013 D23Expo, the fan event for the official Disney Fan Club. Why is Disney investing in ARGs? Scott Trowbridge, vice president of creative at Imagineering Research and Development, explained that with an ARG, "You are participating in the story, not just being told a story." Imagineering didn't stop at creating its own ARG. It is also investing in the genre. Imagineering's Living Worlds (www.disneylivingworlds.com) program invites transmedia storytelling submissions with a goal of nurturing a community of storytellers. The top submissions will be produced by Imagineering.

The Optimist story began with a character named Amelia and her hunt for clues about a story her grandfather sold to Walt Disney.[41] Through blog posts, tweets, and images, players found clues based on history that were woven into the fictional story. Many ARGs are based on futuristic themes, but The Optimist's use of historical fiction served to pay homage to the cultural expertise of Disney fans.

Clues related to the 1964 World's Fair, where It's a Small World first debuted, and many of Walt Disney's favorite locations. Real-world meetups provided opportunities for players to meet with the game characters playing a part of Walt's secret society (which used the symbol 1952—the year the Imagineering Research and Development group was established) and receive additional game paraphernalia. Puzzles in the game couldn't be solved alone, ensuring that fans collaborated. Even fans playing from afar could participate using the game websites and, if registered, even receive mailings and audio recordings. Curious about the entire story? A full history of the plot and clues as they were revealed is available at Inside the Magic.[42]

The official word is that The Optimist ended at the 2013 D23Expo, but rumors abound that The Optimist is somehow connected to a film called *Tomorrowland*, set to be released in May 2015. Originally *1952*, the film written by Brad Bird and Damon Lindelof was retitled *Tomorrowland*. The 1952 symbols seen on *Tomorrowland* project materials are identical to those used in the ARG, leading fans to ask whether this ARG is really over.[43] Perhaps Amelia's Twitter account (@storyorbit) is a clue – her last tweet references seeing a beautiful tomorrow. Could it be a clue for *Tomorrowland?* A recap of The Optimist, told from Amelia's point of view, is available at www.storyorbit.com/tomorrow and on YouTube.

Table 7.1   Pros and Cons of Using an ARG as a Social Entertainment Branding Channel

PROS	CONS
Reach can be substantial. In addition to active players, lurkers and rubberneckers may also see the messages.	ARGs require a lot of effort from initial conception through planning and execution. And, because the storyline can change depending upon the response from players, ARGs require constant monitoring and input from the game architects through and even beyond (as players are debriefed) the game's end.
The games attract media attention, resulting in earned media in the form of publicity.	Because the game can evolve in ways the architects did not originally plan, there is a risk involved. As fans drive the plot, the game can progress in ways the sponsor didn't anticipate.
Exposures earned last longer than do those for traditional media.	Hardcore brand loyalists may resent the influx of new people who express interest in the game.
ARGs are high-engagement messages. The games pull enthusiasts (players, lurkers, and rubberneckers) into the story and encourage them to seek out new information as it is presented in the game.	ARGs are unlikely to reach the same number of prospects as a brand could attract if it used mass media.
Players welcome brand-sponsored ARGs because they do not invade people's space with a brand message.	

streaming music providers like Pandora and Spotify. It's important to reiterate that there is a difference between advertising around social entertainment spaces and truly utilizing social entertainment as a social media marketing opportunity. Technically speaking, advertising in and around social entertainment spaces is digital advertising – online or mobile. It is not in and of itself social, even if the site is social. Despite this, we will cover these options briefly.

In-Network Advertising

Social music is primarily based around cloud services providing streamed sound. Though podcast sites have long provided streamed audio, we classify podcasts as a form of media-sharing site used primarily for social publishing. iTunes, Google Play, and Amazon Music are retailers of music that may also be cloud-stored and streamed and, though these providers have some social features such as ratings and rankings, we consider these more consistent with social commerce. What then are we referring to when we suggest that marketers consider using social music for promotions? Brands can include many types of ads on social music sites, including audio ads, display ads, billboard ads (which serve as a screensaver that appears when a listener has gone inactive), and homepage takeovers (which ensure all site visitors are exposed to the ad). More integrated forms of advertising with social music include the use of branded playlists and the use of microsites within the social music vehicle.

Why should marketers consider social music sites as possible ad vehicles? Like games, these social sites offer targeting and reach capabilities. Advertisers can target using age, gender, preferred music genre, and location. Ad impressions are charged on a CPM basis (cost per thousand). A benefit with social music is that production may be provided by the site (at least for Pandora and Spotify at the time of this writing). As noted, simply posting an ad in the social media space is not social media marketing. That action offers the benefit of reach and frequency but not that of truly engaging.

Immersive Branding

Brands that want a more integrated option need to find ways that the brand itself can add value to the content that the target audience values. Recent examples include branded playlists and branded microsites that focus around artists or styles of music that target markets value. This enables the brand to truly leverage the social community aspects of the vehicle in question. The key here is for brands to find ways to add value to music that people are already passionate about. This is not unlike what sponsorship marketing has been doing ... except now we are doing it among social media communities. Coca-Cola's Placelists campaign provides a good example. Placelists is a social music app hosted by Spotify. Visit www.coca-cola.com/placelists to experience it for yourself. The concept is based on existing music and existing places. Do you have a place that you love? Is there a sound that always brings you back to that place? That's how one of us feels about the Gypsy Kings. Wherever she is, whatever she is doing, if she hears a song by the Gypsy Kings, she is transported to Europe, sitting at a café watching people go by. That's just what Coca-Cola Placelists seeks to do. Or even more! Do you wish to know what people are listening to now in Argentina? Placelists can do that too and let you feel that you are a part of that experience. It's all a part of a Coca-Cola Spotify app. The app uses folksonomies too – with people tagging songs to geographic memories. Are you worried your favorite locale doesn't have a Placelist? Not to worry! Coca-Cola has activated the campaign by seeding the app with 30 locations, 40 songs per location. Coca-Cola wants every place in the world to have its own Placelist. Importantly, as a social media campaign, you and others can influence Placelists.

Another example? BMW – clearly a leader in the development of digital, branded content, it too sought to inspire fans with music. With the campaign objective of increasing awareness and consideration of the BMW 320i, it created a branded app on Spotify that enabled a music set based on iconic American road trips. Each road trip generated a custom playlist curated for that location. What's your favorite road trip? The drive down U.S. 1 viewing the Pacific Coast is a favorite. Of course, the brand is never far from reach and the playlist is shareable.

These are Spotify examples, but Pandora has done well too! Toyota has created Toyota Sessions, a custom station featuring emerging artists. In this regard, Toyota has aligned itself with the culture of Pandora, providing a discovery engine for worthwhile artists.

These examples suggest the ways brands can truly integrate with the passion fans feel for music and provide something meaningful. To our knowledge, no brand has fully adopted social music to the extent of developing branded music. But this area is new and developing … we'll see!

Social TV

ClickZ dubbed 2014 the year of social TV.[44] It defined social TV as "technology that supports communication and social interaction in either the context of watching television, or related to TV content." For social TV to be social media marketing, it not only needs to be designed to meet marketing objectives, but also must be participatory and shareable. We say this because we believe that most examples of social TV to date leverage social community. They are engaging in conversations around the social object of the show or the characters. In this regard, they belong in Zone 1 – Social Community. However, we will cover this area of social media here due to its close affiliation with social entertainment. We also recognize that the development of technologies could rapidly create a situation that enables the true socialization of entertainment programming.

Primarily, social TV means that technology has enhanced the experience of watching video programming through the use of social media. This is to be expected given the prevalence of media multitasking. Surely you've done it! That means to consume one medium while engaged in one or more other media. One of my favorite annual pastimes is to tweet using the hashtag #brandbowl while watching the Super Bowl. That's media multitasking. But it is also the basis for what we now call social TV—video programming with a social twist.

It's especially powerful because television was built on theatre, something that was once a shared experience but now may not be. Still, we glean more from what we see and hear if we share it with others. That is clear from the organic development of Twitter communities around programming like *Scandal*.

That's pure social media, but marketers can leverage that power. How? Twitter knows. It's acquired Bluefin Labs, which has technology that identifies content in television and ties that content to social media conversations.[45] With that, ads can be delivered in real time as you watch television. The result of the data is known as the TV Genome. It allows for media analysis and social media commentary on a large scale.

There's much to be seen still in the development of social entertainment. Outside of the social realm, we see entertainment hubs like Netflix shifting from syndicated content to original content. Amazon is now competing in the area of syndicated streaming video content and also producing original content. So is Hulu. These providers are socializing their own brands, but, to date, have not socialized individual offerings – whether branded entertainment or not. Is that far behind? We anxiously await the answer.

SHOW ME!

Scandal benefited by encouraging conversations and then leveraging them, having characters engage in tweets and conversations during episodes. *Scandal* was not marked for success – until Twitter chatter released a wave of interest that was met with engagement from *Scandal* actors. Watching in real time (not DVR time) is relevant because the viewer can participate in the Twitter dialogue alongside the content. That's powerful. ABC credits social media dialogue with the success of the show.

Photo 7.2

Kerry Washington: HYPERLINK s_bukley / HYPERLINK Shutterstock.com

Social Celebrity

Advertising has long relied upon celebrities to hawk their wares and social media are no different. Increasingly, brands are calling upon social media celebrities to highlight their respective brands. Brands may use ghost writers, but some brands wish to leverage the popularity of social media stars. These stars typically specialize in a particular vehicle and have amassed fan bases of their own. That's led to a whole new breed of celebrity. Social media talent agencies like Niche and GrapeStory represent social media celebrities. You could be one! These celebrities don't have movies or fashion shows under their belt. Instead, they are experts at user-generated content (like we talked about in Chapter 6 on social publishing). Indeed, these celebrities built their own brand using social publishing techniques and talent. They may focus on photography, video, or narrative and may feature a specific vehicle like Vine, Instagram, or Pinterest. What they have in common is a unique POV (point of view) that relates with an audience – so much so that they've been able to attract millions of followers and brands are willing to pay to reach them. They are the social media versions of Lady Gaga or Beyonce. Just as brands will utilize celebrities for affinity or expertise in advertising, they will leverage them for reach in social media. Even dogs are getting in on the game! Check out Biggie's endorsement of BarkBoxes.[46]

CHAPTER SUMMARY

How can social media marketers use social entertainment to meet branding objectives? What are the types of social entertainment? Why is social entertainment an effective approach for engaging target audiences?

Social entertainment provides opportunities for marketers to reach people with content that is welcomed and with which people want to spend time. By developing marketing messages in, around, and integrated with social entertainment, marketers can ensure the target audience spends more time with brand messages. Social entertainment includes social games, social music, and social TV.

What is branded entertainment? How is it distinguished from content marketing used in social publishing?

Branded entertainment is entertaining content that is produced by a brand rather than by a third party. The Chipotle-developed Hulu series, Farmed and Dangerous, is an example. It is a type of content marketing. Content marketing is also used in social publishing strategies for social media marketers, though social publishing strategies focus primarily on content that provides opportunities for thought leadership. Also, social publishing can be utilized by users (to publish user-generated content).

What are the characteristics of social games and gamer segments? How can marketers effectively use social games? How are alternate reality games different from other social games?

A social game is a multiplayer, competitive, goal-oriented activity with defined rules of engagement and online connectivity among a community of players. Most social games include a few key elements such as leaderboards, achievement badges, or buddy lists that allow players to compare their progress with other players. Traditionally we distinguished gamers as either casual or hardcore, depending on how much time they spent playing and how important the games were to them. This distinction is blurring as more "mainstream" players get involved. Today there are many women and older people who are avid gamers in addition to the base of young, male players.

An organization may choose to promote its message in an existing game property. In these cases the brand can advertise in and around the game using display advertising and product placements, sponsor aspects of the game, and integrate the brand into game play. In addition, a brand can take an even bigger step and develop its own customized advergame that delivers a more focused and pervasive branded message.

Players tend to be in a receptive mood when gaming and branding efforts result in more positive brand attitudes. In addition, it's possible to finely target users because most games attract a fairly distinct type of player. And, it's relatively inexpensive to use this medium, brand exclusivity is available (where a sponsor is the sole advertiser in a gaming environment), and metrics are available to measure just how well the game works to attract players.

ARGs are a type of social game. They begin with a scripted scenario. However, the game changes as the network of gamers participates in the game by discovering clues, sharing information with others, and literally changing the structure and plot of the game with their responses. The games unfold over multiple forms of media and utilize many types of game elements, each tailored to specific media platforms. ARGs may utilize websites (story sites and social networking sites), telephones, email, outdoor signage, T-shirts, television, radio play, and more to reveal story clues, compose scenes, and unite gamers. ARGs are best suited to brands that want to reach people who are willing to invest the time to engage in this kind of activity.

How are brands using social music, social television, and social celebrity for brand messaging?

Brands add value by curating content for fans, engaging content around conversations about social television, and affiliating with social celebrities. The brand is not the main focus in these activities but they add value by understanding why fans are participating in the respective form of social entertainment.

KEY TERMS

action games
advergame
alternate reality game (ARG)
branded entertainment
casual gamer
casual games
collective detective
core games
counterarguing
curtain
dark marketing
dark play ARG
display ads
dynamic ads
first-person shooter (FPS)
game clutter
game console
game platform

genre
hardcore gamer
immersive fiction
in-game advertising
in-game immersive advertising
internalization
lurkers
meaning transfer model
milieu
MMORPG
mode
narrative transportation
   theory
performative
plot placement
product placement
puppet master
puzzle games

rabbit hole
role-playing games (RPGs)
rubberneckers
screen placements
script placements
simulation games
social game
social music
social TV
static ads
steganography
strategy games
TINAG
trail
transactional advertising
transference effect
transmedia social games
TV Genome

REVIEW QUESTIONS

1 What is social entertainment? What are the types of social entertainment?

2 How do casual gamers differ from hardcore gamers? Are social gamers casual, a hybrid of casual and hardcore, or a new segment of gamer all together?

3 What are the four major game genres? Provide examples of each. What is the distinguishing characteristic associated with each genre?

4 What makes a game social? Explain the characteristics of social games.

5 Explain the differences between pre-roll, post-roll, and interlevel in-game advertising.

6 What is an advergame? How do we distinguish it from other social games?

7 How is brand integration and immersive in-game advertising different from other forms of branding in social games?

8 Define transactional advertising and provide an example.

9 Why is the entry clue to an alternate reality game called a rabbit hole? What term refers to the game's writer and director? Why are lurkers and rubberneckers just as valuable to brand sponsors as players?

10 What is social music?

11 How can entertainment brands leverage social TV?

EXERCISES

1 Are branded offers in social games ethical? Choose a side and debate this issue with a classmate. Then post your opinions and find out what your social graph thinks of this common practice.

2 Choose a social game to play. As you interact with the game, keep a journal of your experience. In particular, note the advertising and branded components and your reactions to them. How does your experience affect your attitude toward the brands?

3 Choose three people you know who play social games. Interview them about the time they spend online as they play social games. Have they responded to branded offers? Write a blog post on their brand experience in social games and their resulting perceptions of the brand.

4 Visit Unfiction.com or argn.com to see what ARGs are playing now. Explore one of the current games. Is it associated with a brand (or is it a dark play ARG, with the brand yet to be identified)? Make a list of non-entertainment brands that could use an ARG to tell their story and immerse their brand fans.

5 Visit our YouTube channel to learn more about The Lost Ring and other campaigns noted in the chapter.

CHAPTER NOTES

1   Jie Zhang, Youngjun Sung, and Wei-Na Lee, "To Play or Not to Play: An Exploratory Content Analysis of Branded Entertainment in Facebook," *American Journal of Business* 25, no. 1 (2010): 53–64.

2   Jie Zhang, Youngjun Sung, Wei-Na Lee, 2010, "To Play or Not to Play: An Exploratory Content Analysis of Branded Entertainment in Facebook," *American Journal of Business*, 25 (1), 53–64.

3   "Brand Engagement in an Era of Social Entertainment," *Edelman Insights,* 2012, http://www.edelman.com/insights/intellectual-property/matter-brand-engagement/, accessed November 14, 2013.

4   "Essential Facts About the Computer and Video Game Industry," *Entertainment Software Association,* April 2014, http://www.thesa.com/facts//pdfs/esa_ef_2014. pdf, accessed June 14, 2014.

5   Entertainment Software Association, "Essential Facts About the Computer And Video Game Industry," April 2014, www.thesa.com/facts/pdfs/esa_ef_2014.pdf, accessed June 14, 2014.

6   Entertainment Software Association, *Essential Facts about the Computer and Video Game Industry,* http://www.theesa.com/facts/pdfs/ESA_Essential_Facts_2010.PDF, accessed July 12, 2010.

7   Steve Hicks, "Does the Video Game Industry Hold the Keys to the Future of Advertising? Engage Consumers via Brain Chemistry," *Adweek,* February 16, 2014, http://www.adweek.com/news/advertising-branding/engage-consumers-brain-chemistry-155531, accessed June 25, 2014.

8   "What Americans Do Online: Social Media and Games Dominate Activity," *NielsenWire,* August 2, 2010, http://blog.nielsen.com/nielsenwire/online_mobile/what-americans-do-online-social-media-and-games-dominate-activity/, accessed December 21, 2010.

9   Paul Verna, "Video Game Advertising: Getting to the Next Level," *eMarketer,* April 2007, http://www.emarketer.com/Reports/All/Emarketer_2000386. aspx?src=report_head_info_site earch, accessed December 10, 2007.

10   Thomas Apperley, "Genre and Game Studies: Toward a Critical Approach to Video Game Genres," *Simulation & Gaming* 37, no. 1 (2006): 6–23.

11   *Interactive Advertising Bureau, Game Advertising Platform Status Report:* LET THE GAMES BEGIN, October 2007, http://www.iab.net/media/file/games-reportv4.pdf, accessed August 8, 2011.

(Continued)

(Continued)

12 Thomas Apperley, "Genre and Game Studies: Toward a Critical Approach to Video Game Genres," *Simulation & Gaming* 37, no. 1 (2006): 6–23.

13 Thomas Apperley, "Genre and Game Studies: Toward a Critical Approach to Video Game Genres," *Simulation & Gaming* 37, no. 1 (2006): 6–23.

14 "Will World of Warcraft Lose Market Share?" *Seeking Alpha,* March 16, 2014, http://seekingalpha.com/article/2073223-activision-blizzard-will-world-of-warcraft-lose-market-share, accessed July 11, 2014.

15 "Social Gaming Industry Global Analysis Report, 2013–2019," *Transparency Market Research*, http://www.transparencymarket research.com/social-gaming-market.html

16 Adam Blumenthal, "Hey Brands: Get Your Game On," *Social Media Today*, March 29, 2014, http://www.socialmediatoday.com/content/hey-brands-get-your-game, accessed March 31, 2014.

17 Minsun Yeu, Hee-Sook Yoon, Charles R. Taylor, and Doo-Hee Lee, "Are Banner Advertisements in Online Games Effective?" *Journal of Advertising* 42, no. 2–3 (2013): 241–250.

18 Chris Rio, "9 Strange Product Placements in Video Games," *List Verse,* August 4, 2013, http://listverse.com/2013/08/04/9-strange-product-placements-in-videogames/, accessed June 17, 2014.

19 "In-Game Advertising Research Proves Effectiveness for Brands Across Categories and Game Titles," June 3, 2008, http://www.microsoft.com/presspass/press/2008/jun08/06-03adeffectivenesspr.mspx, accessed August 8, 2011.

20 "The MediaBrix Social and Mobile Gaming Report," *MediaBrix,* March 2014, http://www.mediabrix.com/wp-content/uploads/2014/03/MediaBrix_Report_Q3-4_2013_FINAL.pdf, accessed July 11, 2014.

21 Cristel Russell, "Toward a Framework of Product Placement," in J. W. Alba and J. W. Hutchinson, eds. [Special issue], *Advances in Consumer Research* 25 (1998): 357–362.

22 Andiara Petterle, "Reaching Latinos Through Virtual Goods," Media Post, June 10, 2010, http://www.mediapost.com/publications/?fa=Articles.showArticle&art_aid=129857, accessed July 13, 2010.

23 Chris Rio, "9 Strange Product Placements in Video Games," *List Verse*, August 4, 2013, http://listverse.com/2013/08/04/9-strange-product-placements-in-videogames/, accessed June 17, 2014.

24 Beth Snyder Bulik, "P&G's Bounty Picks Up Fans From Social Gaming," *Ad Age*, June 30, 2011, http://adage.com/article/news/p-g-s-bounty-picks-fans-social-gaming/228506/, accessed June 15, 2014.

25   Michelle R. Nelson, "Recall of Brand Placements in Computer/Video Games," *Journal of Advertising Research* 42, no. 2, (2002): 80–92.

26   Nancy Huehnergarth, "Water Is the Enemy, Gatorade Mobile Game Tells Youth," January 8, 2014, *Huffington Post,* http://www.huffingtonpost.com/nancy-huehnergarth/water-is-the-enemy_b_4557456.html, accessed July 12, 2014.

27   "Public Enemies Week on Zynga's Mafia Wars," *AppsSavvy,* http://www.appssavvy.com/publicenemies/, accessed July 11, 2010.

28   Tracy Tuten and Christy Ashley, "Do Social Advergames Affect Brand Attitudes and Advocacy?" *Journal of Marketing Communications,* 2013, http://www.tandfonline.com/doi/abs/10.1080/13527266.2013.848821#.U8UVUpRdWSp

29   City One Game, IBM, August 10, 2010, http://www-01.ibm.com/software/solutions/soa/newsletter/aug10/cityone.html, accessed June 17, 2014.

30   Dawn Anfuso, "Why You Need to Get in the Game," *iMedia Connection,* July 12, 2007, http://www.imediaconnection.com/content/15741.asp, accessed December 10, 2007.

31   Jack Loechner, "Advergaming," Research Brief, *Center for Media Research,* Media Post, October 24, 2007, http://blogs.mediapost.com/research_brief/?p=1550, accessed December 10, 2007.

32   Zachary Glass, "The Effectiveness of Product Placement in Video Games," *Journal of Interactive Advertising* 8, no. 1 (2007), http://jiad.org/vol8/no1/glass/index.htm, accessed December 10, 2007.

33   Grant McCracken, "Who Is the Celebrity Endorser? Cultural Foundations of the Endorsement Process," *Journal of Consumer Research* 16, no. 3 (1989): 310–321.

34   Jennifer Escalas, "Imagine Yourself in the Product: Mental Stimulation, Narrative Transportation, and Persuasion," *Journal of Advertising* 33, no. 1 (2004): 37–48.

35   Ralf Terlutter and Michael Capella, "The Gamification of Advertising: Analysis and Research Directions of In-Game Advertising, Advergames, and Advertising in Social Network Games," *Journal of Advertising* 42, no. 2–3 (2013): 95–112.

36   "Unfiction Glossary," *Unfiction,* http://www.unfiction.com/glossary, accessed July 18, 2010.

37   David Kiley, "Advertising of, by and for the People," *BusinessWeek Online,* July 25, 2005, http://www.businessweek.com/magazine/content/05_30/b3944097.htm, accessed July 13, 2010.

38   Jim Hanas, "Games People Play," *Creativity* 14, no. 1 (2006): 14.

(Continued)

(Continued)

39   David Kiley, "Advertising Of, By and For the People," *Business Week Online*, July 25, 2005, www. businessweek.com/magazine/content/05_30/b3944097.htm, accessed July 13, 2010.

40   "Glossary," http://www.unfiction.com/glossary, accessed July 18, 2010.

41   Michael Anderson, "Disney's The Optimist," *Wired*, July 2013, http://www.wired.com/2013/07/disney-the-optimist-arg/

42   "Inside the Magic, Inside The Optimist: Solving Disney's Alternate Reality Game," *Inside the Magic,* http://www.insidethemagic.net/inside-the-optimist-solving-disneys-alternate-reality-game-what-we-know/, accessed July 10, 2014.

43   Bryan Bishop, "'The Optimist': How Disney Imagineering Is Bringing Alternate Reality Games to the Mainstream," *The Verge*, August 20, 2013, http://www.theverge.com/2013/8/20/4639110/the-optimist-disney-imagineerings-push-to-bring-alternate-reality, accessed July 12, 2014.

44   Marko Muellner, "2014: The Year of Social TV," *ClickZ*, October 15, 2013, http://www.clickz.com/clickz/column/2300252/2014-the-year-of-social-tv, accessed July 13, 2014.

45   Douglas MacMillan, "Twitter Acquires Bluefin Labs to Add Social TV Tools," *Bloomberg News,* February 6, 2013, http://www.bloomberg.com/news/2013-02-06/twitter-acquires-bluefin-labs-to-add-social-tv-tools.html, accessed July 12, 2014.

46   Sheila Marikar, "Turning 'Likes' Into a Career," *New York Times*, July 13, 2014, http://www.nytimes.com/2014/07/13/fashion/social-media-stars-use-instagram-twitter-and-tumblr-to-build-their-career.html?_r=0, accessed July 13, 2014.

Visit the companion website for free additional materials related to this chapter: study.sagepub.com/smm

 # Social Commerce

LEARNING OBJECTIVES

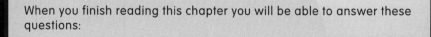

When you finish reading this chapter you will be able to answer these questions:

1   What is the relationship between social commerce and e-commerce?

2   How do ratings and reviews provide value for consumers and e-retailers?

3   How do social shopping applications and tools affect consumers as they move through the consumer decision-making process?

4   What are the psychological factors that influence social shopping?

The Zone of Social Commerce

When was the last time you went shopping? Yesterday? Last weekend? Were you online or in your local mall? Did you go alone or with someone else, or maybe even with a group? Shopping is at its heart a social activity. Doing it with others makes the activity more enjoyable—even when your shopping buddies don't agree with your choices. Our shopping companions, known among marketers as purchase pals, help us to think through our alternatives and make a decision. They validate the choices we make. When we don't have a purchase pal with us, we might turn to surrogate pals like sales associates and other shoppers. Shopping together can be a shared activity that strengthens our relationships with others, but it also reduces the risks we associate with making purchase decisions. Perhaps this has been one reason for the prevalence of in-store shopping over online shopping. E-commerce may finally have a solution for those who hate to shop alone but who would still rather browse online while they hang out at home in their pajamas: social commerce.

Social commerce is a subset of e-commerce (i.e., the practice of buying and selling products and services via the Internet). It uses social media applications to enable online shoppers to interact and collaborate during the shopping experience and to assist retailers and customers during the process.[1] Encompassing online ratings and reviews, numerous shopping related apps, deal sites and deal aggregators, and social shopping malls and storefronts, social commerce is the fourth zone of social media (Figure 8.1).

Historically, wired shoppers have relied heavily on the Internet as an information source during the decision process—but many then turn to offline stores to complete the purchase.

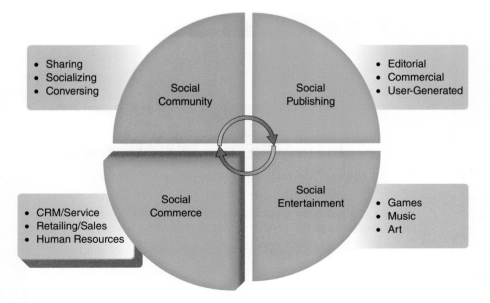

Figure 8.1   Social Commerce Zone

Increasingly though, these online researchers are converting to online shoppers—today over 82% of those who conduct research online also shop online.[2] Online shopping offers many benefits to shoppers, such as the ability to comparison shop easily and efficiently, convenience, enhanced selection, and cost savings. With advances in social commerce, online shopping can finally offer a shared experience too—the experience of social shopping. Though, importantly, social commerce is influencing offline as well as online purchase decisions.

At its core, social shopping refers to situations where consumers interact with others during a shopping event. Of course, just as in the physical world this changes the dynamic of shopping because it opens the door for others to influence our decisions.

Social media applications allow us to share product information electronically; easily post opinions and access the opinions of others; and communicate with friends, family, and associates about shopping decisions without regard to place or time. Whenever consumers navigate product information online using social commerce tools, such as bookmarking their favorite products, emailing product summaries, and subscribing to RSS feeds of other users' favorite product lists, they are social shopping. Social shopping provides utility to our shopping experience because it lowers our perceived risk.[3] We can feel more certain, by using social shopping tools, that we got the best price, made the best choice, and know whether our friends will approve of our decision. It's the digital answer to our desire as consumers to shop with others—but with the added convenience and power of online technologies.

Social Commerce: The Digital Shopping Experience

It's a cold day in mid-December, and David is spending some time on Facebook reading about his friends' recent activities. A social ad for 1-800-Flowers appears on the side of his news feed that promotes flowers as a Christmas gift and provides an endorsement that thousands of people like 1-800-Flowers. Remembering that he hasn't yet sent a Christmas gift to his grandmother in Texas, David gets a brainstorm—he really doesn't have the time to spend hours at the mall looking for something for Grammy. He clicks the ad to reach 1-800-Flowers' Facebook page. There he sees a promotion for 20% off his order if he "likes" the page and a "Shop Now" call to action. With a click of the Shop Now button on the Shop tab of 1-800-Flowers' page, David

Photo 8.1

can browse flower selections and price points. Not sure whether 1-800-Flowers is the best choice, David first visits 1-800-Flowers' Wall. Comments from past customers fill the page, and David can read the posts from satisfied and dissatisfied customers along with the responses from company service representatives. He chooses three arrangements he likes, but then he posts a message to his two sisters to help him decide which is best. They both respond within 10 minutes (and as usual, they both pick the same one!). Now David is confident he's got a winner, so he uses the Buy button where he chooses the arrangement and completes his transaction. Share technologies post to David's Wall—"David bought a holiday arrangement at 1-800-Flowers" and "David likes 1-800-Flowers." Once the flowers arrive and David knows how well Grammy liked them, he plans to return to the page to share a review on 1-800-Flowers' Wall. From there, the cycle begins again as another individual sees shared posts about the brand and/or social ads. Figure 8.2 illustrates how David's actions map to the consumer decision-making process—and he went through the whole process without leaving Facebook!

We all know some people who shop simply for the sport of it, and others (like David) whom we have to drag to a mall. Shopping is how we acquire needed products and services, but social motives for shopping also are important. Shopping is an activity that we can perform for either utilitarian (functional or tangible) or hedonic (pleasurable or intangible) reasons.[4]

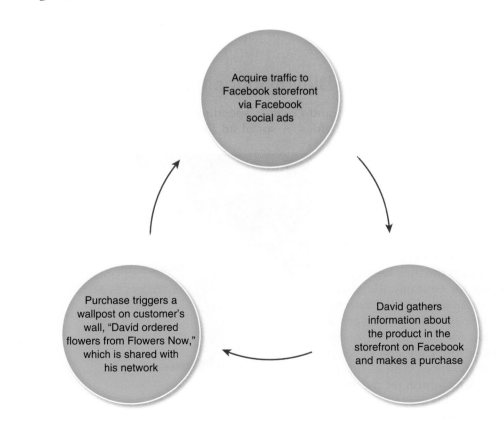

Figure 8.2   Social Commerce and the Customer Decision-Making Process

A shopper's motivation influences the type of shopping environment that will be attractive or annoying; for example, a person who wants to locate and buy something quickly may find loud music, bright colors, or complex layouts distracting, whereas someone who is there to browse may enjoy the sensory stimulation.[5] How such environments translate to social commerce shopping experiences is still unknown. But we can still see where these motives may play a role in social shopping. Hedonic shopping motives include social experiences (the social venue as a community gathering place), opportunities to share common interests with like-minded others, the sense of importance we experience when others wait on us, and the thrill of the hunt.[6] After all, the role of hunter/gatherer has long been ingrained in the human psyche.

Surely, too, there are utilitarian motives at play for social shoppers. E-commerce enabled shoppers to find alternatives and a wealth of pricing information with the click of a mouse. Consumers benefit from the convenience and ease of shopping with more choices and better information. Social commerce further enables shoppers to access opinions, recommendations, and referrals from others within and outside of their own social graphs, again potentially improving the ability for consumers to make the most rational and efficient decisions. But there's one more benefit offered by social commerce that was missing from e-commerce—the social aspect of shopping that people got when they shopped in person with their purchase pals. Social commerce provides that missing ingredient to the e-commerce equation. For example, David trusted his sisters' judgment a lot more than his own when choosing a gift for Grammy (though he would probably consult other purchase pals before he buys a new gaming console).

It was only a few years ago that retailers scrambled to figure out how to present their store offerings online and worried as to the effect of e-commerce on their traditional business models. Now, things are changing again as they assess the influence of consumer desires to shop online socially.

Social Commerce and the Shopping Process

At the end of the day, *shopping online is still shopping*. Sure, the way we locate and purchase products may not look the same—but the successful marketer understands that our basic shopping orientations (e.g., to obtain a needed product or service, to connect with others, to stimulate our senses, etc.) are the same as our ancient ancestors possessed.

Furthermore, it's helpful to break down the process of shopping in terms of the stages of consumer decision making. Though we may make some simple decisions in fewer steps, important decisions require five steps:

- Problem recognition
- Information search
- Alternative evaluation
- Purchase
- Post-purchase evaluation.

When we look at these stages we realize that what seems at first to be an "obvious" and quick decision ("throw something in the cart") is in fact a lot more complicated. On the bright side, many current social media applications are out there to help consumers make it through each of these stages. Table 8.1 summarizes the decision-making stages and illustrates some of these social media and social commerce tools that already are changing how we shop (but not why we shop!).

So social commerce is a part of e-commerce, and it leverages social media to aid in the exchange process between buyers and sellers. That seems straightforward enough, but social media are sufficiently complex and broad to influence e-commerce in all five of the consumer decision-making stages.

We noted earlier that even for offline purchases, wired consumers tend to search online for information prior to making an actual purchase. In a book sponsored by Google, Jim Lecinski explains the process, coining the term, ZMOT – Zero Moment of Truth.[7] The concept is based on a related concept long understood by retailers, and particularly those in the consumer-packaged goods industry. It draws from the notions

Table 8.1   Social Commerce Tools for Purchase Decision Stages

DECISION STAGE	SOCIAL COMMERCE TOOLS
Problem Recognition	Social ads on social networking sites Shared endorsements from friends posted in activity streams Curated images and lists on sites like Pinterest Location-based promotions (e.g., Foursquare)
Information Search	Comments (influence impressions) throughout social channels (opinions posted on a brand's Wall, tweets about an experience, etc.) Queries and responses within social networks (e.g., LinkedIn and Facebook) Ratings and reviews posted on sites (e.g., Yelp, Zagat, Citysearch) Product and pricing information available Deal directories Wish lists, gift registries
Evaluation of Alternatives	Bar code scanning/price comparisons Recommendations, testimonials, recommendation agents, and popularity filters ("ask your network" apps, video testimonials such as VideoGenie, and top lists from retailers such as Amazon) Referrals
Purchase	Shop within network options (e.g., Facebook Buy) Social stores and social shopping malls (e.g., Wanelo) Group buys (e.g., LivingSocial, Groupon)
Post-Purchase	Share opinion posts in activity streams Ratings and reviews on review sites and retailer website Reviews and product experiences posted on blogs

of First Moment of Truth (FMOT), the moment a consumer chooses a product from the store shelf, and the Second Moment of Truth (SMOT), the moment the consumer uses the product and feels satisfaction or dissatisfaction. ZMOT emphasizes that consumers today may be influenced in several moments online prior to making a purchase decision. Though the number of sources and types of sources vary by region and product category, on average consumers will use more than 10 sources of information before a purchase. These sources may be owned media content vetted by the brands in question, paid media in the form of an ad, or content posted by users in social media channels. Savvy brands will strive to be involved in this part of the purchase process, earning positive word-of-mouth and other forms of influence impressions, leveraging the content by encouraging its spread online, and facilitating the development of the content.

ZMOT information, whether a Pinterest board of favorites at Macys.com or a review of pizza places on Yelp, may or may not be social, but much of it is. This information, particularly that provided by reviews and ratings, influences consumers at multiple stages in the buying process. Reviews are assessments with detailed comments about the object in question. Ratings are simply scores generated by users that reflect assessments of attributes like perceived quality, satisfaction, or popularity on a scale. Estimates vary from study to study, but research consistently shows that the vast majority of Internet-connected shoppers globally search for product information online first.[8] Where people search varies but most start with a search engine and consequently can find all kinds of online content, including user-generated and brand-generated content on social channels. This search for information online may take place in social channels including social networks like Facebook, review sites like TripAdvisor, social marketplaces like Amazon, and more. Although shoppers may not always complete their purchases online, many do turn to the Internet to gather information prior to making a purchase. Sixty-four percent of shoppers said they spent 10 minutes or more reading reviews prior to making a purchase.[9] Nearly 40% reported reading eight or more reviews. In other words, this isn't a casual behavior. Shoppers are intensely studying reviews to improve their purchase decisions. Researching products online makes sense—it can save time, increase confidence, and reduce risk that might be associated with the purchase. It also ensures better, more credible information. Besides using opinions early in the decision process, consumers may also use ratings and reviews as a form of validation just prior to purchase. This is called verification.[10] That's right—today buyers seek out information online early in the purchase process, and then many return to validate the decision. Many later also write reviews and rate products in the post-purchase stage (the Second Moment of Truth – SMOT). Because reviews are so influential, retailers are inviting customers to rate their experience and write a review soon after products are delivered.

This information influences the consumer's alternative evaluation stage, with shoppers reporting that they read reviews to evaluate options both for products and retailers, compared prices and checked for deals, and considered the opinions of others. Even with 25% of online shoppers noting that they don't always consider online reviews to be fair or trustworthy, shoppers read the content and judge for themselves whether they feel a review is useful.[11] Consumers trust information provided online by other consumers more than television, magazine, radio, or Internet advertising, more than sponsorships, and more than recommendations from salespeople or paid endorsers.

By the time the shopper reaches the purchase point, he or she has used an average of 10 sources of information with about half being a source delivered via social media. The Second Moment of Truth (SMOT) is just as relevant as it always was. At the point of product use, the consumer evaluates the purchase and has the opportunity to feed others' ZMOTs with their shared experience and opinions.

The Marketing Value of Social Commerce

Marketers will be influenced by social commerce activities whether they chose to engage or not. That's because the reputation economy in which we live ensures that there is a publishing platform for individuals. We see content creation increase with access to social channels and communities, social software, and digital devices. Regardless of whether a brand is active, this content will be generated and will be accessible by a search online. For instance, one study of Yelp reviews looked at over 4,000 small businesses with reviews on its site. None of the businesses were also engaging in advertising on Yelp. Fortunately for them, they still benefited. The study revealed that the unsolicited, organic Yelp reviews were associated with increases in revenue of $8,000 annually on average. What's more is that brands that facilitated a presence on Yelp saw an average uptick of $23,000.[12] Another study found that for independent restaurants, a one-star rating increase on Yelp was associated with an annual increase in revenues of 5% to 9%.[13]

Influence impressions can take on many forms when it comes to user-generated content that relates to social shopping. The cornerstone is reviews. But ratings, recommendations, and referrals are also relevant. Recommendations can also include user-generated curated content such as shopping lists, Pinterest boards, Instagram photos, and more.

Whereas ratings and reviews are visible to everyone who wishes to see them, recommendations and referrals originate from the recipient's social graph. This makes them more influential than reviews and ratings because they leverage the social capital of the referrer. In fact, a Harris Interactive poll found that 71% of respondents said recommendations from family and friends have substantial influence on their purchase decisions.[14] And while we tend to trust reviews from strangers, we are more trusting of recommendations from people we know; 90% in the survey said they trust an online recommendation from someone in their network.[15]

Recommendations from friends and family are all around us, and the prevalence of social media in the lives of wired consumers heightens our ability to share these opinions. WOMMA claims that the average consumer mentions specific brands in conversations with others more than 90 times a week.[16] Just imagine how those influence impressions can travel when shared via social networks. This number could increase as people use social media to seek out recommendations. A study from researchers at Penn State found that 20% of Twitter posts were from people asking for or providing product information.[17]

Recommendations and referrals can be simple or integrated in their execution. Facebook's "like" button, now available on millions of external webpages, is a form of recommendation. When you click it, you publicly announce that you recommend the content on the page. While others can see the total number of "likes," anyone in your network can also see that you personally made a recommendation.

The Value of a Review

Ratings and reviews are not always useful. Companies like Amazon ask users to rate the reviews according to helpfulness to improve the quality of reviews. *Helpfulness ratings* (yes—a rating of a rating!) give a quality indicator to other users before they invest time reading and also provide feedback to those who complete reviews. What goes into a valuable rating and review? Ratings are a heuristic; a mental shortcut consumers use to help them with decision making. For instance, if you want to choose a restaurant near the amphitheatre where you are attending a concert this weekend, you might pull up all the restaurants in the area and then choose the one with the highest average rating. Reviews provide more detailed information for those who want to evaluate the choice at a deeper level. Consequently, a good review should include product information such as features and specifications, an overall impression of the product with a positive or negative judgment, a list of pros and cons, experience with the product, and a final recommendation.[18] With these components, the review will have sufficient information for the readers to judge relevance and credibility and apply the content to their purchase situation.

Increasingly, reviews are questioned. Why? Deception. Estimates suggest that as much as 30% of online reviews is fraudulent. Reviews likely to be deceptive tend to include information that is not related to product use and to lack verified purchase information. These reviews may be provided by marketers (on their own products or for competing brands) or by customers who have not actually bought the product in question. Researchers estimate that legitimate reviews may come from as few as 1.5% of reviewers.[19]

Benefits to E-Retailers

Product opinions affect shoppers, but that isn't the only way they impact the marketing process. Online reviews generate increased sales by bringing in new customers. Further, people who write reviews tend to shop more frequently and to spend more online than those who do not write reviews. Those who review products make up just a quarter of online shoppers, but they account for a third of online sales.[20] And consumers are willing to pay a price premium for products with higher ratings.[21] For e-retailers, this means that it makes good business sense to host rating and review features. Ratings and reviews also enhance organic search traffic to the website. Organic search results improve because reviewers tend to use the same keywords (tags) in their product descriptions that searchers will use. Petco, a pet supplies retailer, found that having customer reviews on its website generated five times as many site visits as any previous advertising campaign. Those who browsed Petco's Top Rated Products had a 49% higher conversion rate than the site average, and an average order amount that was 63% higher than the site average.[22]

Reviews result in better site stickiness—customers reading reviews will stay at a retail site longer than they would otherwise. They can also enhance the effectiveness of offline promotional strategies. For example, Rubbermaid added review comments from its website to the content included in its freestanding inserts. When reviews were included, coupon utilization increased 10%.[23] Lastly, the reviews and opinion posts become a source of research data for the business, highlighting consumer opinions in a frank yet unobtrusive fashion. Some businesses believe the data resulting from online reviews to be more valuable than data from focus group research. Businesses can learn whether consumers like a competitor's brand better and why, how consumers react to positive or negative press, what stories are being spread about the brand, and which customers are being evangelical and which ones are acting as "brand terrorists." In Chapter 9, our focus will be on how marketers can use social media content as a source of consumer insight.

While many forms of user-generated content known to influence the consumer decision-making purchase process will occur organically, savvy marketers can encourage this phenomenon, facilitate it by providing social software tools designed for social shopping, and partner with social marketspaces. We organize the descriptions of social commerce strategies in this way.

Social Commerce Strategies

Encouraging and Facilitating Influence Impressions

The first level of social commerce strategy is to utilize user-generated content, encourage it, and facilitate it with social sharing and shopping functionalities customers want—providing tools that make content creation and sharing easy and by incentivizing the behavior. At the simplest level, an online retailer can include share tools on its website. These tools may enable visitors to tweet an item, pin a picture to Pinterest, or save an item to their Wanola. More engaging tools include those that enable site visitors to create social video testimonials using their mobile phones (with social software apps like VideoGenie) or "share stories" in an onsite gallery. eMarketer estimates that 94% of major online retailers now include such social sharing tools on their websites.[24]

Online retailers can also enable other features that, while not user-generated, are based on user behavior and still represent a kind of social recommendation. These include features like wish lists, gift lists, and similarity recommendations (e.g., "others who bought this also bought").

Here's a summary of the opportunities online marketers can provide to encourage social commerce sharing that may facilitate sales:

- Share tools: social software plug-ins that enable easy sharing of products sold on a retailer's website to social networks. The most popular plug-in today for retailers is Pinterest. This sharing is a form of recommendation in that others in the user's social graph can treat the pin as an endorsement.
- Recommendation indicators: simple buttons that provide an onsite endorsement of a product. The most common options are Facebook's "like" and Google's +! buttons.
- Reviews and ratings: onsite reviews and ratings with tools for writing and rating.
- Testimonials: a form of recommendation that enables users to share a more personal story about their experience, possibly as a video endorsement.

- User galleries: virtual galleries where users can share their creations, shopping lists, and wish lists. This approach is sometimes called user-curated shopping and may occur onsite or offsite with a community like Wanelo.
- Pick lists: lists that help shoppers share what they want onsite, typically in the form of a wish list.
- Popularity filters: filters that enable the shopper to show products by most popular, most viewed, most favorite, or most commented.
- User forums: groups of people who meet online to communicate about products and help each other solve related problems.

Best Practices to Leverage Social Reviews and Ratings

Ultimately, it's important to remember that users are reading online reviews because they want to know what people like themselves think of a product. They must be able to trust those reviews; if they can't, the reviews won't be effective. To make the most of the opportunity, marketers should develop a social commerce approach with these characteristics:

- Authenticity: accept organic word-of-mouth, whether positive or negative.
- Transparency: acknowledge opinions that were invited, incentivized, or facilitated by the brand.
- Advocacy: enable consumers to rate the value of opinions offered on the site.
- Participatory: encourage consumers to contribute posts.
- Reciprocity: acknowledge the value of the opinions customers offer.
- Infectiousness: make it easy for users to share reviews on blogs and social networking platforms.
- Sustainability: online opinions are so influential because they live on in perpetuity. If a consumer tells a friend about a satisfying brand experience on the phone, the story once told is no longer retrievable or trackable. If the opinion is posted in a company-controlled review site (e.g., if you post a review of the leggings you bought from LegLuxe on its review area), the opinions can be moderated and the brand has an option not to publish.

What does this mean for marketers? First, marketers must ensure high standards when it comes to product quality and service if they wish to survive in the world of social reviews. It is so easy for anyone to tell everyone about his or her brand experiences, whether good or bad. That means those experiences had better be good—very good! Those that fail will have their sordid story broadcast to the social world as customers submit reviews and those reviews are shared via social networks. Second, brands should embrace, not hide—because really, online there is no place to hide—from consumer opinions. Instead, organizations can engage in word-of-mouth marketing by actively giving people reasons to talk about the brand while facilitating the conversations. The Word of Mouth Marketing

Association (WOMMA) identifies five key components to word-of-mouth marketing on its website, www.womma.org, all of which can be applied to managing online product opinions for brand value:[25]

- Educating people about your products and services
- Identifying people most likely to share their opinions
- Providing tools that make it easier to share information
- Studying how, where, and when opinions are being shared
- Listening and responding to supporters, detractors, and neutrals.

In other words, marketers should encourage the conversation by informing consumers about the brand, offering consumers a forum for expressing opinions about the brand, and responding (making the communication two-way) to comments consumers make on the forum and elsewhere. Customers can be invited to offer reviews, resulting in more engagement and the propagation of positive word-of-mouth communication about the brand. Perhaps most important is the final component of word-of-mouth marketing—listening. There is valuable information about the need for product improvements like product features and service quality embedded in ratings and reviews.

Why Don't All E-Retailers Offer Reviews and Ratings on Their Sites?

Aside from the problem that marketers and advertisers have overlooked their value and influence, the most commonly cited reason given for not allowing online reviews on sites is the fear that dissatisfied customers will use the review feature as a venue to *flame* a brand. Given the old adage that negative word-of-mouth communication is more damaging than positive word-of-mouth communication is beneficial, some retailers have erred on the side of caution when it comes to offering a review feature. The ratio of negative to positive reviews found on various sites suggests that this fear is unfounded. Bazaarvoice, a firm that provides a customer review and rating service for e-tailers, reports that 80% of its user-generated reviews are positive.[26]

In reality, retailers can benefit from negative reviews and should welcome them. Consumers want to see negative reviews to be able to accurately assess the degree of product risk they face when purchasing. They seek to minimize perceived performance and financial risk associated with purchases. Negative reviews give them the information they need to assess risk. The negative reviews also enhance credibility. Consumers often assume that if the reviews seem too good to be true, they probably are. Lastly, negative reviews give valuable information to the retailer on products that should be improved, augmented, or discontinued. The other primary deterrent for e-retailers is more operational in nature. There are challenges related to acquiring and managing reviews and the review process as well as site maintenance. Companies such as Bazaarvoice and PowerReviews provide solutions; they service retailers by providing the technology to capture and display customer feedback.

Social Promotions and Partnerships

In addition to leveraging user-generated content both through on-site tools and cross-platform partnerships, marketers can also facilitate sales using sales promotions offered through social deal partners and shopping carts in social vehicles like Facebook and Twitter. This is the second level of social commerce strategies.

The most extensive format would be to truly socialize the shopping function on the retailer's website. A few adventurous retailers gave this a shot (most notably, Levi's) but thus far, full implementation has not gained momentum. Amazon is perhaps the world's most friendly retailer for social shopping but synchronous, shared online shopping experiences are still not featured.

Another form is to provide for shopping from within the user's feed on his or her preferred social community. Facebook first offered a similar service known several years ago with shopping carts and transactions completed on the brand's Facebook page. While 62% of retailers tried the functionality in 2012, just 15% are estimated to still use that functionality.[27] More recently, Facebook and Twitter began offering shopping from within one's feed.[28] This allows the retailer to suggest products that are likely to be impulse purchases with social influence. It overcomes the issue of searchability within a large catalog of products, which caused frustration in the earlier versions of in-network social shopping.

Marketers can also partner with other sites for social shopping experiences. Sites like Motilo, Fashism, and GoTryItOn claim to provide a digital shopping experience akin to the one you'd have face to face with friends, known as Shop Together functionality. In addition, marketers may wish to offer sales promotions, short-term deals designed to generate demand in a specific time period, using social shopping communities like LivingSocial or Groupon. These sites have come under fire in recent years. They were originally seen as a panacea but as many businesses suffered from an inability to meet demand (remember our discussion on scalability?) and a negative return on investment, businesses became more reluctant. These communities still offer a way to provide a sales promotion to a large number of socially connected consumers, but should be closely evaluated. LivingSocial has redefined itself as a deal marketplace and includes features that speak to the referral power noted above. With its Me+3 option, when three friends buy a featured deal, the referring friend gets the deal for free! Geo-location communities and apps like Foursquare also offer partnership opportunities for social promotions.

Social shopping portals and partnerships can also be relevant. Wanelo enables users to share products they "want, need, love," which are linked to the product's page on the retailer's website. This enables conversion from browsing to truly buying. Wanelo thinks of itself as a digital mall where users can post favorite items, and comment and share with friends. Users link their favorites to specific retailer websites so that sales can be driven from Wanelo to the retailer's own site. It can be described as a multi-retailer catalog built as a social network. Products are listed with a Buy button that connects to the retailer. This kind of conversion is possible with other social sites too, but Wanelo has a critical mass that makes it especially relevant to marketers. For example, Urban Outfitters has fewer than 200,000 followers on Pinterest, but over 2 million on Wanelo. Facebook is the most used partner, with 86% of retailers identifying it as their most important social network for promoting specific products. Shopify reported that Facebook drove two thirds of the visits to Shopify-operated stores in 2013 with an average order value worldwide of $55.00. Pinterest had an average order value of $58.95 but drove fewer visits. The best vehicle with which to partner also depends upon the type of retailer. Pinterest generated 74% of social orders in the antiques and collectibles industry at Shopify-operated stores.[29]

A developing area in this realm is one known as "participatory commerce," which is sometimes also called social funding. It is part of social commerce because it enables entrepreneurs to include individuals in the development of a commercial venture by

THE DARK SIDE OF SOCIAL MEDIA

People write reviews of their experiences and they can do this on their own blogs, on branded sites, or on review sites like TripAdvisor and Yelp. If a person wants to be heard, there are hundreds of social sites that can publish the content. Most marketers want this coverage. We know from research assessing the reviews online that 80% of online reviews are positive. Among ratings, most brands earn on average a 4.3 of 5 stars. The fans are the ones critiquing, and happily, most of the time! But the negative review is also of value. It's valuable to those who might patronize the brand if it weren't for the information, and to the brand itself, in the form of research that can enable customer service recovery and product improvements.

Still, not everyone believes in the process. And the process may become increasingly regulated. That's what blogger Caroline Doudet learned after posting a review of the restaurant Il Giardino in Cap-Ferret, France. The restaurant owner sued Doudet claiming that Doudet's review ranked so high in the organic search engine results for the restaurant that it was thwarting its ability to do business. This is of course at the heart of why social publishing for a brand is relevant, and also why brands should truly seek to deliver on their promises. Alas, though Il Giardino's owner admitted to failing when it came to providing a good experience for Doudet, he believes it is unfair for one experience to influence the choices of others. The court agreed, fining Doudet and requiring her to pay court costs as well.[30]

The case is related to an ongoing EU controversy on the so-called right to be forgotten. The ruling makes search engines like Google responsible for eliminating or removing search results that provide links to past stories people and businesses don't want exposed. It's quite a controversy since the ruling makes the search engines, which did not create and do not control the content, responsible. Online advocates argue that this goes against the very culture of the Internet, which stands for openness and transparency. If onerous regulations force social networks to censor what is posted, will the democratic promise of the Internet evaporate?

funding at different levels. It is related to the microlending phenomenon. Interested in social funding? Check out the current projects featured on Threadless or Kickstarter.

To summarize, these more integrated approaches e-retailers can take for social commerce include offering sales promotions and social shopping opportunities, often with a partnering company. Marketers can use social commerce in several ways. The most simple approach is to encourage social sharing of the brand's offerings by providing share tools on the site. Some of these tools will result in recommendations and referrals. Other content can be encouraged by enabling a space for reviews and ratings or by developing a campaign that encourages fans to develop user-curated shopping lists. Conversion can be enhanced with social deals and campaigns planned with partners and with in-network shopping functionalities.

Social media marketers who want to win customers find it helpful to understand what we know more generally about the psychology of influence—the factors that make it more or less likely that people will change their attitudes or behavior based on a persuasive message. In particular, some social shopping tools play to our cognitive biases. This term refers to the "shortcuts" our brains take when we process information. Unlike computers that impassively process data and produce the same result each time (when they work!), humans aren't so rational. Two people can perceive the same event and interpret it quite differently based on their individual histories, gender, and cultural biases. For example, our reactions to colors are partially "colored" by our society, so a North American might interpret a woman in a white dress as an "innocent bride" while an Asian might assume the same woman is going to a funeral since white is the color of death in some eastern cultures.

Cognitive biases are important when we look at purchase decisions, especially because they influence what we may pay attention to and how we interpret it. Even though consumers have access to more information than ever before when it comes to purchase decisions, they are also faced with the limitations of bounded rationality. Bounded rationality captures the quandary we face as humans when we have choices to make but are limited by our own cognitive capacity.[31] As consumers, we typically approach an identified need with an information search followed by alternative evaluation. In a world of search engines and social media, though, our information search could potentially be limitless. With thousands of online retailers carrying products, millions of product reviews to sort through, and hundreds of "friends" to ask for recommendations, online commerce is fraught with information overload; there's simply too much data for us to handle.

When consumers are confronted with more complexity than they can manage comfortably, bounded rationality kicks in. We adjust to the overload by finding ways to make decisions without considering all the information for an optimal choice. Instead, we often satisfice—this means we expend just enough effort to make a decision that's acceptable but not necessarily the one that's "best." We call the shortcuts we use to simplify the process heuristics. This term describes "rules of thumb" such as "buy the familiar brand name" and "if it's more expensive it must be better."

This process of using heuristics to simplify the decision-making process is sometimes referred to as thinslicing, where we peel off just enough information to make a choice.[32] When we thinslice we ignore most of the available information; instead we "slice off" a few salient cues and use a mental rule of thumb to make intuitive decisions. Research on the psychology of influence identifies six major factors that help to determine how we will decide.[33] Let's review them and illustrate how social shopping applications and tools harness these heuristics.

Social Proof

We arrive at many decisions by observing what those around us do in similar situations. When a lot of people select one option (e.g., a clothing style or a restaurant), we interpret this popularity as social proof that the choice is the right one. There are several ways that marketers use social proof. For instance, identifying brands as the #1 choice, market leader, and so on, all point to evidence of social proof. In social commerce applications, tools can enable shoppers to see the social proof related to the product. As more people jump on the bandwagon a herding effect can occur.[34] Herd behavior occurs when people follow the behavior of others.[35]

Although in every age there certainly are those who "march to their own drummers," most people tend to follow society's expectations regarding how they should act and look (with a little improvisation here and there, of course). Conformity is a change in beliefs or actions as a reaction to real or imagined group pressure. In order for a society to function, its members develop norms, or informal rules that govern behavior. Without these rules, we would have chaos. Imagine the confusion if a simple norm such as stopping for a red traffic light did not exist.

We conform in many small ways every day—even though we don't always realize it. Unspoken rules govern many aspects of consumption. In addition to norms regarding appropriate use of clothing and other personal items, we conform to rules that include gift-giving (we expect birthday presents from loved ones and get upset if they don't materialize), sex roles (men often pick up the check on a first date), and personal hygiene (our friends expect us to shower regularly).

We don't mimic others' behaviors all the time, so what makes it more likely we'll conform? These are some common culprits:[36]

- *Cultural pressures:* different cultures encourage conformity to a greater or lesser degree. The American slogan "Do your own thing" in the 1960s reflected a movement away from conformity and toward individualism. In contrast, Japanese society emphasizes collective well-being and group loyalty over individuals' needs.

- *Fear of deviance:* the individual may have reason to believe that the group will apply *sanctions* to punish nonconforming behaviors. It's not unusual to observe adolescents who shun a peer who is "different," or a corporation or university that passes over a person for promotion because she or he is not a "team player."

- *Commitment:* the more people are dedicated to a group and value their membership in it, the greater their motivation to conform to the group's wishes. Rock groupies and followers of TV evangelists may do anything their idols ask of them, and terrorists can be willing to die for their cause. According to the principle of least interest, the person who is *least* committed to staying in a relationship has the most power because that party doesn't care as much if the other person rejects him or her.[37] Remember that on your next date.

- *Group unanimity, size, and expertise:* as groups gain in power, compliance increases. It is often harder to resist the demands of a large number of people than only a few—especially when a "mob mentality" rules.
- Susceptibility to interpersonal influence: this trait refers to an individual's need to have others think highly of him or her. Consumers who don't possess this trait are *role-relaxed*; they tend to be older, affluent, and have high self-confidence. Subaru created a communications strategy to reach role-relaxed consumers. In one of its commercials, a man proclaims, "I want a car . . . Don't tell me about wood paneling, about winning the respect of my neighbors. They're my neighbors. They're not my heroes."[38]

In Table 8.2 you can see that several of the social shopping tools we covered earlier influence shoppers with social proof. Any content that we can share with others includes a social proof component. When you choose items for an online wish list and then share that list with your network of friends, you've given your friends social proof that the items listed are desirable. And, testimonials have long been a source of social proof that a product is the right one to choose. New social tools such as VideoGenie make it possible for customers to share their stories with video clips they record with their mobile phones or web cams. At one time, testimonials were limited to those of typical person endorsers, celebrity endorsers, or word-of-mouth communication. Now, users can share testimonials with a written story, comments, or a video.

Authority

The second source of influence is authority. Authority persuades with the opinion or recommendation of an expert in the field. Whenever someone has expertise, whether that expertise comes from specialist knowledge and/or personal experience with the product or problem, we will tend to follow that person's advice. We can save time and energy on the decision by simply following the expert's recommendation. In advertising, we see the use of authority in ads for pain relievers that state "9 out of 10 doctors recommend." A doctor should know which medicine is best for pain, and the copy in the advertisement delivers this advice.

However, the use of authority is also in play when we see ads from someone who has experience with choosing a product for a specific functional need. For example, when Mia Hamm or Peyton Manning endorses Gatorade products, it's based not on credentials in the area of nutrition, but rather on their personal experience with needing a beverage that can rehydrate them efficiently. We listen to them because, as elite athletes, they ought to know which product is best. In the realm of social media, authority can be activated in several ways, including referral programs, reviews (from experts as well as from existing customers who can speak with the voice of experience), branded services, and user forums.

Although citizen endorsers are not paid agents representing a brand, they do hold a position of authority in the minds of other consumers. Professional experts and reviewers, whether book critics, movie critics, doctors, or lawyers, have authority in specific, relevant product categories but so do citizen endorsers who have actually used the product. In other words, one's experience with the product serves as the source of authority.

Table 8.2   Social Shopping Tools and Sources of Influence

SOCIAL SHOPPING TOOL	SOCIAL PROOF	AUTHORITY	SCARCITY	AFFINITY	CONSISTENCY	RECIPROCITY
• "Ask your network"				*	*	
• Brand butler services					*	*
• Deal directories			*			
• Deal feeds			*	*		*
• Filters	*					
• Group buy			*			*
• Lists	*			*	*	
• Recommendations	*	*		*	*	
• Referral programs	*	*	*	*		*
• Reviews	*	*			*	
• Share tools	*			*		
• Shop Together				*		
• Storefronts				*		
• Testimonials	*	*				
• User forums	*	*				*
• User galleries	*			*		*
• Geo-location promotions			*		*	

Affinity

Affinity, sometimes called "liking," means that people tend to follow and emulate those people whom they find attractive or otherwise desirable. If we like someone, we are more likely to say yes to their requests or to internalize their beliefs and actions as our own. We talked about how advertising often uses endorsers as a source of authority. They can also be used as a source of affinity. While Peyton Manning is an expert when it comes to whether Gatorade is the best choice for hydration during times of physical exertion, he is simply a likable celebrity when he endorses Timex watches. With social media, affinity is almost always present because the social shopping is tied to your social graph—to your friendships. Some tools that leverage affinity as a source of influence are "ask your network" tools that enable shoppers to request real-time recommendations from their friends, deal feeds (where friends share deals), shopping opportunities posted in friends' news feeds, pick lists, referral programs, sharing tools, and shop together tools.

Scarcity

We tend to instinctively want things more if we think we can't have them. That's the principle of scarcity at work. Whenever we perceive something as scarce, we increase our efforts to acquire it—even if that means we have to pay a premium for the item and buy it before we would otherwise have wanted. Marketing promotions that use scarcity as an influence tool might focus on deals that are time-sensitive, limited-edition products, or products that are limited in supply. In social commerce, scarcity applications include deal feeds, news feeds with special offers, group buy tools, referral programs, and deal directories.

Reciprocity

The rule of reciprocity basically says that we have an embedded urge to repay debts and favors, whether or not we requested the help. Reciprocity is a common norm of behavior across cultures. We reciprocate kindnesses in part because we feel it is the fair and right thing to do (a social contract we have with others) and in part because reciprocation is important to well-functioning relationships. Reciprocity influences daily interactions all around us. It may be as simple as choosing a birthday present for someone for whom you wouldn't normally buy a present, but you do because they gave you a gift on your birthday. Marketers activate the rule of reciprocity to encourage consumers to choose a specific brand and to show loyalty to the brand over time. The key is to initiate an offer of some kindness, gift, or favor to the target audience. The targeted consumers will then feel compelled to respond in kind.

This is the basic principle behind the sales promotion technique of sampling; where a marketer offers a free trial of a product to consumers. The free trial illustrates the relative advantage of the product, but it also creates the perception of having received a gift in the minds of consumers. Consequently, sales of sampled products are higher than those of products that are not sampled. Some retailers send birthday and holiday cards to their top clients. Even something as simple as a greeting card can be perceived as a kindness that should be reciprocated. In social commerce, several tools can be perceived as a favor or kindness offered by the brand. These include deal feeds, group buy, referral programs, and user forums.

Consistency

People strive to be consistent with their beliefs and attitudes and with past behaviors. When we fail to behave in ways that are consistent with our attitudes and past behaviors, we feel cognitive dissonance, a state of psychological discomfort caused when things we know and do contradict one another. For example, a person may believe it's wrong or wasteful to gamble, yet be drawn to an online gambling site. To avoid this discomfort, we strive for consistency by changing one or more elements in the situation. Thus, our gambler may decide that he or she is betting the house only due to "intellectual curiosity" rather than due to the thrill of betting. The need for consistency is a fairly broad source of influence because it can be activated around any attitude or behavior. Marketers may instigate the need for consistency with image ads, free trial periods, automated renewals, and membership offers. Some of the social shopping tools that include a consistency component include ask your network tools, social games, pick lists, share tools, shop together tools, reviews, forums, and galleries.

FROM BYTES TO BUCKS

Social Commerce Leverages Fan User-Generated Content to Drive Sales

Goran Bogicevic / Shutterstock.com

Photo 8.2

Smart brands are actively thinking about how the products fans share to social networks like Pinterest and Instagram are generating awareness, celebrating the brand, and ultimately driving clicks to purchase. They also understand how users might incorporate brand images on both these sites differently. Curalate, a company that provides tools for brands to integrate user-generated content for branding and demand-generation marketing activities, thinks of this relationship among different visually oriented social networks as optimizing brand celebration (Instagram) with aspirational content (Pinterest).

Urban Outfitters used Curalate's Fanreel product to integrate user-generated photos into its e-commerce site and then used those photos to drive customer loyalty and sales. In their first two months of using Fanreel, Urban Outfitters was able to collect more than 13,000 user-generated images of people celebrating their Urban Outfitters style. These inspirational images were linked to relevant product pages, giving browsers an immediate path to purchase. In fact, user-generated content on Urban drove a 15% clickthrough to product pages. The picture is clear: social proof sells.

Urban Outfitters' customers now upload between 100 and 200 Instagram photos a day via the hashtag #UOOnYou, which populate directly into Curalate's Fanreel. From there, Urban Outfitters can choose images and link them to its digital catalog. Because the system enables links from user photos to a product number, visitors can easily click on a user-generated photo and purchase an item. The system allowed Urban Outfitters to leverage the user-generated content for engagement by rewarding fans with onsite exposure while driving online sales. Most importantly, Urban is celebrating the customers who are celebrating the brand. Additionally, since Fanreel analytics include insights like page views, impressions, and interaction duration, Urban can now easily recognize which user images are resonating with consumers and use those photos to inform other marketing decisions.

Benefits of Social Commerce

So far we've talked about the ways that marketers can approach social commerce. But what benefits does social commerce offer to marketers?

1 It enables the marketer to monetize the social media investment by boosting site and store traffic, converting browsers to buyers, and increasing average order value.

2 It solves the dilemma of social media return on Investment (ROI). ROI is a metric for understanding how much value was created by an investment. We'll explore this concept in depth in Chapter 10. Some criticize social media for their lack of accountability, but linking sales to social media eliminates this criticism.

3 Social commerce applications result in more data about customer behavior as it relates to the brand.

4 Social shopping applications enhance the customer experience. They make online shopping fun and functional, which should mean higher levels of customer loyalty and better long-term customer lifetime value.

5 Social shopping makes sharing brand impressions easy. The brands earn referral value with these easy-to-use word-of-mouth tools.

6 Brands can keep up with the competition, and maybe differentiate themselves from others in the e-commerce space.

CHAPTER SUMMARY

What is the relationship between social commerce and e-commerce?

Social commerce is a subset of e-commerce (i.e., the practice of buying and selling products and services via the Internet). It uses social media and social media applications to enable online shoppers to interact and collaborate during the shopping experience and to assist retailers and customers during the process. Encompassing online ratings and reviews, applications, numerous shopping related apps, deal sites and deal aggregators, and social shopping malls and storefronts, social commerce is the last zone of social media.

How do ratings and reviews provide value for consumers and e-retailers?

Ratings are simply scores people, acting in the role of critic, assign to something as an indicator. The rating may reflect perceived quality, satisfaction with the purchase, popularity, or some other variable. Reviews are assessments with detailed comments about the object in question. They explain and justify the critic's assigned rating and provide added content to those viewing the content. Both serve as a source of research during the information search and evaluation of alternatives stages of the buying process and as a tool for verifying a decision before purchase. For retailers, positive reviews generate increased sales by bringing in new customers. Further, people who write reviews tend to shop more frequently and to spend more online than those who do not write reviews. Consumers are willing to pay a price premium for products with higher ratings, too. Ratings and reviews also enhance organic search traffic to the website.

Explain how social shopping applications and tools affect the consumer decision-making process.

Table 8.1 indicates which social shopping applications primarily affect each stage of the consumer decision-making process. Many of these applications are influential in the information search and evaluation of alternatives stages, but to some extent social shopping is relevant throughout the process.

Describe the psychological factors that influence social shopping.

Research on the psychology of influence identifies six major factors that help to determine how we will decide; these can be applied to social commerce. These sources of influence include social proof, authority, affinity, scarcity, consistency, and reciprocity. Social proof occurs when we can see what others would choose or have chosen. Authority persuades with the opinion or recommendation of an expert in the field. Professional experts and reviewers, whether book critics, movie critics, doctors, or lawyers, have authority in specific, relevant product categories but so do citizen endorsers who have actually used the product. Affinity, sometimes called "liking," means that people tend to follow and emulate those people for whom they have an affinity. With social media, affinity is almost always present because social shopping is tied to your social graph—to your friendships. We tend to instinctively want things more if we think we can't have them—that's the principle of scarcity at work. In social commerce, scarcity applications include deal feeds, news feeds with special offers, group buy tools, referral programs, and deal directories. The rule of reciprocity basically says that we have an embedded urge to repay debts and favors, whether or not we requested the help. In social commerce, several tools can be perceived as a favor or kindness offered by the brand. These include deal feeds, group buys, referral programs, and user forums. The final source of influence is our tendency to be consistent. People strive to be consistent with their beliefs and attitudes and with past behaviors. Some of the social shopping tools that include a consistency component include ask your network tools, social games, pick lists, share tools, shop together tools, reviews, forums, and galleries.

KEY TERMS

affinity
authority
bounded rationality
cognitive biases
cognitive dissonance
conformity
First Moment of Truth (FMOT)
herding effect
heuristics
information overload
principle of least interest
principle of scarcity

psychology of
  influence
purchase pals
ratings
reviews
rule of reciprocity
sales promotions
satisfice
Second Moment of Truth
(SMOT)
share tools
Shop Together

social shopping
social shopping
  portals
social video testimonials
susceptibility to interpersonal
  influence
testimonials
thinslicing
user-curated shopping
user forums
user galleries
verification

REVIEW QUESTIONS

1   Explain the concept of purchase pals. Do you pull your offline and online purchase pals from the same pool of friends and family, or are they different somehow?

2   How is social commerce related to e-commerce? In the future, will e-commerce be able to exist without social applications? Why or why not?

3   What are the benefits that accrue to businesses implementing social shopping applications?

4   Explain the two approaches retailers can take toward social commerce.

5   How are reviews different from recommendations?

6   Why are ratings an important cue to include with a review site?

7   Explain the concept of bounded rationality as it relates to social shopping.

8   Which stage of the decision-making process is most affected by the dimensions of social commerce? Explain.

9   What is thinslicing?

10 Explain the six sources of influence prevalent in social commerce applications.

EXERCISES

1   Search Wanelo for brands you like. Can you buy the products you find? Is a recommendation tool included in the page? Can you add products to your shopping cart and check out from within the page? In your opinion, what could make the site more effective?

2   Which are more influential—reviews from experts or reviews from customers? Explain.

3   Review the list of social shopping applications presented in the chapter and visit some of the sites that use these applications. Social shopping applications provide functionality for customers, such as enhanced organization, price comparisons, risk reduction, and access to product information, but they also make the shopping experience more fun. Tag the list of applications based on the benefit the application provides—utility or fun. Which aspect of social shopping is most important to shoppers?

CHAPTER NOTES

1   Adapted from "Simple Definition of Social Commerce (With Word Cloud & Definitive Definition List)," *Social Commerce Today*, November 17, 2009, Updated June 2010, http://socialcommercetoday.com/social-commerce-definition-word-cloud-definitive-definition-list/, accessed July 28, 2010.

2   Jeffrey Grau, "US Retail E-Commerce Forecast: Room to Grow," *E-Marketer*, March 2010, http://www.emarketer.com/Reports/All/Emarketer_2000672.aspx, accessed July 28, 2010.

3   J. Shen, "Social Comparison, Social Presence, and Enjoyment in the Acceptance of Social Shopping Websites," *Journal of Electronic Commerce Research* 13, no. 3 (2012): 198–212; cf. J. Shen and L. Eder, "An Examination of Factors Associated With User Acceptance of Social Shopping Websites," *International Journal of Technology and Human Interaction* 7, no. 1 (2011); J. Shen, L. Eder, and J. D. Procaccino, "Social Comparison and Trust in the Acceptance of Social Shopping Websites," *International Journal of Electronic Business* 8, no. 4 (2010).

4   For a scale to assess these dimensions of the shopping experience, see Barry J. Babin, William R. Darden, and Mitch Griffin, "Work and/or Fun: Measuring Hedonic and Utilitarian Shopping Value," *Journal of Consumer Research* 20 (March 1994): 644–656.

5   Velitchka Kaltcheva and Barton Weitz, "When Should a Retailer Create an Exciting Store Environment?" *Journal of Marketing* 70 (2005): 107–118.

6   Mark J. Arnold and Kristy Reynolds, "Hedonic Shopping Motives," *Journal of Retailing* 79, no. 2 (2003): 77–95.

7   Jim Lecinski, *ZMOT Handbook*, Think with Google, 2012, http://www.thinkwithgoogle.com/collections/zero-moment-truth.html, accessed May 23, 2013.

8   Yubo Chen, Scott Fay, and Qi Wang, "The Role of Marketing in Social Media: How Online Consumer Reviews Evolve," *Journal of Interactive Marketing* 25, no. 2 (2011): 85–94.

9   "5 Social Shopping Trends Shaping the Future of Ecommerce," *Power Reviews and the eTailing Group*, 2010, http://www.powerreviews.com/case-studies.php, accessed January 1, 2011.

(Continued)

(Continued)

10   "New Research Reveals Best Approach to Harness the Power of Online Influence on Purchase Behavior," *Cone,* http://www.coneinc.com/consumers-confirm-recommendations-online, accessed July 29, 2010.

11   Ayaz Nanji, "Do Consumers Trust Online Reviews," *MarketingProfs.com,* September 5, 2013, http://www.marketingprofs.com/charts/2013/11563/do-consumers-trust-online-reviews, accessed July 13, 2014.

12   Sebastian DiGrande, David Knox, Kate Manfred, and John Rose, "Unlocking the Digital-Marketing Potential of Small Businesses," *BCG Perspectives,* March 19, 2013, https://www.bcgperspectives.com/content/articles/digital_economy_marketing_sales_unlocking_digital_marketing_small_businesses/, accessed July 20, 2014.

13   Michael Luca, "Reviews, Reputation, and Revenue: The Case of Yelp.com," Harvard Business School Working Paper Series, 2011, http://www.hbs.edu/faculty/Pages/item.aspx?num=41233, accessed June 12, 2012.

14   Quoted in "Social Commerce Statistics," *Bazaarvoice,* http://www.bazaarvoice.com/resources/stats, accessed July 30, 2010.

15   Jake Hird, "Online Consumers Trust Real People, Not Companies," *eConsultancy,* July 8, 2009, http://econsultancy.com/blog/4175-online-consumers-trust-real-people-not-companies, accessed July 30, 2010.

16   "Buyers Guide," *WOMMA, The Keller Fay Group,* http://buyers.womma.org/companies/keller-fay-group/, accessed July 30, 2010.

17   "20% of Tweets About Brands," *Social Media Today,* September 14, 2009, http://www.socialmediatoday.com/SMC/123878, accessed July 30, 2010.

18   Warren Barnes, "5 Components a Written Product Review Must Have," *ezinearticles.com,* http://ezinearticles.com/?5-Components-a-Written-Product-Review-Must-Have&id=4160024, accessed July 29, 2010.

19   Eric Anderson and Duncan Simester, "Reviews Without a Purchase: Low Ratings, Loyal Customers, and Deception," *Journal of Marketing Research* 51, no. 3 (2014): 249–269, http://web.mit.edu/simester/Public/Papers/Deceptive_Reviews.pdf, accessed July 20, 2014.

20   "Leading Retail Analyst Shows Retailers Can Gain Market Share Through Consumer-Generated Product Ratings and Reviews," *Bazaarvoice,* August 15, 2006, http://www.bazaarvoice.com/about/press-room/leading-retail-analyst-shows-retailers-can-gain-market-share-through-consumer-generated-product-rati, accessed January 1, 2011.

21 "Online Consumer-Generated Reviews Have Significant Impact on Offline Purchase Behavior," *comScore*, November 29, 2007, http://www.comscore.com/Press_Events/Press_Releases/2007/11/Online_Consumer_Reviews_Impact_Offline_Purchasing_Behavior, accessed July 30, 2010.

22 Don Davis, "Customer Reviews Help Cut Product Return Rate at Petco," *Internet Retailer*, June 26, 2007, http://www.internetretailer.com/2007/06/26/customer-reviews-help-cut-product-return-rate-at-petco, accessed July 30, 2010.

23 "Rubbermaid Products with Reviews Show Increased Revenues," *Bazaarvoice* Case Study, January 2010, http://www.bazaarvoice.com/resources/case-studies/rubbermaid-products-reviews-show-increased-revenues, accessed July 29, 2010.

24 "Social Commerce Roundup," *eMarketer,* July 2014, http://on.emarketer.com/Roundup-07012014-SocialCommerceRoundup.html, accessed July 20, 2014.

25 "An Introduction to WOM Marketing with Definitions," *WOMMA,* http://womma.org/wom101/, accessed January 1, 2011.

26 "Leading Retail Analyst Shows Retailers Can Gain Market Share Through Consumer-Generated Product Ratings and Reviews," *Business Wire*, August 15, 2006.

27 "Social Commerce Roundup," *eMarketer,* July 2014.

28 Silicon Republic, "Tweet-Commerce: Social Media Giants Gear Up for Future of Shopping," July 18, 2014, http://www.siliconrepublic.com/new-media/item/37682-tweet-commerce-social-medi/, accessed July 19, 2014.

29 "Social Commerce Roundup," *eMarketer,* July 2014.

30 Kadhim Shubber, "French Blogger Fined €1,500 for Bad Restaurant Review," *Wired,* July 17, 2014, http://www.wired.co.uk/news/archive/2014-07/17/french-blogger-fined-google, accessed July 19, 2014.

31 Gerd Gigerenzer and Reinhard Selten, *Bounded Rationality: The Adaptive Toolbox* (Cambridge, MA: MIT Press, 2002).

32 Paul Marsden, "How Social Commerce Works: The Social Psychology of Social Shopping," *Social Commerce Today*, December 6, 2009, http://socialcommercetoday.com/how-social-commerce-works-the-social-psychology-of-social-shopping/, accessed July 29, 2010.

33 Robert Cialdini, *Influence: The Psychology of Persuasion* (New York: Collins, 1998).

34 J. H. Huang and Y. F. Chen, "Herding in Online Product Choice," *Psychology & Marketing* 23, no. 5 (2006): 413–428.

(Continued)

(Continued)

35   Wenjing Duan, Bin Gu, and Andrew Whinston, "Analysis of Herding on the Internet—An Empirical Investigation of Online Software Download," *Proceedings of the Eleventh Americas Conference on Information Systems,* Omaha, NE, USA, August 11–14, 2005, http://www.hsw-basel.ch/iwi/publications. nsf/ bc26b92ec161bc8fc 12572180036eb62/592d 9e78196c07fec 125722e00292418/ $FILE/VIRTCOM01-1424. pdf, accessed July 20, 2010.

36   For a study that measures individual differences in proclivity to conformity, see William O. Bearden, Richard G. Netemeyer, and Jesse E. Teel, "Measurement of Consumer Susceptibility to Interpersonal Influence," *Journal of Consumer Research* 15 (March 1989): 473–481.

37   John W. Thibaut and Harold H. Kelley, *The Social Psychology of Groups* (New York: Wiley, 1959); W. W. Waller and R. Hill, *The Family, a Dynamic Interpretation* (New York: Dryden, 1951).

38   Bearden, Netemeyer, and Teel, "Measurement of Consumer Susceptibility to Interpersonal Influence"; Lynn R. Kahle, "Observations: Role-Relaxed Consumers: A Trend of the Nineties," *Journal of Advertising Research* (March–April 1995): 66–71; Lynn R. Kahle and Aviv Shoham, "Observations: Role-Relaxed Consumers: Empirical Evidence," *Journal of Advertising Research* (May–June 1995): 59–62.

PART III

Social Media Data Management and Measurement

Social Media for Consumer Insight

LEARNING OBJECTIVES

When you finish reading this chapter you will be able to answer these questions:

1 How do companies utilize social media research? What are the primary approaches to social media research?

2 What is the research process for collecting, processing, and analyzing residual social media data used in social listening and monitoring?

3 What are the common errors and biases associated with social media research?

4 How do brands manage the social listening process?

5 What is the process for netnographic research in social media communities?

The Role of Social Media in Research

To plan a social media marketing strategy that will meet objectives, marketers need to understand their consumers and their environment. They need to know the answers to questions about consumer personalities and past experiences, motives and fears, responses to campaigns, brand loyalties, and media usage. They may need to listen to consumer complaints. They may need to assess the effectiveness of a marketing campaign. Why? Because every decision we make as marketers is based on what we know about the target audience and the marketing environment. From the product benefits to the brand image to the creative strategies used in the campaign to the media placement of the message, we make decisions based on what we know. And, we make better decisions when we understand the environment within which we compete. Gathering market insight and competitive intelligence are critical steps to develop strategy. Relying upon research—market, competitive, and consumer—to make more informed marketing decisions is standard practice for marketers.

Marketers rely on several variants of marketing research to make decisions. Our options include both secondary and primary research. Secondary research is information already collected and available for use. It may be internal, published publicly, or available via syndicated sources. Secondary data might include background on the market, industry, competitors, and the brand's history. In contrast, primary research is collected for the research purposes at hand. Primary data can help marketers to understand consumers in the market, including psychological makeup, spending and media consumption patterns, and responsiveness to message appeals and offers. We conduct primary research via exploratory, qualitative methods such as observation, focus groups, and in-depth interviews; descriptive techniques such as surveys; or with experimental techniques such as simulations and test markets. None of that changes when we work in social media—only the techniques that we use to collect this information.

Social media provides new sources of data and information that were once difficult to collect or altogether unavailable. In this chapter, we discuss the developing area of social media research and how social media marketers can utilize social content as a valuable source of marketing information. Social media research is the application of scientific marketing research principles to the collection and analysis of social media data such that valid and reliable results are produced.[1]

Social media research can include both secondary and primary research. As we participate in the social media zones, we leave residual evidence of our activities and opinions (our social footprint). Such residue can become rich sources of data (this is currently the main focus of social media researchers). In addition, we can utilize social media channels and communities as modes for data collection, conducting interviews, focus groups, surveys, and experiments. We're not going to go into detail about the foundations of marketing research in this chapter (are you relieved?). However, we will highlight the basic process for social media listening as well as some of the tools that improve an organization's ability to understand what its customers want and how they relate to its offerings.

Social media have expanded the outlets for consumer expression; they have shifted the importance of utilizing user-generated content to a higher level. Content is shared by many users across many forms of social media communities. The content includes opinions, experiences, and facts expressed in text, audio, and video. Conversations are built around the content. As conversation has increased in quantity, quality, location, and format, it has also become more useful and significant to marketers. Every piece of content shared socially online is data. It is residual data that can be collected and analyzed to help marketers provide customer service and service recovery (social customer care solutions), insight for developing marketing strategies, and assessments of the effectiveness of past marketing choices in meeting marketing objectives. Companies can utilize these social data by strategically using social listening and monitoring functions.

Social Customer Care

Brand mentions can be used to identify service satisfaction issues. In this way, listening to social media conversations is a key activity for marketers involved in social CRM tactics. For instance, customer service teams can monitor social media to detect posts by people who write to vent about a "disservice" experience they had with a company. While 75% of social media users are thought to write posts that are at times brand-related, 26% of people are complainers. And, of those, 80% expect a company response to their posted complaint.[2] If an organization learns about complaints quickly, it can respond quickly as well. It may have a chance to salvage a customer relationship it would have lost if the wound had been allowed to fester.

Some brands are better than others at this! Which global brands are the most responsive to customer posts? Halo BCA has been the world's leader with an average response time of 3 minutes. National Rail responds on average within 6 minutes. Movistar Panama responds within 9 minutes. American Airlines typically responds within 10 minutes and Jet Blue within 12 minutes.[3] You can see more social responsiveness scores at www.socially-devoted.com.

As an added bonus, it may actually turn lemons into lemonade because word spreads about the positive actions the organization took to address the problem. Consider this real-life example: A man took his car for servicing at the auto maintenance shop at a Sears in Honolulu, Hawaii. When he picked up his car he found it in a decidedly different condition from when he first dropped it off. Snack wrappers and empty water bottles were in the car and, interestingly, it had less gas! It seems someone had decided to joyride in his car during its stay at the Sears shop. Appalled, he tweeted about his experience on Twitter. Within hours, a Sears service representative reached out to him, made an offer to make things right, and arranged a time for the man to bring the car in for detailing. How does this customer feel about Sears now? He's one of the retailer's biggest fans.[4]

Market Research

Social media research can inform many decisions facing the marketing strategist. These might range from ideas for new product development to target audience insight to concepts for new campaigns. It can alert marketers to impending trouble for crisis communications that might be marked by a shift in the velocity of brand mentions. It can also track brand mentions on competitors' brand names. Tracking brand mentions of key competitors and comparing those points to those for the brand enable marketing managers to learn how the brand is positioned in the marketplace.

Campaign Assessment

Social media research can also be useful for providing feedback on how a campaign or other brand communication was received by others. For example, Dove released its "Patches" video as part of its ongoing "Campaign for Real Beauty." Historically, the campaign, which emphasizes the unique beauty in each woman, has performed well, earning kudos from its global target market and critics alike. The campaign includes traditional media components, including print ads in magazines, billboard ads, and broadcast video adverts, but has always included a strong social media focus. Videos with a longer message than typical for a television commercial are posted on Dove's YouTube channel and garner millions of views. Past videos have even inspired parodies, suggesting that Dove's message has taken on the characteristics of a meme.

SHOW ME! 👁

Dove patch: bikeriderlondon / Shutterstock.com

Photo 9.1

The *Patches* video, created by Ogilvy & Mather Brasil, documents a study of women who are told they are in a test group for a new pharmaceutical treatment. They are asked to wear a patch for several days and keep a diary of their experiences. The patch is associated with feelings of self-confidence and beauty among the women and then the video exposes the big reveal—it's just a patch. There is nothing in the patch at all. By the numbers, the video was a success. It garnered millions of views globally in just a few days. Still, while other Dove videos were acclaimed, critics were outraged. But Dove doesn't sell to critics. It sells to women. Social media research helped Dove understand how its target audience felt about the video. Radian6/Salesforce Marketing Cloud found that a sample of comments in social media (20,000) were overwhelmingly positive, with a 92% positive sentiment score.[5]

Social Media Listening: The Research Process

Observational research involves recording behavior or the residual evidence of behavior. Researchers in offline contexts have done this for years; they watch people as they shop in stores, or perhaps count the number and type of candy wrappers people throw out after a party to see what they're eating. Online this kind of residual data exists in abundance. Not all of it is available to social media researchers. Some is privacy-protected. But much of these data are not. Social listening tools can draw from anything that's publicly available in the social media space. That means marketers can utilize content shared across all four zones of social media including conversations in social networks and forums, blog posts and comments, product reviews, photos shared in sites such as Instagram, videos shared on sites such as YouTube, social bookmarks and comments, and microblog posts. This content can be very useful, because it offers insight marketers can use in segmentation, needs analysis, and customer profiling. Conversations that include influence impressions provide information about brand awareness, attitude toward a brand, competitive advantage, and more because these brand mentions are explained in the context of an online discussion. Companies may approach the collection and analysis of these social data in different ways, but before we discuss the degrees of social media listening, let's review the basic process.

An Overview of Social Media Listening and Monitoring

Social media listening and monitoring is the most popular approach to social media research. It literally means to monitor conversations and content in social media channels by "listening." This listening works with the aid of software that systematically searches key words it finds in social spaces such as blogs, social networks, and forums. By carefully choosing and searching the appropriate key words and the relevant social communities, the researcher can gather insight into customer decision making, perceptions of the brand, perceptions of competitors, and more. Early in the development of social media research, the difference between listening and monitoring was in the consistency of the approach to the process; listening was done on an ad hoc basis, whereas monitoring occurred more systematically. Today, these terms are used interchangeably. An automated monitoring service may be retained to crawl the web (much as search engine bots do), collecting conversations according to established criteria (called scraping) for inclusion in a database. From that database, conversation volume, source, and sentiment can be gauged. At this point, analysts have access to both quantitative and qualitative data.

Monitoring explains what was said, when, by whom, and how many times. Thus, this process answers four basic questions:

1 How many times was the search term found?
2 When was the search term found?
3 Where was the search term found?
4 Who mentioned the search term?

The content of the data collected using monitoring is of great use to marketers. Positive comments can turn into customer testimonials for use in retailing and promotions. Comments about competitors serve as competitive intelligence. Conversations among like-minded groups of friends and connections provide consumer insight that's useful for targeting and positioning. But it gets even better: monitoring results in the development of a detailed database that analysts can use to create more insights as they synthesize the comments of thousands of people. In well-designed systems, these data can be merged with data from other channels. For instance, a brand using Radian6 could merge the data from social monitoring with data collected from its salesforce.

Unlike a lot of traditional survey research, which is quantitative (i.e., in numerical form), much of the data collected are qualitative. Typical types of data include verbatims (the actual comments people post in English or other languages) as well as other identifying information such as the time the item was posted and the site on which it appeared. Multimedia posts can also be analyzed.

The approach requires the specification of a formal research design before any data are collected. The research design specifies a plan to collect and utilize data so that desired information can be obtained with sufficient precision and/or so that hypotheses can be tested properly. It includes decisions on the study approach (exploratory, descriptive, or experimental), the sampling plan to be used and procedures for data collection, and data analysis decisions. This in turn gives the researchers more confidence if they wish to generalize their findings to a larger population (e.g., many or all of their customers). When we apply a scientific approach to gathering data for social media research, we plan a research design to maximize the reliability and validity of our study. In addition to collecting data systematically using software that can collect and scrub relevant content, we pay special attention to the minimizing sources of error that could create bias in our results. We do so as we consider our research design decisions and set data collection protocols. Next we discuss some of these specific approaches, such as text mining, sentiment analysis, and content analysis.

Sentiment Analysis

Sentiment refers to how people think or feel (especially feel) about an object such as a brand or a political candidate. Sentiment is heavier on emotion than reason but it captures an opinion about something. In that regard, collecting and analyzing sentiment data can provide an alternative to attitudinal surveys of consumers—if, and it's a big if, people are talking about what you need to know in social spaces.

How can marketers use sentiment analysis? They can analyze product reviews to obtain insight into the mix of features people want, and the product's strengths and weaknesses. News mentions of a company can be analyzed to indicate perceptions of the company in terms of product quality, service quality, performance, and value. Customers can use sentiment analysis to systematically utilize reviews when they make purchase decisions.

Sentiment analysis is at its core attitudinal research. In fact, sometimes it is called opinion mining. In the context of social media conversations, it means at a very basic level to analyze content to determine the attitude of the writer. When we employ social media research to assess attitudes toward a brand, we essentially seek to determine whether the relevant conversations are positive or negative. Certain emotions are strongly related to specific words. When people feel a particular way they are likely to choose certain words that tend to relate to the emotion. From these words, the researcher will create a word-phrase dictionary (sometimes called a *library*) to code the data. The program will scan the text to identify whether the words in the dictionary appear. The words and phrases in the dictionary are also used as text classifiers, in that once data are retained for further analysis, the data can also be classified according to the words and phrases in the dictionary. That might sound simplistic, but it doesn't mean it's easy to analyze sentiment. It's incredibly labor-intensive when analyzed by human coders and complex when analyzed with text mining software.

Consider this example based on Canon's PowerShot A540. A review on Epinions, a product review site, included this statement: "The Canon PowerShot A540 had good aperture and excellent resolution." A sentiment analysis would extract the entities of interest from the sentence, identifying the product as the Canon PowerShot A540 and the relevant dimensions as aperture and resolution. The sentiment would then be extracted for each dimension; the sentiment for aperture is "good" while that for resolution is "excellent." Of course, at this level, the coding is probably managed by text mining software. Many users post assessments; the individual sentiments are obtained and stored in a database for further analysis and reporting. Let's review the steps to conduct a sentiment analysis:[6]

Step 1:	Fetch, crawl, and cleanse. Data from the sources are collected using web crawlers. These simple applications move through the designated websites and collect and store the content they find. These are the same types of programs search engines use to catalog webpages. Using the word-phrase dictionary, the crawlers select only the content that appears to be relevant based on matches with the dictionary. This process is called **fetching** or **web scraping**. The scraped data need to be cleansed to eliminate unnecessary formatting prior to moving forward. A text classifier (from the dictionary) is then applied to the data to filter any irrelevant content that made it into the data set.
Step 2:	Extract entities of interest. From this filtered set of content, relevant posts are extracted. Remember, a blog post might contain information on several brands, not just the ones of interest in the study. The data are filtered again using rules to tag the entities of interest and further narrow the data set.

| Step 3: | Extract sentiment. From there, the analyst can begin sentiment extraction using sentiment indicators. These are words or other cues used to indicate positive or negative sentiment. In what proximity to the brand mention must they be to serve as an indicator? Accuracy is best when proximity is close. That's one reason why sentiment analysis of tweets tends to be more accurate than that of blogs; the message intent is easier to interpret when the data per content piece are smaller.[7] A **sentiment dictionary** specifies sentiment indicators and rules to be used in the analysis. For instance, if the word "high" is in close proximity to the word "price," the sentiment may be scored as negative. The rules are in place in part to deal with sentence structure patterns. For instance, negation words such as "no," "not," or "never" can totally transform the meaning of a sentence; the analysis will need to be programmed to properly extract the sentiment intended. |
| Step 4: | Aggregate raw sentiment data into a summary. Raw sentiments are then aggregated creating a sentiment summary. |

However, as with any technique there are challenges associated with sentiment analysis:

- First and foremost is accuracy in gauging sentiment with automated tools. The sheer volume of conversation creates an information overload issue for most brands wanting to use social media monitoring and research. The solution is the use of an automated system, but these systems still struggle with accuracy in the coding of meaning. Systems that use a mix of human analysis, keyword meaning, and natural language processing tend to provide the best accuracy scores.

- Cultural factors, linguistic nuances, and differing contexts all make it difficult to code text into negative, neutral, or positive categories. Consider this example: Perhaps we want to know the attitudes toward the movie *Chef*. We could scrape the social Web for comments about *Chef*. But could a machine accurately code those comments? For example, the word "hunger" might be denoted as a negative term. But since this movie is about the restaurant industry, a comment about hunger could be positive. A person could understand that this statement was positive for the movie, but the software program couldn't. Linguistic nuances make it difficult for mining software to achieve better accuracy levels. A chocolate torte described as wickedly sinful would be coded as negative, when it fact the descriptor is positive.

- Defining the sentiment dictionary can also be a challenge, ultimately affecting whether the right words are extracted. Words can have many meanings. Take BP, for instance. As the oil spill in the Gulf of Mexico created a public relations crisis for the company, measuring sentiment before and after recovery steps and announcements is a useful tool to gauge damage control for the brand's image. But in a world of acronyms, BP may mean blood pressure, border patrol, business plan, Brad Pitt, or bipolar disorder.

- Accuracy in the categorical data needed to make better use of data is also an issue. It's difficult to gauge who is making comments (which segments they represent) in terms of demographic and geographic descriptors. Conversation origin may be identifiable using the URL, the IP address, or the language used, but all of these methods have flaws. The URL and IP address are not always helpful (take Facebook, for instance, with users around the world). Language indicators likewise leave a lot to be desired.

Content Analysis

Sentiment analysis is a form of text mining: the gathering and analysis of text data from relevant sources. Sentiment analysis uses a bottom-up approach to extract patterns from text. Human coders identify the sentiment indicators and interpret patterns, but the emphasis is on software manipulation of the data based on extraction rules.

In contrast, content analysis, an analysis approach used to identify the presence of concepts and themes within qualitative data sets, uses a top-down approach that applies theory or empirical evidence to the coding process. For example, a researcher might test a hypothesis that TV commercials reinforce traditional sex-role attitudes by sampling a large number of ads that aired during a certain period of time and comparing the occupations that male versus female actors portrayed.

Both sentiment analysis and content analysis can include quantitative analysis, but the intent is to enable the researcher to make inferences about messages in the content relevant to the research questions. Because content analysis is used to study the meanings relayed through content, the content used as sources is broadly defined. It is most often text-based but may include multimedia. The content could originate from books, essays, interviews, newspaper headlines and articles, speeches, advertising, and so on. For social media researchers most content originates from social conversations and user-generated content posted online. The primary *unit of analysis* is the word.

Table 9.1   Coding Categories for Content Analysis

TYPE OF CODE	PURPOSE
Context codes	Provide information on the source of the comment
Respondent perspective codes	Capture the general viewpoint revealed in the comment
Process codes	Indicate when over the course of the campaign a comment occurred
Relationship codes	Indicate alliances within social communities
Event codes	Indicate unique issues in the data
Activity codes	Identify comments that require response

To conduct a content analysis, the text is coded, or broken down, into manageable categories on a variety of levels—word, word sense, phrase, sentence, and theme—and then examined further for interpretation. Using codes, labels that classify and assign meanings to pieces of information, analysts can use the comments to determine any themes that are reflected in the comments. Table 9.1 summarizes major coding categories researchers use and provides examples to illustrate each.[8]

Caution! Research Errors and Biases

When we look at research results, it's tempting to jump to quick conclusions about what is going on "out there." However, we need to be very careful about doing so because a variety of potential other explanations for the results exist. Numerous biases and errors may complicate the story. Every study has a certain amount of error that we cannot precisely specify; our goal as researchers is to minimize that error. Ultimately we want our research to provide as close an estimation of the truth as it is possible.

Let's briefly review several types of errors that are particularly dangerous for social media research. Market researchers should remain vigilant against potential sources of bias that could interfere with the reliability and validity of the research outcomes. Though numerous errors are possible at every stage of research, our focus is on minimizing coverage error, sampling error, measurement error, and nonresponse error. Interpretation error is also an issue for social media research, but we will address that error in the section on analysis.

Coverage and Sampling Errors

One of the first decisions we must make (after we identify the need for research information and our research approach) is to establish the population from which we need to collect data. If we were collecting primary data using survey research or interviews, we would specify the units of interest, likely the people or families to which we wish to generalize the study results. This is known as defining the population. That's because we want to select participants for our study who represent the people in our population. If we were to study the whole of the population rather than a subset (known as a sample), this would be called a census (like the one the U.S. government conducts every decade). We would then define a sample frame, an available list that approximates the population and from which we draw a sample to represent the population.

Alas, in social media research it generally isn't possible to identify unique people as units in a defined population, though we still want to ensure that our content is representative. It also isn't possible for us to scour the entire Internet every day for every single brand mention to conduct a census of brand mentions. Instead, we define the population as the social communities to which our audience belongs. We create a sampling frame of selected social communities and websites based on their descriptions; these include membership demographics, purpose, location, and activity. In other words, rather than identifying a population of consumer units that matches our target audience and then defining a sampling frame that provides a list from which to draw access to that population, we define a population of relevant communities for those consumer units.

The sample refers to the units of content we draw from the frame for inclusion in data analysis. In this case the sampling plan should also include specifications on identifying relevant content and the time period in which content is drawn. For example, let's say we want to understand how our new video game product fares in relation to other games that are similar. We define our population as members of gaming sites such as GamesForum and Gaming Bay. Our sampling frame could be all members who post on these two forums over a 4-week period, including 2 weeks prior to and 2 weeks post video game launch.

The first source of potential error we need to address is coverage error. This occurs when there is a failure to cover all components of a population being studied. It represents a gap between the sampling frame we use and the population we define. For social media research, the researcher must ask, "Which social media platforms and sites should be (and can be) included in data collection?" We are limited in coverage by the need to access publicly posted commentary. For instance, tweets are largely public content, so Twitter is one platform researchers commonly include in social media research studies. Coverage error occurs if we fail to specify the places where the people we want to study choose to hang out. It would be hard to justify a sample of hard-core gamers that did not include members of the *GamersTalk* forum. If we failed to include this group, our sample might suffer from coverage error.

Sampling refers to the process a researcher uses to select specific cases from a sampling frame for inclusion in a study (note that sampling in research, discussed in Chapter 1, refers to a different process than the kind of sampling that takes places as a form of sales promotion). It is almost always used in research because in most cases it is financially or logistically impossible to use a census. That's especially true for social media that literally include several platforms, thousands of sites, millions of pages and profiles, and zillions of individual pieces of content that could serve as data. A well-devised sampling plan helps ensure that a small portion of the data in the sampling universe can provide as accurate a depiction of the truth as we could get if we actually took a census of the entire population. The issue is, what is the truth? Sampling error is the result of collecting data from only a subset, rather than all, of the members of the sampling frame; it heightens the chance that the results are wrong. In our example, we would commit a major sampling error if we somehow sampled only female gamers who are in their fifties.

In survey research, sampling error is associated with how we draw our sample, using either a probability or non-probability method. For social media research, we will utilize these guidelines in collecting data, but two situations create additional concerns in the area of sampling error for social media researchers: (1) the echo effect and (2) the participation effect. The participation effect is when only some people are participating, and some participate at a high rate, effectively inflating the number of conversations that relate to the research. The actual number of conversations may not always be what it seems.

The echo effect, also called online echo, refers to the duplication in conversation volume that tends to occur in social media spaces. Online echo exists because people who share content online tend to share it in more than one community, and people in the sharer's network may then also share the same content. In Twitter, this is called *retweeting*, but sharing another person's content is common (and encouraged) throughout social media. Thus, the question is how should retweets and reposts be counted in a study?

There are also other forms of irrelevant content that can create sampling error. Spam is increasingly common in social communities and signature lines but it does not represent real conversations we should include in the data set. Further, some marketers pay bloggers and other social media influencers to discuss their respective brands. These paid brand mentions could also be collected during the sampling process, but again, they do not reflect real conversations. To make it even more complicated, organic conversations could grow around these paid brand mentions. Some content is also duplicate content that is simply retweeted automatically by bots programmed to spread messages with specific keywords.

How should researchers handle these issues in the collection of data? The solution to these issues is not as simple as creating a rule to not include duplicate content. If a comment is shared by other people, the extent of sharing is an indicator of increased exposure of the message and sentiment in that someone felt the message worthy of passing along, even if the sharing didn't express an original thought. How we handle different types of mentions and duplicates is something that we must agree to before we start the study.

Nonresponse Bias

There is the potential for nonresponse error in social media research due to the participation effect. In survey research, nonresponse error is the potential that those units that were not included in the final sample are significantly different from those that were. If there are relevant differences, the results based on participating units may not accurately reflect the population of interest. For example, people who are willing to take a 30-minute phone survey may be different than those who aren't. This can result in nonresponse bias, a skewing of the results of a survey.

In social media research, we can sample from any public content posted on the sites we specify in our sampling frame. So why are we concerned about nonresponse bias? Because we've specified our population based on the communities where our customers are likely to be, but our ultimate interest is the attitudes and behaviors of people, not sites. Our specification of social media communities served as a proxy for access to the people. But not all people who are members of social communities participate actively or at the same level. We know from Chapter 3 that most people are not generating original content. Some people consume content, some join and lurk, and some are not active in social communities at all. That means there are people who may use a brand but who are not represented in the social media research analysis.

It is important to keep in mind that searches of social content may not be systematic or exhaustive. They may not be representative of the possible sites where relevant content is posted. In research terms, this form of search is akin to a *convenience sample*; the information we get is suggestive, but it's difficult to generalize it to the broader population. Though there are vast amounts of content available for analysis, we must also remember

Table 9.2   Category Distribution of Offline and Online Word-of-Mouth for the 700 Most Talked About Brands

CATEGORY DISTRIBUTION OF OFFLINE AND ONLINE WORD-OF-MOUTH

	% OF OFFLINE	% OF ONLINE
Beauty products	5%	1%
Beverages	13%	3%
Cars	10%	17%
Children's products	2%	0%
Clothing products	7%	3%
Department stores	5%	4%
Financial services	4%	2%
Food and dining	12%	4%
Health products and services	3%	1%
Home design and decoration	1%	1%
Household products	2%	0%
Media and entertainment	9%	32%
Sports and hobbies	3%	8%
Technology products and stores	13%	17%
Telecommunications	9%	7%
Travel services	3%	1%

In a study of online and offline conversations of 700 of the most discussed brands, researchers found that what is talked about varies considerably. Offline, there are product categories that make up a large percentage of the overall conversation, but no one category dominates the discussions. Online, however, things are a bit different. A third of all conversations relate to media and entertainment brands, and cars and technology make up another third. There is very little conversation about the other product categories.

Source: Mitchell Lovett, Renana Peres, and Ron Shachar, "On Brands and Word of Mouth," *Journal of Marketing Research*, 2013 (August), 50 (4), 427–444.

that many conversations about consumer needs and brands are still held offline—some estimate that as much as 90% of word-of-mouth conversations potentially of interest to marketers is conducted offline.[9]

What consumers talk about online in social channels and offline may vary considerably.) One study of offline and online conversations of 700 brands in 10 product categories over a 3-year period found that online conversations gravitated heavily to media and entertainment products, technology products and services, and cars.[10] In contrast, offline conversations included heavier coverage for beverages, food and dining, cars, and technology but with no specific areas dominating the discussions. Table 9.2 illustrates the percentage of discussions by category offline and online.

Also, the content people share varies for different forms of social sites. Those who post tweets on Twitter are far more vocal than those who share feedback to videos they see on YouTube, but both sites may be included in our sampling frame. This issue must be addressed and can be managed after data collection by using weighting. Sampling weights are adjustment factors applied to adjust for differences in probability of selection between cases in a sample. For example, less than 9% of all Internet users are on Twitter, but Twitter generates up to 60% of content that social media monitoring tools monitor. This means that to get a more accurate picture of all users we might want to sample relatively fewer tweets than other kinds of posts. Without weighting, the data will be skewed based on the sites we choose for data collection.

THE DARK SIDE OF SOCIAL MEDIA

Is It Ethical to Mine Social Conversations?

Social media research is a hotbed of discussion among researchers. Ethical guidelines for the treatment of human subjects are well developed for direct forms of observation. But in social media research, much of the data are public. What responsibility does a researcher have to actually get informed consent?

When researchers conduct research with human subjects, they operate under a policy of informed consent. Participants are made aware of the research and its benefits and implications, and they are given the opportunity to withdraw or move forward. In social media environments, monitoring is akin to data mining of residual traces of consumer behavior, except the traces include opinions, stories, photographs, and videos. Given the often personal nature of the content shared, should researchers seek permission to collect and analyze content? Is it even feasible to acquire the equivalent of informed consent in social media communities?

How should you handle the attribution of comments analyzed and quoted? When it comes to social media research, the data may come entirely from unsolicited comments. Assuming identity can be identified, would the original source want attribution or prefer to have his or her identity protected? Researchers using public social media posts rely upon the fact that the posters could have chosen to protect the post to justify the lack of informed consent for their research. However, many social media posts reference another person—a person who is then inadvertently embedded in the research study without an explicit action to suggest he or she agreed.[11]

In some situations, the researcher may engage in social media communities to have access to data (passive data collection) and perhaps also to tease out conversations on particular topics of interest (social media's version of "man-on-the-street interviews"). In the passive version, the monitoring requires membership to access the content in closed communities. The researcher lurks or eavesdrops by playing the role of community member. But once a member, the researcher can also pose questions and post opinions that may elicit responses from others. Should researchers disclose their affiliations to such communities?

As a start toward developing ethical guidelines for social media researchers, one blogger has proposed a set of rules he adapted from the guidelines a major marketing research organization (ESOMAR) applies to members who collect observational (or passive) data in the physical world:[12]

- If content has been posted to a truly public domain (i.e., there is no gate to viewing data such as registration), it can be used by the researcher.

- If content is posted in a "gated community" to be available to members only, researchers should announce their presence and request cooperation. Researchers should never pretend to be something or someone they are not when they interact in social communities.

- Assess whether the data to be collected will include personally identifiable and/or sensitive information. If they do, take steps to comply with relevant policies and protect the interests of the affected individuals. Processing of personally identifiable data should require informed consent, or at a minimum the implication of deemed consent.

- Prior to reporting and sharing of data, analysis, or results, all data should be made anonymous.

- Take steps to ensure that no harm is done due to researcher behavior or research uses.

Social Data Management

Try this simple exercise: Visit Twitter and search the term "Starbucks." How many hits did you get? Hundreds of mentions even within the past hour, most likely. For a brand like Starbucks, listening is a challenge. There are simply too many conversations going on to monitor them on an individual basis—to do so would probably require hundreds of employees who would need to drink a lot of lattes to keep up with the torrent of comments.

Organizations can approach social media listening anecdotally or more systematically. At the early stages of maturity, many organizations essentially just listen to what users say in cyberspace. Analysts collect content haphazardly and inconsistently as they try to track the comments people post about their brand. For instance, they may compile a list of comments people make on a brand's Facebook fan page or the company blog. At times, they may run searches using tools such as Google Alerts, Twitter Search, and Blog Pulse to get a sense of how many times their brand is mentioned in posts. Deep Sherchan, CMO and co-founder of *Simplify360*, criticized this approach, succinctly stating, "Doing Google is not listening. That's like saying, I listen to my customers when I want to."[13] Fortunately, as organizations recognize the value of residual data shared in social channels, their approaches are likely to become more systematic and grounded. At that point, social media listening becomes social media monitoring and is fully integrated into the company's marketing functions. The social web is rich in tools for searching social conversations. The following list highlights the top tools for simple social media listening:

- BoardTracker
- Google Blog Search
- Omgili
- TweetDeck
- BackType
- Twitter Search
- Hootsuite
- HowSociable
- Topsy
- Google Alerts
- Google Trends
- Social Mention

When organizations have more complex research needs and/or face managing potentially hundreds of thousands of incidences of conversation around specific terms, they will likely shift to a more advanced use of social media research. For companies that manage social media monitoring in-house, social media listening becomes a part of the social media command center, a central hub for visually monitoring social data related to the brand's marketing objectives. Stations in the center focus on specific data such as brand mentions by influencers and customer complaints. Walmart e-Labs, for instance, acquired the social media listening service, Kosmix, to fully integrate these capabilities into its command center. Twitter acquired Trendrr, another social media listening service, to improve its offerings for its advertisers. Others may utilize either a social listening software program like SAS Social Media Analytics, a product of SAS Institute, Inc., or partner with a vendor providing enterprise social listening. Forrester defines it as "the management and analysis of customer data from solicited and unsolicited feedback channels, used to find insights and activate and recalibrate marketing and business programs."[14] Importantly, the leading vendors for enterprise social listening have the capability to pull global data from across the Internet, integrate these data with other important data sources to enable multichannel analysis, provide an easy-to-use dashboard, and aid in the interpretation of data and in devising strategy based on the results. Some of the leaders in the space include Radian 6/Salesforce Marketing Cloud, Crimson Hexagon, and Netbase.

FROM BYTES TO BUCKS

An In-Depth Look at Social Listening Analysis

Radian 6, part of the Salesforce suite, allows organizations to track, monitor, and react to customer comments. The system enables real-time insights to guide decisions drawing from over 650 million sources from Twitter, Facebook, YouTube, blogs, news, and more.

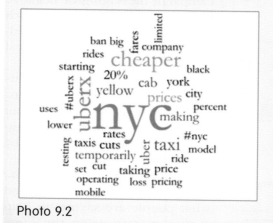

Photo 9.2

The system enables brand managers to see what people are saying about the campaign, understand who is saying what, and possibly why ... because themes may appear. We can see the results in word clouds and in sentiment analysis. The analyst can access information from the campaign and company, but also about the competitors and their campaigns.

A simple word cloud, drawn from comments in social sources, can provide insights for marketing managers.

Let's take Uber and New York City's taxi industry as an example. Uber is a ride-sharing service. People with the Uber application on their smartphone can post a message requesting a ride. The driver closest to the prospective passenger has up to 15 seconds to accept the request. The drivers charge a fee, but no money changes hands. Fees are exchanged through the app using the passenger's credit card information. Anyone can provide a ride. This means that Uber drivers compete with taxi services in metro areas.

In an area of high demand, like New York City, Uber may want to assess how its service (and independent drivers) compete with New York City taxi drivers. The analysis reveals social conversations about taxi fares in the city. The analysis also reveals momentum around a current event that relates to our industry. We can evaluate the commentary and choose to act if relevant ... or not.

UberX Social Listening for Consumer Intelligence
what are people talking about, where and why?

Photo 9.3

UberX Social Intelligence, Real-time Trends, Consumer Voices
what are people talking about, where and why?

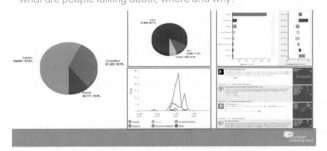

Photo 9.4

UberX Summarized Insights for Enhanced Targeted Campaigns
when people are most active, on what channels

Photo 9.5

The analysis provides a social snapshot of our campaign. We can isolate the social conversations to see topics of interest, themes, advocates, and specific social channels and do so in a way that provides a comparison to competitors. That's not all. We can also do this by segmentation bases.

Using Radian6, we can accurately analyze how a product, campaign, or services compare against the competition and industry.

For Uber, we can view when conversations spike in time and whether spikes are associated with campaign messaging or negative feedback. We can also assess which social vehicles are being used. What's more, we can do this in real time.

The data provide us with insights and intelligence about our prospects as well as how they feel about the brand, macro views by country and language, micro views by top influencers, and more.

Radian6 easily isolates the best conversations to understand what people are saying, to help ensure we are using the same terms to drive SEO and website traffic. These charts are totally interactive, so we can easily look at questions, complaints, or which social channel each theme is happening on. We can look at who is influencing the conversation from trending hashtags, to who is being influenced by whom. Sentiment analysis helps determine any sudden change of feeling (good or bad) that our community has toward our company, campaign, or products. Conversations can be ranked by influence and sentiment—but also classified for quick action into areas like service cases, complaints, sales leads, or general questions.

A social media marketers' dream? Imagine a world of just in time marketing, imagine knowing who you are reaching, the interests that each demographic from gender to location to specific age groups are rallying around, so that you are always relevant with your content, your promotion or the method in which you engage. Radian6 gives that level of detail with a click of a button. It illustrates how each audience talks and feels about your company or brand. Are the 18- to 25-year-olds more active on Twitter than the 46- to 55-year-olds? What are the popular hashtags and why? Whatever the questions are, knowing is better than not knowing.

Primary Social Media Research

Thus far in this chapter, we've introduced two approaches to marketing research using the residual data that people leave behind as they interact in social channels. These sources of data are valuable because they provide marketers with insights into consumer opinions, interactions, and behaviors. Importantly, as secondary data, these traces are readily available and inexpensive for organizations that choose to mine the social Web. However, using residual data is not the only approach marketers can take to social media research. Organizations can collect primary data in social spaces, too. The possible approaches include the use of consumer diaries, interviews and focus groups, surveys, and experiments—all conducted within channels of social media.

For instance, Firefly MB, a global qualitative research company, conducted a global study of consumer views of social media and social media marketing.[15] Participants from 15 countries were recruited using message boards, Facebook, Twitter, and Craig's List. Firefly's research design included asynchronous one-to-one interviews conducted via consumer blogs, focus groups conducted within Facebook Groups, and a hybrid approach using a proprietary online community, IDEABlog, to engage participants in a multi-day forum.

The company's report, *The Language of Love in Social Media*, touts the benefits of the Firefly approach (not surprisingly). Though the participants were queried on specific topics, Firefly notes several advantages to hosting the process in social channels:

- The participants were comfortable being in an environment they frequent regularly, and the community setting led to a feeling of trust and camaraderie during the group sessions. While it can be a challenge to encourage respondents in traditional research studies to open up, the context of social media is already framed with the expectation of sharing.

- Traditional market research is sometimes criticized for its reliance on so-called professional respondents, and this approach filters out these people.

- It's easier to reach people in niche groups. Recruiting can often be a challenge, but the many specialty communities and groups in social media make finding participants with specific characteristics easier.

Harris Interactive, another large market research company, pursues another approach to gathering social media insights. Remember when we said that social media monitoring relies upon public content posted in social channels? The public aspect can be a detriment to market researchers because it may not reflect the whole truth. Many people may post only to those in their networks, and they maintain a wall of privacy around the content they share. The Harris Interactive Research Lifestreaming approach solves this issue of access to private content. Harris Interactive maintains a large panel of participants who have agreed to respond to surveys periodically. By asking these panel members if Harris Interactive could "friend" the members (on Facebook, Twitter, LinkedIn, and Bebo), Harris Interactive gained access to content that was otherwise protected. Harris Interactive still scrapes and mines content, but this content is content otherwise unavailable because of network privacy settings. In addition, because the Research Lifestreaming data are collected from people who have agreed to participate in surveys, Harris Interactive can supplement what it finds in the social content with survey data.

Ethnographic Research

When marketing researchers want to understand how "real" consumers use their products, they may conduct field research where they visit people's homes and offices to observe them as they go about their everyday lives. For example, a team of researchers that wanted to learn about how teenage girls actually talk about beauty care products sponsored a series of sleepovers where they sent (female) employees to hang out overnight and record what they learned when conversation turned to cosmetics, skin treatments, and the like.

Now, some social scientists adapt these methods to rigorously study online communities.[16] Netnography is a rapidly growing research methodology that adapts ethnographic research techniques to study the communities that emerge through computer-mediated communications. Like monitoring, the approach uses information available through online forums such as chat rooms, message boards, and social networking groups to study the attitudes and behaviors of the market involved. The primary difference is based on how the study takes place. In monitoring, data are collected passively. Web crawlers scour the sites designated in the sampling frame to collect the relevant content and save it to our database.

Netnography is an unobtrusive approach to research with a key benefit of observing what is likely to be credible information, unaffected by the research process. Many marketers already use a very informal and unsystematic form of netnography by simply exploring relevant online communities. However, to minimize the limitations of netnography, researchers should be careful in their evaluations by employing triangulation to confirm findings whenever possible.

How can we use netnography? One researcher recommends the following steps:[17]

- Identify online venues that could provide information related to the research questions.
- Select online communities that are focused on a particular topic or segment, have a high "traffic" of postings, have a relatively large number of active posters, and appear to have detailed posts.

- Learn about the group's culture, including its characteristics, behaviors, and language.
- Select material for analysis and classify material as social or informational and off topic or on topic.
- Categorize the types of participants involved in the discussions to be analyzed.
- Keep a journal of observations and reflections about the data collection and analysis process.
- Be straightforward with those in the online community about your purpose for participation by fully disclosing the researcher's presence in the community as well as his or her intent.
- Utilize "member checks" following content analysis of the discourse to ensure that members feel their attitudes and behaviors have been accurately interpreted.

CHAPTER SUMMARY

How do companies utilize social media research? What are the primary approaches to social media research?

Companies use social media research to answer the same kinds of questions traditional marketing research can answer. The advantage is that there is an enormous amount of data available in social media channels. Brands use these data to inform social customer care initiatives, marketing research that guides marketing mix decisions, and the evaluation of campaign effectiveness. Most social media research uses some form of social media listening/monitoring but it is also possible to conduct surveys, focus groups, and interviews in social communities.

What is the research process for collecting, processing, and analyzing residual social media data used in social listening and monitoring?

Social media monitoring uses software to systematically search key words it finds in social spaces such as blogs, social networks, and forums. By carefully choosing and searching the appropriate key words and the relevant social communities, the researcher can gather insight into customer decision making, perceptions of the brand, perceptions of competitors, and more. These data are scraped and then analyzed using keyword analysis, natural language processing, and human analysis of content.

Sentiment analysis is a similar approach that emphasizes how people think or feel about an object such as a brand or a political candidate. Content analysis identifies the prevalence of concepts and themes within data sets; it uses a top-down approach

(Continued)

(Continued)

that applies theory or empirical evidence to the coding process. Analysts assign codes to classify pieces of information they gather so they can determine any themes that are reflected in a lot of users' comments.

What are the common errors and biases associated with social media research?

Social media research is prone to coverage error, sampling error, and nonresponse error. Coverage error occurs when there is a failure to cover all components of a population being studied. Sampling error is the result of collecting data from only a subset, rather than all, of the members of the sampling frame. Nonresponse error is the potential for those who did not participate to differ significantly from those who did.

How do brands manage the social listening process?

Brands can manage this process informally using free tools. However, a more systematic approach is to view social listening as a part of a bigger social data management approach. These brands may develop in-house capabilities and may use software for this function or may partner with a vendor providing enterprise social listening.

What is netnographic research in social media communities?

Brands can also use social media in ways that do not incorporate social listening. One of the most useful approaches is known as netnography. In this approach, the researcher embeds herself or himself in the social community and observes behavior. This approach enables the researcher to draw conclusions related to the culture of the community.

KEY TERMS

census
codes
content analysis
coverage error
echo effect
enterprise social listening
fetching
informed consent
netnography
nonresponse bias
observational research
online echo

opinion mining
participation effect
population
primary research
research design
sample
sample frame
sampling
sampling error
sampling weights
scraping
secondary research

sentiment
sentiment analysis
sentiment dictionary
social media listening
social media monitoring
social media research
spam
text classifier
text mining
verbatims
web scraping
word-phrase dictionary

REVIEW QUESTIONS

1 What is social media research?

2 Why is social media research valuable for marketers? How do marketers use it?

3 What are the sources of data for social media researchers?

4 What sources of error are common in social media research?

5 Explain the steps in sentiment analysis.

6 When should a researcher use content analysis versus sentiment analysis?

7 What is enterprise social listening?

8 How can researchers use netnography?

EXERCISES

1 Visit Social Mention and run an analysis on a brand of interest to you. Do you agree with the analysis? Read the information provided from Social Mention on the sites from which it pulls data. Should you be concerned about coverage or sampling error in the analysis revealed?

2 Identify five videos on YouTube that include mentions of a single brand.

The videos should include at least one corporate piece but the others may be user-generated. View the videos and read the accompanying comments; then conduct a content analysis of the material you find. What insights are you able to glean?

3 Visit Netbase.com and view one of its webinars on using social listening. What insights were provided?

CHAPTER NOTES

1 Home page, *Conversition*, http://www.conversition.com, accessed September 2, 2010.

2 Deep Sherchan, "Why Brands Fail When It Comes to Social Media Listening," *Simplify360*, February 14, 2014, http://simplify360.com/blog/brands-fail-comes-social-media-listening/, accessed June 5, 2014.

3 R. Vasquez, "Most Responsive Socially-Devoted Brands," *Social Bakers,* http://www.socialbakers.com

4 Personal communication, January 13, 2011.

(Continued)

(Continued)

5   Jack Neff, "Dove's 'Real Beauty' Hits a Rough Patch," *Adage,* April 14, 2014, http://adage.com/article/news/dove-s-real-beauty-hits-a-rough-patch/292632/

6   Mukund Deshpande and Avik Sarkar, "BI and Sentiment Analysis," *Business Intelligence Journal* 15, no. 2 (2010): 41–50. See also Robert V. Kozinets, *Netnography: Doing Ethnographic Research Online* (London: Sage, 2009); and Robert V. Kozinets, "The Field Behind the Screen: Using Netnography for Marketing Research in Online Communities," *Journal of Marketing Research* 39 (February 2002): 61–72.

7   "Turning Conversations Into Insights: A Comparison of Social Media Monitoring Tools," *FreshMinds*, May 14, 2010, http://shared.freshminds.co.uk/smm10/whitepaper.pdf, accessed August 19, 2010.

8   R. B. Bogdan and S. K. Biklin, *Qualitative Research for Education: An Introduction to Theory and Methods*, 3rd ed. (Needham Heights, MA: Allyn and Bacon, 1998).

9   Ed Keller, "Wharton Study Shines New Light on Online Versus Offline Word of Mouth," *MediaBizBloggers.com*, December 16, 2010, http://www.mediabizbloggers.com/media-biz-bloggers/111949889.html, accessed December 27, 2010.

10 Mitchell Lovett, Renana Peres, and Ron Shachar, "On Brands and Word of Mouth," *Journal of Marketing Research* 50, no. 4 (August 2013): 427–444.

11 Tristan Henderson, "Ethics and Informed Consent in Online Social Network Research," July 27, 2012, http://responsible-innovation.org.uk/torrii/resource-detail/1473

12 *Guidelines for Social Media Monitoring*, adapted from Ray Poynter's *The Future Place Blog* at http://thefutureplace.typepad.com/ the_future_place/2010/01/what-are-the-ethical-guidelines-for-blog-and-buzz-mining.html, accessed August 7, 2011.

13 Deep Sherchan, "Why Brands Fail When It Comes to Social Media Listening," *Simplify360,* February 14, 2014, http://simplify360.com/blog/brands-fail-comes-social-media-listening/, accessed June 5, 2014.

14 Allison Smith, "The Forrester Wave: Enterprise Listening Software," *Forrester,* January 22, 2014, http://converseon.com/sites/default/files/forrester_wave_listening_platforms_2014.pdf?sid=5916, accessed July 16, 2014.

15 "The Language of Love in Social Media," Firefly MB, 2010, personal communication, COO Cheryl Stallworth-Hooper and presented at Ad Tech 2010, New York, November 3, 2010.

16 Kozinets, *Netnography: Doing Ethnographic Research Online*; Kozinets, "The Field Behind the Screen: Using Netnography for Marketing Research in Online Communities."

17 Robert Kozinets, "E-Tribalized Marketing? The Strategic Implications of Virtual Communities of Consumption," *European Management Journal* 17, no. 3 (1999): 252–264.

Visit the companion website for free additional materials related to this chapter: study.sagepub.com/smm

10 Social Media Metrics

LEARNING OBJECTIVES

When you finish reading this chapter you will be able to answer these questions:

1 What is the role of metrics in social media marketing programs?

2 What are the steps in the DATA approach to measurement?

3 What characteristics do most commonly used social media metrics share?

4 How do we calculate social media ROI?

5 How do we assess the costs and benefits of a social media marketing program?

6 How do we track social media results?

The Numbers Just Don't Add Up

A funny thing happened on the way to the CMO's office.

Between the realization of an eye-opening, game-changing insight gleaned from advertising test results and Web behavior data, the report you're gleefully ferrying to the C-Suite wilted, turns brown at the edges, and starts to dribble a slimy substance with a conspicuous stench.

The CMO immediately develops a nose-squint. The VP of Corporate Communications has that "Oooo, you're in for it!" look in her eye and the VP of Advertising nudges the Director of Direct Marketing and says *sotto-voce*, "The golden boy is about to find out his day in the sun has turned him to toast."

The CMO points to (but does not touch):

- a traffic report from comScore
- a traffic report from Hitwise
- a chart from Compete.com
- an ad banner report from Atlas
- a traffic report from Omniture and
- another from Google Analytics

"It's like the old joke," she said with no humor at all. "If you take all the economists in the world and line them up end-to-end, they all point different directions. What the hell is going on with these numbers? Are we getting thirty two and a half million people on our website or forty-four million?"

The first time you ran into this nest of nettles, you hopped over to the white board and cheerfully explained all about:

- cookie deletion
- cookie blocking
- multiple machine browsing
- multiple browser browsing
- multiple people on the same cookie
- non-human traffic
- dynamic IP addressing
- page caching
- javascript loading
- called pixel placement

You didn't even get to the good stuff about comparing miles to gallons and about:

- different tools using
- different date cut-off routines and
- different methods to capture
- different types of data to store in
- different kinds of databases with a
- different method of data cleansing and
- different slicing and dicing segmentation to produce
- different kinds of reports that ended up in
- different feeds for integration into
- different data warehouses

... before you were thanked for your help and shown the door—permanently.

You don't fall for it this time.

This time you explain that the world of online marketing has been suffering from a delusion of precision and an expectation of exactitude.

You tell them that we live in a world of statistics and probabilities. We can't count all the stars in the sky, so we don't try. We don't try to get an actual count of

- television watchers
- radio listeners
- magazine readers
- billboard readers
- bus poster readers
- floor sticker readers
- airline ticket jacket readers
- sandwich board readers

Instead, we count some and estimate the rest.

You share the good news that we can do this better than any of the above—and we've got some astonishing tools and techniques for dynamically targeting the audience and optimizing each one's experience.

You say, "We get 36.3 million people coming to our website."

The CMO lowers her half-glasses and gives you the look you last saw when caught using the office copy machine for party invitations. So you add, "With a 4% margin of error and it's a benchmark we can compare month over month from now on."

"So somewhere between 34 and a half and 38 million," she says.

"Pretty much right between them, in fact."

Disparagingly, she asks, "You really can't give me a more accurate number of how many people saw this digital marketing masterpiece that costs me tens of millions a year?"

"I can tell you whether our digital visitors are more engaged with our brand, come back more often, buy from us and discuss our products with their friends. How many people buy our products who saw our ads on CNN and 'Oprah' that cost you hundreds of millions a year?"

The VP of Advertising makes himself visibly smaller.

"I came here to show you a way that could save four million dollars of search marketing while boosting online sales by 6 to 8%," you say.

The scowl leaves the CMO's face. The odor of dubious data dissipates. Her eyes narrow as she leans forward and says, "Show me."

The numbers don't have to be precise—just compelling.

Source: Jim Sterne, "The Numbers Just Don't Add Up," *Media Post*, October 2, 2009, www.mediapost.com/publications/?fa=Articles.showArticle&art_aid=114723, accessed October 15, 2010. Used by permission of Jim Sterne, Founder of the eMetrics Marketing Optimization Summit and Chairman of the Web Analytics Association.

What Matters Is Measured

We've shown you throughout this book that brands can benefit when they participate in the social media space. With social media, brands can engage consumers, enhance brand reputation and image, build positive brand attitudes, improve organic search rankings, service customers, and drive traffic to brand locations, both online and off. But no social media marketing campaign will conclude unless objectives are set and effectiveness has been assessed. The challenge is to identify the right measures to use. It's harder than it sounds—in fact, marketers continue to wrestle with these decisions as they seek concrete ways to illustrate the value of these techniques to others in their organizations who hold the purse strings. Nearly 90% of marketers report wishing they had better financial measures for assessing the effectiveness of social media expenditures and strategies.

Not that long ago, social media marketers felt that there were no standard metrics we could apply to social media marketing campaigns. Some believed that applying metrics to something as organic as social media was "mission impossible"—the metrics were bound to be meaningless at best because social media were not about quantitative monetary accomplishments. Many still feel this way! This sentiment is at the heart of an article touting the death of social media ROI.[1] Why? Social media are meant to be about participation and relationships between brands and consumers. In a short period of time, we've developed a host of valuable metrics, but these also come with an important caveat. The metrics we use must be appropriate for the objectives we set for the campaign. Counting followers and fans, retweets, and blog comments is relevant only if those behaviors relate to the goals of the brand's social media activity. Smart social media marketers are focusing on assessing the extent to which objectives were met and measuring reach, engagement, and sentiment for social media efforts.

In many ways, social media marketing mimics online advertising in terms of the viable metrics available to measure how effective these messages are. Advertisers can measure reach (the number of people exposed to the message) and frequency (the average number of times someone is exposed), and analyze site stickiness (the ability of a site to draw repeat visits and to keep people on a site) and the relative pull (a comparison of how well different creative executions generate a response) of creative advertising. Brands can monitor clickthroughs (the number of people exposed to an online ad or link who actually click on it), sales conversions (the number of people who click through who go on to purchase the product), and viewthroughs (the number of people who are exposed and do not click through, but who later visit the brand's website).

A First Date or a Marriage?

Some metrics such as number of unique visitors, page views, frequency of visits, average visit length, and clickthrough rates may be irrelevant or simply fail to capture information appropriate to the reasons we use them. When we want to demonstrate the value of what we're doing, we love to count—we count impressions, visitors, friends, posts, players, even how often we count! There's no doubt that numbers are important. For instance, knowing the number of community members involved in a brand-related conversation can serve as an indicator of exposure, and the number of message threads and lines of text within a thread can serve as proxies of conversation depth. The CMO Survey found that the most often used metrics for social media included hits/views (41%), followers on social media accounts (31%), replies to social activity (21%), and organic buzz (word-of-mouth mentions of the brand in social channels (16%). Under 10% reported using measures like conversion rates and acquisition costs.[2]

However, simply counting the quantity of interactions consumers have with a brand doesn't tell us much about the quality of these touchpoints. We also need to know the degree of engagement people feel during and after their participation, the interaction with the brand, and how these experiences influenced their feelings about the brand. For this reason we also try to collect other numbers that are a bit more diagnostic, such as measures of brand likeability, brand image, brand awareness, brand loyalty, brand affiliation, congruency, and purchase intent. Eight O'Clock Coffee may have more than 20,000 Twitter followers, but what does the number of followers tell us about how the target audience *feels* about Eight O'Clock Coffee? As one analyst observed, "Four thousand two hundred and thirty-one is a measurement. Without context, it is merely a number. When compared with your personal best, company expectations, or your competitors' efforts, that number becomes a metric. It is now indicative of value, importance or a change in results."[3]

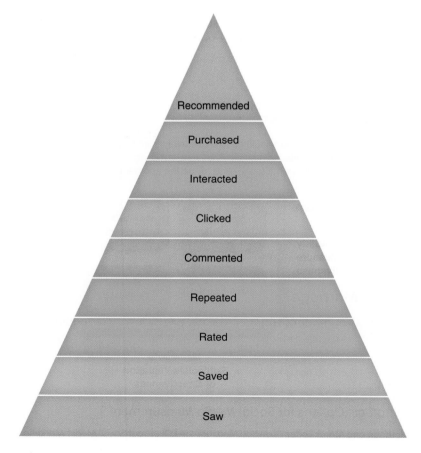

Figure 10.1   The Engagement Food Chain

Engagement is a complex construct made up of several individual accomplishments. The Engagement Food Chain illustrates the hierarchy of effects we seek from our target audience as it reaches increasing levels of engagement with our brand. Figure 10.1 demonstrates how we look for different outcomes depending upon the consumer's level of engagement with the brand.

Because engagement is such a complex phenomenon, we need to be choosy about just what measures we collect and which ones are important. Key performance indicators (KPIs) are those metrics that are tied to organizational objectives.[4] But, there's a catch: in order for KPIs to be valuable, we first must be sure the objectives they're supposed to measure are well defined. As the old geek saying goes, "Garbage in, garbage out."

The Strategic Options for Social Media Measurement provide a simple way to view the choices social media marketers make in terms of developing strategy and assessing success.[5] It explains that social media marketers may approach measurement along a continuum of fuzzy to quantifiable and may see effectiveness along a continuum of failing to succeeding. The result is a simple matrix indicating that social media marketers may see social media as a dead end (fuzzy measures, ineffective), in need of measurement and adjustment (quantified measures, ineffective strategies), naively optimistic (fuzzy measures, effective strategies), or as an iterative process (quantified measures, effective strategies). The framework is shown in Figure 10.2.

STRATEGIC OPTIONS FOR SOCIAL MEDIA MEASUREMENT

Every manager's goal should be to move away from fuzzy measurement and towards quantifiable metrics. That way, a manager can understand what's working and what's not—and revise the approach accordingly.

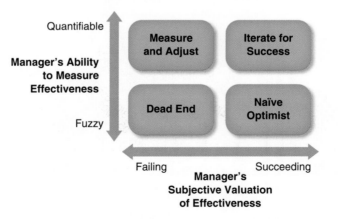

Figure 10.2   Strategic Options for Social Media Measurement

Source: Donna Hoffman and Marek Fodor, "Can You Measure the ROI of Your Social Media Marketing?" *MIT Sloan Management Review*, Fall 2010, 52 (1), 41–49, p. 47.

To review where we are so far:

- Measurements within a defined context are metrics.
- Measurements require context to provide useful feedback.
- Metrics that are tied to objectives are key performance indicators.
- Objectives must be well defined before we can identify key performance indicators.

Campaign Timelines and Metrics

To make matters a bit more complicated, it's important to remember that the metrics we use may shift as a campaign progresses. For example, in the early days just following launch we primarily may be interested in awareness—are people in cyberspace tuning in to what we're doing? As the campaign progresses, we may not be so impressed with that as the pressure builds to show tangible results such as a boost in sales. For example, when Gap ran a group deal with Groupon offering $50 of Gap apparel for $25, it was excited to sell 441,000 Groupon coupons in a single day—$11 million in revenue. But Gap's social commerce tactic wasn't meant to act solely as a single sales promotion to improve sales revenue and deplete inventories. Gap also wanted to remind consumers about the Gap brand and encourage consumers to utilize Gap's website. Later measures of the campaign showed that 70% of the Groupon users went on to browse Gap online, meeting a key objective for the tactic.[6] Figure 10.3 provides a sample campaign timeline to illustrate how a campaign evolves over time. Metrics should be tied to each stage in the campaign timeline.

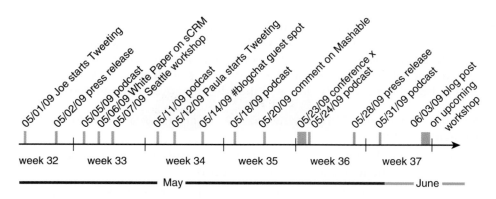

Figure 10.3   A Sample Social Media Campaign Timeline

Source: Based on Oliver Blanchard, "Social Media ROI—Part 8: An Introduction to Timelines," *BrandBuilder*, http://thebrandbuilder.wordpress.com/2009/07/21/social-media-r-o-i-part-8-an-introduction-to-timelines/, accessed December 27, 2010.

The Evaluation and Measurement Process: DATA

When it comes to social media marketing—or any form of marketing, for that matter—measurement isn't optional. It's a necessity for organizations that are serious about adjusting their strategies and tactics to better meet their objectives. Some may feel intimidated about specifying what it is they want to see happen when it comes to their social media activities; perhaps they believe this sets them up to fail because they're not sure they can actually define or attain specific goals. Others may still be in the early stage of the social media maturity life cycle we discussed in Chapter 2; because they're still "playing" with social media, they don't yet feel the need to define what results they would like to see. But ultimately social media will have to answer to the same masters as other kinds of traditional media—the bean counters who need to see value for their money. The investment in social media marketing will require justification. Strategists will want to understand what's working and what isn't in order to decide if a campaign needs fixing or if it's worth continuing at all. Welcome to the cold cruel world of budgets!

In reality, devising a measurement plan is a relatively straightforward process (at least on paper!). We organize our plan according to a four-step process known as the DATA approach:[7]

1 *Define:* Define the results that the program is designed to promote.
2 *Assess:* Assess the costs of the program and the potential value of the results.
3 *Track:* Track the actual results and link those results to the program.
4 *Adjust:* Adjust the program based on results to optimize future outcomes.

Let's dive deeper into each of these four steps.

Define

Our first—and arguably most critical—task is to define just what we want to occur and what we need to measure. Quite simply we have to define the objectives of the social media marketing campaign. After all, if we don't have clear objectives, how do we know when we've reached them? The specific objectives we might identify can vary dramatically from brand to brand but it's likely they will include three overarching issues:

1 *Motivating* some behavior from the target audience (such as visits to a website or purchases of the product)
2 *Influencing* brand knowledge and attitudes (particularly among those who are likely to spread the message to their own networks)
3 *Accomplishing* the first two objectives with fewer resources than might be required with other methods.

For instance, if we use Twitter to identify customer complaints early on and resolve those complaints online, we can potentially influence attitude toward the brand, inspire the customer to share the experience with others, and do so online at a cost far less than it normally takes a call center to resolve. Remember that organizational objectives will tie directly to the applications it has selected. If social media are being used as a customer service venue, we will identify service-oriented results in this step. If social media are a part of the brand's promotional strategy, we will identify communication objectives. If social media are a source of data for customer insight, we specify research objectives.

From a philosophical perspective, defining what's important may mean changing the way we think about marketing. Historically, marketers have addressed measurement from the perspective of company investments in customers and the extent to which those investments generated positive results. However, because social media are largely customer driven, we may need to view measurement from the perspective of the customers' investments in the company.[8] How much time are customers investing in our socially published content? How much social capital are customers putting at risk to recommend our brand?

FROM BYTES TO BUCKS

Simple Measurements in Social Media

To assess social media marketing, marketers must set clear objectives and then measure those same variables. The variables may be quite simplistic but still reveal what the campaign team needs to know.

Photo 10.1

For example, consider the case of Blendtec blenders. Blendtec utilizes a social media strategy based almost entirely on social publishing. It creates demonstration videos (at a cost of about $1,000 each) and publishes them on YouTube. It also shares coupons using Twitter and Facebook. From there, it can use basic measures such as coupon code tracking, YouTube analytics, Twitter analytics, and Facebook Insights to make assessments. Has the strategy worked? Blendtec videos have been viewed and shared millions of times and sales increased over 700% in the first year of the strategy.

For more on Blendtec's YouTube analytics, visit: http://www.trackalytics.com/youtube/user/blendtec/.

Tatiana Mihaliova / Shutterstock.com

Are Your Objectives SMART?

How can we be sure our objectives are clear enough that we can adequately measure them? The key is to state them so they have SMART characteristics:

- Specific
- Measurable
- Appropriate
- Realistic
- Time-oriented

To understand how objectives can be SMART or not, consider the following two examples:

> "We will tell everyone we can about our new Facebook page and see if they like it so much they'll buy more of our product."

> "We will promote our new Facebook page in print advertisements we will place in the June issues of *Rolling Stone, Sports Illustrated,* and *Maxim.* On July 15 we will count the number of Facebook users who 'like' our brand and compare sales to the same period last year."

The second objective is SMART; the first, not so much. However, defining objectives in a specific manner is not as easy as it sounds. Even the most desirable of outcomes (brand engagement and cost-efficiency, for instance) must be clearly defined if they are to be useful in assessment. It may seem difficult to shift from thinking about the benefits we can derive from social media marketing to ways we can measure those values. The benefits may seem intangible ("create lots of buzz!"), so an early step is to find a way to quantify results that may not lend themselves to numerical measurement. Here are some examples:

- One benefit of hosting a blog is that the target audience may use it to educate themselves about the company's product line. It is difficult to measure the value of consumer education, but there are tangible benefits we should see due to greater knowledge about a brand. Assuming that people like what they see, these efforts should move blog visitors to the e-commerce site and from there to transactions. Thus, the benefit of consumer education is valuable if it results in increases in site traffic and sales.

- Another common goal of social media marketing is search engine optimization, as we discussed in Chapter 6. We can see whether our site is optimized when we test the search rankings we achieve. In addition, better search results should lead to higher traffic to the site. Aha! Something we can measure.

- Reaching a specific audience with our brand message is a valuable outcome. Here we may need to measure impressions, but we can also compare the cost of reaching

Table 10.1   Commonly Used Social Media Metrics

1   WOM Metrics Buzz volume

    a   Number (volume) of posts, comments, retweets/shares, bookmarks by channel
    b   Frequency, momentum, recency, seasonality

2   Asset popularity, virality

    a   Sharing, viewing, bookmarking, downloads, installs, and embedding of branded assets such as videos, pictures, links, articles
    b   Changes over time

3   Media mentions (earned media)

4   Brand liking

    a   Fans, followers, friends
    b   Growth in fans, followers, friends
    c   Likes, favorites, ratings, links back

5   Reach and second degree reach (influence impressions from others)

    a   Readers, viewers
    b   Subscriptions
    c   Mentions, links

6   Engagement

    a   Comment volume
    b   Uploads, contest participation
    c   Subscriptions (RSS, podcasts, video series, document series)
    d   Registrations
    e   Time spent with social pages

7   Quality

    a   Ratings, bookmarks

8   Search engine optimization

9   Website effectiveness (traffic, clicks, conversions, viewthroughs)

10   Share of voice in social media and overall

11   Influence

12   Sentiment

    a   Nature of comments, tag attributes
    b   Attitudes

13   Customer value

    a   Sales changes online, offline
    b   Customer lifetime value shifts, customer retention, lower customer acquisition costs

Source: Based on David Berkowitz, "100 Ways to Measure Social Media," *MediaPost Social Media Insider*, November 17, 2009, http://www.mediapost.com/publications/?fa=Articles.showArticle&art_aid=117581, accessed October 15, 2010.

the target audience with social media to the cost of doing so using traditional media. Social media are valuable for showing responsiveness to consumer concerns, but what is the value of the increased responsiveness? We can track customer satisfaction and retention to assess this value.

Metrics

The next step is to decide on the metric, or specific standard of measurement, we will use to measure the objective. When we specify our metrics, we need to match these to the results we are concerned about—whether attitude shifts and behavioral responses from our target audience or efficiency and profitability measures resulting from cost savings and/or increased sales. Table 10.1 lists some of the most commonly used metrics.

A Social Media Marketing Metrics Matrix

The list of possible measures applicable to social media can be overwhelming. Applying a framework to manage the types of measures is useful. The matrix shown in Table 10.2 illustrates the types and characteristics of social media metrics. The three types of metrics include activity metrics, interaction metrics, and return (financial) metrics:

- Activity metrics measure the actions the organization takes relative to social media. For instance, an organization might set goals in terms of the number and timing of blog posts, white papers, tweets, videos, comment responses, and status updates it may contribute in social venues.
- Interaction metrics focus on how the target market engages with the social media platform and activities. Interaction measures include the number of followers and fans, comments, "likes," recommendations and reviews, and the amount of shared content. Interactions are essentially made up of all the ways in which users can participate in a social media relationship with the brand.
- Return metrics focus on the outcomes (financial or otherwise) that directly or indirectly support the success of the brand. They include return on investment measures, cost reduction measures, and other performance metrics. In addition to these categories, social media data can be characterized as qualitative or quantitative. Using both forms provides the hard numbers that CFOs (chief financial officers) require to fund investments in social media strategy while also valuing the soft benefits of social media such as stories, buzz, and image.

A common metric to gauge success is return on investment (ROI). ROI is a measure of profitability. It captures how effective a company is at using capital to generate profits. To determine ROI we assign a financial value to the resources we use to execute a strategy, measure financial outcomes, and calculate the ratio between inputs and outcomes. Return on investment answers the question, "How much income was generated from investments in the activities?" When we apply this concept to a brand's investment in social media marketing, we call the measure social media return on investment (SMROI). SMROI answers the question, "How much income did our investments in social media marketing generate?"

Table 10.2   A Social Media Metrics Framework

CATEGORY/ CHARACTERISTIC	QUANTITATIVE MEASURES	QUALITATIVE MEASURES
Activity (input)	Number, frequency, and recency of: Blog posts Updates/posts Comments/reply comments White papers Photo posts Video posts Activity across media channels	Creative messaging and positioning strategy Resonance/fit of campaign appeal Social media involvement
Interaction (responses)	Number, frequency, and recency of: Registrations Bookmarks/favorites/likes/ ratings Comments/posts/mentions/ tags Links/trackbacks Downloads/installs/embeds Subscriptions Fans/followers/friends Share/forward/invite/refer Reviews/testimonials Traffic/visits/views/ impressions Time spent on site Profile development UG content contributed Discount/deal redemption rate Echo effect/virality	Sentiment Engagement Influence effects Recommendations Buzz/virality
Performance (outcome)	Cost/prospects Lead conversion rate Average new revenue per customer Cost efficiencies across marketing functions Customer lifetime value Earned media values Shifts in average sales/site Traffic/ search engine ratings Share of voice Return on investment	Attitude toward the brand Brand loyalty Customer satisfaction Service quality perceptions

Source: Adapted from Mike Brown, July 14, 2010, 6, "Social Media Metrics You Should Be Tracking," *Social Media Today,* http://www.socialmediatoday.com/mikebrown1/146589/6-social-media-metrics-you-should-be-tracking, accessed September 2011.

It's natural to want to quantify the value of a corporate activity and to use that value as justification to continue and expand the activity. The challenge when it comes to social media is the qualitative, viral, pervasive nature of the outcomes of social media advertising. Investments in social media generate goodwill, brand engagement, and momentum, and analysts must define how those constructs will be assessed.

Analysts have proposed several ways to calculate SMROI that are appropriate to measure the financial return on social media depending on the objective that is relevant. In addition to SMROI, we can view other returns that may be generated as a result of social media marketing efforts. Let's review some other approaches.[9]

- The return on impressions model demonstrates how many media impressions were generated by the social media tactics employed. An impression is simply an "opportunity to see" for the target audience. When a brand buys advertising space, it purchases opportunities for the target market to be exposed to the ad. Social media also provide impressions but the media space is not purchased. The costs are different. The opportunity for exposure to the brand message might be delivered as part of a virtual world event, on a social networking profile site, and with consumer-generated ads, product reviews, and so on. Impressions are valuable, according to this model, because we assume that impressions lead to changes in awareness, followed by changes in comprehension, changes in attitude, and ultimately changes in behavior (sales). Using the percentage of people reached who ultimately purchase as a way to calculate sales value, we can then determine a return on impressions by taking the gross revenue estimated minus the cost of the social media advertising program divided by the cost of the program. For example, if we estimate that Dunkin' Donuts earns $500,000 in gross revenue due to its Twitter presence, at a cost of $100,000 in time investment, the ROI for the microblogging activity is 400%.

- The return on social media impact model attempts to track coverage across media and in different markets against sales over time. It requires the statistical technique of *advanced multiple regression analysis* to analyze variables that may affect sales, including the mix of advertising and promotional tools used at each time and place. This approach offers the greatest potential for social media marketers, because it can include lagged measurements that control for time order of events taking place online (e.g., the timing of an event in a social world, the point at which a profile was activated, the timing of a contest conclusion, and subsequent posting of consumer-generated ads). Return on social media impact promises to determine how sales can be attributed to each element in a marketing mix and to tactics within the social media advertising strategy. Content generation and consumption are tracked and assigned algorithm scores to dictate the weight of relative influence. Sales are also tracked at the same intervals, and then statistical analysis is used to determine how sales trends shifted according to the timing of the social media marketing.

- The return on target influence model relies upon survey data to assess the effectiveness of social media marketing. Surveys assess whether participants were exposed to the social media tactics and what perceptions they formed as a result of exposure.

The model then calls for calculating the change in the probability of purchase based on the exposure.

- The final approach is that of return on earned media model. This approach uses a metric called advertising equivalency value to equate publicity in news media outlets to its paid advertising equivalent. In other words, if a brand had paid for a mention in a specific space, what would it have cost? For social media advertising, an AEV would attempt to equate the following with paid advertising value: source authority, source prominence, depth of brand mention, and recommendation. To calculate advertising equivalency, the cost to purchase a display ad on a site would be used to assign a dollar value to the impressions achieved socially. For example, if we spent $50,000 on social display ads on Facebook, we could assign an earned media value of $50,000 to a thousand page views of our brand profile on Facebook. The value can also be adjusted by the subjective importance of the earned media in question. For example, one might believe that profile visits are more valuable than a display ad rotation because it suggests that visitors sought out the brand interaction. The earned media value can be adjusted to account for variables such as the popularity of the location, the relative influence of the source, and so on. The ROI calculation is then based on the difference between the AEV and the cost of the social media advertising program divided by the cost of the program. If the AEV for the Facebook profile is $50,000 but it cost $5,000 in time for its development and maintenance, the incremental gain is $45,000. The gain divided by the cost of the program expressed as a percentage reveals an ROI of 900%. This measure may be among the easiest to execute for those social media spaces that also sell display advertising. However, it is not truly a return on investment measure so much as it is a measure of effective resource utilization.

Assess

As you've begun to see from the discussion of returns, we need to know something about costs and values in order to calculate outcome measures. This is the second step in the measurement planning process—to identify the investments required for specific activities and how to value the outcomes. What does it take to participate in social media marketing and what is it worth? What is the value of a customer or of a lead? What does it cost to gain a lead or a customer? What does it cost to maintain a blog? To promote and manage a social game? To maintain an active Twitter presence? What is the value of an ad impression? These are the kinds of questions an organization must answer in order to calculate returns. Here are some of the costs we need to consider:

- Opportunity cost: What else could employees or volunteers have done if they weren't spending time contributing to the brand's social media activity? For example, what's the time value of the person tasked with creating content for the corporate blog or posting responses to irritated customers on Facebook when without these tasks he or she could have spent time on other revenue-generated tasks?

- Speed of response: Social media enable companies to identify crisis situations quickly and respond quickly. It can be difficult to quantify the value of speed, but we know it is valuable.

- Message control: Brands accept a risk that the brand's message will be shared or manipulated in ways that the brand would rather not have happen. But if we want to capitalize on the value of virality and the echo effect that we discussed in Chapter 9, then we also have to be willing to sacrifice some control. For example, Comcast Cares grew out of negative tweets customers made about the brand on Twitter. Comcast took those tweets as an opportunity to right wrongs and ensure customer satisfaction.[10] But some brands may take the approach that they'd rather not have customers speaking openly about their experiences. In fact, many businesses set their Facebook walls to "Brand only" posts so that contributions from others are hidden to visitors. Unfortunately, these brands won't benefit in the same way that Comcast did.

A simple approach to assessing costs and value is to develop a cost-benefit analysis table. Table 10.3 illustrates an example of a cost-benefit analysis to start and maintain a corporate blog.[11] The analyst needed to make several assumptions about value, and he or she researched costs to complete the assessment. The possible value associated with the corporate blog has been included and financial figures have been estimated for those benefits. If the assumptions are correct, the brand should pursue the corporate blog because the benefits outweigh the costs to maintain it.

The brand could also calculate the return on investment for maintaining the blog using the figures in the table or it could calculate the blog's Blog Value Index (BVI).[12] The BVI is a simple equation that enables a company to assess whether the blog adds more value than it costs. If the BVI is under 1, the blog costs money, but if it is greater than 1, the blog yields a profit. The cost of software and hosting is assumed to be zero because presumably the organization is already covering the cost of website hosting and additional costs for the blog would be negligible.

$$BVIa = [adh (aay/1,000)] \div [abt \times ehw]$$

where

adh = average daily hits
aay = average advertising yield
abt = average number of hours spent per day blogging
ehw = employee hourly wage of the blogger

The equation itself is straightforward, but sometimes our input figures are difficult to assess in social media. For instance, it can be a challenge to identify how many unique blog readers one has. Feedburner, a service from Google that enables blog subscriptions and tracks analytics, reports a measure of reach: the total number of people who have taken action on the content in your feed. It also includes a subscriber measure of how many people are subscribed to your feed. But readers can also view blog content via a news filter site or blog search engine, which can limit the accuracy of the reach figures.

Table 10.3 Cost-Benefit Analysis of a Corporate Blog

ESTIMATED COSTS

Start-up costs	
Planning and development	$25,000
Training for blogger	10,000
Ongoing costs (annual)	
Blogging platform	25,000
Brand-monitoring service	50,000
IT support	3,000
Content production	150,000
Review and redirection	20,000
Total costs (Year One)	**$283,000**

ESTIMATED BENEFITS

Advertising value (visibility/traffic based on 7,500 daily)	$7,000
PR value (24 stories at 10,000 each)	240,000
WOM value (370 posts at $100 each)	37,000
Support value (50 calls daily avoided at cost of $5.50/call)	69,000
Research value (5 focus group equivalent at $8,000 each)	40,000
Total benefits (Year One)	$393,000
Net value for Year One	**$110,000**

Track

In the tracking stage we collect and organize the data we will use to determine our results. The tracking step in the DATA process involves the following components:

- Identify tracking mechanisms
- Establish baseline comparisons

- Create activity timelines
- Develop transaction data
- Measure transaction precursors
- Overlay timelines and look for patterns

There are many tracking tools useful for marketers. Companies may use comprehensive systems such as those reviewed in Chapter 9 (e.g., Radian6) or may use individual tools focused by social media vehicle. Facebook offers Facebook Insights, Twitter offers Twitter Analytics, and YouTube offers YouTube Analytics. There are also services that focus on specific forms of measurement. For example, Keyhole enables the tracking of the spread and reach of a hashtag. Bit.ly enables the tracking of shortened URLs. Even Hootsuite, one of the social media content management tools, provides many forms of analytics.

Tracking is not only concerned with determining how we will collect the data we need for making assessments. It is also concerned with organizing the data in a way that enhances their utility. There are three approaches to tracking that reflect different ways to do this: (1) forward tracking, (2) coincident tracking, and (3) reverse tracking:[13]

1 Forward tracking means that the tracking mechanisms are developed prior to launching the activity or campaign. Forward tracking is the most accurate approach because it enables the account team to develop a mechanism for tracking exactly the data desired. Ideally, then, the measurement plan will be created as part of the strategic social media campaign plan and the tracking mechanisms identified up front. If the organization has set SMART objectives, forward tracking should already be in place.

2 Coincident tracking begins during the activity or campaign. Coincident tracking can be effective in that it relies on residual data (which become the data scraped for social media research) left at the point of interaction or point of sale. It doesn't necessarily require that a unique tracking mechanism be developed. Moreover, it is interaction or outcome oriented because tracking occurs only when people leave traces of their activity or opinions. This is an imperfect approach. Searches won't necessarily reveal relevant information unless the consumer who posted used keywords or hashtags.

3 Reverse tracking is conducted after an activity or campaign has concluded. Reverse tracking also uses residual data and may include primary data collection such as surveys to assess the effects of the campaign. For instance, it would be simple to count the number of pieces of content uploaded to a microsite. However, without forward tracking in place, the microsite would have been missing key share technologies, making it more difficult to track the shared content originating from the site.

THE DARK SIDE OF SOCIAL MEDIA

In order to assess the effectiveness of social media, we need to track if or how people interact with our messages. As you might suspect, the downside of evaluating performance is that the greater the need to track people's activities, the greater the risk of violating their privacy. Companies can utilize tracking software to collect and record information about social media users. Have you approved an app's use of your social media accounts? If so, you've enabled that application to track information. They don't release the names of individuals, but they do enable clients to utilize the data and may also sell data to interested marketers.

Data like these can be powerful for targeting as well as tracking.

The companies that collect these data do so anonymously; they strip out information that identifies an individual before they sell it. However, this practice may create a sense of false security—someone who is determined (and smart) can potentially trace profiles back to real people. Recently two computer scientists at the University of Texas–Austin did just that. They developed an algorithm that looks at relationships among all the members of a social network to retroactively pinpoint individuals. The professors found that one third of those who are on both Flickr and Twitter can be identified from the completely anonymous Twitter graph. Even though it's estimated that there is only about a 15% overlap between the two platforms, members of each have many other common members in their social network, so there was no hiding from the computer.[14] Although not everyone is (or knows) a high-powered computer scientist, companies that track our online behavior will need to be held to greater scrutiny as the pressure mounts to follow our online journeys.

Baselines

One useful way to track a campaign's effectiveness is to construct a baseline. This is a metric (often expressed visually) that allows a marketer to compare its performance on some dimension to other things such as how competitors are doing or how its own efforts fluctuate over time. Figure 10.4 provides a simple baseline comparison between a marketer's efforts pre-social media campaign and post-campaign.

Measurement Maps

A measurement map displays the types of branded messages produced and distributed (e.g., written vehicles like blog posts and white papers; ads in the form of display ads or rich media video; podcasts) and invitations for consumer engagement with the brand

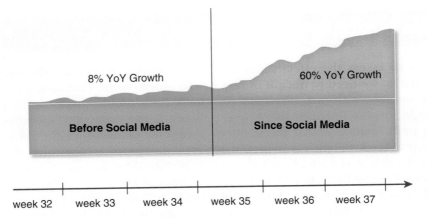

Figure 10.4   A Baseline Graphic

Note: YoY = Year over Year

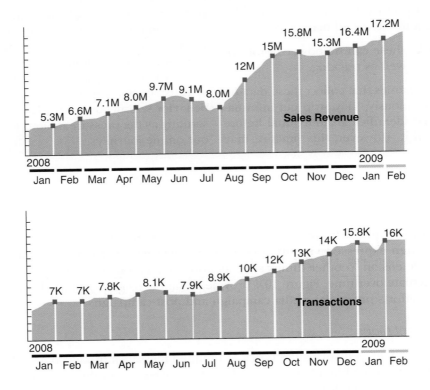

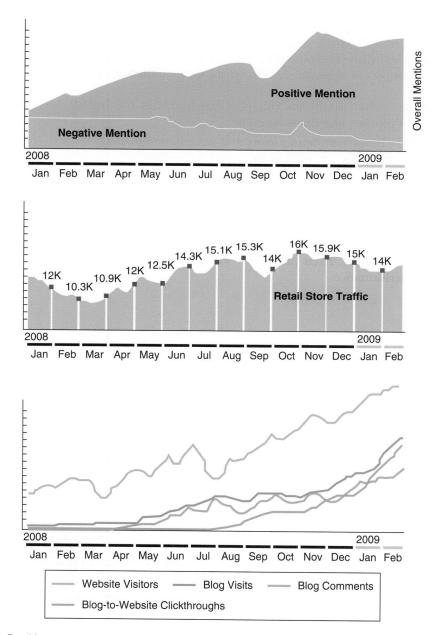

Figure 10.5   Measurement Maps Illustrate Changes in the Tracked Outcomes Over the Course of the Social Media Campaign

Source: Adapted from Oliver Blanchard, "Social Media ROI—Part 8: An Introduction to Timelines," *BrandBuilder*, http://thebrandbuilder.wordpress.com/2009/07/21/social-media-r-o-i-part-8-an-introduction-to-timelines/, accessed December 27, 2010.

(e.g., games, consumer-generated advertising contests, promotions, and interactive brand experiences) as well as the online location for these materials.[15] It should also include online locations where content relating to the brand may be distributed by others. Here are some examples of opportunities to create measurement maps:

- Are there viral videos on YouTube that highlight the brand? Are there product reviews on sites like Epinions.com?
- Are there blogs with brand icons and information posted?
- Are people tweeting about the brand?
- Are members of Reddit tagging the brand's website and are Digg members voting for branded content?

Once the analyst identifies all the sources of brand information, the map should sketch out the chain of potential touchpoints. Figure 10.5 illustrates several different examples of measurement maps. Each provides a vivid visual report about some aspect of the campaign's performance.

Adjust

The final step in the process is adjusting. There is little value in measuring without a process for applying what is learned to future activities and investments.

Simple Ways to Start Measuring

Clearly, we can choose from a variety of criteria, approaches, and tools to measure the effectiveness of a social media campaign. Some marketers, however, will want a simple start before they dive in and develop a full measurement program for their social media marketing campaigns. This list highlights a few metrics that provide a good start:[16]

- *Content consumption:* Who is interacting with and consuming the brand-generated and consumer-generated content? Is it who you want to consume your content?
- *Content augmentation:* Who is adding to or changing your content by continuing the conversation with response posts? In what ways is the content augmented? Is it consistent with what you want from the campaign?
- *Content sharing:* At what rate are those exposed to the brand messages sharing the content with others using share tools? Does the rate of sharing suggest campaign momentum?
- *Content loyalty:* How many consumers have subscribed to branded content with RSS feeds or by registering for site access?
- *Content conversations:* Who is discussing the brand? Who is linking to brand websites? What is the comment-to-post ratio?
- *Content engagement:* Is the number of friends to brand profiles growing? Are people contributing content like comments and photos?

CHAPTER SUMMARY

What is the role of metrics in social media marketing programs?

Metrics are measures to which marketers can compare results that relate to specific marketing objectives. Metrics allow us to determine the extent to which our strategies have been successful, if at all. Without metrics, we would be unable to assess the effectiveness of our campaigns.

What are the steps in the DATA approach to measurement?

We organize a measurement plan according to a four-step process known as the DATA approach: define, assess, track, and adjust. This process allows us to clearly specify what the program should accomplish for the organization and then confirm the plan works. If it doesn't, the DATA approach encourages the organization to modify the plan to make it more likely it will yield the desired results.

What are characteristics the most commonly used social media metrics share?

One way to describe social media metrics is in terms of what they measure: activity metrics measure the actions the organization takes relative to social media. Interaction metrics focus on how the target market engages with the social media platform and activities. Interaction measures include the number of followers and fans, comments, "likes," recommendations and reviews, and the amount of shared content. Return metrics focus on the outcomes (financial or otherwise) that directly or indirectly support the success of the brand. They include return on investment measures, cost reduction measures, and other performance metrics.

How do we calculate social media ROI?

ROI is a measure of profitability. It captures how effective a company is at using capital to generate profits. To determine ROI we assign a financial value to the resources we use to execute a strategy, measure financial outcomes, and calculate the ratio between inputs and outcomes. Return on investment answers the question, "How much income was generated from investments in the activities?" When we apply this concept to a brand's investment in social media marketing, we call the measure social media return on investment (SMROI). SMROI answers the question, "How much income did our investments in social media marketing generate?" We calculate SMROI with one or more of the metrics listed in Table 10.2.

How do we assess the costs and benefits of a social media marketing program?

Social media marketing programs have the potential to provide direct and indirect benefits to organizations. In some applications the returns will be direct and fairly easy to measure because a campaign will cause consumers to buy the product.

(Continued)

(Continued)

Other applications are more indirect and may be evident only in the long term; these include buzz-building and awareness campaigns that motivate people to talk to one another about a brand or to seek out more information about it. Social media programs overall tend to be less expensive than traditional marketing campaigns, but they also contain hidden costs. In particular, they may require the organization to allocate employee' time to monitoring, so personnel costs need to be included in the budget.

How do we track social media results?

Forward tracking requires the analyst to develop tracking mechanisms prior to launching the activity or campaign. Forward tracking is the most accurate approach because it enables the account team to develop a mechanism to track exactly the data desired. Coincident tracking begins during the activity or campaign. This method relies on data we gather at the point of interaction or point of sale. Reverse tracking is conducted after an activity or campaign has concluded. This approach also uses residual data and may include primary data collection such as surveys to assess the effects of the campaign.

KEY TERMS

activity metrics	key performance indicators	return on social media
advertising equivalency	(KPIs)	impact model
value	measurement map	return on target influence
baseline	message control	model
Blog Value Index (BVI)	opportunity cost	reverse tracking
coincident tracking	reach	sales conversions
DATA approach	relative pull	social media return
engagement	return metrics	on investment
forward tracking	return on earned media model	(SMROI)
frequency	return on impressions model	speed of response
interaction metrics	return on investment (ROI)	viewthroughs

REVIEW QUESTIONS

1 What is a metric?

2 Explain the meaning of SMART objectives.

3 How can marketing managers apply the DATA process to evaluate social media marketing efforts?

4 Describe the differences among activity metrics, interaction metrics, and return metrics.

5 Explain the strategic options for a social media measurement framework and what it means for social media marketers.

EXERCISES

1 Identify a student organization that uses social media to promote its activities and membership opportunities. Briefly review the social media zones in use by the organization and define three SMART objectives for the organization's use of social media.

2 Using the SMART objectives developed in Exercise 1, identify two metrics appropriate to measure the success of each objective.

3 If you are using Hootsuite University, explore the analytics available in the program.

CHAPTER NOTES

1 John Heggestuen, "The Death of Social ROI," *Business Insider*, October 22, 2013, http://www.businessinsider.com/the-myth-of-social-roi-2013-10, accessed November 12, 2013.

2 Kyle Wang, "What Is the Value of Social Media Engagement?" *Forbes*, May 13, 2014, http://www.forbes.com/sites/kylewong/2014/05/13/what-is-the-value-of-social-media-engagement/, accessed May 24, 2014.

3 J. Sterne, *Social Media Metrics* (Hoboken, NJ: Wiley, 2010), p. 4.

4 J. Sterne, *Social Media Metrics*. (Hoboken, NJ: Wiley, 2010), p.4.

5 Donna Hoffman and Marek Fodor, "Can You Measure the ROI of Your Social Media Marketing," *MIT Sloan Management Review* 52, no. 1 (Fall 2010), 41–49.

6 Zachary Sniderman, "5 Winning Social Media Campaigns to Learn From," September 14, 2010, http://mashable.com/2010/09/14/social-media-campaigns/, accessed December 27, 2010.

7 J. R. Roy, "Marketing Metrics and ROI: How to Set Up a Measurement System That Can Double Your Profitability," 2009, http://www.marketing-metrics-made-simple.com/index.html, accessed September 19, 2010.

8 Donna Hoffman and Marek Fodor, "Can You Measure the ROI of Your Social Media Marketing," *MIT Sloan Management Review* 52, no.1 (Fall 2010), 41–49.

9 Fraser Likely, David Rockland, and Mark Weiner, "Perspectives on the ROI of Media Relations Publicity Efforts," *Institute for Public Relations*, 2006, http://www.

(Continued)

(Continued)

instituteforpr.org/research_single/perspectives_on_the_roi/, accessed December 26, 2010.

10   Rebecca Reisner, "Comcast's Twitter Man," *BusinessWeek*, January 13, 2009, hrrp://www.businessweek.com/managing/content/jan2009/ca20090113_373506.htm, accessed December 26, 2010.

11   Charlene Li and Josh Bernoff, *Groundswell* (Boston, MA: Harvard Business Press, 2008), p. 113 (note that *Groundswell* includes similar tables for calculating the ROI of ratings and reviews and of a forum).

12   Jason Stampler, "The ROI of Blogging, and Whether Jonathan Schwartz's Blog Pays for Itself," *Computer Business Review,* April 4, 2006, http://www.cbronline.com/blogs/technology/the_roi_of_blog, accessed December 27, 2010.

13   Roy, "Marketing Metrics and ROI: How to Set Up a Measurement System That Can Double Your Profitability."

14   Arvind Narayanan and Vitaly Shmatikov, "De-anonymizing Social Networks," presented at IEEE Security & Privacy '09, http://randomwalker.info/social-networks/, accessed October 19, 2010.

15   Chris Brogan, "Measuring Social Media Efforts," September 24, 2007, http://www.chrisbrogan.com/measuring-social-media-efforts/, accessed December 27, 2010.

16   Michael Brito, "Measuring Social Media Marketing: It's Easier Than You Think," *Search Engine Journal,* June 30, 2007, http://www.searchenginejournal.com/measuring-social-media-marketing-its-easier-than-you-think/5397/, accessed August 7, 2011.

Visit the companion website for free additional materials related to this chapter: study.sagepub.com/smm

CASES

Increasingly, brands are integrating social media into their marketing communication campaigns or creating stand-alone social media campaigns to meet marketing objectives. Here we showcase examples to illustrate how social media can be used in regional, national, and global initiatives.

Case: Bellisio Foods' Michelina's Engages Frozen Foodies
Jacqueline Rae Evans

Brand: Michelina's

Bellisio Foods, Inc., is a frozen food manufacturer whose longest standing brand is Michelina's. Michelina's is the little green box located in the frozen food aisle. It was founded by Jeno Paulucci just a few years after his family moved to America from Bellisio Solfare, Italy. Jeno was born in 1918 and always had an entrepreneurial outlook and a strong work ethic. He made food his life. While Jeno was growing up, his father worked in the iron mines of Minnesota and his mother cooked and catered to the families in the area. Always being a family man, Jeno later founded the frozen food brand and named it in honor of his mother, Michelina, and her authentic recipes. Currently, Bellisio Foods is the third largest frozen food manufacturer in the country and makes over two million Michelina's entrees per day. While Bellisio Foods is a leader in the frozen food category, it was not even considered a follower, or fan, of social media until April 2013.

In January 2013 Bellisio Foods, headquartered in Minneapolis, Minnesota, partnered with a digital marketing agency to develop a new, responsive website for Michelina's. The new website sought to improve the user's experience and serve as a source of information. In April 2013, the digital agency and Bellisio spearheaded Michelina's social media initiative to drive awareness to the brand and participate with social consumers. It did so using the brand persona of Mama Michelina. This persona is used across all channels and vehicles. The strategy was based on enabling organic content from brand fans, but eventually included a social media campaign, paid search engine advertising, contests, and more.

After numerous ideation and brainstorming sessions, it was agreed that the first ever campaign would be Make it Your Michelina's. A type of appeal for user-generated content, Michelina's challenged their fans and followers to submit pictures of how they put their own unique spin on the brand's already delicious recipes. Before the campaign was opened for user submission, Bellisio and the agency created their own recipes to aid in inspiring fans and followers to put their creative aprons on and get to cooking.

Bellisio also partnered with a third-party company that connects social media content creators with brands. This third-party company carefully selected multiple bloggers to make their own Michelina's meal and write about how convenient and fun it is to put your own twist on things. Bellisio provided the bloggers with $10 gift cards that allowed them to purchase a Michelina's frozen meal of their choice along with whatever ingredients they wanted in order to make it their own so that they could get to blogging! This was all part of the strategy to drive attention and awareness to the campaign and to Michelina's brand. Bellisio and the agency also incorporated social advertising to reach more people in the target audience with Facebook social ads and promoted posts, a form of native advertising.

What was the incentive to inspire user-generated content behind the Make it Your Michelina's campaign? A year's worth of Michelina's! For 4 weeks, the agency chose a weekly winner who won a week's worth of Michelina's, and in the fifth week of the campaign, a grand prize winner was awarded 365 days of Michelina's. This campaign was also a good gateway for the brand to enter Pinterest. Within the Make it Your Michelina's Pinterest board were pins of the pictures Bellisio and the agency had created to inspire fans as well as all of the entries of consumers. After numerous submissions and a creative strategy to vivaciously promote the campaign, the first milestone of Michelina's was accomplished: a successful B2C social media marketing campaign. In the month of September Michelina's had a 45% increase in fans on Facebook, and an over 300% post-reach increase due to organic engagement and paid ads due to the heightened number of posts featuring the campaign. The brand's Twitter account increased 30% in September with an engagement increase of over 500% and a Retweet Reach increase of over 300%. Why? Clearly, the Make it Your Michelina's campaign showed the importance of communicating with consumers and keeping them intrigued and knowledgeable about the brand.

Within a year of launching the Michelina's digital initiative, the brand was able to achieve 65,000 "likes" on Facebook and currently has over 5,200 followers on Twitter. The brand continues to produce engaging content and strives to keep consumers happy and in the know.

For Discussion

1   Did the Make It Your Michelina's campaign inspire an experience worth participating in and sharing? Explain.

2   How would you describe the target audiences for Michelina's? How did the Michelina's campaign address different types of social media participation?

3   How did Michelina's leverage the use of paid, owned, and earned media with its campaign?

4   How could Michelina's use the campaign to grow fans through the levels of fan engagement?

Case: A Startup Seeks to Solve Age-Old Problem With Social App

Amanda Steeley

Brand: TheGiftIWant.com

Before there was Facebook, there was Myspace. Before there was Google, there was NetScape. Innovation, by Google's definition, includes the process of changing, altering, or revolutionizing.

TheGiftIWant.com is a company that began development in late 2013 with the intention of innovating the gift-giving and gift-receiving industry online.

The concept is familiar: TheGiftIWant.com is a way to create and send gift lists online. Anyone who has used Amazon.com's gift lists or has created an online gift registry for a wedding (Target.com) or a baby shower (BabiesRUs.com) is at least familiar with what an online gift registry is. It's a fast and easy way to select the gifts you want, and communicate these interests to friends and family.

The innovative quality supplied by TheGiftIWant.com is that gift lists created on the site can seamlessly include products from Amazon.com, Target.com, and BabiesRUs.com. In fact, the list can include products from virtually any e-commerce site—all with one click of a downloadable applet.

The idea for the website originated after founder and CEO, Tony Emma, "received one too many paperweights" from his wife's sisters for Christmas. He began to ask people if they had ever received a gift they really didn't want, or given a gift they weren't sure was appropriate. From kid's birthday parties to college graduations, everyone could relate.

The company plans to engage thousands of users in the first 2 years following launch. With 25 years of experience in the marketing industry, Emma is optimistic about reaching these numbers. His energies thus far have been focused on working side by side with developers to create the site he has envisioned; however, he sees great potential for exponential growth as the site gains exposure.

The type of URL aggregation that TheGiftIWant.com provides is similar to the one-click ease of Pinterest. In addition to easily being able to add gifts to lists, users will be able to share lists via social media and email. As the site develops, users will be able to make lists public or private, pursuing gifts using keywords for ideas. If the idea is as sticky as the company hopes, TheGiftIWant.com will replace all other online gift lists.

For Discussion

1 TheGiftIWant.com is an online start-up company that will rely on social media for consumer participation. What social media marketing channels should they focus their strategy on? What vehicles should they use? Why?

2   In the summer of 2013, the company stated the goal of achieving 10,000 engaged users by the end of 2014. Keeping in mind that the majority of their investment has gone into website development, how would you suggest they achieve this goal? Do you think it's a reasonable goal? Why or why not?

3   Go to TheGiftIWant.com website. Create a gift list. Include five things your heart desires. Do you think the site is capable of replacing all other online gift lists? What did you like? What would you do differently?

4   What metrics would you use to track the growth of TheGiftIWant.com users? How would you reinforce early adopters so that they remain engaged? How long would you wait before "inviting" a dormant user back to the site? How would you incentivize them to return?

Case: The Gnome Experiment

Steven Shugartt

Brand: Kern

Kern is a precision scales manufacturer, founded in 1844 in Southern Germany. Despite that long history, audience analysis verified that low brand recognition existed for their primary product. Furthermore, the product was a commodity with very little recognition regarding quality, reliability, or precision. As for social media? Well, no significant discussions on social media were occurring, despite a key unique selling proposition of "calibrating scales for local gravity."

How could that be?! So Kern partnered with Ogilvy PR/London and OgilvyOne and made magic.

Kern's goals included brand building, differentiation, and market share growth in the science and education sectors. Specifically, Kern sought to:

1. Drive sales of scales to the education and science sectors by enhancing Kern's brand visibility and preference amongst these key markets.

2. Generate conversations internationally around gravity's influence on weight measurement—explaining the importance of Kern's USP = calibration scales for local gravity.

3. Raise awareness of Kern's reputation for accuracy within and beyond its existing customer base.

The brand needed a social media strategy consistent with its brand positioning. How is the brand positioned? Kern is a family owned company, founded in 1844. Its website touts continuity and consistency as key attributes. The philosophy states: "Consultation, sales and service from one source is efficient and reasonably priced." The key target audience is the millions of educational and scientific labs all over the world that use measurement equipment in experiments. This includes high schools and universities in every corner of the globe as well as tens of thousands of companies that use this equipment.

What did Kern do? It incorporated the support of influencers. It sent kits to invited scientists and existing Kern customers, and then asked them to send the kits on to colleagues. This created a built-in third-party endorsement from every person who participated in the experiment.

How did Kern engage fans to participate and share? Ogilvy PR/London created a garden gnome called Kern. Gnomes are famous for their love of traveling and this tied into the central idea for the campaign—verifying gravity's influence on weight. Gnomes are also from the same area of Germany where the company is located. By developing a blog and website, www.gnomeexperiment.com, they were able to engage consumers and create a personality for the gnome—scientifically irreverent.

The Gnome experiment was featured on Kern's website, on a microsite just for the experiment, www.gnomeexperiment.com, and in paid media. On www.gnomeexperiment.com, visitors were told about how the earth's gravity varies depending on where we are in the world so the gnome will weigh slightly more or less, and that only Kern's scales are sophisticated enough to correct for this difference. Visitors are invited to use the Kern scale to weigh the gnome where they are and then enter data to the website and upload a video to the company's YouTube channel. Sending the travel kit on to the next participant added to the interactivity of the campaign. Switzerland, South Africa, the United Kingdom, the United States, and Canada were some of the key countries targeted when sending out gnome kits to scientists in an attempt to spark local conversation but in a global way. The campaign truly engaged people.

The campaign is content heavy. YouTube videos and photos of people all over the world weighing Kern, the gnome, and the accompanying stories were critical to success. The gnome was even sent from the South Pole to the CERN particle collider.

Before the gnome experiment, the only social media channel used by Kern was community, with a company Facebook page and Twitter feed. For the campaign, Kern developed a blog and website, gnomeexperiment.com, to engage the target audience, as discussed earlier. Social media news releases were sent to international media directing everyone to the gnomeexperiment.com website as well. Community was also used with Facebook and YouTube.

How did Kern perform? Within 2 days of the campaign launch, 355 million people visited the website and requested the travel kit so they could weigh the gnome. This resulted in 3 requests per minute from all over the world. After 1 month, it became a Top News Story with 16,386 websites linking to www.gnomeexperiment.com. It paid off in terms of search engine optimization! The campaign pushed Kern from page 12 on Google search to page 1. Oh, and sales increased 21%. Return on Investment was measured at 1,042%.

For Discussion

1 How did Kern utilize the four zones of social media marketing?
2 How did Kern create an experience worthy of participation and sharing?

3   Was the campaign targeted well? Did it anticipate the likely motives and behaviors of the target audience?

4   What else could Kern do?

CIPR: Corporate and Business Communications Campaign—Case study. (2013). Retrieved February 14, 2014, from http://www.cipr.co.uk/content/events-awards/excellence-awards/results

David, E. (2013, December 12). *Top 10 influential social media marketing campaigns of 2013*. Retrieved February 14, 2014, from http://www.adherecreative.com/blog/bid/152638/Top-10-Influential-Social-Media-Marketing-Campaigns-of-2013

Davis, B. (2013, June 26). *Kern & Sohn precision scales*. Retrieved February 14, 2014, from http://econsultancy.com/blog/62977-five-great-social-media-campaigns-and-their-metrics

Kern: The Gnome Experiment. (2013). Retrieved February 14, 2014, from http://www.ogilvyprlondon.com/our-work/kern-gnome-experiment

APPENDIX

Sample Social Media Marketing Plan: Raceway

Introduction

Raceway, located in the Southeastern United States, is the home of memorable motor races, a top-of-the line drag strip, dirt racing, auto fairs, and numerous events that attract racing lovers from a large area. It sits in a 2,000-acre complex and boasts a capacity of 140,000 fans. Although Raceway has a sizeable fan base, the management team wants to create more awareness of its offerings, polish its brand reputation, and strengthen relationships with fans. With a minimal promotional budget, Raceway's leadership recognizes the value of incorporating social media into its communications program.

Raceway offers racing enthusiasts the opportunity to attend races, car shows, and other special events such as the Christmas Lights Show. It attracts visitors from all over the region and even from other parts of the country. Raceway consists of a super speedway, a zMax dragway, and a dirt track, so it can offer a portfolio of events to cater to the interests of a diverse fan base. The venue also offers a variety of ticket pricing options. These range from affordable tickets and discounted group packages to high-priced VIP tickets that come with a variety of perks. Raceway promotes events and special deals using traditional outlets such as radio and television advertisements and its website. Recently it developed a Facebook page and Twitter account, but now it wants to more fully incorporate social media into its promotional mix.

Situation Analysis

Raceway has a strong loyal fan base that visits the track at least once per season. It also has fairly good ticket sales to corporate offices that buy tickets to support the community and provide incentives to employees. Families enjoy Raceway for its family-friendly environment and the ability to tailgate before and after events. However, a day at Raceway can be expensive for families, one of the primary targets for race events. This has become an even greater problem given current economic conditions. On a positive note, there are no other tracks within a 3-hour radius of Raceway. Still, races are entertainment and there are many forms of entertainment available, whether simple weekends at home or an outing to a movie.

Raceway needs not only to stay top-of-mind in its target audiences' minds for weekend entertainment, but the venue also needs to minimize media spending on advertising to offset weaker ticket sales than in past years. The rise in social media usage is an opportunity for Raceway to shift some of its promotional focus to less expensive media.

Overall, Raceway has a strong brand and brand awareness, but a questionable value position compared to other forms of entertainment. It also faces competition in the form of alternative entertainment activities. A campaign should build on the Raceway brand, differentiate Raceway events from other entertainment, and utilize social media to reach underserved target markets.

Marketing Objectives

- Create awareness of Raceway's VIP offerings including networking opportunities and corporate functions among at least 60% of the target audience.
- Develop a multidimensional relationship with the target audience by incorporating Raceway events and communications into fans' social and family lives.
- Increase visits to Raceway's homepage by 25% within a 6-month period.
- Increase visits to Raceway's social media profile pages by 30% within a 6-month period.
- Increase ticket sales by 20% within a 6-month period.

Target Audience

Raceway already successfully targets motorsports fans and families within a 2-hour radius of its location. The social media strategy will not only encompass this existing audience but also focus on a secondary market for Raceway—professional working adults. These individuals are highly motivated, active, and career-oriented with a passion for success. They are familiar with motorsports but are not fans. However, they view motorsports events as suitable social experiences for time with work colleagues, friends, and family members. They are tech-savvy owners of smartphones. They spend time online for work and pleasure and maintain at least two social media profiles (typically including Facebook and LinkedIn). As we discussed in Chapter 3, they use social media to perform the roles of conversationalists, joiners, spectators, and collectors. Though they live busy lives, members of this target market enjoy spending time online and using their smartphones; they frequently play short social games like Angry Birds. This audience spends less time with traditional media because of their work schedules, active social lives, and time spent online. With incomes upward of $75,000 annually and large networks personally and professionally, they are ripe for targeting.

Social Media Strategy

Given the campaign objectives and the target audience's characteristics, the social media strategy most appropriate for Raceway utilizes three of the four zones of social media: community building, social publishing, and social entertainment. Raceway's slogan, "Life's a Race. Get on Track," will integrate the social media plan with Raceway's other promotional work. Raceway's homepage will be repositioned as the hub of all activity related to the speedway. Links to all social media sites will be prominent on the site and feeds from some social media activities will be shown on the site.

Integrate Zone 1: Social Community

Raceway should develop and maintain a presence with the social networks that the target audience uses most heavily. These include Facebook and Twitter. LinkedIn may be used at a later point to announce business-focused networking events. The campaign will also feature a mobile app that will be developed specifically for this initiative. Tabs will be created on Raceway's Facebook page for each element of the campaign, including (1) Information, (2) Events, (3) Speedway Club, (4) Special Promotions, (5) Fan Forum, and (6) the Fan Track, a section for user-generated content. The Wall will feature several posts each week including event and ticket sales reminders, Raceway news updates, specials, featured user-generated content, and questions to fans. Wall content will vary so as not to over push sales information. The Information tab will include links to all other forms of online presence for Raceway. Participation from fans will be encouraged, with calls for shared photos, videos, and testimonials. The Fan Forum is a place to encourage interaction among fans.

Twitter will be used as a reminder device. Rather than bombard followers with prices, events, and specials, Twitter will be used creatively to post fan and racer quotes, links to user-generated content, quirky thoughts, fan questions, and requests for service quality recommendations.

A mobile app will be developed and branded the *Raceway Track App*. The app will serve as a mobile hub for all things Raceway. It will stream feeds from all social media posts related to Raceway, allow users to post to the Facebook Wall from within the app, and feature a calendar component to allow the target audience to keep track of their own personal upcoming events along with events hosted by Raceway.

Integrate Zone 2: Social Publishing

Raceway will harness and create several forms of content for use in the social publishing zone of its social media strategy. The content will include live streams of races and other events from Raceway cams (cameras positioned in the garage, infield campgrounds, and other vital areas), blog posts including articles about racers, featured fans, stories from the perspectives of the teams racing, and video footage. This content will require ongoing development. A Director of Content will be needed to guide the creation and development of the content used in the social publishing zone.

The Raceway website will include a blog called *The Track,* which will serve as the primary publishing channel for original branded content. RSS feeds will ensure that the content is syndicated to fans. New content will be promoted using Facebook, Twitter, and the mobile app. Fans will be encouraged to comment on blog posts. While the social relationship activity will include daily updates, the blog will include new stories at least twice per week such as interviews with drivers or gossip about the racing community. Immediately preceding events, blog activity will increase to drive traffic to the ticketing section of the website.

Video content will be published on the Raceway website and on a new Raceway YouTube channel. Videos will include race uploads, Raceway cam video captures, interviews with fans and drivers, and fan videos. New content will be promoted on all other social venues.

Major events and interview engagements with star racers also will be promoted with a Social Media Press Release. The press release will help ensure additional online links to Raceway social content. The social publishing portion of the strategy ensures a strong linkwheel for fans to find other content and optimizes Raceway's search engine rankings.

Integrate Zone 3: Social Entertainment

The final zone used in Raceway's social media strategy is social entertainment. A social game titled Raceway: The Game will be developed and launched. Players can play Raceway: The Game on Raceway's website and within Facebook, much like the popular Farmville game. Racing is a popular video genre and social games are gaining rapidly in popularity. By developing a game that simulates the Raceway experience while allowing fans to drive their own virtual car, Raceway will ensure that fans spend more time online and in social venues with the Raceway brand. The game also encourages players to share the game with friends and it provides advertising inventory in the game that can be sold to sponsors as an additional stream of revenue. Branding within the game will be consistent with Raceway's slogan of "Life's a Race. Get on Track."

The Experience Strategy

Raceway's campaign theme is "Life's a Race. Get on Track." The social media strategy must support this theme. The campaign will position Raceway as a way for professionals to escape the hustle and bustle of the workplace while still staying connected and "on track." The campaign is centered on the concept that it doesn't have to be "all work, no play" and that Raceway offers great opportunities for corporations and working individuals to socialize, enjoy themselves, and be productive—all at the same time. The "Get on Track" slogan is a fun pun; it will inspire the target audience to get themselves to the Raceway track. From a creative perspective, the most appropriate approach is that of an experiential strategy—the promotional messages should encourage the target audience to imagine the experience of being at the track, seeing and hearing a race, and feeling the pleasure of time spent with others. The core message is to become involved in Raceway, online and in person, by buying tickets and attending events. By becoming involved, new fans will have a better awareness of Raceway and its events and begin to see Raceway as a viable entertainment alternative.

In each zone there are opportunities for the target audience to experience Raceway and, importantly, to engage and to share with others in their networks. The Facebook page will enable the creation and sharing of user-generated content and discussions in the fan forum. The Twitter account will be used to share quirky messages designed to encourage sharing with others. The mobile app will make Raceway a part of a user's mobile experience—for hours each and every day. With the campaign theme, "Life's a Race. Get on Track," users will be able to integrate short- and long-term goal planning and time management activities in a fun and aesthetically pleasing branded mobile application. The social publishing activities provide interesting and entertaining content designed to be consumed and shared. Lastly, the game is an experience in itself. Even people who are not at the track can be in the game.

Activation Plan

- Assign a Director of Content to develop and maintain fresh streams of content on an ongoing basis.
- Redesign Raceway's website to establish it as a hub for all activity, develop *The Track* blog area, and provide engaging links to social media presence.
- Redesign the Facebook page to include new tabs. New content should be posted in tabs, on a regular basis. Banners on Raceway's website will promote the Facebook page.
- Develop the mobile app and plan launch schedule.
- Install Raceway cams and set up live feeds to sites.
- Develop Raceway: The Game and plan launch schedule.

More precise budget estimates will be developed as the activation plan rolls out. The budget allocation for the social media campaign is $350,000. This includes sufficient funding for the development of the social game (budgeted at roughly $200,000), the mobile app (budgeted at roughly $25,000), a content staff member (budgeted at $50,000), and other development costs.

Management and Measurement

Performance will be measured using a mix of activity and outcome measures including website traffic, blog trackbacks and comments (quantity and content), Facebook fans, Twitter followers, YouTube average views/video, mobile app downloads and usage rates, players in the game, engagement duration (for time spent with the brand per interaction), and peer impressions shared socially. Online ticket sales originating from Facebook and other social sites will be tracked. Search engine rankings will be assessed weekly.

SOCIAL MEDIA PRESS RELEASE

CONTACT INFORMATION:

Client Contact
Tracy Tuten
555.555.0328
tracy@theraceway.com
www.raceway.com

Agency Contact
Social Media, Inc
555.555.4385
info@socialmediainc.com

Raceway Releases "Track App" for iPhone

Raceway announces its new application for the iPhone, the "Track App." The application is set to release on April 17, 2015.

Core News Facts

- The application will be a hub for all activity at Raceway.
- The "Track App" will stream feeds from Facebook and Twitter to the user.
- It will allow users to post directly to Raceway social media pages.
- A calendar component will allow fans to save events from Raceway's Facebook page and they will automatically integrate into its calendar.
- This mobile application is perfect for the on-the-go user who wants to stay up-to-date on events at the speedway.
- For more information, go to www.theraceway.com/trackapp.

Pre-Approved Quotes

"This application is great for our on-the-go fans. They will be able to sync with our social media sites and our calendar and never miss an announcement or an event."—Sarah Rowe, Marketing Agency Representative

"The 'Track App' will hopefully drive traffic to our social media sites and allow our fans to stay informed on what is happening at Raceway."—O. Bruton Smith, Chairman

Additional quotes upon request.

Raceway features a 2,000-acre complex and a capacity of 140,000. The 1.5-mile track is home to the Race for the Win, Brands 600, and the Raceway 500. Building on the basic philosophy of putting fans first, and keeping its competitors in the rear-view mirror at all times, Raceway continues to be a leading promoter and marketer of motorsports activities in the United States.

INDEX